CRIME SCENE UNIT MANAGEMENT

Crime Scene Unit Management: A Path Forward is a must-have resource for anyone involved with forensic investigations and the search for evidence at the crime scene. The book provides standards for how to manage a crime scene so that evidence is collected and preserved without errors and includes guidelines for how to implement the standards and set up regional training programs for smaller jurisdictions with tighter budgets. Key features include examples, checklists, and flow charts for evidence handling and routing. CSIs, fire investigators, homicide investigators, accident investigators, police executives, and students of forensic science will benefit from this thorough approach to how the crime scene – and the personnel charged with tending to the evidence – should be managed.

Edward W. Wallace, Jr. was the Director of Forensic Training at the New York City Office of Chief Medical Examiner from December 2008 to December 2014. He is also Senior Adjunct Instructor and Weapons of Mass Destruction Training Course Developer for Louisiana State University at the National Center for Biomedical Research, which is a provider of emergency responder training for the US Department of Homeland Security, Office of Domestic Preparedness. He retired in 2004 after 20 years with the New York Police Department, where he served as training officer, crime scene investigator, and counter-terrorism investigator, among other roles. Wallace has given testimony as a forensic expert in 393 trials, and is co-author of *Crime Scene Investigation*, 3rd edition (Routledge/Anderson, 2014).

Michael J. Cunningham is a retired New York Police Department 1st Grade Detective. He served for 26 years as a latent fingerprint officer, evidence technician, and crime scene investigator, and assisted in developing standard operating and quality assurance procedures for the crime scene unit. He teaches at the National Center for Biomedical Research, which is a provider of emergency responder training for the US Department of Homeland Security, Office of Domestic Preparedness. He also teaches crime scene investigation techniques internationally on behalf of the US State Department's Anti-terrorism Assistance Program. Mr. Cunningham is a recognized expert in shooting reconstruction and 3D laser scanning. He currently works with Leeds LLC to provide Crime Center case management solutions to the law enforcement community.

Daniel Boggiano is an active law enforcement Investigator in New York City and has been serving as a crime scene investigator for more than a decade. In addition to investigative responsibilities, he is responsible for quality assurance issues and the development, coordination, and delivery of training for investigators. This includes basic training for newly assigned investigators, advanced training for tenured investigators, and coordination of the IAI (International Association for Identification) certification program for crime scene investigators assigned to his unit. Boggiano holds an M.S. degree in Forensic Science and has completed course work toward a Ph.D. in Criminal Justice (Forensic Science Concentration) at John Jay College of Criminal Justice. Boggiano has offered testimony in many criminal cases and has been deemed an expert in crime scene investigation and reconstruction disciplines. He currently teaches crime scene investigation for the John Jay Graduate Criminal Justice Program.

This text will be an invaluable asset to a wide spectrum of individuals/groups who are concerned with the management of crime scenes or adequate preparation for investigating major incidents including university programs in forensic science, line supervisors of crime scene units, upper management of police departments, and professional development planners and instructors.

Peter A. Pizzola, Pace University

CRIME SCENE UNIT MANAGEMENT

A Path Forward

Edward W. Wallace, Jr., Michael J. Cunningham, and Daniel Boggiano

Routledge
Taylor & Francis Group
LONDON AND NEW YORK

First published 2016
by Routledge
711 Third Avenue, New York, NY 10017

and by Routledge
2 Park Square, Milton Park, Abingdon, Oxon, OX14 4RN

Routledge is an imprint of the Taylor & Francis Group, an informa business

Library of Congress Cataloging in Publication Data
Wallace, Edward W., Jr., 1963-
Crime scene unit management : a path forward / Edward W. Wallace, Michael Cunningham, Daniel Boggiano.
pages cm
Includes bibliographical references and index.
ISBN 978-1-138-89925-4 (hardcover : alk. paper) — ISBN 978-0-323-24324-7 (pbk. : alk. paper) 1. Crime scene searches. 2. Criminal investigation. 3. Evidence, Criminal. 4. Forensic sciences. I. Title.
HV8073.W3336 2016
363.25'2—dc23
2015025789

ISBN: 978-1-138-89925-4 (hbk)
ISBN: 978-0-323-24324-7 (pbk)
ISBN: 978-1-315-65235-1 (ebk)

Typeset in Bembo
by FiSH Books Ltd, Enfield

CONTENTS

FIGURES

PREFACE

This first edition of *Crime Scene Unit Management: A Path Forward* was written to assist those practicing, studying, and managing crime scene investigations to develop and implement organizational systems that ensure professional standards are maintained and high quality work is produced. The book is written from the practical point of view of professionals with many years of experience in processing crime scenes and instructing CSIs.

Why This Book Was Written

Society in the United States is resolute in apprehending its criminals and holding them accountable, especially when violence has occurred, but society also insists on a system of justice that ensures fairness in its convictions. The work of forensic science is critically important to this system of justice. So much so that in 2009 the National Academy of Science (NAS) completed a landmark study in collaboration with the Department of Justice and issued a report on forensics. This report, titled "Strengthening Forensic Science in the United States; A Path Forward" (known as the "NAS Report") triggered shock waves throughout the forensic science field, the effects of which will continue to be felt in crime labs and crime scene units for some time to come.

Many initially interpreted the NAS Report as being overly critical of the methods used in the field and assumed a defensive posture. It was unclear at first what was intended by the nation's top scientists seemingly criticizing the hard work and accomplishments that had been made in forensics and what the implications of such a report would be. It was even unclear to some whether or not the report considered CSI work to be a part of the greater forensic science field. But as time passes it's becoming quite clear that the report actually laid the foundation that can make implementing large-scale meaningful change in forensics, including crime scene investigation, a real possibility. The changes on this path forward are what will enable the practitioners in the field to continue to expand the amazing possibilities that forensic science brings to crime solving.

The Authors of *Crime Scene Management: A Path Forward*, Daniel Boggiano, Edward W. Wallace and Michael J. Cunningham, have dedicated their professional lives, in the public, academic, and private sectors, to the forensic discipline of crime scene investigation (CSI). After reflecting on their observations of the trend towards accreditation and certification triggered by the NAS Report, and also recognizing that the CSI community had a need for references to assist in implementing such programs, they used their many years of professional experience to collaborate on this book.

About This Book

Each of the book's authors have worked as crime scene investigators (totaling over 60 years of experience) and at some point in their career they worked together solving cases. Ed Wallace completed a career with the New York City Police Department and held the position as Director of Forensic Training at the New York City Medical Examiner's Office. He currently has a private forensic practice and also works to provide National and International forensic training. Daniel Boggiano served many years as a CSI Detective and is also an Adjunct Professor in the Forensic Science Program at John Jay College of Criminal Justice in New York, a position that allows him a unique perspective on policy issues in forensics. Michael Cunningham completed a career with the New York City Police Department as a CSI Detective and has provided National and International forensic training. He is currently an instructor in the private sector teaching forensic mapping and 3D crime scene reconstruction to law enforcement agencies.

The authors present a unique perspective of crime scene investigation work in that the organizational aspects of crime scene investigation are covered in much more depth than the practical aspects of scene processing. Processing methods such as how to develop fingerprints or how to cast footwear impressions have been covered well in a great many texts, but how to organize and manage a unit of investigators who are charged with these duties has not been previously examined in full.

This book covers the following important topics:

- The need for a path forward in crime scene investigation
- Crime scene unit personnel assignments and management
- Investigator safety issues and regulations
- Crime scene contamination prevention
- Unit accreditation and CSI training and certification
- Developing written protocols
- CSI equipment procurement, use and maintenance
- Managing the crime scene team during the field process
- Scene documentation procedures and requirements
- Quality assurance methods and policies
- Pre-incident planning for critical incidents
- Business records management requirements and distribution policies

At the time of this writing the National Commission of Forensic Science has issued written recommendation to the Attorney General that all forensic science service providers in the United States (CSI units included) should be accredited to national standards. It would appear inevitable that this will indeed become a mandatory requirement on forensic sciences path forward.

The challenge along this path forward for CSI units is to develop sound policy and quality assurance systems that will improve their forensic work and allow them to achieve accreditation without dampening the investigative reasoning process employed by CSIs. Quality CSI work has always required combining the art of a detective with the science of forensics. Removing investigative reasoning from the process reduces the CSI to a technician who blindly runs tests and collects samples. Such a dampening of investigative reasoning would actually weaken the overall criminal investigation process.

This book outlines the methods to develop good policy while maintaining an investigative approach to CSI work and it will help readers meet challenges facing the field of crime scene investigation.

The crime scene is the beginning of the whole evidentiary process, indeed the whole forensic process. It is where evidence is recognized, documented and preserved or forever overlooked. It is, perhaps, the place in the chain where the most damage can occur. Within the crime scene investigation there is a higher chance of degradation, or destruction of evidence than anywhere else in the forensic process. The stakes are high and everyone involved must agree that society should be absolutely assured that its CSIs strive to produce the best results possible. Our system of justice and the people it serves (victims and the accused alike) deserve no less. To this end, it is hoped, this book will be a helpful guide to students, investigators and managers to chart a path forward for successful crime scene investigations.

ACKNOWLEDGMENTS

The authors would like to acknowledge those individuals who toil day and night at crime scenes and in our nation's crime labs dedicated to their work while remaining mostly unseen by others. It is their efforts to find the truth and speak on behalf of victims who cannot speak for themselves that has inspired us to this work. We also wish to thank our mentors who took the time and patiently offered guidance throughout our careers, especially Peter Pizzola PhD and Peter DeForest D. Crim.

Perhaps most importantly we would like to thank our families. Without their understanding and support we would never have been able to carry out our mission.

INTRODUCTION

The "CSI" franchise of TV shows has portrayed the forensic sciences in a favorable and glamorous light. Unfortunately occurrences over the past years, poor behavior by individual practitioners, and egregious errors by others, have exposed flaws in how forensic scientists conducts business and have now attracted governmental scrutiny.

Such criticism can be an opportunity to institute constructive change. Foreseeing problems and responding with ways to conduct business better, can achieve the same goal without the unnecessary negative attention. To this end, forensic science has in the past seen a need for, and initiated systems to ensure, a better quality product. These systems have taken the form of accreditation and certification. Current criticisms (such as the "NAS Report") should not be spurned, but embraced as a positive means to bring change where needed.

Even with these types of quality ensuring systems in place there are still events and issues that can cause disruptions to good quality service. Whether the current criticisms of forensic science are warranted or not, public entities such as the criminal justice system must be assured that they are receiving the best product possible.

This is true not only with forensic laboratories but with crime scene investigation as well. Forensic science starts at the crime scene. Quality analysis of the evidence starts at the crime scene. So many things that can happen at the crime scene investigation level affect everything else that comes after. What is done at the crime scene cannot be undone at the laboratory.

Crime scene investigation is not just experts from opposing sides showing up to reconstruct events and issue their opinion at trial. It is the beginning of the whole evidentiary process. It should, and must, share equal status with the other forensic subspecialties. In reality, the administration, accreditation, and certification of its professionals has been woefully neglected by the profession, and it is, perhaps, the link in the chain where the most damage can occur. Within the crime scene investigation lays the highest risk of diminution, degradation, or destruction of evidence.

The subspecialty of crime scene investigation cannot wait for its clients to demand change and improvement. Like other lab sections, crime scene investigation must foresee problems and improve without outside catalysts.

Before an organization can look towards accreditation and certification as a means of demonstrating this commitment to quality, it must first take measure of the operation. This is a critical first step. Assurance of a quality product is paramount. That is what this text hopes to accomplish. It is not checklist for getting a crime scene investigation unit accredited or its personnel certified. Nor is it a step-by-step guide to perfection. It is experience combined with ideas that have worked to improve the quality of crime scene investigation services.

The ideas in this text, along with meaningful methods to implement them are meant to be a springboard or starting point for both managers and practitioners alike, a means to help find ways to make what they do better.

It is the intent of this text to help an organization be introspective, with a critical eye to improvement and success. It is about finding ways to ensure that evidence entering the lab is as it should be, undiminished by contamination or degradation as well as documented and recovered by well trained, highly competent practitioners.

It is hoped that this sharing of ideas will spur organizations forward to examine their operations with a critical eye. Whether the operation is currently experiencing issues, or the organization is simply looking to create a new, singular program that it doesn't already have, it is hoped that this resource will be a good starting point for any such review and a useful path forward.

1

THE NEED FOR A PATH FORWARD

Overview

The criminal justice system consists of many parts, each part working together to administer justice. These parts include lawyers, judges, administrators, witnesses, law enforcement, and juries. In a perfect world, each part works as it should in order to ensure a correct outcome. Society desires the correct outcome. In a criminal case, the desired outcome is that the guilty are found guilty and the innocent are found innocent.

An incorrect outcome does no one any good. Finding a guilty party innocent allows someone to remain free in society to commit more crimes. Finding an innocent person guilty punishes and attempts to rehabilitate an individual who does not deserve punishment nor need rehabilitation. In the end it achieves no worthwhile purpose.

Forensic science and its practitioners often play an important role in this aspect of the criminal justice system. Physical evidence collected from the scene will be analyzed and presented to the jury accompanied by expert testimony. The interpretation of this evidence and the testimony given by the forensic expert can significantly affect the outcome of the trial. The nature of the evidence, the results of the analysis, the interpretation of those results and, ultimately, the testimony given can sway a jury towards a verdict. To say that this is a very big responsibility is a gross understatement.

The responsibility for the outcome of the analysis should not rest solely on the scientist or forensic expert sitting on the witness stand at the time. In order for the best possible analytical outcome to occur, the evidence must be in the best state that it can be in; uncontaminated, unadulterated, not diminished in any way. What we are talking about here is making sure that nothing bad happened to the evidence so the information it can give to the jury can reach its maximum potential.

To make this happen, all of forensic science must play its part, from beginning to end. Each link in the chain has to show that it did everything the way it was supposed to be done, by employing best practices. If this happens, then all those people who rely on the products that forensic science produces can be assured that the results of the analysis can be relied upon.

The Need for a Path Forward

In November of 2005, the United States Congress through the Science, State, Justice, Commerce and Related Agencies Appropriations Act of 2006, tasked the National Research Council to, ostensibly, study the state of the forensic sciences in America.[1] As a result, in the fall of 2006, a committee was formed to set about this task.[2] The committee was comprised of a cross section of stakeholders in the criminal justice system. It included members of the forensic science community, the legal community, and other scientists.[3] The committee held hearings in which it heard testimony from many people. The committee met on eight occasions to deliberate.[4] The result of its work, published in 2009, was a report titled "Strengthening Forensic Science in the United States: A Path Forward." The task was, to say the least, monumental. The report covered a lot of ground, endeavoring to identify issues facing forensic science today and supply solutions for them.

A comprehensive review of the NAS Report is not the purpose of this chapter or book. We are neither equipped to, nor do we desire to, give either a detailed summary of the report or reasoned arguments for or against its merits. The fact is, without regard to what one believes are the motivations for the report, or what one thinks of those who spurred the movement of the selection of those who sat on the committee, the report is here to stay. There are issues highlighted by the report that pertain to the various subspecialties within the forensic sciences. There are issues that practitioners from all subspecialties should be aware of. The fact is that some topics of this report will touch all of forensic science in some way. If readers desire an in-depth review of the report, it is suggested that they seek out a more authoritative and comprehensive treatment, or download the report from the internet and read it for themselves. This report is the start of the path forward.

The goal of this chapter is to explore what this report may mean to crime scene investigation, the beginning of the forensic process. We want to draw the attention of executives, managers, bureaucrats, administrators and investigators that create, evaluate or have to live with the policies and procedures they create for their crime scene investigators and crime scene investigation units, to what the report has to say. We would like to explore what the report says in a general sense about forensic science, forensic science practitioners and some of the methods used and how they will (or must) integrate in the future to ensure an acceptable, reliable product. We would like to try and figure out where this is all going to go, so we can figure out the best way to get there also.

Some basic knowledge of the report is needed in order to understand how it will encourage forensic science to ensure a reliable product. When we try to understand the report, we must frame the issues in a way that all of the players can understand. The stakeholders must also articulate their needs in language that everyone can understand. Not all forensic practitioners come to the profession with an understanding of what forensic science is, its unique philosophy, or how the services it provides differ from other scientific endeavors. Not all administrators will be forensic scientists. This may be especially true for those entities traditionally run by law enforcement agencies. Not all law enforcement agencies will have trained forensic scientists or practitioners in their ranks to run these entities, nor will they have trained forensic scientists or practitioners who are effective managers and policy creators. Sometimes, it seems, this is a fact of the way government works. As a result, those who find themselves in supervisory positions within forensic units may not have formal knowledge about the work methods that those they are supervising actually perform.

Here are some quick points that those who are new to the forensic sciences should know before we move on. The various forensic science subspecialties do not operate in a vacuum. Some of the issues that affect one subspecialty may affect some or all of the others. There will be more than one process to any forensic investigation. Evidence may be recovered from a crime scene unit then pass through multiple areas of a lab before all analyses are complete. Issues affecting the quality of the evidence at Step 1 may affect the evidence at Step 2, and so on. Everyone with a stake in the outcome of the criminal justice system will expect assurances that, from the time an item of physical evidence was initially collected to the time it was analyzed and then stored, it was handled correctly.

We think it is fair to say that many, if not all, responsible practitioners already recognize this. The committee recognized this also. (Believing that, just because the report didn't directly address crime scene investigation on one specific point or another means that it is not our problem, is wishful thinking.)

Although many stakeholders in the criminal justice system have different desires regarding the outcome of any particular case, there are several ideals that the NAS Report points to that all stakeholders can and should agree on. These ideals are not new, nor are they novel. They are simply that all of society has a desire to see the right person prosecuted and convicted for the crime. No one is served when the wrong person is convicted for a crime they did not commit.

The NAS Report – Strengthening Forensic Science in the United States: A Path Forward

A Brief Recap of the Basics

The NAS Report doesn't say a whole lot about crime scene investigation directly. This does not mean that crime scene investigation practices are perfect nationwide or exempt from an obligation to strengthen forensic science. The report makes it clear that the committee could not address every question or find a solution to every problem. It could only reach consensus on the most important issues that affect forensic science today, and offer recommendations for improvement for them.[5] It seems at its core that the report wishes to understand the problems that lead to faulty convictions. The whole basis of our criminal justice system is to get it right. In the end, wrongful convictions and acquittals make us less safe.

Of course, the report places some of these problems at the feet of forensic science. Although they note some of the advances forensic science, as a discipline has made over the years, work still needs to be done. More, systematic advances, they say, will help law enforcement by identifying people with a higher level of reliability.[6]

One of the issues the report points to is the lack of uniformity within the forensic community. This includes funding, training, instrumentation, certification and accreditation. Any system, they indicate, needs to lessen this lack of uniformity and create consistent practices.[7]

Disparity exists among the various disciplines and from one jurisdiction to another within the same discipline. Standards, in the form of education, training, certification and accreditation will help to remedy these issues.[8] Although the report does not address any one discipline directly it can be construed that it is addressing all disciplines, crime scene investigation included.

Another problem that the report takes note of is the disparity in the types of conclusions analysts can make from various kinds of evidence. The report simplifies this by drawing our attention to analyses based on analytical methods (DNA) and analyses based on expert interpretation (e.g. pattern evidence).[9] Analytical methods draw stronger conclusions with regard to certainty than those based on expert interpretation. Further, different disciplines that rely on expert interpretation are at different places with regard to established protocols, research and the like. On top of that, varying practices from one jurisdiction to another truly hamper the ability to understand how "good" a particular item of evidence is. As a result, the report points out that the scientific validity of the methods used may not be robust enough to support such results.[10]

The report is concerned with the underlying knowledge base of forensic science and how to address the limitations and capabilities of the disciplines. In doing this, stakeholders will know what valid information can be expected from evidence. The report notes that this present fragmentation can cause the quality of the evidence and of its interpretation to vary widely from one place to another. It suggests that funding may reduce backlogs but will not necessarily fix these other issues.[11] True, unless some of this money is earmarked for research, training and the like.

The report gives some recommendations about how these problems might be remedied. Starting at the top, it advocates the creation of a federal department as a means to set a national policy and direction for all of forensic science. This department would work to, among other things, establish best practices, standards for accreditation and certification, promote research, improve and standardize education and training and to strengthen knowledge of forensic methods.[12]

The report recommends that this federal department create standard terminology for testimony and reporting as well as address issues of accuracy, reliability and validity.[13] In more common words, what evidence is "scientific", what is "expert interpretation" and what makes it good or bad evidence?

Recommendations with regard to individual certification and organizational accreditation were also included in the report. The ability to create uniformity rests to a certain degree on both of these items. Also, accreditation and certification create the ability to enforce a code of ethics and of quality assurance, which were included in the list of recommendations.[14]

Another pointed recommendation made by the report was the creation of committees in conjunction with the National Institute of Standards and Technology (NIST) to "fix" problems in various disciplines and methods. Some issues that the committees might look at are the identification and creation of best practices and rules for measurement and interpretation.[15]

This is just a very, very small snapshot of this document. The report is over 300 pages long and contains many important concepts. No review can, in reality, give it the treatment it needs in order to truly understand the breadth and scope of what the members of the Committee who produced it felt was important enough to recognize and investigate further. Again, one should read the report for a better understanding.

The NAS Report and Crime Scene Investigation

The authors of the NAS Report note that collectors can be anybody and everybody, from uniformed officers to hospital medical personnel. This clear fragmentation has the potential for "inconsistent policies and procedures as well as bias." They note, however, that very often the crime scene investigator is a sworn officer.[16]

This variability in practice, the authors feel, is a direct result of the lack of standards and proper training. This can contribute to difficulties in the laboratory when drawing conclusions from the evidence once it has been tested.[17] It is not clear to us what they mean here, but our feeling is that they are indicating once something is missed or done improperly the damage cannot be undone in the laboratory. Whatever information is lost with regard to context or because of degradation of the evidence as the result of mishandling cannot be recovered by laboratory techniques.

Summary

If one seeks guidance from the NAS Report about the direction that the nation will be taking with regard to forensic science, it is easy to find. The authors discuss the same themes in very general terms. They are things like the use of best practices, standardization (techniques, reporting, etc.), reliability, and the demonstration of these through accreditation and certification.

They do not offer much guidance about the degree with which these, and other issues, will apply to any particular area or subspecialty of forensic science. In fact, they spend very little time discussing crime scene investigation specifically, about one page of the whole document. But, if we infer a doomsday scenario based on our interpretation of this section of the report, they seem to take notice that crime scene investigation is the start of the forensic process. Mistakes at this stage are perpetuated throughout and down the line. It is interesting, however, that if this is the case, why the authors spent so little time discussing crime scene investigation specifically in the report. The reason may be very simple, because the issues they discuss in general about forensic science also apply to crime scene investigation.

The NAS Report only tells some of the story as it did not spend a lot of time discussing implementation of the recommendations. Some deeper thought about how to do this has started to come, and will continue to come in the near future.

What Has Happened Since

National Institute of Standards and Technology Organization of Scientific Area Committees – NIST OSACs

There are a few events we must discuss before we move on. Two of them are a direct response to the NAS Report. The first is the creation of new Organization of Scientific Area Committees (OSACs) by the National Institute of Standards and Technology. As of March 2014, those responsible for beginning the process have already started to outline the various groups and Scientific Area Committees that will be used to get the ball rolling.

These OSACs seem to be the entities that will replace the SWGs. One of the main criticisms that the NRC Report had about the Scientific Working Groups (SWGs) was the variability. Some disciplines had SWGs and some didn't. Some disciplines used the SWGs for different purposes than others. There was no standardization for the SWGs. The OSACs managed by NIST aim to be more coordinated in their structure and uniform in output.

On October 29, 2014, NIST announced that 402 individuals had been assigned to serve on the various OSACs to, "bring a uniform structure to what was previously an *ad hoc* system with the goal of improving the quality and consistency of forensic science in the United States."[18] The individuals will serve on the 23 subcommittees of the five Scientific Area Committees. What is interesting about this particular information are the OSACs (or subcommittees) comprising the "Crime Scene/Death Investigation Scientific Area." The organizational chart on this web page[19] and recreated in Figure 1.1 might leave a crime scene investigator with many questions. Those on the outside looking in may be somewhat confused. The OSACs comprising the Crime Scene/Death Investigation area are anthropology, disaster victim ID, dogs and sensors, fire scene and explosives, medical legal death investigation and odontology. A crime scene investigator might be curious to know where some of the more

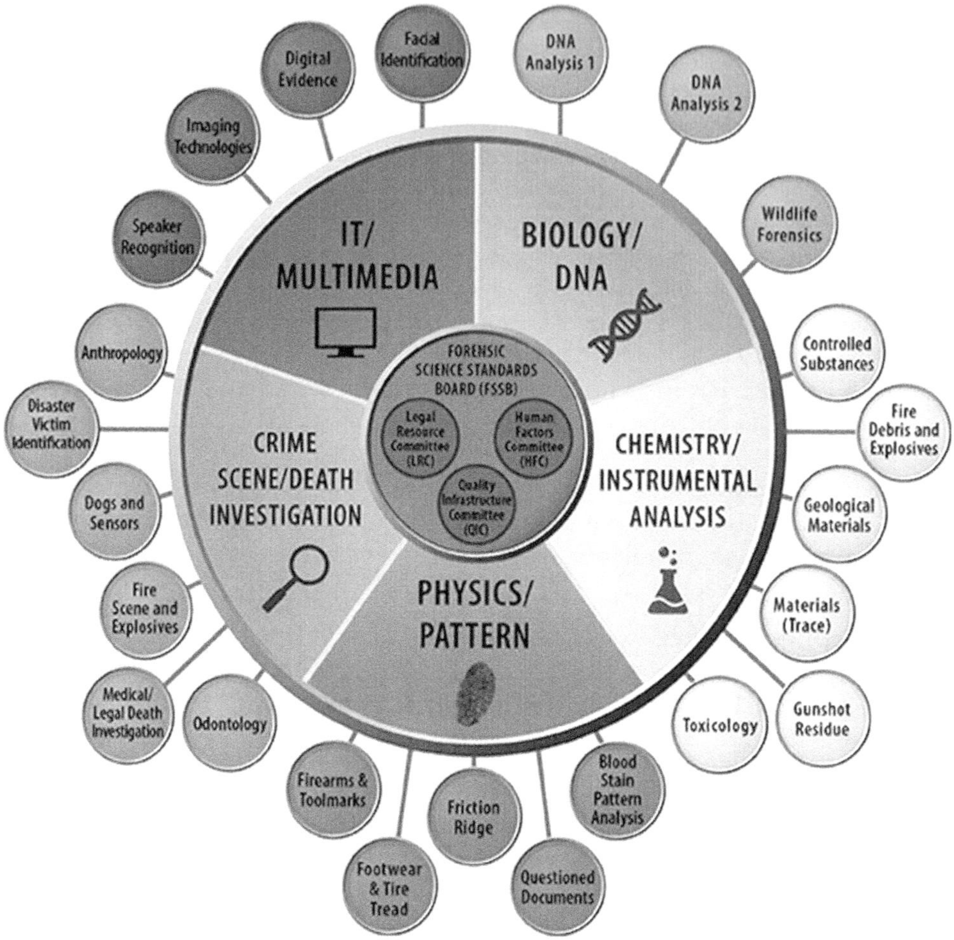

FIGURE 1.1 Organizational chart of NIST Scientific Area Committees as of March 2014

"traditional" crime scene investigation tasks might be assigned. Areas such as evidence collection and preservation, documentation, mapping and reconstruction techniques are not mentioned. According to the release, the Scientific Area Committees are planning on holding public hearings in 2015.

National Science and Technology Council (NSTC) Committee on Science Subcommittee on Forensic Science – Strengthening the Forensic Sciences

A second event that should be noted is the release of another report, this one by the Executive Office of the President, National Science and Technology Council. This report is titled "Strengthening the Forensic Sciences." The document indicates what policies the committee feels to be the most important and some general ideas on how it might be implemented nationwide.

The NSTC is, "the principal means by which the Executive Branch coordinates science and technology policy."[20] Its objective is to "establish clear national goals for Federal science and technology investments."[21]

In July of 2009, in response to the NRC Report, the White House Office of Science and Technology Policy established a subcommittee on forensic science. The culmination of this committee's work is this report, which details findings that, it hopes, will help create a collaborative dialogue to enhance policy, research and practice.[22]

This report, which is downloadable from the White House website, covers only a few areas important to our discussion: accreditation of forensic service providers; certification of forensic examiners; proficiency testing of forensic examiners and a national code of ethics. This is but a very small part of the issues discussed in the NRC Report.

This report differs from the NAS Report in several ways. Like the NRC Report, it discusses the reasons why these policies will improve forensic science in the United States but it also includes a discussion of ways to implement the policy as well as the implications of implementation. (This report is more of a how do we do this and what might happen if we do it.)

This report does not mention any particular subspecialties; it speaks about forensic science as a whole discipline. Since much of forensic science is based in the laboratory, it speaks from a laboratory perspective.

Accreditation

The authors of this report also recognize the usefulness of accreditation as a means of recognizing competence by an independent auditing authority. They also point out that accreditation is a useful method of any lab to take measure of how it is doing things on an ongoing basis. This continual reexamination works to uncover issues before they become problems, which then can be addressed and remedied. Accreditation requires the implementation of a quality management system which works to decrease errors in testing results, interpretation and opinions. They recognize that accreditation is a measure of a laboratory's total operation, from management to the laboratory environment.[23]

In the same breath, it recognizes that accreditation is not a cure-all. Accreditation cannot overcome all of the shortcomings that have been identified by the NRC Report. Laboratories can be accredited without using best practices all the time. Accreditation does not cure issues inherent with certain types of evidence (e.g. limitations). It does not stop people from over-stating the potential of evidence to create linkages.[24]

Accreditation is often voluntary and variable. There is no universal accreditation mandate in the United States. Some states have legislation requiring accreditation and some do not. Universal, mandatory accreditation will be a challenge. The first challenge, is to identify just exactly who is considered a forensic science service provider. The main or more common subspecialties are easy; however there must be a clear policy adoption. The authors of the report feel that the easiest way is to create a broad, loose definition of who is a forensic science service provider. They write,

> The most comprehensive approach to increasing standardization within the forensic sciences – and the simplest in terms of policy, is not the simplest to implement – would be to make all entities performing forensic testing, even on a part time basis, subject to mandatory accreditation requirements.[25]

This has big implications for everyone, including crime scene units. If your unit performs forensic testing, your unit will have to be accredited if this policy is adopted. What they do not define is what a "forensic test" is. However, if we use a little common sense, a presumptive test would be considered a forensic test. So, by extension, if a crime scene unit uses catalytic presumptive tests for blood, the unit would need to seek accreditation under this policy.

The authors do take note of the challenges this would create on a national level. The fact is, these same challenges present themselves for all the policies that they would seek to implement, whether it is accreditation, certification or proficiency testing. Some of these are: lack of funds, lack of central guidance, and staffing limitations. Any or all of these issues, and possibly others, can lead to problems, which can culminate in the loss of services by forensic providers. They also recognize that the current accreditation methods available today may not be ready to handle universal accreditation. New standards and educational materials might need to be created, and increased accrediting capacity may be required.[26]

The authors offer four ideas for implementing these policies. The first is national legislation defining who will be required to seek accreditation, and setting a time limit. The second approach is to bring together a broad cross section of the criminal justice community with an eye to creating consensus on a uniform law and getting all of the states to adopt it. Third, mandate accreditation in order to receive federal monies for things like training and other needs. The fourth approach is some combination of all of these.[27] In sum, if a unit performs forensic testing, they will be required to become accredited.

Certification

Like accreditation, certification should be a universal mandatory requirement for individual forensic science professionals. Certification brings recognition that the individual has, "acquired and demonstrated specialized knowledge, skills, and abilities in the standard practices necessary to execute the duties of their profession."[28]

Certification programs are not universal in the forensic science community. Only a few, related disciplines have a certification body: the other disciplines and processes do not. Each certification has different requirements with regard to education, experience, testing and the like. In other words, certifications for different disciplines are different. There is no uniform or standardized approach to certification. If there was, there would be some consensus as to what one would have to go through to become certified. There would be some standardization with regard to what type of written test is acceptable, what kind of practical testing is acceptable, what levels of education are required, what role proficiency testing will play on an ongoing basis and what continuing education and training is required. (Additionally, the authors feel that there is no fully independent accrediting body.)

Many challenges exist when it comes to universal, mandatory certification. They are similar to those facing universal, mandatory accreditation in that resources will be needed to achieve the goal. Resources in terms of money, individual preparation for tests, more personnel needed to backfill and other, common issues when manpower stops analyzing cases and starts to study for a test. Time and resources will always be an issue.

Other challenges are presented because there are many disciplines for which there are currently no certifications and creating them is a considerable undertaking. They cite the need for multiple levels of certification within the same discipline and the need to create study and educational materials to accompany certification exams. In addition, some practitioners may need to be certified in multiple disciplines based upon the types of analysis they carry out.[29]

In some cases, where there are not a lot of practitioners certification, providers might be hesitant to create certifications because it will not be profitable enough to do it. In cases such as these, alternative means of training, educational support and proficiency testing, where available, may be required in place of certification. Finally, there would be need to accommodate longstanding practitioners who do not meet current certification requirements.

At any rate, the authors admit that the implementation of mandatory, universal certification will be a complex process to say the least. At the present time, there is no central responsibility for implementing certification and all of the trappings that go along with it. It will also be very difficult for governmental entities to legislate mandatory certification, especially where no certification exam and no responsibility for it exists. They recognize that, in the case of certification, distributing grant money to jump start the process may be the best way to go.[30]

Proficiency Testing

The authors recognize the recommendation of the NRC Report for wide use of proficiency testing to be an important one. Proficiency tests emulate realistic casework and so they are a valuable means of improving feedback and identifying shortcomings in forensic science practices. Proficiency tests help evaluate technical competence and provide insight into the overall performance of both individuals and laboratories. As a result, both the NRC and the NSTC seem to agree that proficiency tests should be a mandatory element of certification programs.[31]

Implementation of proficiency testing will be as difficult as all of the other wishes and desires of the NRC Report. The span of control will necessarily need to be larger. Everyone involved in the proficiency testing must be accredited including the proficiency test providers and the bodies that accredit the proficiency test providers. In addition, some of the same issues that will effect resource availability with regard to certification will also effect implementation of proficiency testing. Primarily the availability of time and money will be required to conduct proficiency testing. For those laboratories that already do this, it's not an issue. For those that do not, proficiency testing will be required according to a schedule. Further, the money spent on these tests will have to come from somewhere else.[32]

Rules governing what and how proficiency testing for crime scene units will be like remain to be scene under a new plan such as this. It remains to be seen if there will be any at all. If blind proficiency testing from an outside source becomes the requirement, the proposition becomes much more difficult.

How to implement mandatory proficiency testing is another question that the NSTC attempts to answer. As one might expect, legislation requiring mandatory proficiency testing or mandatory proficiency testing as a condition of accreditation is a definite choice. Achieving the consensus of the stakeholders and passing a uniform law in all states or linking the use of proficiency testing to certain financial incentives such as the availability of grant money or training are other, viable choices.[33]

To this end, in the fall of 2014, the National Commission of Forensic Science Policy published a policy paper advocating universal accreditation.[34] In it they noted that there are 7,000 to 10,000 forensic science service providers (FSSPs) employing between 35,000 to 50,000 persons, a majority of which are not accredited. They define an FSSP as anyone who "applies scientific practices to recognize, collect, analyze, or interpret physical evidence and issues test results, provides laboratory reports, or offers interpretation, conclusions, or opinions through testimony with respect to such evidence."[35]

This certainly can be construed to include crime scene investigators. And, if a crime scene investigation unit is an FSSP under this definition, then it can further be extrapolated that, in order to become accredited, the members providing this service will need to become certified in order to meet accreditation standards.

As one might suspect, the proposed implementation strategy would tie federal funding to accreditation. In addition, they propose that federal prosecutions rely only on analysis conducted by accredited FSSPs after January 2020.[36]

Summary

Accreditation, certification, and proficiency testing are all intertwined together. One cannot be affective without the other in some way. The implementation of mandatory accreditation, certification and proficiency testing all come with difficulties. They recognize that there are problems with the current models for each of these topics. Standing along, not one of these things can or will make forensic science better. Even as a group, they cannot completely solve all issues that might arise.

Consider these issues. Should a forensic science service provider be accredited? Can a forensic science service provider (for example a laboratory or crime scene unit) be accredited if its personnel are not certified? Can the personnel be certified if they are not tested? It obviously depends on what an individual believes, however, in the end it will truly rest on what the policy makers believe. It seems that the policy is shifting in the direction of accreditation and certification. Proficiency testing will be a part of this scheme.

The Criminal Justice and Forensic Science Reform Act

A third event to note is the introduction of the Criminal Justice and Forensic Science Reform Act in the United States Senate by Senators Leahy and Cronyn. The wording of the bill seems an attempt to legislate some of the recommendations for many of the issues described in both the NAS Report and the National Science and Technology Council Report. A description of the bill can be found under the press releases section of Senator Leahy's website.[37] A synopsis of the legislation can be found on the IAI website.[38]

In general, the bill aims to accomplish a few things. It aims to promote national accreditation and certification standards in order to strengthen oversight of labs and practitioners. It seeks to promote the development of best practices as well as a national research policy.

Specifically, the legislation would create the Office of Forensic Science within the Department of Justice which will coordinate efforts with NIST. It would also create a Presidential Forensic Science Board. This legislation would seek to enact the recommendations of both the NAS Report and the NSTC recommendations.

What Might this Mean and Where Do We Go From Here

The path forward will be paved with good intentions and, it seems, will begin with some sort of accreditation and certification policy. It will apply to any service provider that performs some kind of forensic testing. Although these reports are aimed at laboratories, the wording cannot be ignored. Even if the initial focus is on laboratory entities, one could argue that the goals of finding and preserving evidence that identifies and convicts the guilty and not the innocent cannot be achieved without proper work being done at the crime scene.

The reasons why crime scene investigation was not specifically mentioned in these documents is not explained nor abundantly clear. Perhaps the authors fail to realize how important crime scene investigation is to the outcome of a forensic investigation. Perhaps they feel that the larger problem resides with the analysis and interpretation of certain types of evidence. It could also be that they recognize that crime scene investigation must evolve as laboratory procedures do and not the other way around. It probably doesn't matter because at some point their attention will turn to crime scene investigation service providers. Once any problems perceived to be occurring in the laboratory setting are fixed, they will realize that any other issues encountered are not as a result of the laboratory, the analysis, or the interpretation. Evidence routinely contaminated at the crime scene investigation stage may be enough to draw the attention of these people. As DNA techniques become more sensitive it will be harder and harder not to contaminate a scene.

We should take a cautionary step back and take stock of how things like accreditation and certification will help crime scene investigation and some of the realities that will accompany them. Only the NTSC report really considers the policy implications posed by mandatory, universal accreditation and certification. (These programs pose issues operationally and financially; however neither accreditation nor certifications are a sure way to achieve the goals that they hope to achieve.)

Generally speaking, accreditation programs for either a forensic laboratory or a crime scene unit use ISO standards that were not truly made for or specific to either. What makes accreditation work with these ISO standards are the additional, supplemental requirements included in the certification requirements by the accrediting bodies (the organizations that come and inspect and see if the lab or crime scene unit is following the ISO and added requirements).

So far as crime scene units are concerned, this is even truer. There are no specific ISO standards that apply to crime scene units, although two standards are being applied currently. As noted in the NAS Report, one of the problems with accreditation is that it does not ensure that best practices are used. Forensic service providers create manuals and procedures that govern everything they do in their laboratory. What they do does not have to adhere to a gold standard or be a best practice. What they must do is live by the manuals. As long as they say what they do and do what they say their accreditation remains safe, so to speak. And so it is true for crime scene unit accreditation.

The problem with this model is that crime scene investigation can be very simple in some respects and very complicated in others. For the sake of discussion, let us not even consider reconstruction techniques such as blood stain pattern analysis and ballistic trajectory analysis. Let us pretend that, eventually, those disciplines, and others that rely on expert interpretation will be separate areas from general crime scene investigation. Let us consider just crime scene investigation in a very narrow definition. Let us say that crime scene investigation involves, very generally, the recognition of evidence, the documentation of evidence, the recovery and preservation of evidence and searching for evidence (which will employ its own set of techniques such as reagents, fingerprint techniques, light techniques and photographic techniques) a gap still exists. Crime scene investigators may still have to deal with these expert interpretation types of evidence at a crime scene in order to process the scene. Unless accreditation mandates having investigators with certain kinds of expertise on hand, the generalist that processes the scene will have to document the evidence in such a way that the documentation can be used satisfactorily in place of attendance at the scene by the particular subject matter "expert."

The reality is that accreditation for crime scene units, if done to the standards that are alluded to in the NAS and NSTC Reports, will be just as complex and just as demanding as any accreditation scheme for a laboratory. Consider just for a moment the need to document evidence so that, if needed, a reconstruction of the events can be attempted. It is not always feasible to reconstruct every crime scene. Depending upon workload, and the types of services performed it may never be feasible to expend the resources to reconstruct any crime scene at the time of the investigation. The data will still need to be collected as if a reconstruction was going to be performed. Simply because there is no one able to perform the reconstruction at that very moment does not mean that the criminal justice system should be deprived of the opportunity later on. Also, the significance of the data may not be recognized at the time, but if properly documented can still lead to useful information later on. Some hybridized accreditation plan for crime scene units may need developing allowing for this data collection but not necessarily a reconstruction, especially if an expert is not available to the crime scene unit for whatever reason.

Whoever is charged with the task of oversight for the accreditation of crime scene units will need to bear all of these issues in mind. Current accreditation schemes may not be robust or specific enough for crime scene units. They may be a great start but if the desired effect cannot be achieved with the status quo, then it may be better to enhance existing standards to create a standard that better achieves the goals.

As was noted in the NAS Report, those with ultimate oversight may have to force some changes in the accreditation standards to include new ideas and mandatory requirements for things such as best practices. That would be a good place to examine the whole with an eye to change what needs to be changed and add what needs to be added.

Since, at this point, there is no certain way to predict what will ultimately be done, the best way to proceed may be to start gearing up for accreditation based upon current standards if the particular crime scene unit's situation allows for it.

Certification of crime scene investigators is a little further along than accreditation. The International Association for Identification has been working on investigator certification for many years. At this time, the main requirement to obtain a certification is passing a written exam. As indicated by the NAS and NTSC reports, this may not be enough. The current certification scheme has no requirements for practical examinations, ongoing proficiency testing, and there is no case review.

Instead of these components, the International Association for Identification outlines minimum training requirements and presumes, perhaps, that the training classes or workshops used to satisfy them will have all of these components built in. For the most basic crime scene investigator certification, the IAI requires a minimum of one year of experience in crime scene related activities and 48 hours of training that is approved by the IAI's certification board. Recertification requires prescribed hours of approved continuing education training in crime scene topics. This is a great start, however flawed when viewed from the position of the NAS and NSTC Reports. The IAI is in the best position currently to create a program that would conform to the desires of the NAS and NSTC Reports.

Crime scene investigation is a very hands on job and having no practical testing is an issue that needs improving if this is to satisfy the requirements alluded to by the NAS Report and the NTSC Report. Although current certification methods are not a perfect solution, the current available IAI certification may be on its way to becoming one as time and attention to the program continue. Perhaps ongoing funding could allow it to be brought to a place where it would be a program that satisfies the sentiment of the NAS and NSTC Reports.

When a crime scene unit considers accreditation and certification, it must be prepared for all of the individual tasks that it will take to make these goals obtainable. Accreditation will require a whole host of changes that a crime scene unit may not be ready for. The unit will have to have a training program and training manual. The unit may come to find that not all of their personnel have the requirements of the current training program and the unit may have to find a way to bring everyone up to that level. The crime scene unit will have to produce a procedural guide (or field manual) that outlines what they do and how they will do it. The unit will need a quality assurance plan which may require hiring personnel to run it. The unit may need a technical manager to run certain aspects of the operation especially if management does not have the requisite forensic background. It will also have to have the tools, materials and personnel to sustain the operations that the unit says it will. The unit will also have to have plans for continuity of operations in the event of large-scale incidents.

Each one of these areas will, in turn, have its own set of requirements. The more the unit does and the larger it is, the larger the amount of work will be. Consider the benefit of implementing some or all of these things, even if the unit does not wish to seek accreditation in the current climate.

Every crime scene unit should do the very best job that it can. One could even argue that there exists a duty to perform the tasks to the highest possible standards. Of course, there are going to be complications and situations that require someone to make judgment decisions quickly; however, if the systems are in place, these decisions will be based on solid training and understanding of the tasks that need to be performed.

The ultimate goals of the crime scene investigation and the crime scene investigator can be debated. Yet there must be some basic goals that everyone can agree upon. If we look at the "guidance" given by the NAS Report, the ultimate goals of all of forensic science should mirror those of the criminal justice system. How each area of forensic science achieves these goals will differ. Crime scene investigation endeavors to recognize evidence (what is it and how does it help tell the story or create a linkage), document it so that the context in which it is found is preserved, and recover it so that it is preserved until analysis. None of these basic tasks can occur unless the whole crime scene operation runs according to plan. Yes, one can be lucky, but it is better to be consistently good than lucky.

Recognition of evidence is more than just seeing something and knowing what it is. It is understanding what role it played in the events and how it will help the investigation either by linking persons and places or by leading to other evidence that will. Recognition is more than just finding ballistic evidence at the scene of a shooting. It can induce an understanding of when other types of evidence, perhaps latent, might be sought. So, the task of recognition is more than just looking around. It is knowing when and how to look for things that may not be apparent.

Documentation takes on a variety of techniques all aimed at the purpose of preserving the context of evidence in the scene and the scene itself. Some of the tasks can be technical in nature, especially those having to do with photography, but there is more. Sketching and measurements are required, especially if a reconstruction might be required later on. These measurements will need to be done with precision and accuracy. The task cannot be taken cavalierly, and requires knowledge, training and skill.

Recovery of evidence must be done in such a way that it is preserved for analysis. Improper handling can lead to contamination or degradation. Any of these things can cause problems with analysis and interpretation. Some items of evidence that otherwise would have led to useful information may now be useless to the investigation. Sometimes circumstances cannot be overcome but, if personnel are well trained and set up for success, they will succeed more often than not.

None of these three tasks can be done successfully if all the pieces are not in place. Personnel must have the right training and the right equipment. Further, the equipment must be available and functioning according to specifications all of the time. None of this will happen if the unit is not running as it should be.

Underpinning these tasks are other areas such as personnel, crime scene practices that prevent contamination, training and certification, procedural guides, equipment needs, managing operations at the crime scene, documenting the crime scene, quality assurance and pre-incident planning, that allow for continuity of services. Each of these areas can be evaluated to ensure that the unit is running optimally. Without these basic needs addressed, the management team leaves to chance that things will just go right. That is not a good way of managing a crime scene unit. All of these tasks work toward the common goal of ensuring that once the investigators are on scene, they can work efficiently and produce the best product possible.

In the end, accreditation and certification are noble goals and tangible ways for the criminal justice system to quickly identify a quality product. However, as they stand now, they are not perfect solutions. Is any solution perfect? Absolutely not. But a crime scene unit could choose to exceed the expectations of minimal standards and seek to do better. The crime scene unit will certainly not be punished for exceeding the accreditation and certification standards already in place and available to them. If the unit exceeds these standards, they are more than ready to seek accreditation and certification. However, running the operations of a crime scene unit in such a way that success is guaranteed on a regular basis is more important than that. It is a manager's duty to embark on a path forward.

What the Book Hopes to Accomplish

This is, primarily, a book of ideas. No one is endorsing any particular accreditation program or certification program. No one is demanding a particular methodology for operations. No one endorses a demand for performing things a certain way. No one is saying that if you don't do what this book proposes then you aren't doing it the right way. The only idea that is endorsed is to do the best job you can do. Do a quality job for the sake of doing a quality job. Do a quality job for the sake of all those who rely on crime scene investigators to do a quality job. Never rest and always strive to find better ways to accomplish the crime scene task. These are not necessarily longer ways, or more strict ways, or more complicated ways, but ways that achieve the goal more efficiently and lead to a better quality product. Consider the ideas offered in this book and understand what problems they attempt to solve. In this way, it may be able to help crime scene units recognize and fix issues before they hamper crime scene investigation operations.

This book does not purport to have a monopoly on truth. The only thing this book offers is experience. These experiences are with issues that caused problems, ideas that didn't solve the problems and ideas that did solve them. Very often, people don't see potentially serious issues before they become big problems. Hopefully the reader will see that the ideas in this book will relate to problems or potential problems they have.

Our hope that this book can help everyone strive to do the best job that can be done, to be aware of pitfalls that can hamper that goal and to run a crime scene unit to the highest level that it can achieve. Although it is hoped that the ideas presented are useful and may help a crime scene unit become accredited and its personnel certified, that is not the main function of this text. The main function of the text is to be helpful without being technical. The subject matter has, hopefully, been presented in a non-technical manner so as not to become a barrier to those that may read it. It is presented in a manner that, hopefully, beginners and seasoned veterans alike will find useful and easy to understand.

The book is primarily written for two groups of people. The first are those who are in leadership positions; those supervisors that affect and/or create policy, and know little or nothing about crime scene investigation and/or forensic science. The second are those supervisors or investigators who may want to examine and improve their operations, may be looking for ways to get started, ideas on ways to assess what they are doing and ideas to try or ideas to modify so that they are more tailored to fit their needs.

As noted already by the NAS Report, many crime scene investigation responsibilities fall to local law enforcement agencies either at the state or municipal level. Although the investigators are trained and aware of what they do and how to do it, supervisors thrust into positions of leadership often have little formal knowledge about crime scene investigation and forensic science. Sometimes, their main exposure comes from investigations that they have been a part of in the past or what they see on television. These supervisors are at a distinct disadvantage. What takes investigators time to learn through study and practice over the course of years, supervisors sometimes must learn at a moment's notice. Many adapt to their situation quickly. Most, if not all, are forced to learn about different issues when problems present themselves and they are forced to react. In these cases, supervision can hopefully look to the investigators to solve the problems for them on an *ad hoc* basis.

Being reactive isn't always the best way to handle all situations, especially when it is avoidable. Many crime scene investigators will find that when they really think about it, they act proactively more often then they realize. When situations and conditions are present at a crime scene, they act in a manner that mitigates whatever "damage" the situation or condition would have caused if no action were taken. They recognized a condition and acted before it became a problem.

Crime scene units, as a whole, shouldn't run this way when it comes to their daily operations. Crime scene investigators do not operate this way. When an investigator finds a better way of doing something they often implement it when and if the situation arises again.

The role of leadership should be to maintain good operations and improve when possible. In order to constantly assess and improve if needed, one should be able to recognize where the pitfalls in the particular operation are. If someone really has no basic idea of what the operation is supposed to be doing in the first place, this will be a hard task. Although knowledge will come in time, it is hoped that this book will decrease the amount of time it would take someone to get up to speed.

Finally, no one is advocating the reinvention of the wheel. It is a simple hope that this book will give investigators and supervisors the information they need to recognize when the wheel might need to be repaired or improved upon.

It is also a hope that, if an agency is starting a crime scene unit from scratch, that this book will be a resource for it to begin the process. The chapters are an outline of some of the main tasks that would need to be considered when starting from the beginning. The ideas offered on how to accomplish this task can help the organizers save time as they might serve as a springboard to reaching the goal. The ideas can be used as is or tailored to a specific operation.

For those that are looking to improve, encountering a problem or endeavoring to learn the basics about topics they didn't already know about, this book could prove useful. The text was designed so that it could be read whole or, if one topic was of interest, the chapter pertaining to it would stand on its own. They were designed to include enough necessary background information so that standing alone, it might prove a useful reference.

Sometimes, trying to improve a complicated, fluid, living operation can be difficult because one may not know where to start. Other times, it may be readily apparent that something isn't working. In some cases, there may be resistance to change because things have always been done a certain way. The purpose of accreditation is to act as a way to measure one's operation against some objective standard. Very often crime scene investigators measure their operations against others that they know of. What some have a hard time with is the recognition that something isn't working or that simple tweaks could improve it greatly.

This book is a text of ideas of varying standards that people could use to take stock of their own operations. Again, no one is proposing that this book is something that a crime scene unit should strive to live up to. These ideas aren't the stuff of legend. A majority of them have been used in one degree or another and have had various levels of success. They are offered as they are just ideas if someone needs them for improvement. At some point, someone will dictate the objective standard that all crime scene units will have to reach. This, most probably, isn't it. Hopefully, the crime scene investigation community will have a large say in what the objective standard will encompass.

How This Book Hopes to Help Its Readers

This book is not so much about how to process a crime scene. There are many good books already in existence that accomplish that task very well. This book is more about how to define, organize and keep the unit going as a whole. The main goal of the crime scene unit management should be to support the crime scene investigation operations. If the unit is running well, it has the maximum ability to support the crime scene investigation task. If this happens, at the very least, the crime scene investigators will have all the support they need to do their job efficiently, safely and reliably. The investigators will be able to arrive at the scene, with all the equipment they need, in proper working order so that they spend little time solving problems that should never have come up. Crime scene investigators should not have to spend time fixing problems that are foreseeable or should have been foreseeable. This wastes time and jeopardizes the crime scene. The operations will be the foundation on which all other investigative tasks are built upon. The time for checking to make sure everything is running smoothly is not when the request for service comes in. By then, it is too late. The time for checking is not at the beginning of someone's shift either. The unit may come in and need to respond immediately. The time for checking and ensuring that the operation is running smoothly is all the time. The crime scene unit must operate on a daily basis so that successful crime scene processing is achievable every day at every scene, and it may take non-investigative personnel to assist in the task.

In order to present the ideas in a logical way, the book is divided into eleven topics. They are: personnel, investigator safety, contamination prevention, training and certification, developing protocols, investigative equipment, the crime scene, scene documentation, quality assurance, pre-incident planning, and records management.

Each of these topics has the ability to hamper unit operations and therefore hamper crime scene operations. Some of these topics will be areas that will be scrutinized if a unit decides to prepare for accreditation. At any rate, they are some of the topics that could be assessed or might be implemented if the unit does not already. In short, these are some of the issues brought up in the NAS Report.

Personnel

The organization of a crime scene investigation unit and its personnel are very important to the efficiency and success of the unit. Recruitment, assignments and deployment should not be left to chance. Recognizing that support staff are just as important to the mission of the unit as investigative personnel are, management should make every effort to incorporate them into the organizational chart.

Recruitment of both support and investigative staff is a task that should be well thought out. Identifying candidates for both types of assignments should strive to identify those with the most likelihood of either excelling in the training program or in logistical assignments. The application process should reflect the jobs and tasks personnel will be asked to perform and certain positions in the future. The positions of Quality Assurance and Technical Manager may be mandatory. They will serve the unit in a functional way.

Another issue that one may want to consider is that some accrediting bodies will require that a crime scene unit have sufficient staff to perform the tasks and functions that the crime scene unit says it will. In order to ensure compliance, the unit may be required to perform the tasks and functions that it claims to do.

Investigator Safety

Investigator safety is always a top priority when performing any crime scene investigation. It starts in the investigator's office and works its way out into the field. Crime scene investigators are constantly exposed to various hazards from the scene, as in the case of blood borne pathogens, damaged structures (post blast or fire scene), from the forensic equipment, such as alternate light sources, and from chemicals used in the processing of evidence, such as fingerprint powders, ninhydrin, luminol, or amido black, to name a few. It's important to be fully aware of any hazards these forensic chemicals pose and what personal protection equipment and or actions must be used to maintain safety and what first aid treatment is required in case of exposure. Under the US Department of Labor's (US DOL), Occupational Safety and Health Administration (OSHA) Hazard Communication Standard (HCS) regulation (1910.1200), your employer must maintain, update, prominently display and make readily available in an easily accessible area, the Material Safety Data Sheets (MSDS) for all potentially harmful substances or materials to be handled or utilized by employees in the course of their duties.

Contamination Prevention

When crime scene investigators prioritize the goals, objectives and operations involved in crime scene investigations, scene/evidence, contamination and destruction, prevention and control, would only be second to the CSI's safety. In medical ethics there is an old adage, that is applicable to crime scene investigations, and that is, "Primum non nocere," which is Latin for, "First, do no harm." As part of our job we must understand Locard's Exchange Principle, which states that whenever two items come in contact, there will be an exchange. Investigators use this principle to help the investigations by establishing links like: whether a person or item was at, or came from, a location; whether a person was in possession of an item; or whether a person interacted with a victim. These are just a few examples of Locard's Principle; there are many more. Having said that, we must be mindful that investigators are subject to this same principle and must take measures to prevent and control our impact on the crime scene and the evidence found therein.

Training and Certification

Whether a unit employs civilian investigators with degrees in forensics or sworn officers, investigators, or detectives, with or without degrees, employers are responsible for the training and certification of the investigators for every aspect of the expected tasks with regard to the crime scene investigation. The crime scene unit must establish a written, detailed, validated and robust training and certification program as a part of its overall quality assurance and quality control (QA/QC) program. Agencies can't rely on degrees, previous training or experiences obtained before employment (or mere assignment to a crime scene investigative unit) to prepare investigators before sending them directly into the field, as this is just our foundation for employment or assignment. Employers must train and certify on the entire unit's forensic protocols, procedures, processes, field tests, methodologies, equipment, and tools, as well as, reports, paperwork, and courtroom testimony requirements. Testing must show proficiency and competency in all the aforementioned areas.

Developing Protocols

Procedures defining the ways and means that the crime scene unit will conduct business will be a requirement in the very near future. This will be especially true if accreditation will be a desire of the crime scene unit or a mandate for the future. When done well, creating and adhering to procedures will ensure that the best methods are followed when processing a crime scene. When considering the path forward, procedures will then be one of several measurable values that the accrediting body and thus the criminal justice system can look at in order to judge a crime scene unit. At this point, this will be true whether an accrediting body is assessing them or not. Standard procedures also serve to ensure consistency in performance as well as efficiency, since all investigators will perform tasks the same way. Mandating or guiding investigators will allow case files to adhere to a consistent model and the work product to be consistent across the board.

Investigative Equipment

Crime scene investigation is an endeavor that requires a large amount of equipment and supplies in order to maintain operations and complete of all of the steps of the process properly. As the demand for forensic evidence continues to increase within the criminal justice system, and forensic science continues on its path forward, the complexities and costs involved with supplying a CSI unit with adequate equipment and supplies will, in all likelihood, also increase. Crime scene investigation units who desire to improve their operations to meet higher standards or to seek accreditation under guidelines set forth by ASCLAD LAB or ISO 17025 may find that the process will require considerable research, planning and acquisition of equipment and supplies that may outpace existing budgets. In the near future, agency managers may be forced to face tough decisions on whether they can commit the required resources to maintain a full-scale crime scene unit. Some agencies may opt to provide some crime scene services in-house but rely on other agencies, or outsourcing (a process familiar to many crime labs) to provide others. As forensics moves forward each agency needs to assess its operations and obligations to the public which it serves to determine how to best plan and manage operations. Part of that process is examining the equipment that is needed to provide quality crime scene processing services.

Today a crime scene investigator uses a small arsenal of equipment to process a scene and complete casework. Upon arrival at the scene the CSI uses an array of tools to document the crime scene and then moves to a second set of tools to search for and recognize probative evidence. Once evidence is located a third set of tools may be required to process or enhance the evidence and then of course additional tools and supplies will be required to collect and package the evidence so it can be safely transported away from the scene for laboratory testing or secure storage. While all of this activity takes place additional tools and supplies are required to protect the scene from contamination as well as protect the investigative team from hazards.

The Crime Scene

Crime scenes vary greatly in size, scope and complexity. Some crime scenes, such as residential burglaries, may be handled routinely by a single investigator being dispatched to the scene with little difficulty arising during the assignment. However, major incidents such as homicide investigations will overwhelm a single individual and instead require a crime scene investigation team (CSI Team) to respond, process the scene and complete the casework and administrative process. CSI Teams vary in size from a small team of two persons to much larger teams depending upon the needs of the investigation; however, regardless of the size the overall integrity, continuity and completeness of the investigation will be improved when an organized team concept is employed. Although the incident at hand will dictate the size of the CSI Team, the basic team structure will remain the same regardless of the incident.

Scene Documentation

Criminal investigation is a core service provided by law enforcement in the United States. When the investigation revolves around the commission of a violent crime then a forensic investigation will likely be required, and at the core of that process is the need for documentation. The crime scene investigation is the beginning of the forensic science process and a large part of that involves collecting scene documentation that is needed to facilitate the remaining steps of the process and present the findings in court. This chapter will look at various forms of documentation and the accepted methods for accomplishing them properly. Where they exist we will look at formal standards for crime scene documentation and where they do not exist we will discuss what might constitute an acceptable level of documentation. We will also build on the topics covered in Chapter 6 for developing standard operating procedures for crime scene documentation.

Quality Assurance

Quality assurance programs will most probably be a requirement in the future for all forensic science service providers, crime scene units included. This is a worthwhile goal. In order to ensure that the final product of any analysis can be relied upon, the quality of every step in the operation must be traceable. This means that quality assurance must start at the beginning, and the beginning is very often at the crime scene level.

Quality assurance is required for two reasons at a the crime scene level: first, to create a chain of quality assurance from collection to the completion of the analysis and second to ensure that the crime scene unit will be unencumbered when time is of the essence. Evidence that is diminished in quality because an action was not able to be taken in a timely manner, or at all is a failure of management which needs to be controlled.

Pre-Incident Planning

When it comes to a crime scene unit's preparedness and response to major incidents, the ability to continue operations in the face of adversity will be important. In order for the crime scene unit to maintain its continuity of operations (Con-Ops), during a high consequent event (HCE), that is to say an incident or event beyond the crime scene unit's normal response capabilities, there must be pre-incident planning, preparation and preparedness, which includes back up facilities, equipment, and other assets.

Management has to understand and prioritize the possible HCE threats to their jurisdiction, such as those events that are announced and planned well in advance, for example the Super Bowl, a political event/convention, a Thanksgiving Day parade or New Year's Eve celebration. In addition to the planned events, let us not forget those unannounced incidents that take us by surprise, such as: terrorist attacks involving a weapon of mass destruction (WMD), transportation incidents (plane or train crash), with or without mass injuries or mass fatalities, and construction incidents involving the collapse of structures (buildings/bridges) or equipment (cranes) with or without mass injuries or mass fatalities, to name a few.

Once this has occurred, the crime scene unit has to understand how each of the identified HCE threats will impact their day-to-day operations. From this a needs assessment is developed and prioritized, so that that the jurisdiction can begin its preparations and preparedness.

Records Management

All of the effort expanded in processing a crime scene must eventually be condensed and described in the form of a written crime scene report. The crime scene report should have a pre-determined format that ensures continuity across casework and comprehensive reporting of all pertinent facts. The report format and style may differ from one agency to another but should remain consistent among various investigators within a single unit. The format and style may be dictated in large part by the parent agency's methods and by what has been historically acceptable. A crime scene unit compiles a large amount of records during the course of business. These records are both physical records which are printed on paper and take up space for storage and, electronic records which are generated by information technology devices. Regardless of their form many of these records have legal connotation to them. This creates responsibility for the Crime Scene Unit Managers to employ robust management systems that are in keeping with good business practice and current legal standing. A crime scene unit's business records created while engaged in scene investigations must be given special consideration in the way they are created and controlled. Since the business of the crime scene unit involves the investigations of crimes which have very long statute of limitations, or no statute of limitations, these records may become required at unpredictable times well into the future. Furthermore even after a case is closed the records must still be maintained for the possibility of appeals or some other action requiring the case to be reopened. The records are also sensitive in nature and they must be maintained in a way that protects the privacy of crime victims and the decency standards demanded by society.

Summary

The path forward for forensic science and crime scene investigation will be paved with good intentions. Hopefully, those laying the bricks will be those most intimately involved in the field. Those most intimately involved are best positioned to implement the needs of the criminal justice system as a whole. In other words, forensic scientists will have to listen to the problems presented to them by the other stakeholders and find ways to solve them.

It will not be an easy task. It will take support and money, but, if forensic science practitioners do not work hard to clean their own house, someone will essentially do it for them. The house is not a total wreck. Forensic science practitioners should not think for a minute that this is a disaster. There have been many-hard working people and groups implementing systems to ensure quality for many, many years before the NAS Report was written. Obviously, forensic science cannot rest upon any gains made and must continue to forge ahead in the quest to improve even more.

Crime scene investigation will not be immune from this situation. The forensic system will require it to demonstrate that it has been, and still is improving its methods. It will be able to do so by adopting systems similar to other disciplines and subspecialties only modified to demonstrate quality for the unique ways in which crime scene units operate.

Following the same line, crime scene units will also be required to demonstrate that their operations are up to the task as well. The unit will need to demonstrate that all aspects of its operation can support the work it does in the best possible way in that it is employing best practices where they exist. This book hopes to assist by outlining ideas that may help in achieving these goals.

Notes

1 Strengthening Forensic Science in the United States: A Path Forward; Committee on Identifying the Needs of the Forensic Sciences Community, National Research Council, The National Academies Press, Washington, DC, August 2009, p.1.
2 Ibid., p.2.
3 Ibid., p.2.
4 Ibid., p.2.
5 Ibid., p.4.
6 Ibid., p.4.
7 Ibid., pp.4–5.
8 Ibid., p.6.
9 Ibid., p.7.
10 Ibid., p.8
11 Ibid., pp.15–16.
12 Ibid., p.19.
13 Ibid., p.22.
14 Ibid., p.22.
15 Ibid., pp.23–24.
16 Ibid., p.56.
17 Ibid., pp.56–57.
18 Press Release. [online] Available at: www.nist.gov/forensics/osac_102914.cfm [Accessed December, 21 2014].

19 Press Release. [online] Available at: www.nist.gov/forensics/osac_102914.cfm [Accessed December 21, 2014].
20 National Science and Technology Council, Strengthening the Forensic Sciences, p.. iii. [online] Available at: www.whitehouse.gov/sites/default/files/microsites/ostp/NSTC/forensic_science___may_2014.pdf [Accessed June 20, 2014].
21 Ibid., p. iii.
22 Ibid., p.1.
23 Ibid., p.4.
24 Ibid., pp.4–5.
25 Ibid., p.6.
26 Ibid., p.7
27 Ibid., pp.7–8.
28 Ibid., p.9.
29 Ibid., p.11.
30 Ibid., p.13.
31 Ibid., p.20.
32 Ibid., p.22.
33 Ibid., p.23.
34 Press Release. [online] Available at: www.justice.gov/sites/default/files/pages/attachments/2-14/10/15/draft_on_universal_accreditation.pdf [Accessed December 14, 2014].
35 Ibid., p.2.
36 Ibid., p.3.
37 Press Release. [online] Available at: www.leahy.senate.gov/press/leahy-and-cornyn-introduce-sweeping-forensics-reform-legislation [Accessed June 21, 2014].
38 IAI Summary of The Criminal Justice and Forensic Science Reform Act. [online] Available at: www.theiai.org/president/cjfsra-one-pager-outside.pdf [Accessed June 21, 2014].

2

UNIT ORGANIZATION AND PERSONNEL

Overview

Whether building a crime scene investigation unit from the ground up or working toward the optimization of a current operation, there are several factors that should be considered when organizing the personnel of a crime scene investigation unit. They include, but are not limited to:

- The organization of personnel, both support and investigative personnel
- The application and selection process of both support and investigative personnel
- Personnel deployment at the crime scene

In this chapter, we will discuss not only the application and selection process of those assigned to the crime scene unit but also the qualification and skill sets that will be required of them.

How a particular agency runs its operation and deploys its personnel should not be left to tradition, especially if those traditions are neither efficient nor effective. The crime scene investigation unit and its personnel must be organized so that the unit runs efficiently but cannot be structured so rigidly that it ceases to maintain the ability to remain flexible as crime scene investigations will always require some measure of flexibility. Although there are no wrong answers (except sticking with those that do not work), there are definite lessons a manager can and should take away from the various ideas presented here. First, don't be afraid to try something new if the current model doesn't work. Second, take the personnel application and selection process seriously. Third, define the tasks that will be required of all of the personnel assigned to the unit and hold each person accountable for their performance. Finally, support of the primary mission, investigating crime scenes, is more important than one might think. It is better to be good than then to be lucky.

The two main groups of personnel requiring organization based upon their functions, are investigative staff and support staff, including both staff-level and supervisory-level personnel.

Investigative staff are those persons tasked with carrying out the primary mandate(s) of the unit: recognizing, documenting, and recovering physical evidence. Support staff are those persons tasked with ensuring that the whole of the operation has the ability to run efficiently and without interruption.

In the perfect world of proper staffing levels and funding, most agencies would prefer to have their staff members dedicated to only one specific or singular task, or at least a small number of tasks that are very closely related. Under the best of circumstances, this would mean persons performing either investigative functions or support functions, but not both. Due to perennial manpower and budgetary limitations, all those concerned must understand that individuals within the unit may be required to wear multiple hats and perform both investigative and support functions. Further, those performing support functions may have to perform more than one support task.

There are other staffing models that management could try. One envisions multiple individuals working on the same group of related tasks. These "working groups" would be responsible for a number of related tasks and no one person would be responsible for any one, singular item. The group would be responsible for all of the tasks assigned to them. This might be a "normal" situation when it comes to operating at a crime scene in that the investigative team completes all tasks required to process the crime scene, however it seems quite abnormal to have more than one person keeping track of the same administrative or support issue. Control and dissemination of information related to the task will become problematic. For example, issues may arise concerning who has the most updated information. The problems created by systems like this are only exacerbated if the agency has a heavy case load, due to either the number of crime scenes the agency responds to, or the amount of time needed to complete each scene.

When personnel are not assigned to a singular task, time management (in this case, the time needed to *properly* complete each task any one single person is assigned to complete), becomes problematic. Having staff dedicated solely to the support of the investigative mission appears, on its face, to allow for a smoother overall operation, especially when an agency is "busy." One's sense is that this is true. When individuals divide their time among multiple tasks, especially if the agency has a heavy work load, the system prevents any one person from devoting the necessary time to his/her assignment. As alluded to earlier, confusion will be created when multiple people are tasked to monitor and/or complete a single task or related group of them (investigative endeavors excluded). When there are insufficient eyes on any one area of an operation, or an "I thought you did it" mindset, gaps and inefficiencies can quickly appear, creating issues for the bottom line. In this case, the bottom line is the efficiency of the crime scene investigation.

Included under the umbrella of personnel is the application and selection process. The selection process will differ if the unit or agency recruits individuals for support assignments and investigative assignments separately. Although there will be a need for an overlap of knowledge, the abilities of support personnel and investigative personnel will differ.

Support personnel will need to understand the job of the investigator and know how the tools used by the investigator work, but will not need to be able to produce the same work product that the investigator will. Support personnel will need to understand how reagents and cameras are supposed to work properly, but will not be required to take a crime scene photograph. Their primary skills will be more logistical in nature and so their skill set will be different.

Investigative personnel will not only need to know the mechanics behind the tasks they perform but they will also actually have to perform them in a competent way, producing a quality product. This includes several tasks such as:

- Photography
- Sketching
- Diagramming
- Descriptive writing
- Report writing
- Tasks that require manual dexterity
- The understanding and application of scientific principles

While considering all of the ideas presented here, management must also work to identify those issues that do and do not apply to them and also identify situations not covered or presented here that may be unique to their operation. Only once these tasks have been completed can managers undertake a true accounting of how to maximize efficiency in their crime scene unit.

Support Personnel

Overview

When considering how to organize and deploy personnel in a crime scene unit, the first group that should receive consideration is support personnel. This idea probably runs contrary to what one normally thinks should happen. Most managers might think that support assignments should generally receive what's left over after the assignments dedicated to the primary mission of the unit are allocated. This makes sense since the investigative functions *must* be filled. Management can then consider how to distribute support functions to whoever is left, or as secondary assignments to investigators. Support of the primary investigative mission, however, is more essential to good operations than many recognize, without regard to how "busy" a particular agency is and management should consider dedicating the proper resources to it immediately.

If an agency is "busy" meaning a large number of requests, and investigators respond to scenes with the wrong equipment, with inadequate, poorly maintained equipment, or non-functioning equipment, the end results can be bad. At the very minimum, there can be a delay in recovering evidence and at most a failure to properly document and/or recover evidence. If an agency is "slow" meaning they have relatively few requests for service, and investigators respond with the same problems related to equipment, the results will be the same.

This should not be taken cavalierly. Delay in recovering evidence, especially evidence that is fragile or subject to degredation because of environmental factors, can quickly lead to failure of the mission. As we know, once evidence is damaged or lost, the information it contains will be damaged or lost and may not be recoverable. In order to maintain fluid operations, management must have a clear idea of what their support staff will need to accomplish on a regular basis in order to allocate the proper resources. Maintenance of data and proper tracking of data (for things such as inventory) will become important to the mission. When one considers what a "regular basis" implies, we generally mean on a daily or an "often" schedule. It is important to remember that some data, such as equipment calibration may have to be tracked on a monthly or yearly basis. Thus, the need to be aware of these dates in advance and plan ahead for them is also something that must be done regularly, even if infrequently.

Someone must always be thinking about important issues that directly affect the primary mission of the crime scene investigation unit such as equipment availability, expendable materials, maintenance, scheduling, and quality assurance. There is nothing more troublesome then running out of essential equipment or materials during a crime scene investigation, but don't believe for a minute that it can't happen.

As previously mentioned, how extensive support staff can be will rest, primarily, on an agency's manpower limitations; and management may find that it has to rely on a small group of people dividing their time among several tasks. It is tempting to leave the decision on support staff to the end as a means to see how much is left in the pot, but, this may not be the best approach. Management must have the forethought to identify what is needed to maintain a fluid and efficient operation. If the management team does not have the experience to accomplish this task, then they must identify and seek help from those that do. The first step will be to consider candidate qualifications and to identify what tasks will be the responsibility of support staff. A partial list of some tasks that are important enough that they should have personnel dedicated to them are:

- Inventory control
- Quality assurance
- Maintenance and calibration
- Vehicle maintenance
- Training
- Communications

Qualifications

Qualifications of support staff members will be a serious consideration for any management team. This is not a position where someone will be responsible for simply ordering stuff. These positions require someone who can, at the minimum, have a similar knowledge base as those in the investigative positions. Support staff personnel must be familiar with the techniques and equipment used to process crime scenes. Support staff personnel must know how to use the equipment so that they may ensure that it functions properly. They must be well organized so that they can efficiently and accurately track large amounts of continuously changing information. Support staff personnel must also be technically savvy. They must be able to use, test and assist others with trouble-shooting equipment when it does not work as expected.

Staff filling roles in training must have the requisite experience, education and training to perform crime scene investigations. Additionally, those assigned as trainers must be willing participants in the process. They will most likely be accepting an increased work load. Trainers must also be willing to move at a pace suitable for the instruction of new investigators for the purpose of exposing a new investigator to the processes used to accomplish the investigation. It may also be useful to seek candidates for training that have good writing skills and teaching skills as well. What follows is a list of tasks and a short description of what it takes to satisfy them. In this way, a manager can decide what tasks his or her unit will need to do, what tasks do not apply to their specific unit and thus, how much in the way of resources they will need to dedicate.

Investigators (i.e. non-support staff personnel) must realize that they hold responsibility for many things. First, they hold responsibility for their work at scenes. They must also realize that they hold at least a secondary responsibility for their equipment needs when carrying out their scene related duties. If the support staff holds primary responsibility for ensuring that vehicles have an adequate stock of materials necessary for operating at a crime scene, investigators cannot in good conscience respond to a scene, either knowingly or unknowingly, without needed materials. If they do, and evidence is lost to the weather, contaminated or its value otherwise diminished, they are equally responsible.

Budgeting

Equipment Management – Inventory Control and Maintenance

Expendable Materials

Every crime scene investigation unit should have an inventory or list of the equipment required to carry out their mandate(s). This will include both expendable materials (swabs, fingerprint powder, tape and bags for example), as well as non-expendable items (alternate light sources, electrostatic dust lifters, casting frames, ballistic trajectory equipment, photographic equipment and the like).

The inventory might be based on several factors. Briefly, what services the unit will provide and how the unit will perform specific tasks will play a large role in these decisions.

As important as knowing what you use is knowing how much is used during a period of time and how much time it takes to replenish unit supplies. How quickly it takes to replenish supplies can be affected by factors outside of the unit's control. Some questions that support staff may want to have answers to are:

- About how much is used?
- About how long do I take to use this amount?
- At what amount will I need to initiate an order?
- How much time will it take to navigate the internal bureaucracy?
- What is the shipping time?

So, in other words, support staff must be assigned to manage equipment and to monitor and control inventory. Inventory control is an essential requirement of any good business, and this applies to crime scene investigation units as well.

The complexity of the task will increase with the amount of and types of items the unit requires to perform services. Simply, the more there is to track, the more complex the tracking becomes. The larger the span of control becomes, the harder it is to control. If a particular crime scene unit handles all types of physical evidence and/or has a high volume of work, the task becomes more difficult, and good control systems are even more essential. Being able to continuously measure usage and replenishment is essential.

These functions will be carried out on a regularly scheduled basis, and there are any number of methods that can be used to achieve good results. These can include, but are not limited to:

- Commercial inventory control systems
- Regularly and/or periodically counting cases or units of items
- Regularly and/or periodically counting individual items
- Displaying individual items in bins with marks indicating approximate amounts (i.e. a measuring cup)

In reality, any system that serves the purpose of quick and roughly accurate inventory measurement will suffice.

As noted, it is important to have some understanding of how quickly the various items are used. Based upon the amount of time it takes from order to delivery, it would be worthwhile to have a trigger point where, when a certain amount is left in storage, an order is placed and stocks are replenished. Management should ensure that there is a clear system in place for this task.

Laying out a physical location for the crime scene unit's home base must include adequate storage for all materials. Consideration should be given to having adequate space where materials can be stored in such a manner that they can be easily accessed and counted. This planning will allow for inventory tracking for as long as the situation is maintained. Storage plans should also take into account the delicate nature of materials such as reagents used by the unit for things like blood detection and electronics like cameras, batteries, computers, total stations, and alternate light sources. Support staff should understand the layout intimately, knowing where all items are.

Reagents, Chemicals and Other Sensitive Items

Reagents, usually in the form of various chemicals or chemical mixtures and perhaps even standards, will require more effort to track. The task is more than just reordering material before it runs out. The task is made more complex because expiration and/or shelf life will also need to be considered. What's more, they will also require special storage conditions. So in the end, inventory control must be mindful, not only of the amount of reagents on hand and the amounts regularly used, but also the amounts lost to expiration and when it is lost to expiration. This is often an imprecise science and requires good record keeping. The unit most probably will not have any control over the expiration dates of the reagents it receives. So the system used to order replacement supplies will need to account for this variable.

Aside from reagents and chemicals, other materials used during crime scene investigations can have a shelf life. This shelf life can also vary depending upon storage conditions. For example, although no expiration date is printed on the box, Mikrosil, according to the Technical Information Sheet from Sirchie, has a one-year shelf life.[1]

A final issue to consider regarding this subject is that other materials, although they have no expiration date, or expressed shelf life, can lose efficacy over time. An example of this are gelatin lifters. According to manufacturers' literature, depending upon storage conditions and packaging condition, the gelatin lifter's color can tint or the lifter can lose tack.[2] So, aside from keeping track of materials that do not have expiration dates or a shelf life, support staff must also keep track of materials with known expiration dates and/or shelf lives and be familiar with materials used and their current storage conditions in order to maintain optimal results for use in the field.

Management should also realize that materials that are deployed require tracking as well. Management should consider controlling the deployment of these kinds of sensitive materials. If reagents or other materials that have expiration or loss of efficacy are deployed somewhere other than storage, its location will need to be known so that it can be recovered when required.

The issue should not be taken lightly. The person(s) assigned to support the mission of the unit must be more than just people who count and order stuff. In reality, they must understand the needs and rules of the mission. Again, it is easier to work towards getting things done right at the beginning than try to repair something that may not be fixable.

Quality Assurance

Another responsibility that will fall to support staff is the maintenance, in some part, of a quality assurance program. This can include:

- The verification of reagents
- The maintenance of standards and associated records
- The maintenance of expiration schedules
- The maintenance of distribution records
- The maintenance of non-expendable equipment including calibration schedules

Reagents and standards may play a large role during the crime scene investigation, and quality assurance will begin when the unit receives either reagents or standards. Ensuring that reagents and standards work (verification), prior to their use at a scene is a mandatory step in the investigative process. False positive results, although not optimal, are something that can be lived with. They increase the lab's workload but do not necessarily diminish the case overall. False negatives, however, are a problem. Failing to recognize evidence, when in fact it should have been recognized, might let the guilty go free. This is particularly problematic if the false negative is the result of malfunctioning reagents, standards or other equipment which are all preventable or, at the least detectable.

Methods for assuring quality with regard to reagents, standards and other equipment will be discussed in more detail in a later chapter; however, supervision should be aware that any reagent or standard received by the unit must be verified. For reagents, verification might include testing a certain percentage of the lot received with a known standard. In the field, all reagents should be verified prior to its use with a known standard. For standards, record keeping such as the cataloging of certificates of authenticity will be required.

As previously mentioned, support staff will need to keep track of when, and to whom reagents and standards are distributed. Problems that develop after receipt of reagents, or the expiration of chemicals will need to be tracked so they can be recovered at the proper time. The complexity of the task will increase with the distribution method and the amount distributed. A simple document that someone is responsible for maintaining will suffice. "Sticky notes" do not constitute a document. A dedicated log book would serve better.

Depending upon how the unit operates, it will be important to note that certain equipment items will not be amenable to storage at extremes of temperature. That means they may not be stored in vehicles that are, in turn, parked outside. This applies generally to reagents, standards and electrical equipment. There are easy solutions. Response bags containing the unit's reagents and standards can be tracked more easily than distributing reagents and standards to individuals or teams. Support staff would then have the added task of replenishing items used in each bag, updating tracking and putting kits back into service. A more thorough discussion of this method will follow in a later chapter. Briefly, the smaller span of control will allow for easier recovery of problematic or expired reagents and standards and will allow for better control of these sensitive items.

Depending on available manpower, a position dedicated largely, or even solely to quality assurance is encouraged. Personnel assigned to quality assurance might also be responsible for administrative and/or technical review of case work, where appropriate.

Non-Expendable Equipment

The maintenance and calibration of non-expendable equipment is another task that will fall to support staff. This includes, but is not limited to items such as cameras, alternate light sources (including portable hand scopes), electrostatic dust lifters, ballistic trajectory kits, blood stain pattern analysis equipment, computers, connectivity devices and measurement tools (e.g. lasers and total stations). This is another class of equipment that may not be storable in vehicles left outside. Extreme temperatures can damage many of these types of equipment.

Typically, this equipment makes use of batteries that will, in turn, require attention. This is especially true of rechargeable batteries. They will need to be maintained on a regular basis. This includes charging, discharging and rotation of batteries as prescribed by the manufacturersh recommendations. Placing these items in a closet and expecting them to work when you pull them out is wishful thinking. Again, those who are responsible for this equipment must ensure that rechargeable batteries are properly conditioned. They must also be aware of routine maintenance (such as the cleaning of digital cameras) and required calibration schedules. Uncalibrated equipment is just as useful as no equipment. As a result, these tasks should also be part of a comprehensive quality assurance program. Equipment that sees minimal scene usage should be routinely tested. Broken parts of any kits should be promptly replaced with compatible parts. Regular maintenance scheduling and rotation of rechargeable batteries should be considered.

Vehicles

Response vehicle maintenance will require much more than regular oil changes and tire rotations. This will be especially true if the vehicles see heavy use or if evidence will be, or the potential exists for evidence to be in the vehicle, even for just a little while. Depending upon the unit's protocols, evidence may be examined or documented, to some extent, inside a response vehicle. At the very minimum, vehicles could be used for temporary shelter and storage in exigent situations where evidence needs protection from issues such as the weather. If there is any chance of unsealed evidence entering a response vehicle, both support and investigative staff will need to be aware of contamination issues and be prepared to take action to minimize the chances of contamination.

Even if evidence will not be in the vehicle, personnel operating in crime scenes will be in and out of the vehicle(s) on a regular basis and so must take measures to prevent contamination from these activities. Even with the best of intentions and using the best practices, there will always be the potential to contaminate the interior of the vehicle. All personnel will have a responsibility and a duty to clean the vehicle as well as any tools and equipment that are used in the scene prior to placing it back into a vehicle.

There are more surfaces that require cleaning (decontamination) than one might realize. First, and most obvious, are those surfaces that have direct contact with evidence or people who have been in a crime scene. This includes floors, table top surfaces, work surfaces and handles/knobs. These surfaces require regular cleaning with appropriate methods such as bleach and water and/or alcohol. Less obvious, however are areas such as the driver and passenger compartments and cabinet interiors. The driver and passenger compartment are often unnoticed sources of contamination. Eventual movement from the work area of a vehicle or crime scene to a driver or passenger seat has the potential to both capture and transfer trace evidence. The same can be true of storage cabinets where tools or other equipment used in the scene eventually go.

Much of these issues can be mitigated by simply being thoughtful and using good practices. Taking off used PPE before getting into the vehicle and cleaning tools before putting them into on-board storage will eliminate some of these potential contamination sources. If the item is decontaminated before it goes into the cabinet, the potential to contaminate the cabinet obviously becomes lower. When evidence enters a vehicle and is examined, cleaning will be required before any other evidence is brought into the vehicle, especially if it is not sealed and will also be examined. Consider also the storage of sealed evidence in a vehicle, especially if that evidence was sealed in the scene. There exists a contamination potential on the exterior of the packaging.

Staff entering vehicles for maintenance purposes should also take precautions against contamination. This all sounds alarmist, however with the increased sensitivity of DNA techniques, it is not out of the realm of possibility to have secondary contaminations (contamination of evidence by someone not at the scene). Of course, it is going to happen. Minimization is the desire.

Aside from maintenance of the actual vehicle itself, and the assurance of cleanliness, it is useful to have staff that work to ensure that adequate quantities of materials are maintained. The value of a clean, properly equipped, and well-functioning vehicle cannot be under estimated. How a particular unit operates will dictate what routine(s) it will need to go through in order to maintain the vehicles properly (even if investigators clean up as they go along, it is advisable to check/clean the vehicles thoroughly on a regular basis to catch the stuff that gets through).

When the fleet is constantly on the go, either because the unit is busy or because there are too few vehicles, management should strongly consider having a mechanism for turning the vehicles around so that they can get back on the road quickly. So, although each investigator has a responsibility, it is advisable to have a dedicated person to perform regular maintenance on the vehicle to include cleaning and material replacement.

Training

Training, in order to maintain current skills and introduce new techniques, is imperative for any crime scene unit in the current climate the field finds itself in. A well thought out and consistent training program will lead, not only to quality work but also to the certification of individuals which may eventually result in the accreditation of the unit. A group within the unit dedicated to managing a training program should be strongly considered.

If the unit has individuals qualified to provide training, these persons should be tasked with creating and delivering not only the unit's in house training program but also with identifying external training that can be delivered to the unit, if budget allows. It may also make sense to have this group maintain educational records for the unit. One will find that a central repository for the staff's training records will lead to efficiency later on. Aside from the training records, this group should also maintain the training materials. Copies of materials, either electronic or paper, should be maintained. This will allow for review by anyone needing a refresher. They might also be responsible for seeking external validation of training. External acceptance of training will facilitate documentation of education and continuing education requirements for certification. In the future, this will also facilitate record keeping for accreditation. Since training will probably not be an everyday occurrence, staff assigned to training may be able to share in some other duties normally assigned to support staff. This will depend on a unit's particular situation.

Although, at this time, there are no standards for those who provide training to crime scene investigative personnel, there are several considerations that supervision might take into account. Those with formal education in the topics pertinent to crime scene investigation who can teach would be the best choice. Formal education can include college level education in science or forensic science. However this should not be the limit. No one comes out of college prepared to operate, or capable of operating at a crime scene. They may have a better understanding of how forensic science applies to crime scene investigation out of the gate but by no means are they necessarily ready or able to teach anyone how to do any one particular task at a crime scene. Formal education must be coupled with training specific to the tasks of the particular unit as well as experience in their application. Record keeping will be an integral part of the training program and, as such, those responsible will be required to keep appropriate records.

The training group should be prepared to deliver the following:

- Basic level training for new investigators
- Advanced and refresher training for current investigators
- Speciality training (e.g. Train the trainer)

Case Files and Communications

The maintenance of case file materials should be done in a systematic and methodical way. Case files, whether they are paper, digital or a combination of the two should be monitored carefully. Although all might require access to the files, this access should be controlled in some manner. There are several systems one can consider to achieve this goal. At the very minimum, a method for tracking the location and maintenance of case records should be maintained by staff.

A second function that staff could serve is maintaining communications between the unit and its clients. Transmission of case files to prosecution, laboratory or others who hold a stake in the information must be maintained. Records of those who received files or copies of files are something that should be controlled.

if your particular unit is not busy, relatively speaking, this task could be handled by the individual investigator responsible for the case. If your unit is busy or you have multiple jurisdictions to deal with, the task is simplified significantly with a dedicated person to perform the tasks.

Conclusions

Management must consider what support they can give to the investigative side of the operation for several reasons. First, it is imperative that the investigation be able to proceed immediately without hindrance. One way to ensure that this can occur is to assign support tasks to dedicated support personnel. What tasks will be delegated to support personnel, and how many people will be assigned to the tasks will be a function of the needs of the unit.

In the end, clear communication is needed in both directions. Further, autonomy to perform tasks such as inventory, ordering, and general maintenance is required. Management must be clear in its expectations of staff (support or otherwise). This is essential. Staff must be aware of operational issues in order to satisfy budgetary issues as well as material needs. If multiple support staff will be drawing from the same resources, then all must be aware of what is available in so far as money is concerned as well as the needs of the unit as a whole.

If the unit is small and workload is on the lighter side, investigators could assume dual roles and take a hand in the support of the unit. Management will be required to allow everyone sufficient time to complete tasks. Rushing through either scene work or administrative work is very rarely a good idea. Rushing means mistakes.

Investigative Personnel

Qualifications and Skill Sets

A crime scene investigation requires much more effort than most people realize. You cannot truly grasp just how physically and mentally taxing a crime scene investigation can be until you have fully participated in one. It is a full contact sport and a test of both mental and physical stamina. There is no training that will fully prepare potential crime scene investigators for what they might encounter. This makes it very difficult for an agency to "know" what qualities will make someone a good crime scene investigator.

The stress a crime scene investigator experiences is both physical and mental and is caused by any number of issues associated with the investigation. Some of the stress can be mitigated through confidence. Ensuring investigators are prepared (as best they can be) for what they will encounter is the best way to mitigate some of the stress they will be put under. A lack of confidence in one's skills will put unnecessary stress on an investigator.

The job of a crime scene investigator is not a job you want your good buddy or the chief's son to have simply because he can. This job requires ability and, at a minimum, management should attempt to identify candidates who have some training, knowledge or aptitude for the tasks that will be required.

Some tasks that a crime scene investigator will be required to do are:

- Successfully complete training, educational or academic requirements
- Computing
- Photography
- Sketching, mapping, diagraming, and related skills
- Scientific understanding
- Other crime scene tasks
- Writing
- Public speaking

Having knowledge of or ability in some or all of these areas, having an aptitude for, and/or the strong desire to learn and master them is one tool management can use to identify candidates for investigator positions.

Education

Traditionally, and as noted in the NAS Report, crime scene investigations are generally handled by law enforcement agencies. As such, crime scene investigators tend to be sworn officers. Their assumption, thus, is that crime scene investigators' education requirements tend to be those requirements needed for employment at that particular law enforcement agency.[3] Largely silent on the specific topic of education for crime scene investigators, the NAS Report does have some commentary on the education requirements of forensic scientists in general. It is hard to gauge what some future state or national requirement might be, but one could be guided by the general tone of the report.

We should be under no illusions about the usefulness of education in the forensic sciences. On balance, it would be better to hire someone with background and understanding out of the gate. It is also usually easier to train someone with background than without. Do not think that a newly assigned person with a college degree in forensic science will be ready to tackle even the simplest of crime scenes. Like every other subspecialty in forensic science, they will require some amount of training and mentoring. The amount of training will rest, specifically, upon what tasks that will be performed at scenes and this, in turn, will be based on the mandates of the unit.

If a law enforcement agency were to consider the educational recommendations of the NAS Report, one might conclude that crime scene investigators would need, at minimum, a bachelors degree in a physical science. A forensic science component would be desirable. All totaled, this would be a minimum requirement just to get into the unit assuming the candidate had no previous crime scene investigative experience. An equivalent standard was, at least, expressed for those working in a forensic laboratory.

On the other hand, however, we aren't discussing a position which would necessarily be staffed by a forensic scientist but rather a position staffed by someone operating at the technician level. If we accept this to be the case, the education requirements may not hold so strictly.

At this point, agencies could strive to recruit candidates with an educational background in science. Unfortunately, not knowing where the educational requirement discussion will go at this time, managers would never know if they got it right or not, only to find out later that they missed the mark at some point down the road. Perhaps a bottom line could be summed up like this. If you have candidates with a science education and a desire and aptitude to do crime scene work, recruit them. If not, then recruit those who want to do this work and ensure they receive all the training possible so they reach the technician level.

There are so many tasks associated with crime scene processing, especially if the unit operates using an approach where an investigator performs all tasks at a crime scene. The aptitude of the applicant or candidate will encompass several disciplines. These disciplines will range from the very technical to the very mundane. When assessing candidates, one should consider methods for judging either their aptitude or desire to learn and master these skills.

Computer Skills

There are a few specialized computer skills that will most probably need to be learned by anyone who is not already engaged in crime scene investigation. These programs tend to be technical in nature and, at the minimum, include computer-aided drafting and perhaps digital darkroom programs. This is aside from the need to be proficient in regular word processing, presentation and spreadsheet type programs for report generation and courtroom testimony and presentations.

Those who are already computer literate can probably learn these other technical programs. Computer-aided drafting programs are not nearly as hard to learn and use as they once were. Those who present no, or very rudimentary computer skills may be less readily amenable to learning some of the tasks that may be required of them. Ask the candidate to provide a list of computer applications that they are proficient or competent in.

If a candidate professes competency in a particular program that is used by the unit, ask them to provide examples of work, or to perform a demonstration, or to describe some of the steps involved in the creation of a product that the unit is interested in.

Photography

Another technical task that will definitely be required of a candidate is photography. The photography skills that will need mastering by an investigator will be a much higher level then point and shoot or program mode photography many of us use at home to take pictures of our families and activities. Although composition does play a part in crime scene photography, technical ability will be the more important skill needed to document crime scenes. Training programs will consist of basic, fundamental photography principles such as:

- Aperture
- Focus
- Shutter
- Depth of field
- Low light/existing light techniques

Topics will also include the requisite knowledge of optics and its effects on the overall camera system. In addition to the basic fundamentals of photography, the candidate will need to learn about the required crime scene photographs and their composition.

Some of these concepts will need to be mastered for all of the various lighting conditions that one might encounter. This includes, but is not limited to daylight (which includes various levels of light from full sun to deep shadow) to even low, existing light and complete darkness. As such, candidates will need to master techniques and retain knowledge about exposure, depth of field and focus for all of these conditions. They will come to realize that this can be challenging at times and will include techniques that will require mastery such as existing light and painting with light.

Aside from demonstrative photography, the candidate will need to learn specialized photography for documenting certain kinds of evidence. Sometimes called examination quality photography or scientific quality photography, these techniques require patience and attention to detail in order to perform correctly. Done properly, these techniques can aid an examiner by giving them additional material to use during their examinations of evidence, in particular pattern evidence.

With todays camera systems, anyone and everyone can take a picture. Realize, however, that these pictures must be not only properly composed but also properly exposed and focused. No one will get it correct all of the time, but with today's digital cameras, mistakes can often be observed at the scene and remedied. It will take a professional photographer to accomplish this task. Those who have formal photography training or who are self-taught and advanced in skill will be an asset to the unit.

Sketching, Mapping, Diagramming and Related Tools

Candidates will need to master the various tasks associated with documenting crime scenes that involve sketching, mapping and diagramming. One does not need to be artistically inclined to perform these tasks well, but the ability to translate spatial relationships from eye to paper certainly helps. The candidate will have to have the desire to practice and the ability to learn some related concepts.

Sketching with pencil/pen and paper isn't always as easy as it looks. The ability to translate spatial relationships to paper does take practice and, perhaps, some mentoring. Practice may not, even after many, years make this task easier, however, learning the different techniques and tools used to perform these tasks will. The use of measurements, graph paper, straight edges and the like can ensure that a rough sketch created at a scene can be used to create a finished diagram that is a fair and accurate representation of the scene as well as informative and ready for court presentation. If the particular unit does not use computer-aided drafting programs and creates a court presentation or finished diagram using pencil and paper, these same tools can be used to accomplish this task outside of the scene at a later time.

The use of total station survey equipment for documenting and measuring scenes has been around for some time now. Particularly useful for outdoor scenes, it helps the investigator create a "sketch" of the scene and capture evidence measurements very efficiently. Many crime scene units and accident investigation units use a total station routinely. Locations that would otherwise be difficult to sketch and translate to a diagram can be made into a coherent map of the local area using this technology. These local maps are especially useful when the scene occurs in remote areas. Generally, scenes are sketched/diagrammed in relation to some landmark. These landmarks can be the walls and doors of a home, an intersection, a curb line or a property or building line. When the scene occurs in a remote area where these kinds of landmarks don't exist, a total station can create a diagram that uses the local landmarks such as trees, rocks, paths and the like to create a diagram that shows proportions, distances and orientations.

In order to take advantage of these tools, candidates will need to understand the techniques and principles that they operate under. They are simply the general coordinate systems used to map scenes. These generally include rectangular, polar and baseline coordinate systems. Whether using a total station or not, this knowledge will help the investigator use the methods and systems most applicable to the situation at hand. Although the total station uses one particular mapping system to locate items in relation to the station itself, it can be combined with other systems such as a baseline and data points. Sometimes, when these systems are combined together, scenes in somewhat remote areas can be related to locations that have better recognized landmarks. Finally, candidates will need to acquire the skills necessary to work with the data in computer-aided drafting programs in order to take full advantage of what the total station has to offer in terms of diagramming and measuring evidence.

Asking candidates to produce a sketch during a selection process as a method to judge ability can be a useful tool in terms of identifying someone who has skills that can be built upon. This does not need to be a complicated test. Ask the candidates, perhaps after the interview to sit in a small room with a few items and draw it out. Provide tools such as graph paper, rulers, pencils and erasers.

Science

Depending, again, upon what tasks the investigator will be called upon to perform, they will have a need to understand the underlying scientific principles that govern them. It's useful to have understanding of these scientific principles so that the investigator has a frame of reference for evaluating results of tests performed at scenes as well as to have the ability to testify in court. It cannot be understated how important it is at trial to be able to answer questions clearly and concisely. These scientific principles extend beyond what one might expect. Knowing why things are the way they are, will most certainly help the investigator solve problems in the field.

Any candidate for a crime scene investigator position, and any investigator for that matter, must be able to understand, execute and articulate the quality assurance plan implemented by the organization. Quality assurance is not a hard concept to grasp, however, the candidate will need to understand the underlying philosophy of the "whys" and "hows..

These concepts fit in with the whole concept of understanding scientific principles. The concepts that apply here have mostly to do with presumptive testing, the use of reagents, and the prevention of false negative results as a result of faulty regents.

The candidate will be required to demonstrate understanding of how presumptive tests work in general as well as how the unit's particular presumptive tests work specifically. It is only through this understanding that the candidate will be able to assess the reagents' performance under specific circumstances. Further, the candidate will need to learn interpretive skills and nuances connected with each test or reagent that they use.

Generally speaking, candidates should learn the processes that occur when both reagents and standards are brought into the unit as well as how and why reagents are verified in the field before use in case work. They will have to document this information either through notes or on captioned forms and may have to discuss or explain the steps and results for each step taken. They will also have to understand and articulate the concept of traceability.

Without scientific training or even forensic training, it is very hard to evaluate a candidates predisposition to learn these things. A possible method of evaluating someone's ability to learn is the candidatest academic record.

Other Crime Scene Tasks

During training, candidates will need to learn other tasks not readily categorized. Generally speaking these are topics dealing with the documentation, collection, and packaging of various types of evidence with instruction about why different types of evidence are packaged certain ways and the effects of improper handling.

More in-depth training will accompany techniques involving the documentation and recovery of certain kinds of evidence. Sometimes, these techniques require manual dexterity and the manipulation of tools and materials. Deviation from procedure or a simple mistake could ruin the evidence. A short list of evidence that falls into this category is:

- Latent fingerprints development and recovery
- Patent blood impressions
- Footwear impression
- Dry and wet origin residue prints
- Tool marks
- Latent blood detection

Investigators will train and practice with techniques and tools in order to recover evidence that is fragile in nature. What is more, the improper use of the tools and materials can easily damage evidence or, if used improperly, fail to recover the evidence and, at the same time, ruin it.

Candidates will train in each of these topics to proficiency. In other words, they will train until they demonstrate consistent results with the various tools and techniques. The techniques include some amount of manual dexterity which can be learned with practice.

Descriptive Note-Taking and Writing

Descriptive note-taking at the crime scene and report writing at the conclusion of investigative activities is a fundamental job of the crime scene investigator. At the scene, investigators will need to be able to make descriptive notes and collect information in order to adequately describe and document many things. These descriptions may apply to photographs, items, people and places. This task is important because it requires the investigator to know what information needs to be collected as well as how to collect it and how to describe it. Descriptive writing is not necessarily an easy thing to do. Some of these tasks can be accomplished by simply writing down single descriptive words (e.g. color(s), size, manufacturer information, serial number, insignia, damage, etc.).

Note-taking in this manner will be simplified to some degree by using captioned forms, check-boxes and pull-down menus. Unfortunately, not everything will be amenable to such treatment and the investigator must be capable of providing a written picture that accurately describes the item, condition, location, and so on. Cameras can capture a lot of information. A picture really is worth a thousand words. Unfortunately the camera cannot capture everything and these things (e.g. sounds, smells, lighting conditions, etc.) will require written words to adequately document and capture them.

In time, an investigator may be challenged to document more complex items and conditions. Specifically, consider the need to make written descriptions of more complex types of evidence. This can include evidence such, bloodstain patterns, ballistic trajectories, and other types of pattern evidence. Free form descriptions, more so than captioning or check-boxes, will do a better job at describing this material. Of course, when candidates receive training in these different disciplines, it is hoped that they will begin to learn the accepted terminology to use and ways to go about descriptive note-taking.

Formal Writing

Formal report writing can be accomplished in several ways, from completely free form to completely captioned. Whatever a particular agency does is up to them. It seems very hard to completely caption a report. Again, some topics just do not lend themselves easily to check-boxes and pull-down menus. The investigator will need to be able to clearly convey information to others, in writing.

No one is suggesting that reports must be award-winning novels. No one is suggesting first drafts must be perfect. All reports should be reviewed by someone in the unit (peer review) prior to their publication. Candidates should be able to demonstrate some ability to clearly convey information in writing.

Public Speaking

Presenting information to other investigators, supervisors, prosecutors, judges and juries will generally be the culmination of all of the effort invested by a crime scene investigator. Any candidate must be prepared to present often complicated information clearly to all parties concerned. In order to accomplish this, the investigator must have the confidence to speak in front of strangers without faltering. Those not accustomed to public speaking will find this difficult at the very least. It is, in fact, not easy. Anecdotally, many find court testimony to be among the most difficult parts of the job. Many feel that the end result of any successful prosecution rests upon their performance at trial.

Confidence with this type of public speaking comes from several sources. In part, it comes from security in one's knowledge of one's job; knowledge of why the investigators did what they did and the means to articulate it. It is very easy to get rattled on the witness stand if an investigator is insecure in or unsure of the basic principles the tasks performed rest upon. Attorneys will have access to the same text books that investigators might use. Generally speaking, many attorneys are smart people and will understand what they read from these books in preparation for the crime scene investigators' testimony. In sum, it will be very difficult to get through testimony if the attorney can explain what the investigator cannot.

Confidence also comes from being prepared. This can be accomplished easily enough by organizing and studying case materials (notes, pictures, logs, reports, etc.) as if the investigator were taking an exam. The investigator may not be able to memorize everything, but at the very least should be familiar enough with the paper work to know where to find the information efficiently while on the witness stand.

Aside from being able to speak to a group of strangers, investigators might need to prepare exhibits for use in court. This is a part of public speaking that many people forget about. Public speaking (court testimony) is essentially a teaching session. The investigator is instructing the various parties involved about the crime scene. Proper instruction may require the use of visual aids, also called exhibits. Exhibits can take several forms. They can be:

- Pictures
- Enlargements of diagrams or maps
- Digital presentations
- Visual examples of concepts presented

In some cases, the investigator might be able to just hand off the materials to the prosecution and they will make up the exhibits. Often, the investigator will not only prepare the exhibits, but will also have some input into their creation.

An agency can use various methods in order to assess a candidate's public speaking skills. During the application process, ask the candidate to supply information about any training or skills that would be useful to the unit's mission. This will give those making the selection an opportunity to ask the candidate questions regarding a subject the candidate knows something about. Management, in turn, can use this as a tool to gain some idea about the candidate's ability to articulate concepts. Taking advantage of a topic the candidate is familiar with might give the interviewer a better sense of how this person could perform when speaking from a position of confidence. This would be a better measure then asking the candidate to speak about a topic of which he has little understanding.

At later, or follow up interviews, ask the candidate to come to the interview prepared to make a formal presentation to a group of people, even if it is a small group. Have the candidate prepare a multimedia presentation about a familiar topic or activity. In this way, the interviewer will be able to make some assessment of the candidate's ability to speak before an unfamiliar group as well to convey information in a logical manner.

Application and Selection of Candidates

During the selection process, management can try a few things to help in the assessment of applicants. Although the types of tasks previously mentioned are not a complete list of those that an investigator will need to perform at a crime scene, it does include some of the harder tasks to learn and execute. These ideas are not all-inclusive and management may need to think of other or additional methods that might be needed based upon the unit's own specific tasks.

Management can easily come up with a list of tasks that are deemed crucial to the mission of the unit and asking the candidates what education or experience they might have that is illustrative of that particular skill. This list can be simply asking for credentials or other experiences in photography, drawing, the use of tools, knowledge of science, and so on. In other words, what education or experiences does the candidate have that give them a knowledge base that can be built upon. Management may also prioritize this list and give more or less weight to different skills, giving more weight to skills that may require more training or knowledge to master.

The application process should also be well thought out and must cover all of the skills that a particular agency seeks. The recruiting process should be multi-directional in that the agency should go out to the applicant pool and seek to recruit those with education, skills or talents that it values. This doesn't mean that everyone who looks good on paper will want to do this job or be able to do this job. It also does not mean that those who do not look good on paper cannot do the job. This is just one possible starting point.

Whoever is charged with seeking candidates for the selection process should first begin by identifying the tasks performed by the unit and the skills required to perform those tasks.

Applications should incorporate the materials management needs and can use during the interview process. If the unit operates whereby a member is responsible for a single task (e.g. photography, fingerprints, mapping, etc.) then this whole job should be easier in that the candidate's skill set can be much less diverse. However, if your unit operates wherein all members are responsible for all aspects of the scene, then the task of identifying and choosing candidates becomes more difficult and, as such the application process must be more robust. The agency must identify candidates with larger skill sets or abilities.

Once the agency identifies the task list, based largely on the mandate of the unit, it should decide what skills candidates for crime scene investigation positions should possess. Only then can it begin to plan out the application and related processes. Management needs to identify which skills they believe can be evaluated and decide on how they will go about evaluating them. Some ideas have been expressed here, but they are not the only ways to go about it. Those ideas offered can be modified to suit a unit's particular needs and, with some thought, new ideas can be added.

Without regard to any rules or regulations imposed or recommended by governmental agencies, certifying bodies, or the like, seeking candidates with education and training in the areas and skills needed by a crime scene investigator is a useful first step. If nothing else, it gives management an objective assessment of a candidatesc potential trainability. Formal education or training is a method of assessment that can be verified through transcripts, diplomas and certifications. If a skill lends itself to a portfolio (such as photography or drawing), the applicants portfolio would be another useful measure of ability.

The application and interview process should be supportive of the selection process. The physical application should include any materials or instructions the applicant should follow. It should include a list of things that the applicant is responsible for producing, handing in or presenting to those who will make the selection. So, if the candidate should have a writing sample of a specific length in a specific format, instructions to that effect should be in the application. This holds for any item required. Some items management might want to see are:

- Photographic portfolio
- Writing sample
- Digital presentation

At the interview, the candidate could be asked to:

- Make an oral presentation
- Produce a sketch
- Create an unrehearsed descriptive writing sample

Organization and Deployment

Organizational plans for investigative personnel (or teams) working at crime scenes have been suggested by other authors. As one might expect, these methods, as well as variations based on them, are used in practice today. Gardner has given terms to some methods of investigative team organization labeling them as the "area" approach and the "functional" approach.[4]

The "functional" approach can be described, generally, as the movement of people with various areas of responsibility or specialty through a crime scene as they are needed. As one might imagine, this method may be hampered by logistical difficulties. This is especially true if the unit is very busy. If the unit typically has multiple operations or has extended operations, the right people may not be available at the right times thus significantly slowing down the operation. Gardner rightly points out that investigators must be available at the right time so they can be moved into the scene in the correct order based upon their particular area of knowledge or expertise. Jurisdictions with well manned units and/or low workload would be able to utilize this method most effectively.

The area approach seems, on its face, to be a much more reasonable method for using manpower. In this method, one team performs all of the tasks at a crime scene until the scene is completed. This method is not without its difficulties. It is a completely reasonable method for processing the normal sized crime scene of moderate duration. Large scenes will take longer to complete, causing problems such the need to for staff to rest during the operation. Anecdotally speaking, at least some units operate like this.

Even if most crime scene units operate this way, it is not always an optimal way to conduct business. Fatigue created from extended operations will cause unnecessary mistakes. Management could keep the crime scene going until completion by relieving teams after a certain point. Now, multiple people will be responsible for the work produced at the scene based upon when they started. This will create issues of accountability and confusion at trial, to say the least.

Another, although less worrisome, consideration that arises with this approach is that all personnel will need to be well trained in all aspects and disciplines needed to successfully complete processing a scene. There are some other approaches that can also be useful and should be considered. They are hybridized approaches based on the functional and area approaches.

As noted, when employing the area approach, difficulties which arise when operating at long, complicated or otherwise protracted scenes can be overcome by designating a primary or lead investigator. This investigator will hold overall responsibility for the scene. This primary investigator will be present at the scene and his assisting investigators will be rotated through the scene on a regular basis, keeping those completing tasks fresh and rested. Processing can be paused so that the primary investigator can rest also.

Another hybridized approach uses the team concept as a primary manpower method. Termed the practitioner approach, all members of the unit are trained from basic to advanced levels in all the disciplines that would be needed to operate utilizing the team approach concept. Each member of the unit, however, would have one or two areas in which they are highly trained. Members trained to a practitioner level or more in various crime scene techniques and methods such as mapping, photography, blood stain pattern analysis and shooting reconstruction, could then be rotated through scenes where they are needed on an *ad hoc* basis.

These hybridized schemes make the most sense. Stringent formulas very rarely work well for everyone. Taking good ideas or methods from several different places and merging them together to fit the needs of particular circumstances allows for a customized fit for each jurisdictions particular requirements. Flexibility, and even coming up with ideas on the fly will be required in order to keep the work going forward, keep personnel sharp and produce a quality product.

Supervision and Management

The more important question regarding supervisors can be summed up by asking whether they should have the same or similar level of training as investigators or not. In the case of crime scene investigation, should supervisors be trained to technician level? There are certainly arguments that can be made for both sides of the issue.

There is no harm in having supervisors trained to the same, basic level as investigators. In fact, in times of crisis or exigency, there may be stronger arguments for it. Another pair of hands during these times will certainly be useful.

Consider, also, how easy it will be train supervisors. If the unit has a formal training program, they can sit in with investigators also taking the course. If, however, the unit trains new investigators using a mentoring model where training is done "on the job" it may become more cumbersome to do. Having to go out when a request for service is made it could interfere with supervisory responsibilities.

Another argument in favor of having trained supervisors is the enhanced ability they will have to liaise with those outside of the unit. This simple task of running interference will allow the investigators to concentrate more on their work and less on briefing those who need or want information.

Crime scene units may want to fall somewhere in between no training and some training. A course covering the same topics but not the hands-on component will give the supervisor the knowledge needed to understand the job but not the training to operate at the same level as the investigators is a workable solution. For example, is there a need to train supervisors to take examination quality photographs or just to a level where they can assist in an emergency?

Perhaps a logical solution to the competing needs is to create a level below technician that will teach the supervisors about crime scene investigation and the techniques used. Basic understanding of crime scene management, documentation steps, and evidence recovery is useful but it may not be necessary to train supervisors in the mechanics of the different tasks to competency. Teach, demonstrate and allow supervisors to do the tasks but without the repetition needed to be able to perform the tasks on their own. It will allow supervisors to be exposed to the techniques but without the time it takes to train an investigator to competency.

If the unit will require supervisors to train the same levels as investigators, then the application process for supervisors should be the same as it is for investigators. If supervisors will receive training to some level below technician, a modified version of the application process should be used.

Conclusions

The tasks of a crime scene unit should be divided into two areas, support and investigative. When possible, support jobs should be filled with personnel dedicated to the tasks. Management will have to decide what tasks are most important to the mission and how many persons can be detailed to accomplish them.

Support is more important than many managers might realize, especially if the unit is busy, either because of the volume of work or the amount of time spent at a crime scene. The maintenance of equipment, vehicles and materials such as reagents will lead to other issues for the unit. Chief among them will be unnecessary delays recovering fragile evidence, contamination issues and malfunctioning equipment. All of these can lead to unfortunate circumstances such as false positive and false negative results at scenes.

Contamination will be also be another unfortunate result of great scene investigations but lacking maintenance. Even with best practices, regular cleaning will be required to ensure tools and vehicles are not the source of contamination. Expecting investigators to spend many hours at a scene then many more hours cleaning and stocking is probably not the best idea for a busy unit.

When it comes to identifying candidates for the unit, management should recognize that different positions require different talents, levels of training and levels of education. If the unit will have members performing strictly support tasks, they will require a similar knowledge base about tools, equipment and their operation as investigators so that they may provide the proper support when needed. Aside from that, support personnel's talents should reside in logistics and record keeping.

Investigators will require a higher level of training then support personnel. At a minimum, they will require training to a technician level. If a candidate brings education or advanced ability in some or all areas of crime scene investigation, so much the better. This candidate will be easier to train and perhaps integrate into the job. As with a laboratory scientist, no one comes out of college ready to conduct either a crime scene investigation or trace evidence analysis. They simply have a foundation on which to build and a proven ability to learn.

Finally, supervisors can either be untrained, partially trained, or fully trained investigators depending upon the needs of the unit. No harm exists in training supervisors to a technician level, but, it may not be practical. Training supervisors to a level at which they can operate as an assistant to an investigator when exigent circumstances exist should be a minimum consideration.

There will be no one recipe for the organization of personnel in any one crime scene unit. Management will need to remain flexible and willing to try new things that will help increase the efficiency of the unit while at the same time limiting any bad outcomes that might occur. Management should not take the organization and distribution of tasks lightly for this reason. Serious consideration should be given to just how many people will be needed and how many can be dedicated to the support mission.

Notes

1 Sirchie (2010). Technical Information. Available at: www.sirchie.com/Assets/Manuals/pdf/UPD/MCM100_TI02-59ENG-REV3E.pdf [Accessed July 20, 2013].

2 BVDA International. Gelatin Lifter Product Information. Available at www.bvda.com/EN/download/en_gellifters.pdf [Accessed July 20, 2013].

3 NAS Report p. 220 in Committee on Identifying the Needs of the Forensic Science Community (2009) National Research Council *Strengthening Forensic Science in the United States: A Path Forward.* National Research Council of the National Academies.

4 Ross M. Gardner (2005) *Practical Crime Scene Processing and Investigation*, Boca Raton, London, and New York: CRC Press.

3

INVESTIGATOR SAFETY

Investigator safety is always a top priority when performing any crime scene investigation. It starts in the investigator's office and works its way out into the field. As crime scene investigator's (CSIs) we are constantly exposed to various hazards from the scene, as in the case of blood borne pathogens, damaged structures (post-blast or fire scene), from the forensic equipment, such as alternate light sources, and from the processing of evidence, such as the use of fingerprint powders, Ninhydrin, Luminal, or Amido Black, to name a few. As CSIs we utilize various forensic chemicals, in solid, liquid, and gaseous forms, which assist us in our investigations, both in the office or laboratory and in the field. It's important as CSIs that we are fully aware of any hazards these forensic chemicals pose to us and what personal protective equipment (PPE) and or actions we must utilize to maintain our safety and, in the case of exposure, what first-aid treatment is required. Under the US Department of Labor's (US DOL), Occupational Safety and Health Administration (OSHA) Hazard Communication Standard (HCS) regulation (1910.1200), your employer must maintain, update, prominently display and make readily available in an easily accessible area, the Material Safety Data Sheets (MSDS) for all potentially harmful substances or materials to be handled or utilized by an employee in the course of their duties.

Hazardous Communication Standard (HCS) under 1910.1200(a)(2) states,

> This occupational safety and health standard is intended to address comprehensively the issue of classifying the potential hazards of chemicals, and communicating information concerning hazards and appropriate protective measures to employees, and to preempt any legislative or regulatory enactments of a state, or political subdivision of a state, pertaining to this subject. Classifying the potential hazards of chemicals and communicating information concerning hazards and appropriate protective measures to employees, may include, for example, but is not limited to, provisions for: developing and maintaining a written hazard communication program for the workplace, including lists of hazardous chemicals present; labeling of containers of chemicals in the workplace, as well as of containers of chemicals being shipped to other workplaces; preparation and distribution of safety data sheets to employees and downstream employers; and development and implementation of employee training programs regarding

> hazards of chemicals and protective measures. Under section 18 of the Act, no state or political subdivision of a state may adopt or enforce any requirement relating to the issue addressed by this Federal standard, except pursuant to a Federally-approved state plan.
>
> *(OSHA)*

All CSIs should make themselves familiar with this OSHA law and its associated laws, such as OSHA 1910.120, "Hazardous Waste Operations and Emergency Response" and OSHA 1910.134, "Respiratory Protection," to understand our responsibilities as CSIs and that of our employers to maintain our safety.

As we all know, our employers are responsible for training and certifying us on all the various forensic methodologies, protocols, and equipment they expect us to perform and utilize in connection with our employment. These certifications require continuing education in these areas and proficiency testing, in order for the certifications to be maintained. And, as you can see from the section of OSHA law quoted previously, we must be trained on the hazards of the chemicals and equipment we are mandated to use. All of this training and proficiency testing, must be thoroughly documented in our personnel folders, and, when requested for official business, should be made available to members of the criminal justice system, such as judges, prosecutors, and defense attorneys. It may also be required by accreditation bodies and federal, state, or local, regulatory agencies such as: the American Society of Crime Laboratory Directors (ASCLAD), International Organization for Standardization (ISO), International Association for Identification (IAI), American Board of Criminalistics (ABC), OSHA investigators, US Environmental Protection Agency (US EPA) investigators, the Centers for Disease Control (CDC) investigators, Public Health investigators, National Institute of Standards and Technologies (NIST) investigators, National Transportation Safety Board (NTSB) investigators, US Department of Transportation (US DOT) investigators, just to name a few. As CSIs, we must read all the MSDSs for all the chemicals that we prepare and utilize in connection with our field and laboratory processing of crime scene evidence: from the basic fingerprint powders to radioactive isotopes and everything in between. The MSDS will provide us with the following information:

- Identification of the material
- Hazard(s) identification
- Composition/information on ingredients
- First-aid measures
- Fire-fighting measures
- Accidental release measures
- Handling and storage
- Exposure controls/personal protection
- Physical and chemical properties
- Stability and reactivity
- Toxicological information
- Ecological information
- Disposal considerations
- Transport information
- Regulatory information
- Other information

Once we read the MSDSs for the various materials we as CSIs are using, you may discover that our employers will need to provide you with certain personal protective equipment (PPE), such chemical protective clothing (CPC): suits, gloves, boots, goggles, face shields, to protect your skin and eyes from exposure or respiratory and gastrointestinal tract protection in the form of half-face or full face respirators and or mechanical engineering equipment, such as fuming hoods, laminar air flow bio-safety cabinets, and glove boxes. Let's look at the MSDS for Amido Black (Figure 3.1).

Upon reading section 2 "Hazardous Identification:" we see that amido black is listed as having the Global Harmonized System, United States (GHS-US) warnings (a link to the GHS-US is provided in the "Required and Suggested Reading", at the end of this chapter):

Flam. Liq. 3 GHS-US Code H226, which means, it has a flash point of ≥ 23°C and ≤ 60°C (140°F).

Skin Corr. 1A GHS-US Code H314, which means, it produces destruction of dermal tissue: visible necrosis in at least one animal, for an exposure of < 3 min. and Observation made in < 1hr.

Muta. 2 GHS-US Code H341, which means, this substance gives rise to an increased occurance of mutations in populations of cells and/or organisms. Category 2 states that the following is "Suspected/Possible": May include heritable mutations in human germ cells; Positive evidence from tests in mammals and somatic cell tests; In vivo somatic genotoxicity supported by in vitro mutagenicity.

Next it lists the Signal Word GHS-US Danger, which is the designation for more severe hazards. Then the GHS-US Hazard statements which states: H226-Flammable liquid and vapor; H314-Causes severe skin burns and eye damage; H341-Suspected of causing genetic defects (Dermal, Inhalation, Oral). Next you will find the Precautionary statements per the GHS-US, and they are quite lengthy, so we will just highlight a few: GHS-US, P260, states, "Do not breathe fume/mist/sprays/vapors". And, according to Annex 3 (Provided at the end of this chapter) the Codification of Hazard Statements, Codification and Use of precautionary Statements and Examples of Precautionary Pictograms, from the United Nations Economic Commission for Europe, who are responsible for the development of the GHS, this means that this material has one or more of the following "Hazard Classes": Acute toxicity-inhalation; Specific target organ toxicity, single exposure; Specific target toxicity, repeated exposure, Skin corrosion; and Reproductive toxicity-effects on or via lactation. So from this we see that respiratory and gastrointestinal protection, in the form of an air purifying respirator, with the appropriate organic vapor cartridge. Next, let us look at GHS-US, P280, states, "Wear protective gloves, protective clothing, and eye protection/face protection". Again referring to Annex 3, means that this material has one or more of the "Hazard Classes": Explosives; Flammable liquids; Flammable solids; Self-reactive substances and mixtures; Pyrophoric liquids, Pyrophoric solids, Self-heating substances and mixtures; Substances and mixtures which, in contact with water, emit flammable gases; Oxidizing liquids; Oxidizing solids; Organic peroxides; Acute toxicity; Skin corrosion; Skin irritation; Skin sensitization; Severe eye damage; Eye irritation; Germ cell mutagenicity; Carcinogenicity; and Reproductive toxicity. So, from this we see that appropriate chemical protective: clothing, gloves and eye protection are required when using this material. If a full face air purifying respirator is utilized, then eye and face protection, as well as, respiratory protection from this chemical are accomplished. So this material is harmful if inhaled, ingested, or absorbed by the skin and can have acute and chronic effects. Doesn't that just give you a warm and fuzzy feeling about using this chemical? What we should take away from this and the other sections of the MSDS, where we find similar statements, is that they really don't know what the effects of chronic exposure to this material are and that no testing has been performed to find out. To repeat, from this section we

Amido Black Liquid

SIRCHIE

Safety Data Sheet

according to Federal Register / Vol. 77, No. 58 / Monday, March 26, 2012 / Rules and Regulations

Date of issue: 01/10/2014 Revision date: 03/10/2014 Supersedes: 01/27/2011

SECTION 1: Identification of the substance/mixture and of the company/undertaking

1.1. Product identifier

Product form	: Substance
Substance name	: Amido Black Liquid
Product code	: LV501L

1.2. Relevant identified uses of the substance or mixture and uses advised against

Use of the substance/mixture	: Laboratory chemical

1.3. Details of the supplier of the safety data sheet

SIRCHIE Finger Print Laboratories
100 Hunter Place
Youngsville, NC 27596 - USA
T 919-554-2244; 800-356-7311 - F 919-554-2266; 800-899-8181
http://www.sirchie.com

1.4. Emergency telephone number

Emergency number	: 1.800.424.9300

SECTION 2: Hazards identification

2.1. Classification of the substance or mixture

Classification (GHS-US)

Flam. Liq. 3 H226
Skin Corr. 1A H314
Muta. 2 H341

2.2. Label elements

GHS-US labeling

Hazard pictograms (GHS-US) :

GHS02 GHS05 GHS08

Signal word (GHS-US) : Danger

Hazard statements (GHS-US) : H226 - Flammable liquid and vapor
H314 - Causes severe skin burns and eye damage
H341 - Suspected of causing genetic defects (Dermal, Inhalation, oral)

Precautionary statements (GHS-US) : P201 - Obtain special instructions before use
P202 - Do not handle until all safety precautions have been read and understood
P210 - Keep away from heat, hot surfaces, open flames, sparks. - No smoking
P233 - Keep container tightly closed
P240 - Ground/bond container and receiving equipment
P241 - Use explosion-proof electrical, lighting, ventilating equipment
P242 - Use only non-sparking tools
P243 - Take precautionary measures against static discharge
P260 - Do not breathe fume, mist, spray, vapors
P264 - Wash all exposed skin thoroughly after handling
P280 - Wear eye protection, protective gloves
P301+P330+P331 - If swallowed: Rinse mouth. Do NOT induce vomiting
P303+P361+P353 - IF ON SKIN (or hair): Remove/Take off immediately all contaminated clothing. Rinse skin with water/shower
P304+P340 - IF INHALED: Remove to fresh air and keep at rest in a position comfortable for breathing
P305+P351+P338 - If in eyes: Rinse cautiously with water for several minutes. Remove contact lenses, if present and easy to do. Continue rinsing
P308+P313 - IF exposed or concerned: Get medical advice/attention
P310 - Immediately call a POISON CENTER or doctor/physician
P321 - Specific treatment (see Contact a physician on this label)
P363 - Wash contaminated clothing before reuse
P370+P378 - In case of fire: Use CO2, dry chemical, foam, water spray for extinction

03/10/2014 EN (English US) Page 1

FIGURE 3.1 Sirchie Amido Black MSDS

P403+P235 - Store in a cool and well-ventilated place
P405 - Store locked up
P501 - Dispose of contents/container to local, regional, national,international regulations

2.3. Other hazards

Other hazards not contributing to the classification : None under normal conditions.

2.4. Unknown acute toxicity (GHS-US)

No data available

SECTION 3: Composition/information on ingredients

3.1. Substances

Name : Amido Black Liquid

Name	Product identifier	%	Classification (GHS-US)
AQUA	(CAS No) 7732-18-5	88	Not classified
acetic acid	(CAS No) 64-19-7	10	Flam. Liq. 3, H226 Skin Corr. 1A, H314
C.I. acid black 1	(CAS No) 1064-48-8	> 5	Skin Irrit. 2, H315 Eye Irrit. 2A, H319 Muta. 2, H341 STOT SE 3, H335
formic acid	(CAS No) 64-18-6	2	Flam. Liq. 3, H226 Acute Tox. 3 (Oral), H301 Skin Corr. 1A, H314

Full text of H-phrases: see section 16

3.2. Mixtures

Not applicable

SECTION 4: First aid measures

4.1. Description of first aid measures

First-aid measures general : Never give anything by mouth to an unconscious person. If you feel unwell, seek medical advice (show the label where possible).

First-aid measures after inhalation : Remove to fresh air and keep at rest in a position comfortable for breathing. Call a POISON CENTER/doctor/physician if you feel unwell.

First-aid measures after skin contact : Wash with plenty of soap and water. Wash contaminated clothing before reuse. If skin irritation occurs: Get medical advice/attention. Specific treatment (see ... on this label).

First-aid measures after eye contact : Rinse cautiously with water for several minutes. Remove contact lenses, if present and easy to do. Continue rinsing. If eye irritation persists: Get medical advice/attention.

First-aid measures after ingestion : Rinse mouth. Do NOT induce vomiting. Obtain emergency medical attention.

4.2. Most important symptoms and effects, both acute and delayed

Symptoms/injuries : Suspected of causing genetic defects.
Symptoms/injuries after inhalation : May cause respiratory irritation.
Symptoms/injuries after skin contact : Causes skin irritation.
Symptoms/injuries after eye contact : Causes serious eye irritation.

4.3. Indication of any immediate medical attention and special treatment needed

No additional information available

SECTION 5: Firefighting measures

5.1. Extinguishing media

suitable extinguishing media : Foam. Dry powder. Carbon dioxide. Water spray. Sand.
Unsuitable extinguishing media : Do not use a heavy water stream.

5.2. Special hazards arising from the substance or mixture

Reactivity : May be corrosive to metals.

5.3. Advice for firefighters

Firefighting instructions : Use water spray or fog for cooling exposed containers. Exercise caution when fighting any chemical fire. Avoid (reject) fire-fighting water to enter environment.

Protection during firefighting : Do not enter fire area without proper protective equipment, including respiratory protection.

FIGURE 3.1 continued

SECTION 6: Accidental release measures

6.1. Personal precautions, protective equipment and emergency procedures

6.1.1. For non-emergency personnel

Emergency procedures : Evacuate unnecessary personnel.

6.1.2. For emergency responders

Protective equipment : Equip cleanup crew with proper protection.

Emergency procedures : Ventilate area.

6.2. Environmental precautions

Prevent entry to sewers and public waters. Notify authorities if liquid enters sewers or public waters.

6.3. Methods and material for containment and cleaning up

Methods for cleaning up : Soak up spills with inert solids, such as clay or diatomaceous earth as soon as possible. Collect spillage. Store away from other materials.

6.4. Reference to other sections

See Heading 8. Exposure controls and personal protection.

SECTION 7: Handling and storage

7.1. Precautions for safe handling

Precautions for safe handling : Wash hands and other exposed areas with mild soap and water before eat, drink or smoke and when leaving work. Provide good ventilation in process area to prevent formation of vapor. Obtain special instructions before use. Use personal protective equipment as required. Do not handle until all safety precautions have been read and understood. Avoid breathing dust/fume/gas/mist/vapors/spray. Use only outdoors or in a well-ventilated area.

Hygiene measures : Wash ... thoroughly after handling.

7.2. Conditions for safe storage, including any incompatibilities

Storage conditions : Keep only in the original container in a cool, well ventilated place away from : Keep container tightly closed.

Incompatible products : Strong bases. strong acids.

Incompatible materials : Sources of ignition. Direct sunlight.

7.3. Specific end use(s)

No additional information available

SECTION 8: Exposure controls/personal protection

8.1. Control parameters

acetic acid (64-19-7)		
USA ACGIH	ACGIH TWA (ppm)	10 ppm
USA ACGIH	ACGIH STEL (ppm)	15 ppm

formic acid (64-18-6)		
USA ACGIH	ACGIH TWA (ppm)	5 ppm
USA ACGIH	ACGIH STEL (ppm)	10 ppm

8.2. Exposure controls

Personal protective equipment : Dust formation: dust mask. Gloves. Safety glasses. Avoid all unnecessary exposure.

Hand protection : Wear protective gloves.

Eye protection : Chemical goggles or safety glasses.

Skin and body protection : Wear suitable protective clothing.

Respiratory protection : Wear approved mask.

Other information : When using, do not eat, drink or smoke.

FIGURE 3.1 continued

SECTION 9: Physical and chemical properties

9.1. Information on basic physical and chemical properties

Physical state	: Liquid
Appearance	: Liquid. blue.
Color	: Blue.
Odor	: Vinegar odour.
Odor threshold	: No data available
pH	: No data available
Relative evaporation rate (butyl acetate=1)	: No data available
Melting point	: No data available
Freezing point	: No data available
Boiling point	: No data available
Flash point	: No data available
Self ignition temperature	: No data available
Decomposition temperature	: No data available
Flammability (solid, gas)	: No data available
Vapor pressure	: No data available
Relative vapor density at 20 °C	: No data available
Relative density	: No data available
Solubility	: Soluble in water.
Log Pow	: No data available
Log Kow	: No data available
Viscosity, kinematic	: No data available
Viscosity, dynamic	: No data available
Explosive properties	: No data available
Oxidizing properties	: No data available
Explosive limits	: No data available

9.2. Other information

No additional information available

SECTION 10: Stability and reactivity

10.1. Reactivity

May be corrosive to metals.

10.2. Chemical stability

Stable under normal conditions. Not established.

10.3. Possibility of hazardous reactions

Refer to section 10.1 on Reactivity.

10.4. Conditions to avoid

Direct sunlight. Extremely high or low temperatures.

10.5. Incompatible materials

strong acids. Strong bases.

10.6. Hazardous decomposition products

fume. Carbon monoxide. Carbon dioxide.

SECTION 11: Toxicological information

11.1. Information on toxicological effects

Acute toxicity : Not classified

formic acid (64-18-6)	
LD50 oral rat	730 mg/kg (Rat)
LC50 inhalation rat (mg/l)	7.4 mg/l/4h (Rat)
LC50 inhalation rat (ppm)	2000 ppm/4h (Rat)

FIGURE 3.1 continued

Skin corrosion/irritation	: Causes severe skin burns and eye damage.
Serious eye damage/irritation	: Not classified
Respiratory or skin sensitization	: Not classified
Germ cell mutagenicity	: Suspected of causing genetic defects (Dermal, Inhalation, oral).
Carcinogenicity	: Not classified
Reproductive toxicity	: Not classified Based on available data, the classification criteria are not met
Specific target organ toxicity (single exposure)	: Not classified
Specific target organ toxicity (repeated exposure)	: Not classified Based on available data, the classification criteria are not met
Aspiration hazard	: Not classified Based on available data, the classification criteria are not met
Potential Adverse human health effects and symptoms	: Based on available data, the classification criteria are not met.
Symptoms/injuries after inhalation	: May cause respiratory irritation.
Symptoms/injuries after skin contact	: Causes skin irritation.
Symptoms/injuries after eye contact	: Causes serious eye irritation.

SECTION 12: Ecological information

12.1. Toxicity

acetic acid (64-19-7)	
LC50 fish 1	75 mg/l (96 h; Lepomis macrochirus; Fresh water)
EC50 Daphnia 1	47 mg/l (24 h; Daphnia magna; NOT NEUTRALIZED)
EC50 other aquatic organisms 1	> 5000 mg/l (5 h; Activated sludge)
LC50 fish 2	94 mg/l (96 h; Oryzias latipes)
EC50 Daphnia 2	95 mg/l (24 h; Daphnia magna; Static system)
TLM fish 1	100 ppm (96 h; Carassius auratus; Fresh water)
Threshold limit algae 1	90 mg/l (192 h; Microcystis aeruginosa; NEUTRALIZED)
Threshold limit algae 2	4000 mg/l (192 h; Scenedesmus quadricauda; NEUTRALIZED)

formic acid (64-18-6)	
LC50 fish 1	175 mg/l (24 h; Lepomis macrochirus)
LC50 other aquatic organisms 1	100 - 1000 mg/l (96 h)
EC50 Daphnia 1	34.2 mg/l (48 h; Daphnia magna)
EC50 other aquatic organisms 1	25 mg/l (96 h; Scenedesmus subspicatus)
LC50 fish 2	46 mg/l (96 h; Leuciscus idus)
TLM fish 1	5000 mg/l (24 h; Lepomis macrochirus; Na-SALT)
TLM fish 2	175 mg/l (24 h; Lepomis macrochirus)
Threshold limit other aquatic organisms 1	100 - 1000,96 h
Threshold limit algae 1	26.9 mg/l (72 h; Scenedesmus subspicatus)

12.2. Persistence and degradability

Amido Black Liquid	
Persistence and degradability	Not established.

C.I. acid black 1 (1064-48-8)	
Persistence and degradability	Biodegradability in water: no data available.

acetic acid (64-19-7)	
Persistence and degradability	Readily biodegradable in water. Inherently biodegradable. Biodegradable in the soil.
Biochemical oxygen demand (BOD)	0.6 - 0.74 g O^2/g substance
Chemical oyxgen demand (COD)	1.03 g O^2/g substance
ThOD	1.07 g O^2/g substance
BOD (% of ThOD)	56 - 69 % ThOD

FIGURE 3.1 continued

formic acid (64-18-6)	
Persistence and degradability	Readily biodegradable in water. Biodegradable in the soil.
Biochemical oxygen demand (BOD)	0.02 - 0.27 g O^2/g substance
ThOD	0.35 g O^2/g substance
BOD (% of ThOD)	40 - 77 % ThOD

12.3. Bioaccumulative potential

Amido Black Liquid	
Bioaccumulative potential	Not established.

C.I. acid black 1 (1064-48-8)	
Bioaccumulative potential	No bioaccumulation data available.

acetic acid (64-19-7)	
Log Pow	-0.31 (Experimental value)
Bioaccumulative potential	Bioaccumulation: not applicable.

formic acid (64-18-6)	
Log Pow	-0.54 (Experimental value)
Bioaccumulative potential	Bioaccumulation: not applicable.

12.4. Mobility in soil

acetic acid (64-19-7)	
Surface tension	0.028 N/m (20 °C)

formic acid (64-18-6)	
Surface tension	0.04 N/m (15 °C)

12.5. Other adverse effects

Other information : Avoid release to the environment.

SECTION 13: Disposal considerations

13.1. Waste treatment methods

Waste disposal recommendations : Dispose in a safe manner in accordance with local/national regulations. Dispose of contents/container to ...

Ecology - waste materials : Avoid release to the environment.

SECTION 14: Transport information

In accordance with DOT

No dangerous good in sense of transport regulations

Additional information

Other information : No supplementary information available.

ADR

Transport document description :

Transport by sea

No additional information available

Air transport

No additional information available

SECTION 15: Regulatory information

15.1. US Federal regulations

Amido Black Liquid
Listed on SARA Section 313 (Specific toxic chemical listings) Listed on the United States TSCA (Toxic Substances Control Act) inventory

FIGURE 3.1 continued

15.2. International regulations

CANADA

No additional information available

EU-Regulations

No additional information available

Classification according to Regulation (EC) No. 1272/2008 [CLP]

Skin Irrit. 2 H315
Eye Irrit. 2 H319
Muta. 2 H341
STOT SE 3 H335

Full text of H-phrases: see section 16

Classification according to Directive 67/548/EEC or 1999/45/EC

Muta.Cat.3; R68
Xi; R36/37/38

Full text of R-phrases: see section 16

15.2.2. National regulations

No additional information available

15.3. US State regulations

No additional information available

SECTION 16: Other information

Data sources	: REGULATION (EC) No 1272/2008 OF THE EUROPEAN PARLIAMENT AND OF THE COUNCIL of 16 December 2008 on classification, labeling and packaging of substances and mixtures, amending and repealing Directives 67/548/EEC and 1999/45/EC, and amending Regulation (EC) No 1907/2006.
Training advice	: Normal use of this product shall imply use in accordance with the instructions on the packaging. Keep in tightly closed container. Keep cool and dry. Avoid all ignition sources - heat, open flame, sparks. Avoid incompatible materials. Avoid dust creation and accumulation. Avoid inhalation and ingestion. Avoid contact with eyes. Wash thoroughly after handling.
Other information	: None.

Full text of H-phrases: see section 16:

Acute Tox. 3 (Oral)	Acute toxicity (oral) Category 3
Eye Irrit. 2A	Serious eye damage/eye irritation Category 2A
Flam. Liq. 3	Flammable liquids Category 3
Muta. 2	Germ cell mutagenicity Category 2
Skin Corr. 1A	skin corrosion/irritation Category 1A
Skin Irrit. 2	skin corrosion/irritation Category 2
STOT SE 3	Specific target organ toxicity (single exposure) Category 3
H226	Flammable liquid and vapor
H301	Toxic if swallowed
H314	Causes severe skin burns and eye damage
H315	Causes skin irritation
H319	Causes serious eye irritation
H335	May cause respiratory irritation
H341	Suspected of causing genetic defects

FIGURE 3.1 continued

Amido Black Liquid
Safety Data Sheet
according to Federal Register / Vol. 77, No. 58 / Monday, March 26, 2012 / Rules and Regulations

NFPA health hazard	: 1 - Exposure could cause irritation but only minor residual injury even if no treatment is given.
NFPA fire hazard	: 1 - Must be preheated before ignition can occur.
NFPA reactivity	: 0 - Normally stable, even under fire exposure conditions, and are not reactive with water.

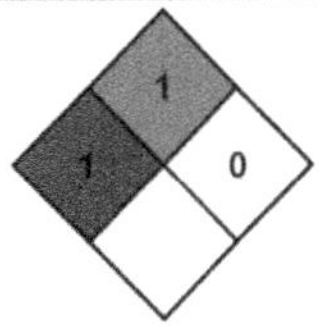

HMIS III Rating

Health	: 1 Slight Hazard - Irritation or minor reversible injury possible
Flammability	: 1 Slight Hazard
Physical	: 0 Minimal Hazard
Personal Protection	: G

SDS US (GHS HazCom 2012)

The information above is believed to be accurate and represents the best information currently available to us. However, we make no warranty of merchantability or any other warranty, expressed or implied, with respect to such information, and we assume no liability resulting from its use. Users should make their own investigation to determine the suitability of the information for their particular purposes.

FIGURE 3.1 continued

immediately know what needs to be protected and that is our: eyes, skin, respiratory and digestive tracts. The next section, section four (4), list the first aid measures, which includes routes of entry, health hazards, signs and symptoms, medical conditions that can be aggravated by exposure to this product, emergency first aid procedures and other health warnings. Now let's scroll down to section seven (7), "Handling and Storage" Under "Precautions for safe handling" we see that this product needs to be used in a well ventilated area and with "Personal Protective Equipment" (PPE). Note, that it doesn't say "chemical protective clothing", but that is exactly what is needed, as it states not to get amido black on skin and clothing.

Given what has just been revealed from this MSDS, and trust us, amido black is not an extreme example of a hazardous material we CSIs may use (look up the MSDS for Luminol, Ninhydrin, Iodine Crystals, or DFO), we just found out that our employers need to provide chemical protective clothing in the form of, chemical resistant suits (Tyvek™, or Tychem™ or similar products, not cotton lab coats), gloves (nitrile, not latex), boots, half-face air purifying respirator with organic vapor cartridges and chemical splash eye protection or, a full face air purifying respirator with organic vapor cartridges. I wonder how many of you reading this actually have been trained and issued this PPE/CPC by your employers, to use amido black. If the MSDS for this product states that this is what is needed to protect you from exposure, then, your employer must now comply with the MSDS and OSHA regulations found in 1910.120 and 1910.134. This is to say, we need a respiratory protection plan. This plan and all the OSHA regulations compliance should be assigned to a health and safety administrator or compliance officer. This person must be a member assigned to the crime scene unit, if the unit is independent of a forensic laboratory. If the crime scene unit is a part of a forensic laboratory then the laboratories' health and safety administrator, can be assigned to monitor its personnel and operations. Next, we need to be cleared by a licensed medical health professional, that we are physically and medically fit to wear the PPE/CPC, suits and air purifying respirators. We need to be fit tested for our own air purifying respirators and these respirators require annual fit testing, because, unfortunately we don't always maintain our ideal weight, throughout our careers, and we need to ensure that mask is sealing properly when we use it. We need a filter program for our mask to ensure we are using the right filters for the threats and that we are replacing and disposing of these filters properly. We need base line medicals, to document our current health and this information needs to be kept on file by our employer. This base line medical may consist of pulmonary function tests, chest x-rays, EKGs, blood and urine laboratory work ups, and all this needs to be performed annually. Once we have been cleared on all of the aforementioned, we need to be trained on all aspects of using this PPE/CPC, and once trained; we require continuing education and proficiency testing in the use of the PPE/CPC to maintain our skills and certifications. Once again all of this needs to be documented in our personnel folders. We would also suggest, you maintain a personal copy of all this information, training, certifications, and medical baselines, and to store them in a safe, secure place.

The following are OSHA laws that are employers are required to follow for all CSIs:

1. OSHA Law, Blood Borne Pathogens 29 CFR 1910.1030
    a. Establishes requirements to take universal precautions for any occupation coming in contact with blood which may expose these occupations to blood borne pathogens
        i. Requires all employees who may come in contact with blood, body fluids, or other potentially infected materials to treat such items/materials as being infected with blood borne disease such as:
            1. Hepatitis B Virus (HBV)
            2. Hepatitis C Virus (HBC)
            3. Tuberculosis (TB)
            4. Human Immunodeficiency Virus (HIV)
        ii. List the required PPE and how to use it
        iii. List procedures and methodologies of equipment use
        iv. List procedures and methodologies for Biohazard waste handling
        v. List decontamination procedures and methodologies

2. OSHA Law, Hazardous Waste Operations and Emergency Response (Hazwoper) 29 CFR 1910.120 for states who have OSHA approved occupational safety and health plans or US EPA law, 40 CFR Part 311, for states who do not.
    a. Establishes requirements for private and public, personnel that respond to hazardous material emergencies.
        i. Requirements:
            1. Emergency response plans, 29 CFR 1910.120(q)(1)
            2. Training, 29 CFR 1910.120(q)(6), (7), (8)
            3. Medical surveillance programs, 29 CFR 1910.120(q)(9)
            4. Emergency response procedures, 29 CFR 1910.120(q)(3)

3. OSHA Law, Respiratory Protection 29 CFR 1910.134
    a. Establishes requirements for respiratory protection
        i. A respirator shall be provided to each employee, 29 CFR 1910.134(a)(2)
            1. The employer shall provide respirators that are applicable and suitable for the

purpose intended

2. The employer shall be responsible for the establishment and maintenance of a respiratory protection program
3. The program shall cover each employee required to use a respirator

ii. Employer must develop and implement a written respiratory protection program, administered by a suitably trained program administrator, with required:

1. Worksite specific procedures
2. Elements for respirator use

a. Procedures for respirator selection, 29 CFR 1910.134(c)(1)(i)
b. Medical evaluations of employees required to use respirators, 29 CFR 1910.134(c)(1)(ii)
c. Fit testing procedures, 29 CFR 1910.134(c)(1)(iii)
d. Procedures for proper use of respirators in routine and reasonably foreseeable emergency situations, 29 CFR 1910.134(c)(1)(iv)
e. Procedures and schedules for cleaning, disinfecting, storing, inspecting, repairing, discarding, and maintaining respirators, 29 CFR 1910.134(c)(1)(v)
f. Respiratory hazards potential exposed to during routine and emergency situations, 29 CFR 1910.134(c)(1)(vii)
g. Training Doning/Doffing, limitations, and maintenance, 29 CFR 1910.134(c)(1)(Viii)
h. Procedures for regularly evaluating the effectiveness of the program, 29 CFR 1910.134(c)(1)(ix)

3. Prohibitive conditions, actions, operations and other requirements, 29 CFR 1910.134(g)
    a. Face piece and seal protection, 29 CFR 1910.134(g)(1)(i)
        i. Facial hair, 29 CFR 1010.134(g)(1)(i)(A)
        ii. Conditions interfering with seal and valve function, 29 CFR 1910.134(g)(1)(i)(B)
        iii. Employee corrective glasses or other PPE interfering with seal, 29 CFR 1910.134(g)(1)(ii)
        iv. Employee user seal check upon donning, 29 CFR 1910.134(g)(1)(iii)
4. Employers required to provide for cleaning, disinfecting, storing, inspecting, and repairing respirators used by employees, 29 CFR 1910.134(h)
5. Employers required to provide effective training to employees, who are required to use respirators. Training must be, comprehensive, understandable, and reoccur annually, 29 CFR 1910.134(k)

4. OSHA Law, Confined Space 29 CFR 1910.146
    a. Definition of confined space, 29 CFR 1910.146(b)
        i. Is large enough and so configured that an employee bodily enter and perform work
        ii. Has limited or restricted means of entry or exit
        iii. Is not designed for continuous employee occupancy
            1. Examples:
                a. Tanks
                b. Vessels

- c. Silos
- d. Storage Bins
- e. Hoppers
- f. Vaults
- g. Pits
- h. Sewers

b. Permit required confined space characteristics, 29 CFR 1910.146(b)
   - i. Contains or has the potential to contain a hazardous atmosphere that may expose the employees to the risk of death, incapacitation, impairment of ability to self-rescue, injury, or acute illness from one or more of the following:
     1. Flammable gas, vapor, mist in excess of 10% of its lower flammable limit (LEL)
     2. Airborne combustible dust at a concentration that meets or exceeds it LEL
     3. Atmospheric oxygen concentration below 19.5% or above 23.5%
     4. Atmospheric concentration of any substance that could result in the employee exposure in excess of its dose or permissible exposure limit
     5. Any other atmospheric condition that is immediately dangerous to life or health (IDLH)
   - ii. Contains a material that has the potential for engulfing an entrant
   - iii. Has an internal configuration such that an entrant could be trapped or asphyxiated by inwardly converging walls or by floors that slope downward and tapers to a smaller cross-section
   - iv. Contains any other recognized serious safety or health hazard

c. Only certified confined space personnel may enter allowed to work in a confined space after a permit is issued

d. The atmosphere must be continuously monitored for:
   - i. Oxygen
   - ii. Flammable gases and vapors
   - iii. Carbon monoxide (CO)
   - iv. Other toxic gases or vapors (e.g. Hydrogen Sulfide [H_2S], Chlorine [CL], …)

e. Rescue services must be immediately available on-site

f. Ensure emergency medical services are immediately available on-site

g. When working in confined spaces, employees must:
   - i. Implement measures to prevent unauthorized entry into the confined space, such as signs or ii.barriers, 29 CFR 1910.146(d)(1)
   - ii. Identify and evaluate the hazards of the permit space before employees are allowed to enter, 29 CFR 1910.146(d)(2)
   - iii. Protect entrants from external hazards by providing signs or barriers, 29 CFR 1910.146(d)(3)(v)
   - iv. Provide necessary communications equipment, 29 CFR 1910.146(d)(4)(iii)
   - v. Provide ventilating equipment as needed, 29 CFR 1910.146(d)(4)(ii)
   - vi. Provide PPE as needed, 29 CFR 1910.146(d)(4)(iv)

5. OSHA Law, Lock Out/Tag Out 29 CFR 1910.147

  a. Regulation designed to prevent the unexpected energization or start up of a machine or equipment, or release of store energy that could cause injury to the employees, 29 CFR 1910.147(a)(1)(i)
     i. Applies if employee required to:
        1. Remove or bypass a guard or other safety device
        2. Place any part of their body into an area of/on a machine or piece of equipment where work is actually being performed upon the material processed (point of operation) or where an associated danger zone exists during the the machines operating cycle, 29 CR 1910.147(a)(2)(ii)(A)(B)

6. OSHA Law, Trenches and Excavations 29 CFR 1926.650, 1926.651, 1926.652
   a. Definition of excavation:
      i. Any man-made cut, cavity, trench, or depression in an earth surface, formed by earth removal, while a trench is a narrow excavation(in relation to its length) that is deeper than it is wide, made below the surface of the ground, and is greater than 4 feet deep, 29 CFR 1926.650(b)
   b. OSHA Requirements:
      i. Each employee in an excavation shall be protected from cave-ins by an adequate protective system designed in accordance with 29 CFR 1926.652(c), unless excavations are less than 5 feet in depth and an examination of the ground by a competent person provides no indication of a potential cave-in
         1. Competent person is one who is capable of identifying existing and or predictable hazards in the surrounding or working conditions that are unsanitary, hazardous, or dangerous to employees, and has authorization to take prompt corrective measures to eliminate the hazards, 29 CFR 1926.650(b)

7. US Department of Transportation (US DOT) Law, Hazardous Material Transportation Regulations, 49 CFR Subchapter C
   a. Noncommercial transport of hazardous material evidence via a law enforcement vehicle is not regulated by these laws, if the law enforcement agency ensures proper hazard classification and proper packaging, and assumes liabilities for the movement of the materials
   b. If commercial shipping is to be used then the DOT and or International Air Transport Association (IATA) regulations apply and they require:
      i. Personnel responsible for shipping the hazardous materials must be trained and certified on how to package and to ship hazardous materials

8. US EPA Law, Resource Conservation and Recovery Act (RCRA)
   a. Regulation which provides management and disposal of hazardous waste by generators and transporters
      i. As CSIs utilizing certain chemical reagents to process our crime scenes we may be subject to these laws, post crime scene investigation as we are the generator of the hazardous waste condition.

ii. As for the removal of hazardous material evidence, this type of evidence is not subjected to RCRA regulations, until such time as this evidence is no longer needed or required, such as after a criminal case has been fully adjudicated (after all appeals have been exhausted), or other reasons, at that time RCRA does apply and licensed hazardous waste contractor must be contracted to deal with this hazardous waste.

Now that we discussed those issues, let us discuss the responsibilities of the CSI who use these chemicals in the field. What if you have a bloody crime scene and you note numerous partial bloody footwear impressions and partial bloody fingerprints throughout the crime scene and you decided to utilize amido black? You spray this chemical where needed and obtain the evidence you were seeking, what now? What is your responsibility? Do you clean up the mess? If you're not cleaning up the mess are you obligated to inform the person(s) who may be tasked with cleaning it up or own the property, the dangers and the precautions required. Once again if we review the MSDS, section 6, "Accidental Release Measures", you will see that the person responsible for the cleanup has to wear the same PPE/CPC as the person spraying it. Next you will note, that the MSDS states to clean it up you must: Evacuate unnecessary personal; Equip cleanup crew with the proper PPE; Ventilate area; Keep materials from sewers and public waters and notify authorities if it enters these areas; Soak up spills with inert solids, such as clay or diatomaceous earth as soon as possible; Collect spillage; Store away from other materials; and while not listed here, we know from section 2.2 we must dispose of this material according to local, regional (state), National (federal) and International regulations." While our use of this chemical is not an "Accidental Release", it still is a release that we created, thus we and our agencies bear the responsibility, to ensure the proper clean up will be performed by qualified, licensed hazardous waste contractor, properly informed of the MSDS for the chemical and in accordance with all applicable; local, state, and federal laws.

Since we are discussing hazardous materials, let's continue with this and why CSIs should be trained and certified as hazardous material technicians, beyond what we have already gone over. Ever since the biological and chemical weapons attacks perpetrated by the Japanese cult, Aum Shinrikyo, in the 1990s (Studies, 2001), the "Ameriathrax Attack" of 2001, and the fixation of terrorists to utilize chemical, biological, radiological, nuclear and explosive (CBRNE) agents, also known as weapons of mass destruction (WMD), CSIs need to be prepared to investigate crime scenes involving the release of CBRNE agents. The CSIs will need to be able to safely operate in these contaminated environments to perform all the forensics conducted as a matter of routine at conventional crime scenes as well as acquiring the abilities to locate, screen, classify, collect and package CBRNE evidence. Many of you reading this may be saying that this is not my job and we say, under the law, it is and that it is just a natural extension of your current duties. It is the statutory authority of law enforcement agencies to investigate and collect evidence at crime scenes, regardless of the type of crime, conventional or non-conventional, such as CBRNE crime scenes. Others reading this may argue that it is the Federal Bureau of Investigation's (FBI) duty to investigate and collect evidence at CBRNE crime scenes. Well, there maybe some truths to this, but there are qualifiers that need to be met to get an FBI response. Then, where are they coming from? How long will it take to get there? How many investigators are coming? What equipment are they bringing? If you don't know the answers to these questions, then I have to ask you, why? It has been over fourteen years since 9/11 and the Ameriathrax Attack. Do you think it's not going to happen in your jurisdiction? Was the Oklahoma City bomb built in Oklahoma City? Was the 1993 World Trade Center Bomb built in New York City? Was the Time Square Bomb built in New York City? The answer to these questions is no. These bombs were built in small towns, out of the state of the attack and transported via vehicles to the target. Is there a possibility that a terrorist could choose your jurisdiction to build their WMD or pass through your jurisdiction in route to the target? In either case, could there not be an accidental release, a premature detonation, or a law enforcement interdiction in your jurisdiction? If you answered yes, you better get prepared. Since all crime scene investigations start out local, the locals ought to be ready to deal with CBRNE scenes independent of the FBI. As CSIs we must know that many of the CBRNE agents are highly transient in nature, and if CBRNE evidence is not located, collected and packaged in a timely fashion, they may be lost forever.

Moving forward, let's talk about safety issues with the CSIs response to the crime scene. It's important when obtaining the dispatch information to obtain as much detail about the crime as possible, to understand what we CSIs will be responding to. For instance if we are responding to an exterior release of a CBRNE agent, it's important to inquire as to what particular agent is suspected to have been released and the environment it was released in, so that the CSIs can understand the agent's properties and threats they pose to the CSIs and their response to the scene. The CSIs should understand how the prevailing weather and geography at the location will affect the dispersion of the agent and thus aid them in identifying the safest route to take to the scene's staging area so they don't inadvertently drive through a contaminated area on the way to the scene, thus exposing themselves to the agent. Similarly, if the CSIs are responding to the scene of an officer involved shooting with a fatality, and this has caused neighborhood unrest, it would be best take a route to the scene to safely avoid the unrest.

Now that we arrived at the scene safely, upon signing into the scene, the CSIs should have the first of several briefings with the following personnel:

- First Officer On Scene/Safe Guarding Officer
- First Supervisor On Scene
- Assigned Detective or Investigator
- Coroner/Medical Examiner's Medicolegal Death Investigator for Body on Scene Deaths
- Prosecutors
- Incident Command System (ICS)
  - Incident Commander (IC)
  - Safety Officer (SO)
  - Investigations and Intelligence Section Chief
  - Forensic Investigation Branch Leader
  - Operations Section Chief

Among other items to be discussed is the safety and security of the scene. Once on scene it's the responsibility of the CSIs to review the crime scene perimeters established by the initial law enforcement responders, prior to the CSIs arrival, to determine if they are of an adequate size for the scene, to correct any deficiencies, and to ensure that the perimeters are properly secured by uniformed law enforcement officers. Next the CSIs should discuss the safety issues of the scene, as discovered by the initial emergency responders and document in your notes. Remember, that the responsibility for your safety falls upon you and not what someone told you. You, as the CSI, have to perform your own independent safety check of the scene, which is typically conducted during the crime scene walk through. Once you have identified the safety issues, you need to document them, then notify those responsible for the scene's safety issues, such as the incident command's safety officer (SO), or someone similar if the scene is not being managed under the incident command system (ICS). You, as the CSI may not have all the required subject matter expertise, or equipment, to deal with all the identified safety issues, and you may not have the ability to obtain all the additional subject matter experts (SMEs), equipment, and personnel, required to mitigate the safety issues that are beyond your expertise to fix. This is why it is important to tell the SO or other persons responsible for scene safety, all the safety issues you identified and which ones you are capable of handling yourself. There is no such thing as a minor safety issue and you should not take unnecessary risks to perform your crime scene investigation. If your gut is telling something is wrong or not safe at the scene, then it is, end of story. You should not let anyone order you to perform any forensic work at the scene, if your assessment is that it is unsafe to do so and that a proper safety plan to accomplish the tasks has not been adequately developed and implemented, and/or you are not properly trained, certified, or equipped to perform the required work in that environment. How many of you reading this can remember a time you performed some work at a crime scene, that your gut told you was unsafe, and afterwards when you gave your actions deeper thought, you realized how dangerous those actions were and how lucky you were to come out of this incident unharmed? And, did you come to the conclusion that you would never do that again? Here are some prime examples that the authors were involved in. On February 26, 1993, al Qaeda supported terrorist, in the second documented attack on United States soil, utilizing a rental van packed with explosives, also known as a vehicle borne improvised explosive device (VBIED), attacked the World Trade Center (WTC) in New York City causing massive damage to the WTC's underground parking areas between the two towers, injuring thousands and causing the deaths of six people. (History.com) The crime scene was massive and contained numerous hazards, such as aerosolized concrete, asbestos, heavy metals, biological (fecal matter) and volatile organic compounds. In additional there were hazards consisting of electrical, trips, falls, cutting, slicing, impalement, water, natural gas, release of oxygen displacing chemical air conditioning refrigerants, crushing, confined space and collapse. The VBIED took out five stories of reinforced steel, concrete flooring, leaving the steel columns without lateral supports. There were large sections of concrete, found at the perimeter of the damaged floors, hanging into the pit and only being held in place by bent and damaged reinforcing metal bars (Re-Bar), and vehicles hanging on the edges of the damaged floors. Yet with all of these dangers clearly visible and identified, the post-blast investigation teams, made up of the New York City Police Department (NYPD) (Arson and Explosion Squad, A&E, Bomb Squad, and Crime Scene Unit, CSU}, Federal Bureau of Investigationm, FBI) (Bomb Technicians and Evidence Response Teams, ERTs, and the Bureau of Alcohol, Tobacco, Firearms and Explosives (ATF) (Bomb Technicians and Post Blast Investigators), were working in, around, and under all of these hazards. It wasn't until a Port Authority of New York and New Jersey (owner of the WTC Site) engineer inspected the site and found the site too unsafe for us to be working in, and we were all ordered out of the crime scene. A contract was awarded to demolition contractor, who removed the hazards, and made it safe for us to continue processing the crime scene. The point being, we should not have been allowed into that crime scene to perform the post-blast investigation crime scene processing, until these hazards were properly identified and mitigated.

FIGURE 3.2 Five-story pit created by the 1993 World Trade Center (WTC) vehicle borne improvised explosive device (VBIED), note the floor systems are gone and the columns have no lateral support at their floor joints due to the missing floor systems

FIGURE 3.3 Concrete slabs and steel hanging precariously over the five-story pit created by the 1993 WTC VBIED

FIGURE 3.4 Concrete slabs, steel, and vehicles hanging precariously over the five-story pit created by the 1993 WTC VBIED

FIGURE 3.5 Concrete slabs, steel, and vehicles hanging precariously over the five-story pit created by the 1993 WTC VBIED

FIGURE 3.6 Post blast investigators working under the debris shown in previous photographs

FIGURE 3.7 Post blast investigators working under the debris shown in previous photographs

FIGURE 3.8 Post blast investigators working under the debris shown in previous photographs

FIGURE 3.9 1993 WTC post blast crime scene work halted so contractors could make the site safe

FIGURE 3.10 1993 WTC post blast crime scene work halted so contractors could make the site safe

FIGURE 3.11 1993 WTC post blast crime scene work halted so contractors could make the site safe

Now by the 2001 WTC Attack, you would think we would have learned our lesson; we did not. The air monitoring and testing, which was tasked to the US EPA, did not properly identify all the hazards in the air at Ground Zero, and thus for many weeks, the emergency responders were told the air was safe and that PPE in the form of chemical protective clothing (CPC) and respiratory protection were not required. By now, all CSIs around the world should be aware that many of the responders working at Ground Zero, the Staten Island Landfill, and the Morgue, were needlessly exposed to a toxic cocktail of chemicals, biologicals, heavy metals, and volatile organic compounds. Many items in this cocktail were identified as carcinogenic compounds. Post-scene investigation and search and recovery operations, there have been thousands of emergency responders sickened and numerous responders have died, from the various cancers, respiratory diseases, gastrointestinal diseases, auto-immune diseases, and other illnesses contracted by their exposure. Included in these responders is one of the authors of this book, who has been diagnosed with several incurable diseases, has had several operations in connection with these diseases, must have constant medical monitoring and take numerous prescription medications to manage the side effects of these diseases (News, 2011). We did

FIGURE 3.12 September 11, 2001 WTC emergency responders working at Ground Zero with improper PPE

FIGURE 3.13 Toxic debris and dust from 9/11 WTC attack

FIGURE 3.14 Emergency responders were allowed to eat and drink in contaminated areas at Ground Zero

FIGURE 3.15 Emergency responders allowed to work under large sections of steel hanging dangerously out of the side of a damaged building at the World Financial Center (WFC)

FIGURE 3.16 Later a crane would be brought in to remove the dangerous steel hanging from the side of a WFC building

not have the proper PPE/CPC at these sites. We were allowed to eat, drink, and smoke in contaminated areas, and there were no decontamination facilities until months into the response. To make matters worse, contractor trailers were leased and brought into the sites to give the various emergency responders a place to operate out of and to rest in. These trailers, having no air scrubbers, allowed the contaminants to build up inside the trailers, to the point that air inside the trailers was worst then the air outside the trailers.

Now these two examples are large-scale crime scenes, involving WMDs, but the lessons learned are applicable to all types of crime scenes, regardless of the size and complexity. We must not rush into any crime scene. A proper safety threat assessment of each and every crime scene must be accomplished first, so we CSIs, don't become victims of our work. Each crime scene is unique and thus, each will have its own safety issues. Typically, the safety issues will be directly associated with the types and manners of crimes, the location or geography, the weather, the lighting conditions, as well as the processes we utilize at these scenes. The following is a list of possible safety issues found at crime scenes based upon the type and manner of crime committed. By no means is this a comprehensive list of all possible safety issues found at these crime scenes:

- Homicides, suicides, assaults, or sex crimes with bloodletting caused by gunshot wounds, sharp force injuries, or blunt force trauma injuries:
  - Blood borne pathogens such as:
    - AIDS/HIV
    - TB
    - Hepatitis
  - Radiological dyes or pharmaceuticals
  - Chemotherapy
    - Routes of entry:
      - Inhalation
      - Ingestion
      - Dermal absorption (damaged skin)
      - Injection
  - Trips and falls

- Death investigations, body on scene with no visible injuries, no bloodletting, no signs of foul play, no evidence of suicide, and no known medical conditions:
  - Possible contagious diseases such as:
    - Meningitis
    - SARS
    - Plague
  - Possible non-contagious diseases such as:
    - Anthrax
    - West Nile
    - Food poisoning
      - Ecoli
      - Salmonella
        - Routes of entry:

            - Inhalation
            - Ingestion
            - Dermal absorption (damaged skin)
            - Injection

- Death investigations, body on scene, victim being treated for cancer:
    - Radiological implants; seeds, wafers or other
    - Chemotherapy
        - Routes of entry:
            - Inhalation
            - Ingestion
            - Dermal absorption (damaged skin or undamaged)
            - Injection

- Suicide by toxic industrial chemicals (TICs) or displacing oxygen, such as:
    - Carbon monoxide
    - Hydrogen sulfide
    - Helium
    - Nitrous oxide
    - Household chemicals
    - Automotive chemicals
        - Routes of entry:
            - Inhalation
            - Ingestion
            - Dermal absorption (damaged skin or undamaged, H_2S)
            - Injection

- Sex crimes with no bloodletting, but possible body fluids present:
    - Sexually transmitted diseases (STDs)
        - Routes of entry:
            - Inhalation
            - Ingestion
            - Dermal absorption (damaged skin)
            - Injection

- Post blast and fire scene investigations:
    - Inhalations and ingestion of toxic debris; chemical and biological
        - Routes of entry:
            - Inhalation
            - Ingestion
            - Dermal absorption (damaged skin)
            - Injection
    - Trips and falls
    - Lighting

- Thermal
- Utility hazards; electrical, water, sewage and natural gas
- Cutting, slicing, and impalement
- Structural damage, collapse, confined space, crushing

- Crime scenes involving the release or non-explosive dispersion of CBRN agents:
  - Inhalation
  - Ingestion
  - Dermal absorption
  - Injection

As you can see there is a lot of information to digest here and most of the crime scenes listed above requires the CSIs to wear PPE/CPC, in the form of chemical protective: suits, boots, gloves, and respiratory protection. This is due to the nature of the hazards at the scene and doesn't even account for the forensic processes to be performed at the scene, which may require additional PPE/CPC requirements above those already identified.

The authors would be remised if we did not touch on one additional issue, which at first, may not seem to be a safety issue but rather a medical one. However, the ramifications of not dealing with this issue could be life threatening. The issue we are referring to is mental health. As CSIs we see, smell, and physically interact with some of the worst acts perpetrated by humans and nature. Over time, regardless of how strong we think we are, these effects, if not dealt with properly, can lead to all manners of substance abuse (alcohol and drugs), severe depression, domestic violence, and even suicide, to name a few possible results. If we are required by OSHA to have baseline medicals and annual fit testing to wear PPE/CPC to work in hazardous environments, then similarly we CSIs should be given a baseline psychological, training on identifying and coping with the stresses of conducting crime scene investigations, and annual psychological reviews. We have seen, that in cases of high profile incidents, such as the 2001, 9/11 attack and many of the mass fatality shootings, that immediately afterwards the emergency responders were given access, mandatory in the case of 9/11, to mental health professionals. This was a lesson learned after the tragic suicides of numerous emergency responders, who responded and worked at the Oklahoma City bombing and why there were far fewer suicides in the emergency responder community after 9/11. Why don't our employers understand that access to mental health professionals should also be provided for chronic exposures to death and violence, and not just the acute exposure of major incidents? We know that in the emergency responder community, especially in law enforcement, there is a stigma attached to being treated for psychological issues and that many emergency responders are afraid to seek help for fear of losing their jobs. Nowadays, many agencies have mechanisms in place so that their employees can obtain psychological help, and with few exceptions, the employee's identity is not reported to the employer. The authors do not have all the answers to this problem. No one does, but we can no longer turn a blind eye to this issue. We must work together to solve these problems to the best of our abilities. All of us are different and can carry different amounts of weight. But there will come a time where we will meet our limits and going forward will require help. There is no shame in seeking help. It doesn't mean we are not strong or incapable of doing our jobs; it just means we are human. And, like vehicles, humans require maintenance from time to time, all kinds of maintenance.

All too often, the authors have heard that smaller local jurisdictions don't have the personnel, equipment, and budget to investigate their crime scenes in the manner that we have outlined. In response to this we state unequivocally, that it is not the authors preaching from on high, or stating, "This is how we do it in the big city, so this is the way you should do it." We suggest to those questioning this, to thoroughly review all of the works published by the various Forensic, Technical and Scientific, Working Groups, sponsored by the US Department of Justice (US DOJ), National Institute of Justice (NIJ), and the FBI, as well as the new NIST, Scientific Working Groups, the NIJ Law Enforcement Guidebook on Crime Scene Investigations, the FBI Handbook of Forensic Services, the ASCLAD/ISO accreditation standards, the National Academy of Sciences' report, Strengthening Forensic Science in the United Sates, A Path Forward, American National Standards Institute (ANSI), US DOT, and the OSHA laws, to understand where this is all coming from. Failure to follow these standards and laws, may cause your agencies to lose their ability to operate and maintain a crime scene unit or forensic laboratory, to suffer severe monetary fines from OSHA and the US EPA for violating these laws, to lose their accreditations for their crime scene units or forensic laboratories, to fight law suits by employees or property owners, and let's not forget the possibilities of having thousands upon thousands of criminal cases reviewed by the courts, prosecutors and defense attorneys. Your agencies or units, may have been conducting their crime scene investigations without complying with the outlined laws and standards for many years and to date, may not have suffered any of the aforementioned consequences for non-compliance, but all it takes is one incident to shine a light on your operations and then instead of possibly having to deal with one or two of these side effects, you may find yourself dealing with all of them at one time. With regards to concerns of budgets, there are numerous grants for equipment and training that can assist your agency with implementing much of what is being advocated in this chapter and, more importantly, by the agencies and organizations listed previously. Grants from the US Department of Homeland Security (US DHS), and US DOJ, NIJ, have been utilized by many law enforcement agencies to obtain personnel, training, and equipment. Also both of these federal departments offer numerous training courses, independent of any grants. Most, if not all of these training courses are delivered to your jurisdictions personnel, at no cost to your agency. Another model to give serious thought to is, to form regional forensic task forces with multiple nearby law enforcement agencies, thus pooling each agency's monies, personnel, training and equipment. The forensic task force model is also advantageous, should your jurisdiction suffer a WMD attack, CBRNE release, or mass fatality incident, as no one jurisdiction or agency, including the largest law enforcement agencies in this country, may have enough qualified crime scene investigators and equipment to handle the requirements and complexities of such a crime scene investigation by themselves.

It is the hope of the authors, that we stimulate your thinking about your current crime scene investigative practices with an eye on safety so that we all perform our forensic duties at crime scenes to national and international, accepted standards. Therefore, regardless of the size of the jurisdiction, we are all working off the same sheet of music to achieve consistency in our forensic disciplines in the safest possible way.

References

History.com. (n.d.). *This day in History, February 26, 1993.* Available at: www.history.com/this-day-in-history/world-trade-center-bombed [Accessed October 14, 2013].

News, ABC. (2011, September 11). *911 First Responders Plagued by Health Problems From Toxic dust and Debris.* Available at: http://abcnews.go.com/Health/Wellness/911-responders-plagued-cancer-asthma-ptsd/story?id=14427512 [Accessed October 14, 2013].

OSHA. (n.d.). *www.OSHA.gov.* Available at: www.osha.gov/pls/oshaweb/owadisp.show_document?p_table=STANDARDS&p_id=10099 [Accessed October 7, 2013].

Studies, M. I. (2001). *cns.miis.edu/reports/pdfs/aum_chrn.pdf.* Available at: http://cns.miis.edu/reports/pdfs/aum_chrn.pdf [Accessed October 13, 2013].

Required and Suggested Reading

American National Standards Institute. *American National Standard Practice for Occupational and Educational Eye and Face Protection* (ANSI Z87.1-2003). American National Standards Institute, New York, 2003.

American National Standards Institute. *American National Standard for Personal Protection –Protective Footwear* (ANSI Z41-1991). American National Standards Institute, New York, 1991.

American National Standards Institute. *American National Standard for Safe Use of Lasers* (ANSI Z136.1-2000). American National Standards Institute, New York, 2000.

Best, A. M. Choose the proper gloves for chemical handling. In: A. M. Best (ed.), *Best's Safety Directory*. Oldwick, New Jersey, 1998.

Bloodborne Pathogens, 29 CFR 1910.1030, U.S. Department of Labor, Occupational Safety and Health Administration, Washington, D.C. Available at: www.osha.gov/pls/oshaweb/owadisp.show_document?p_table=standards&p_id=10051.[Accessed May 28, 2015].

Conforti, J.V. *Confined Space Pocket Guide*. Genium, Schenectady, New York, 1996.

The Control of Hazardous Energy (Lockout/Tagout), 29 CFR 1910.147, U.S. Department of Labor, Occupational Safety and Health Administration, Washington, D.C. Available at: www.osha.gov/pls/oshaweb/owadisp.show_document?p_table=standards&p_id=9804. [Accessed May 28, 2015]

Gorman, C. *Hazardous Waste Handling Pocket Guide*. Genium, Schenectady, New York, 1997.

Hazardous Materials Table, 49 CFR 172.101, U.S. Department of Transportation, Washington, D.C. Available at: www.access.gpo.gov/nara/cfr/waisidx_05/49cfr172_05.html [Accessed May 28, 2015].

Hazardous Waste Operations and Emergency Response, 29 CFR 1910.120, U.S. Department of Labor, Occupational Safety and Health Administration, Washington, D.C.: Available at: www.osha.gov/pls/oshaweb/owadisp.show_document?p_table=standards&p_id=9765. [Accessed May 28, 2015]

International Air Transport Association. *Dangerous Goods Regulations*. 44th ed., Montreal, Canada, 2003.

National Research Council. Committee on Hazardous Substances in the Laboratory. *Prudent Practices for Handling Hazardous Chemicals in Laboratories*. National Academy Press, Washington, D.C., 1981.

Occupational Foot Protection, 29 CFR 1910.136, U.S. Department of Labor, Occupational Safety and Health Administration, Washington, D.C.: Available at: www.osha.gov/pls/oshaweb/owadisp.show_document?p_table=standards&p_id=9786. [Accessed May 28, 2015]

Office of Environmental Health and Safety. *Laboratory Survival Manual*. University of Virginia, Charlottesville, Virginia, 1998. Available at: http://ehs.virginia.edu/chem/home.html. [Accessed May 28, 2015]

Permit-Required Confined Spaces, 29 CFR 1910.146, U.S. Department of Labor, Occupational Safety and Health Administration, Washington, D.C. Available at: www.osha.gov/pls/oshaweb/owadisp.show_document?p_table=standards&p_id=9797. [Accessed May 28, 2015]

Requirements for Protective Systems, 29 CFR 1926.652, U.S. Department of Labor, Occupational Safety and Health Administration, Washington, D.C. Available at: www.osha.gov/pls/oshaweb/owadisp.show_document?p_table=standards&p_id=10776. [Accessed 28 May, 2015]

Resource Conservation and Recovery Act, 40 CFR 3001–3020, U.S. Environmental Protection Agency, Washington, D.C. Available at: www.epa.gov/region5/defs/html/rcra.htm. [Accessed May 28, 2015]

Respiratory Protection, 29 CFR 1910.134, U.S. Department of Labor, Occupational Safety and Health Administration, Washington, D.C. Available at: www.osha.gov/pls/oshaweb/owadisp.show_document?p_table=standards&p_id=12716 [Accessed May 28, 2015].

Scope, Application, and Definitions Applicable to This Subpart, 29 CFR 1926.650, U.S. Department of Labor, Occupational Safety and Health Administration, Washington, D.C. Available at www.osha.gov/pls/oshaweb/owadisp.show_document?p_table=standards&p_id=10774 [Accessed May 28, 2015].

Specific Excavation Requirements, 29 CFR 1926.651, U.S. Department of Labor, Occupational Safety and Health Administration, Washington, D.C.: www.osha.gov/pls/oshaweb/owadisp.show_document?p_table=standards&p_id=10775 [Accessed May 28, 2015].

Transportation, 49 CFR 100–185, U.S. Department of Transportation, Washington, D.C.: www.access.gpo.gov/nara/cfr/waisidx_05/49cfr172_05.html [Accessed May 28, 2015].

Upfal, M. J. *Pocket Guide to First Aid for Chemical Injuries*. Genium, Schenectady, New York, 1993.

4

SCENE/EVIDENCE, CONTAMINATION, AND DESTRUCTION PREVENTION

When Crime Scene Investigators (CSIs) prioritize the goals, objectives and operations involved in crime scene investigations, scene/evidence, contamination and destruction, prevention and control, would only be second to the CSIs safety. In medical ethics there is an old adage, that is applicable to crime scene investigations, and that is, "Primum non nocere," which is Latin for, "First, do no harm." As part of our job we must understand Locard's Exchange Principle, which states, whenever two items come in contact, there will be an exchange. As CSIs we use this principle to help us with our crime scene investigations by establishing links like: whether a person or item was at, or came from, a location; whether a person was in possession of an item; or whether a person interacted with a victim. These are just a few examples of Locard's Principle; there many more. Having said that, we must be mindful that we CSIs are subjected to this same principle and must take measures to prevent and control our impact on the crime scene and the evidence found therein.

In terms of evidence destruction and contamination, prevention and control, it would be helpful to first list some of the possible types and sources of crime scene and evidence, destruction and contamination, and we can follow up on them individually. By no means is this meant to be a comprehensive list of all the possible sources of crime scene and evidence, destruction and contamination.

Possible sources of crime scene and evidence destruction and contamination:

1. The suspect(s)
2. The victim(s)
3. Witnesses, bystanders, and crowds
4. Civilian vehicles, public transportation, and commercial vehicles/transportation
5. Indigenous wildlife, pets and other animals/insects
6. The first responders
    a. Law enforcement; vehicles, personnel, equipment, operations
    b. Fire department; vehicles, personnel, equipment, operations
    c. Hazardous material units (if independent from the fire service); Vehicles, personnel, equipment, operations

   d. Emergency medical services; vehicles, personnel, equipment, operations
7. Weather, natural disasters
   a. Precipitation
      i. Rain
      ii. Hail
      iii. Snow
   b. Wind
      i. Gale force
      ii. Tornados
      iii. Hurricanes
   c. Water
      i. Tidal surge
      ii. Tidal waves
      iii. Flooding
   d. Temperature
      i. Heat
      ii. Cold
   e. Sun/UV
8. Other natural disasters
   a. Earthquakes
   b. Volcanic activity
   c. Sink holes
   d. Mud slides
   e. Avalanches
   f. Land/rock slides
9. Mechanical:
   a. Heating
   b. Air conditioning
10. Lighting
11. Structural damage/collapse
12. Fire
13. Explosion
14. Chemical, biological, radiological, or nuclear (CBRN) exposure
15. Office of emergency management; vehicles, personnel, equipment, operations
16. Public works; vehicles, personnel, equipment, operations
17. Public utilities; vehicles, personnel, equipment, operations
18. Search and rescue; vehicles, personnel, equipment, operations
19. Emergency construction/demolition: vehicles, personnel, equipment, operations
20. Coroner's/medical examiner's; vehicles, personnel, equipment, operations
21. Crime scene investigator's; vehicles, personnel, equipment, operations

From this brief list, we see that there are numerous natural and manmade examples of how crime scenes and evidence maybe destroyed or contaminated. Let's take a look at the manmade examples first. If your primary assignment is a CSI and you work in a 24/7 "crime scene unit," then you are not a first responder. You are assigned to a specialty unit and are typically referred to as a secondary responder, who are called to a crime scene at the request of the first responders or assigned investigator/detective. However, in smaller jurisdictions, a patrol officer, or an investigator/detective, may wear multiple hats and also be the CSI or Evidence Tech, who may be dispatched to the scene to handle the initial 911 call, then if needed, transitions into the CSI or Evidence Tech. Regardless of which model you find yourself working in, CSIs have always been taught that life safety comes before the crime scene. While this is true, it doesn't give the first responders a license to be a bull in a china shop. The responsibility to protect a crime scene and safeguard its evidence falls to every emergency responder, who find themselves responding to and or, physically at a crime scene, regardless of their agency. That is to say, all emergency responders, fire agencies, emergency medical service agencies, and others, who respond and enter a crime scene, are responsible to identify and safeguard the scene and its evidence. It is not just a law enforcement responsibility. All this being said, it is our responsibility as CSIs to educate all the emergency responders in our jurisdiction, law enforcement and non-law enforcement, on the proper steps to take to safeguard a crime scene and to protect the evidence in it. The first thing that is required is to give these emergency responders the basics on the various types of forensic evidence that may be found at a crime scene and an understanding of their importance and use in a criminal investigation. Once the emergency responders grasp this, then they should be educated on how their work at a crime scene can alter, contaminate, and or destroy, the various types of forensic evidence they may come in contact with. Immediately follow this up with reasonable alternative methodologies, where possible, that they may utilize to safeguard the evidence, while still allowing them to perform their assignments in a safe, time appropriate, and effective manner. The bottom line is that your alternatives must be well thought out, validated by testing, and reasonable. In order for us to do this, we must first educate ourselves on the responsibilities and methodologies that the other emergency responders may be performing at our crime scenes, such as law enforcement, clearing a scene for hostiles and additional victims, a hazardous materials unit conducting a public safety sampling operation, and everything in between. We must also work with personnel from the other agencies who are understanding of the issues and willing to work with us on them. Only after we do our due diligence, will our suggestions be given the consideration they deserve. We know what some of you are thinking right about now, and no, we are not delusional. We know that this may work in some jurisdictions, typically the smaller ones; in other jurisdictions there still will be a long road to hoe with changing the policy and methodologies of another agency. In those cases you will need to get your agency's management involved to discuss these issues with the management of the agencies of concern. Even then, there's no guarantee that there will be effective, meaningful change. In fact the authors are aware of several similar incidents where issues couldn't be resolved amongst the agencies and the mayor had to step in to resolve them. We have also heard of agencies having local and state laws enacted to resolve similar issues. Obviously the last two examples are extreme cases and most issues won't require such measures and while you may not be able to affect change on an agency level, you may be able to affect some change on an individual responder level, if you are professional, respectful, and your message is on target. This is why it is important to pick your battles carefully. One such message we found to be effective and that the emergency responders were very receptive to, is when we taught the responders the *"RAIN"* principle. *RAIN* is an acronym that stands for:

Recognize: an item as potential forensic evidence.
Avoid: touching, moving, altering, contaminating, and destroying the forensic evidence, where and when reasonably possible.
Isolate: the identified forensic evidence from yourself and others.
Notify: the personnel trained to deal with this item of forensic evidence (CSIs), of all the details associated with the evidence and your actions.

Now, as stated previously, many CSIs are secondary responders, while others are first responders who are also CSIs or Evidence Techs. For the secondary responder CSIs, we can't control what happens at the scene before we get there, where as to some degree, the first responder CSIs "may" have a bit more control at the crime scene. And, we say "may," because we are sure we can all relate horror stories where our crime scenes were overrun by; the well intentioned first responder, the curious morbid seeking responder, the media seeking responder, the medal/award seeking responder, the clumsy responder, the brain dead/inept responder, and management. We all know that in many cases, in the early stages of the incident, the scene is very chaotic and unorganized, as the first responders are trying to: make the scene safe; identify victims, suspects/perpetrators, and witnesses; render aid to victims; apprehend suspects/perpetrators; interview witnesses; and make notifications. As we said earlier, life safety comes before the crime scene. It would be nice if the emergency responders would don booties, listing their agency on the bottom, and gloves, before they make the initial entry into the scene, but this is not reasonable or logical given their primary duties upon arrival at the crime scene.

Some of the typical duties of the first officer on scene are:

1. Ensure the safety of all involved persons, civilians and responders
2. Render reasonable aid to the injured
3. Make arrests where possible
4. Do not add/remove or touch anything, to/from the crime scene unless there is a safety/medical issue or the evidence will be lost, altered, and/or contaminated
5. Document any changes/alterations made to the crime scene and the justification for the change/alteration
6. Detain all witnesses where possible and obtain identification of all persons at the crime scene upon your arrival
7. Establish a crime scene or re-evaluate the crime scene perimeters if established before arrival; make it as large as possible, remove all unauthorized persons from the crime scene, and protect it
8. Notify a supervisor to respond if dispatch hasn't done so
9. Create a crime scene log to record the names, agencies, identifications, dates and times of arrival of all responding personnel, date and times of entry into the crime scene of authorized personnel, and keep all unauthorized personnel out of the crime scene
   - The following personnel are typically authorized to enter a crime scene:
   - First/safeguarding officer and back up unit(s)
   - Assigned supervisor
   - Assigned detective
   - Assigned crime scene investigators
   - Assigned EMS
   - Assigned prosecutor

- Assigned coroner/medical examiner, medicolegal death investigator

10. Ensure all authorized personnel making entry into the crime scene are wearing the appropriate personal protective equipment, and deny entry if not
11. Keep accurate notes of observations made upon arrival to the crime scene, especially safety issues
12. Make yourself available to the first supervisor, assigned investigator/detective, the assigned CSIs, the assigned prosecutor and the assigned coroner/medical examiner, medicolegal death investigators, and document all briefings

Remember, the first officer is the most critical link in any crime scene investigation. What they do, or fail to do, in the first crucial moments of the investigation can be the difference between identifying the guilty and protecting the innocent, as well as, obtaining a just guilty verdict, verses an unjust acquittal.

Once order has been established at the scene and it is reasonable, the first responding officer, preferably from the responding law enforcement agency, but if no law enforcement personnel is on scene yet, then someone from the on-scene emergency responder agencies command, should order the crime scene perimeters be established and to keep all unauthorized persons from entering the scene. Remember from your National Incident Management System (NIMS) training, that the Incident Command System (ICS) or Unified Command System (UCS) will be utilized. This means that the initial command of the scene will fall to the first responder agency on scene and the command will transfer to the agency or agencies, with highest priorities, or most emergency responsibilities at the scene, as dictated by the jurisdiction's statutory authorities. If the crime scene perimeters were established by non-law enforcement personnel, then the first law enforcement officer, upon arrival and upon completing their entire initial on-scene protocols and procedures, shall take control of the scene from the incident commander (IC) responder who established the scene. The officer should obtain the personal information and agency of the IC and interview this responder to document: their actions at the scene, the actions of the agency under their command, and to understand how and why the perimeters were established the way the officer found them upon their arrival. All of this must be documented in the officer's notes. This officer is now in charge of the scene and must follow their agency's response protocols and procedure.

Upon transfer of the scene's command to the first law enforcement on scene, this officer should correct any deficiencies in the crime scene perimeters and security of the scene. If no additional law enforcement personnel are on scene, or not enough law enforcement personnel are on scene yet to properly secure the scene, seek assistance with this task from the on-scene emergency responder agencies, via their command. Ensure additional law enforcement assets, including a supervisor, are responding; open the crime scene log, and, once sufficient law enforcement personnel arrive on scene, relieve the assisting agencies personnel from their scene security duties. The first officer will remain in charge of the scene until their supervisor arrives.

Once the first on-scene law enforcement supervisor arrives on scene, the first officer will transfer incident command to them. The first on-scene law enforcement supervisor will be in command of the crime scene until the assigned investigator/detective arrives on scene. This supervisor must interview the first on-scene law enforcement officer to understand what the officer has learned about the incident and what actions the officer has taken regarding arrests, victims, witnesses, evidence, and the scenes; alteration, security and safety. This supervisor will then delegate the first officer on scene as the scene's safeguarding officer and ensure that the officer has opened the crime scene log. Some of the typical duties of the first law enforcement supervisor on scene are:

1. Respond to the scene immediately upon notification
2. Confer with the acting incident commander (first/safeguarding officer) upon arrival and document
3. Assume control of the scene
4. Confirm that reasonable aid is being administered to the injured
5. Verify any arrest
6. Supervise an immediate search for suspects, if needed
7. Note and address any safety issues
8. Verify that:
   - the crime scene has been established and the log haas been opened
   - the crime scene is an appropriate size
   - all unauthorized persons are being kept out
   - there is sufficient personnel at the scene to conduct a search for suspects, evidence, and to protect the scene
9. Re-evaluate the crime scene perimeters if established before arrival and make alterations if required
10. Ensure that no one adds/removes or touches anything, to/from the crime scene unless there is a safety/medical issue or evidence will be lost, altered, and/or contaminated
11. Supervise and document any changes/alterations to the crime scene
12. Ensure that all witnesses are properly identified and take preliminary statements from those who were detained and won't wait for the assigned investigator/detective
13. Notify the investigators/detectives and any other appropriate notifications
14. Make yourself available for: assigned investigator/detective, the assigned CSIs, the assigned prosecutor and the assigned coroner/medical examiner, medicolegal death investigators, and document all briefings
15. Ensure all authorized personnel making entry into the crime scene are wearing the appropriate personal protective equipment, and deny entry if not
16. Turn over control of the scene to the assigned investigator/detective, upon arrival and document

Upon arrival of the assigned investigator/detective, the first on-scene law enforcement supervisor will transfer command of the crime scene. The assigned investigator/detective will be in command of the crime scene until the assigned CSIs arrives. The assigned investigator/detective must interview the relieved incident commander (the assigned supervisor) and the first on-scene law enforcement/safeguarding officer, to understand what these officers have learned about the incident and what actions these officers have taken regarding; arrests, victims, witnesses, evidence, and the scene's alteration, security and safety. The assigned investigator/detective will then delegate the relieved supervisor to oversee the safety and security of the crime scene. Some of the typical duties of the assigned investigator/detective on scene are:

1. Respond to the scene immediately upon notification
2. Confer with the acting incident commander (first supervisor) and the first/safeguarding officer, upon arrival and document
3. Assume control of the scene
4. Confirm that reasonable aid is being administered to the injured

5. Verify any arrest
6. Supervise an immediate search for suspects, if Nneeded
7. Note and address any safety issues
8. Verify that:
    a. the crime scene has been established and the log has been opened
    b. the crime scene is an appropriate size
    c. all unauthorized persons are being kept out
    d. there is sufficient personnel at the scene to conduct a search for suspects, evidence, and to protect the scene
9. Re-evaluate the crime scene perimeters if established before arrival and make alterations if required
10. Ensure that no one adds/removes or touches anything, to/from the crime scene unless there is a safety/medical issue or evidence will be lost, altered, and/or contaminated
11. Supervise and document any changes/alterations to the crime scene
12. Ensure that all witnesses were properly identified and first, take statements from those who were detained and want to leave before canvassing the location
13. Address any/all search and seizure issues
14. Notify the crime scene investigators, if not already on scene, and any other appropriate notifications
15. Make yourself available for: the assigned CSIs, the assigned prosecutor and the assigned coroner/medical examiner, medicolegal death investigators, and document all briefings
16. The assigned investigator/detective should remain on scene to brief the assigned CSIs, the assigned prosecutor and the assigned coroner/medical examiner, medicolegal death investigators, if the assigned investigator/detective cannot, ensure that an investigator/detective, the assigned supervisor, and the first/safeguarding officer has all the information developed thus far and document
17. Bring a digital camera to take photos of victim's position/injuries, if the victim must be moved/removed prior to the CSIs and the assigned coroner/medical examiner, medicolegal death investigators, arrival and note
18. Ensure all authorized personnel making entry into the crime scene are wearing the appropriate personal protective equipment, and deny entry if not
19. Turn over control of the scene to the assigned CSIs, upon arrival and document
20. Inform the CSIs of any new developments which would impact their work at the crime scene/lab and document
21. Confer with the crime scene unit with regards to the closure of the crime scene and document
22. Stay in contact with the CSIs assigned, during the course of the investigation

Upon arrival of the assigned CSIs, the assigned investigator/detective will transfer command of the crime scene. The assigned CSIs will be in command of the crime scene until the completion of the crime scene investigation. The assigned CSIs must interview the relieved IC (assigned investigator/detective), the assigned supervisor and the first/safeguarding officer, to understand what these officers have learned about the incident and what actions these officers have taken regarding; arrests, victims, witnesses, evidence, and the scene's alteration, security and safety. Some of the typical duties of the assigned CSI are:

1. Respond to the scene immediately upon notification
2. Upon arrival at the scene, the CSI confers/interviews/conducts briefing and documents with:
    a. The first/safeguarding officer
    b. The assigned supervisor
    c. The assigned investigator/detective
    d. Witnesses and victims (when applicable)
    e. Assigned coroner/medical examiner, medicolegal death investigators
    f. Fire personnel (when applicable)
    g. EMS Personnel (When Applicable)
    h. Prosecutor
3. The CSI should ensure that the preliminary crime scene perimeters have been established, secured from unauthorized entry, and that a crime scene entry log has been opened and maintained
4. The CSI should address any/all search and seizure issues, and document
5. The CSI should address any/all safety issues, and note
6. Assume control of the scene
7. Re-evaluate the crime scene perimeters and make alterations if required
8. Ensure that no one adds/removes or touches anything, to/rrom the crime scene unless there is a safety/medical issue or evidence will be lost, altered, and/or contaminated
9. Supervise and document any changes/alterations to the crime scene
10. Notify the coroner/medical examiner, medicolegal death investigators, if not already on scene, and any other appropriate notifications
11. Whenever possible, the CSIs and coroner/medical examiner, medicolegal death investigators, should work the scene together
12. Upon pre-entry briefing conclusion the CSIs and the coroner/medical examiner, medicolegal death investigators, should don personal protective equipment (PPE) and conduct a walk through or scene survey
13. Ensure all authorized personnel making entry into the crime scene are wearing the appropriate personal protective equipment, and deny entry if not
    a. Before entering the scene have the PPE checked for contamination (foreign Materials)
    b. Remember the walk through is not a physical search, it is a visual search (plain view):
        i. Don't touch or move anything during the walk through unless:
            1. Safety issue
            2. Evidence issue
    c. Scene walk through typically conducted with the coroner/medical examiner, medicolegal death investigators when body on scene and they respond in a timely manner
    d. Extensive written and sketching documentation occurs during the walk-through
    e. Used to develop plans on how to process scene:
        i. Identify safety/hazard issues
        ii. Identify the types of forensic evidence present and conduct a threat, processing and collection, prioritization assessment
        iii. Photographs
        iv. Identify required forensic equipment
        v. Decedent
        vi. Identify the need for forensic specialty disciplines

14. Upon entering the scene:
    a. Identify/document any/all safety issues/hazards and ensure all persons authorized to enter the scene are aware of them
    b. Notify/request required personnel to mitigate the safety issues if beyond the CSIs' capabilities
    c. Do not perform any work in an unsafe environment until the conditions are corrected or can be safely accomplished with the appropriate PPE and safety plan
    d. Establish a safe path to follow through the scene and ensure all persons authorized to enter the scene are utilizing the path:
        i. Avoid walking through blood and contaminating PPE, if possible:
            1. Change contaminated PPE and dispose of properly
    e. Identify a location, free of evidence and contamination, to set up your work station and stage your equipment
    f. Document the scene conditions, plain view evidence and any decedents:
        i. Written descriptions
        ii. Measurements
        iii. Sketch
    g. Locate plain view evidence and ensure its safety:
        i. Determine the transient nature of the evidence
        ii. Determine if the evidence is in danger of being contaminated, altered, lost or destroyed
        iii. Take required corrective actions and document
    h. Identify evidence in, around, and on the body, that may interfere with a thorough examination of the body by the coroner/medical examiner, medicolegal death investigators
        i. Formulate a plan with the coroner/medical examiner, medicolegal death investigators to deal with these issues and document
    i. Identify if the location where the body is at is appropriate for a thorough examination of the body, If not formulate a plan with the coroner/medical examiner, medicolegal death investigators to deal with this issue and document
        i. Full body scene examinations are not conducted during the walk through
    j. Upon completion of the visual examination of the body, the walk through should be completed
    k. Before exiting the scene:
        i. Have your PPE checked to ensure you are not exiting with anything belonging to the scene, then doff and dispose of properly
15. Upon exiting the crime scene, the CSIs and coroner/medical examiner, medicolegal death investigators will conduct a post walk-through briefing the purpose of which is to discuss the findings of the walk through and formulate plans to deal with:
    a. Safety issues
    b. Forensic specialty disciplines
    c. Photographic documentation
    d. Evidence issues
    e. The decedent(s)
16. The post walk-through briefing will be conducted with the following personnel:
    a. The first/safeguarding officer
    b. The assigned supervisor

    c. The assigned investigator/detective
    d. Witnesses and victims (when applicable)
    e. Assigned coroner/medical examiner, medicolegal death investigators
    f. Fire personnel (when applicable)
    g. EMS personnel (when applicable)

17. Upon completion of the post walk-through briefing, and mitigation of any safety issues or implementation of the safety plan, the CSIs coroner/medical examiner, medicolegal death investigators, will don new PPE and reenter the crime scene to photograph and process the scene/victim(s)
18. Stay in contact with the CSIs assigned, during the course of the investigation

At this point we will stop with the typical duties of a CSI and highlight the crime scene and evidence, destruction and contamination issues and possible counter measures that can be implemented. As stated earlier, during the chaos of the initial response, the first responders will be altering the scene and possibly damaging or destroying potential evidence. For instance as the first responders make entry into the scene to conduct their primary objectives, some of the first types of evidence to be inadvertently altered, contaminated or destroyed, include: possible trace/transfer evidence, such as; hairs and fibers, possible impression evidence, such as; tire impression, footwear impression, tool mark impression and fingerprint impression (latent or visible), possible ballistic evidence, such as discharged cartridge casings, and fired projectiles (bullets), possible ballistic damage evidence, such as bullet holes and ballistic impact marks, and possible blood and bloodstain pattern evidence. Again, life safety comes first and while we wish we could stop any of this from happening, there is just no reasonable way it can be done. The best we can do is to try to limit it as we described earlier, by giving crime scene forensic evidence awareness training to the first responders. That being said, it is still the responsibility of the first responders to document any scene/evidence; alterations, damage or destructions, they knowingly caused during their initial emergency response and to notify the CSIs or the incident commander, of these facts, so that this information can be relayed to the CSIs.

Once the emergency response phase is completed, now it's time, to fully implement the crime scene/evidence, contamination and destruction controls. The first actions will be the identification and careful removal of all unauthorized persons, civilians and responders, from the crime scene. Before these persons are allowed to leave, they should be thoroughly examined for any evidence they may have inadvertently transferred to them, as well as, possibly obtaining; footwear exemplars, elimination fingerprints, hairs and fiber exemplars, and DNA exemplars, if the CSI's interview of these individuals identifies that this is required. Next will be the identification of the full extent of the physical area of the crime scene, setting up of the crime scene perimeters, and securing these perimeters, from unauthorized entry. When establishing the crime scene perimeters the physical location, the natural boundaries, and the locations of where evidence has been identified in the crime scene, as well as a jurisdictions ability to secure the scene, will dictate how this will be accomplished. Additional factors to consider are whether the crime scene is an exterior scene, such as a street scene, an inside scene, such as inside a residence, or a combination of the two. Another factor that will impact the perimeters will be whether the crime involves the release of hazardous materials such as toxic industrial chemicals (TICs) or chemical, biological, radiological, nuclear, or explosive (CBRNE) agents or materials, also known as weapons of mass destruction (WMDs). If this is the case then, there will be specific guidelines which need to be followed in setting up the crime scene perimeters, as outlined by US

Environmental Protection Agency (US EPA) and the US Occupational Safety and Health Administration (US OSHA). Due to the nature of these scenes, they require at a minimum three crime scene perimeters, also known as hazard zones. The zones are: the exclusion zone, also known as the hot zone, which is the area of the hazardous contamination; next is the contamination reduction zone, also known as the warm zone. This is zone where the responders must pass through to enter the exclusion zone and where they will exit, drop off their contaminated equipment/debris and be decontaminated, next is the support zone, also known as the cold zone, which is where all the staging, preparation, and commands are located. To establish these zones requires training and certifications in hazardous materials and hazardous material emergency response operations. Besides all the aforementioned considerations, listed for establishing the crime scene perimeters for a conventional crime scene, we must now consider the possible agent and its characteristics, and the extent of the contamination, as well as, the meteorological conditions, the geography of the area, and much, much more. With regards to hazardous materials, there are numerous reference guides and computer plume modeling software which con assist in identifying these perimeters. All of these considerations, whether for a conventional or non-conventional crime scene, will assist in these decisions as well. As a general rule, for conventional crime scenes, the crime scene perimeters should be made as large as reasonably possible, to ensure that all the evidence is contained within the crime scene perimeters. Once the crime scene perimeters have been identified, then one ingress and egress will be logically located and established. The first/safeguarding officer will be assigned at this entry point with the crime scene entry log and will only allow authorized personnel to enter the crime scene if wearing the appropriate PPE and only after they have been properly identified and logged in. This officer will also be responsible for ensuring that the authorized entry personnel's PPE and their equipment are free of exterior contaminants before they are allowed to enter the crime scene, as well as being free of scene evidence when exiting the crime scene. It would be extremely useful for this individual to utilize a forensic light source to assist with these examinations. It would also be ideal if the first/safeguarding officer, had a table or two, some chairs, waste cans for bio-hazards and ordinary waste, a pop-up canopy or tent, all the required PPE, access to electric, lighting and all other required forensic equipment, at this ingress/egress point. The authorized persons should be donning and doffing their PPE at this location, just outside the entrance to the crime scene.

With regards to the forensic equipment that the CSIs require to process a crime scene, a robust quality assurance/quality control (QA/QC) program should be established and maintained to ensure that all cases or kits, transporting, any forensic or other required equipment, all non-disposable, reusable equipment, such as cameras, forensic light sources, evidence tents, stainless steel hemostats, blood bridging pads or stepping pads, portable collapsible tables and the like, that will be transported from the office to the scene or from scene to scene, are examined, cleaned, tested and repackaged or sealed, between each crime scene response, before these items can be re-used at another crime scene. This must be documented in a log and this information must be given to and maintained by, the QA/QC Manager. Where ever possible, the CSIs should identify, obtain, and utilize, new, clean or sterile, individually packaged, single/one time use, disposable, forensic field tests, evidence protection, processing, collection, and packaging equipment. Continuing with equipment, there are two schools of thought on bringing forensic equipment kits into a crime. One school says don't do it. Set up a clean, as close to sterile as possible, work station outside the crime scene, and retrieve the equipment as needed. This means a lot of entering and exiting, but it keeps the majority of the equipment from being exposed to the scene. The next school says to identify an area in the scene, free of any involvement with the crime and where no evidence will be altered, contaminated, or destroyed. Then utilizing a new, unopened plastic drop cloth, create a clean work space to set up and stage the equipment. The upside is, no repetitive in and out of the scene; however, all of the equipment is now exposed to the scene. We have utilized both methodologies, as dictated by the crime scene, because sometimes there are no, appropriately sized, clean, uninvolved areas without evidence at the scene.

Sometimes during the preliminary crime scene walk-through we CSIs see that the first responders have placed clean paper coffee cups (to go cups), procured from a nearby diner, or something of this nature, over ballistic evidence, such as discharged or ejected cartridge cases or deformed bullets. This was done during the chaos of the initial response in an effort to protect this evidence from being stepped on, kicked, blown away, rained on, lost in the snow, or any number of similar reasons. While this is considered "Altering the Crime Scene," it is perfectly acceptable, as they are attempting to protect the evidence. As long as the first responders wear new, clean gloves and the items they are using are clean and unused and most importantly, they tell us the who, what, where, when, and why of it, then we document it, its fine. When we conduct our crime scene walk-through, one of our priorities is to identify the evidence that is endangered of being contaminated, altered, lost or destroyed. This will require us to have various types of equipment or materials to protect and save the evidence. Whenever possible, we should try to use; new, clean or sterile, individually packaged, single/one time use, disposable items for these tasks. However, there will be times where reusable items will be utilized and they will be subjected to the same QA/QC decontamination/cleaning and testing procedures outlined previously. Some equipment that can be utilized to safeguard various types of evidence against; water, rain, snow, crushing, kicking, winds, sun/uv, volatilization liquids are:

Single, individual, small sized items (e.g. – ejected cartridge cases, single hair or fiber, single blood drops, insect, volatile organic compound liquids):

1. Sterile plastic wide mouth, screw top, specimen (urine) cups:
   a. Open an place over the item, base up
2. Quart or pint, fire evidence cans:
   a. Open an place over the item, base up
3. Chinese takeout containers wax coated paper
   a. Bottom side up
4. Plastic take out or food storage containers with plastic lids
   a. Bottom side up for containers
   b. Top side up for lids
5. Disposable plastic drinking cups
   a. Bottom side up
6. Disposable hot liquid drinking cups
   a. Bottom side up
7. Disposable plastic or Styrofoam bowels
8. Bottom side up plastic food storage containers with plastic lids
   a. Bottom side up for containers

Multiple, individual, small sized items, covering small, tight areas:

1. Tripod mounted umbrellas
2. Plastic evidence transport bins (mailbox bins)
   a. Bottom side up
3. Top side up for lids
4. Plastic stackable clothing bins with plastic stackable lids
   a. Bottom side up for bins
   b. Top side up for lids
5. Plastic or Styrofoam coolers with removable lids
   a. Bottom side up for coolers
   b. Top side up for lids
6. Five gallon buckets
   a. Bottom side up
7. PVC stackable lawn side tables
8. Stackable stainless steel laboratory instrument trays with stackable stainless steel covers
   a. Bottom side up for tray
   b. Top side up for covers
9. Stackable plastic dishwashing pans
   a. Bottom side up
10. Disposable aluminum cooking pans
    a. Bottom side up
11. Stainless steel or Pyrex cooking pans
    a. Bottom side up
12. Metal stacking garbage cans and garbage can covers
    a. Bottom side up for cans
    b. Top side up for covers

Multiple, individual, small sized items, covering medium to large areas, medium to large items, body(ies), vehicle(s):

1. Pop-up beach/sun shelters or tents
2. Portable, collapsible pop-up canopies/tents, 10′ × 10′ or 12′ × 12′
3. Inflatable children's pools
   a. Bottom side up
4. Stackable plastic children's pools
   a. Bottom side up
5. PVC folding tables or card tables
6. PVC piping and plastic sheeting
7. PVC Tarps and strapping (rope, bungee cords, straps)
8. Portable body privacy screens

Running or flowing liquids:

1. Spill:
   a. Barriers
   b. Dikes
   c. Berms
   d. Containment booms

Proper lighting is another important crime scene/evidence, contamination and destruction control. When the crime scene doesn't have proper lighting, it can cause accidental scene/evidence, alteration, contamination, and/or possible destruction, as well as causing us to miss or not find crucial items of forensic evidence. If our crime scenes do not have the proper lighting, then we must obtain the lighting to use in our scenes, but bringing portable lighting, extension cords, rechargeable portable battery power supplies, and or portable gas powered electric generators, into our scenes will have the same QA/QC issues concerning their cleanliness and contamination. These items must be certified clean and contaminant free or they cannot be utilized in the crime scene. When the scene permits, it's best to illuminate the scene while keeping the lighting and power supplies outside of the crime scene. This will be easier to accomplish for outdoor crime scenes then indoor scenes. If we are working in crime scenes which have electricity, then it's best to power the lights this way, but try to keep the lighting equipment as close as possible to the electrical outlet so we limit the use of extension cords. If no electricity is present, then next best option is to utilize a portable, rechargeable battery power supply. Placing a clean tarp of the appropriate size on the floor of the area where we are placing the lights and the power supply is highly recommended. Another trick to maintain the light's cleanliness and to keep it from getting contaminated is to place new, clean plastic bags or new, clean nitrile gloves over the legs of the light stand. The bags or gloves can be held in place with new, clean tape, rubber bands or wire ties. This technique can be used for similar forensic equipment, such as tripods and for cameras, 3D laser scanners, total stations, and high end GPS units. As stated earlier it's best to place the battery power supply, right next to the light so we don't have to run extension cords all over our scenes. The last and least of the acceptable methods for powering our lights is to use portable gas powered electrical generators. These generators should never be brought into our crime scenes, especially if our crime scenes are; indoors (carbon monoxide exhaust), a fire scene or a post-blast scene (gasoline). Unfortunately, this will require us to utilize extension cords, which, if we are working an indoor crime scene, will stretch from the outside of our crime scenes and into our scene.

As CSIs we have all come across at least one scene that we will never forget due to the extraordinary volume of blood found in or throughout the crime scene. Scenes with so much blood present that the first responders couldn't navigate through the scene without stepping in the blood and creating bloody footwear impressions and trails throughout the scene. As we stated earlier, during the emergency response phase, life safety comes before the crime scene. But once the emergency response phase, also known as the operational phase is completed and we transition into the crime scene phase, then from this point on, those authorized to enter the crime scene must be wearing PPE, with booties. Before we move on, just a note about those bloody footwear impressions possibly left by the first responders. These impressions will have to be documented and an investigation will have to be conducted determine whose footwear impressions they are. Are these bloody footwear impressions potential evidence involving the crime, the victim(s), and/or the suspect(s) or were they created by the first responders? Interviews of all the first responders must be conducted to assist in the identification of the first responders who may have made the bloody footwear impression at/in the crime scene. Once specific first responders have been identified as possible sources, and then their footwear impression elimination exemplars will have to be obtained and examined against the documented footwear impressions found at/in the scene. This can only be performed by a certified footwear impression analyst. Getting back to the PPE booties, these disposable booties are now made with 3D words on their soles which spell out the various first responder disciplines, such as: FIRE, EMS, POLICE and so forth. If these booties are utilized by those authorized to enter the scene during the crime scene phase, and these persons walk thought blood, regardless of the reason, then the blood impressions and trails they leave are now easily eliminated as evidence and we can easily identify which agencies personnel made them. Whenever possible, it's best to avoid stepping in the blood. One way to do this is to use clean, contaminant free blood bridging pads or blood stepping pads, which limit the surface contact with the blood to the four corner feet of the pads. We can take additional steps to limit the contamination of the pads by covering the four feet of the pads in the same manner as described for the tripods. Continuing with this theme, during the course of the photographic documentation of the scene and its evidence, it will become necessary to alter the scene by placing evidence identification numbers and scales into the scene. These numbers and scales are subjected to the same QA/QC controls for cleanliness and contamination, outlined previously. However, we can provide additional protection of the scene and the numbers/scales, by sealing these numbers/scales in plastic bags before placing them into the scene.

Post documentation of the crime scene, we will now enter next phase of the crime scene investigation where we will begin our evidence collection, processing, and packaging. During the crime scene walk through we documented all of the plain view evidence and we conducted a threat assessment of the evidence which helped us establish the order of collection, processing and packaging of the evidence, from the most transient or endangered of being altered, contaminated, lost or destroyed first, and working our way through to the evidence with the least of these issues left to the end. When performing these operations it can become very easy for us to contaminate or cross contaminate the evidence found at the crime scene. Here are some aseptic techniques we can utilize as part of our crime scene/evidence, contamination and destruction controls. After our post walk through briefing, while outside the crime scene in our designated clean work area, just outside the scene, the lead CSI and their partner, should don new PPE, with new clean gloves and begin to build and label, all the collection, processing, and packaging kits for all the evidence identified and documented during the crime scene walk through. When building our forensic evidence collection kits we will have to prepare evidence labels. The standard labels consist of preprinted adhesive labels which require the CSIs to fill in the required information per your agencies' protocols. Typically the CSIs will utilize a pen or permanent marker. These writing implements cannot be the same writing instruments we utilize, for our everyday business (home and office), and that we touch with our bare hands. These pens and markers are contaminated by biological materials containing our DNA and are thus a source of potential scene and evidence contamination/cross contamination. Therefore we must utilize pens and markers that will only be used at our crime scenes. These dedicated pens and markers must be kept clean, packaged and safeguarded from contamination in between scenes. They are only to be touched, packaged, and stored, as well as, retrieved and utilized, when wearing new, clean, uncontaminated gloves at our crime scenes. More recently computer generated and printed bar code evidence labels are being utilized at our crime scenes and can help in lessening some of the contamination/cross-contamination concerns associated with the use of pens and markers. However it doesn't fully eliminate all of these concerns as many CSIs are required by protocol to initial their custody seals, tamper tape, or heat seals placed on our evidence packaging. Our kits will contain new disposable (where possible), individually wrapped or packaged, clean or sterile: collection tools (e.g. swabs, hemostats, tweezers, gloves), forensic processing equipment (e.g. dionized water, latent fingerprint powder, latent fingerprint powder application brushes), and primary packaging containers (gun boxes, swab boxes, zip lock plastic bags, heat seal bags, specimen cups, zip ties). They will also contain a clean work surface towel, new, clean nitrile gloves, and pre-labeled custody seals or tamper tape. All of the components of these kits will be put in individual plastic zip lock bags, labeled with the unique evidence identification number assigned to this item of evidence and then placed in a clean evidence transport bin. Once all the evidence kits are built and placed in the evidence transport bin, a "Murphy Kit," named for Murphy's Law, containing extra collection, processing, packaging equipment, and new clean gloves, will be built, sealed in a zip lock bag, and placed in the evidence transport bin. Before moving on to the CSIs continuing our on-scene activities, we would like to discuss another model for dealing with building evidence collection kits that we feel could be beneficial in reducing the possibility of scene/evidence contamination and destruction. In this model the crime scene unit's (CSU) equipment/supply manager, can utilize all of the unit's evidence collection protocols to aseptically build these kits for the collection, processing, packaging and labeling of the various types of forensic evidence they are tasked to collect and process. These evidence kits should be built in the clean, sterile environment of the forensic laboratory dedicated for this purpose. The kits can have new unused barcode labels pre-attached to the packaging and duplicate bar codes, required for placement on the evidence itself, where and when required, sealed in the kits to be used out at the scene. These evidence bar codes can be scanned into the system out in the field, where all of the evidence data/information can be attached to this bar code via the computer and its evidence tracking software. These kits, once completely built must be sealed in packaging, stored securely, and distributed to the CSIs as needed. This whole process must be subjected to a very rigorous QA/QC program to ensure that these kits are clean and contaminate free and that their integrity is protected. While there are pros and cons for both models discussed here, we feel that this model can eliminate a lot of the field kit building contamination/cross-contamination issues. Returning back to our field processing, the CSI team will doff their gloves utilized to build their evidence collection kits and don new, clean nitrile gloves, and then assemble their in-scene clean work space equipment (e.g. tarps, tables, heat sealers, debris/garbage container). Once this is accomplished they will change their gloves again, gather all of their prepared equipment and head into the crime scene to the identified work area. Once at this location, they change their gloves again, discarding the entry gloves into their debris container, and then set up their workstation. Once set up is complete, they will perform an aseptic glove change. At this point the lead CSI, is referred to as the "collector" and the assistant CSI, is referred to as the "facilitator." The collector will collect, process, package and seal all of the evidence and the facilitator will set up all of the evidence kits, aseptically transfer all of the collection, processing, packaging, and sealing equipment to the collector, and perform any additional required documentation. Aseptic transfers of equipment is achieved by the facilitator, opening the collection and processing tools, by the handle end of the tool or the end of the tool which does not touch the evidence, peeling back the tool's packaging or wrapper, exposing the handle end, but not removing the tool from its packaging. The facilitator will then point the open end of the tool downward and the collector will retrieve the tool from below the facilitator's hands. The collector will never obtain or transfer items from or to the facilitator, with the collector's hands above the facilitator's hands. The facilitator's hands will always be above the collector's hands. This will assist in keeping the facilitator from potentially being cross-contaminated by materials falling off the collector's possibly contaminated gloves. The facilitator will also transfer all evidence collection and processing gloves, as well as packaging and custody seals, in the same manner. The facilitator will discard all used equipment packaging/wrappers, used clean work surfaces, and the facilitator's gloves into the debris container after the evidence has been collected. The facilitator will don new, clean nitrile gloves, and set up the next evidence collection, processing, and packaging kit. The collector will discard all their used equipment in the debris container, place the packaged and sealed evidence in the evidence transport bin, then doff their used gloves and discard these gloves in the debris container. The collector will then stand by while the facilitator sets up the next evidence kit. Once this is accomplished the whole process will be repeated for the next piece of evidence and it starts with the aseptic transfer of the evidence collection kit's gloves to the collector by the facilitator. There is no doubt that this process is tedious, but it is best practice for crime scene/evidence contamination and destruction control. These methodologies must be written into our protocols and we must be trained and practiced in them. Annual refresher training and proficiency testing of these methodologies and protocols is required as well, as these are perishable skills.

The next area in our crime scene/evidence contamination and destruction controls to be addressed is the hierarchal order and timing of the various crime scene processing methodologies. For instance, due to the nature of fingerprint powders becoming aerosolized when processing the physical crime scene and or individual items of evidence, the powder inadvertently spreads throughout the scene, thus potentially contaminating other locations and evidence found at the scene. It's usually best practice to document, collect, process, and package, all of the forensic evidence found at the scene that can be altered, contaminated, damaged or destroyed by being exposed to the fingerprint powders, before processing the physical scene for fingerprints and we typically make processing the scene for fingerprints one of the last tasks we perform at the crime scene. Similarly, we must follow the same guidelines as outlined previously for the latent fingerprints, when utilizing liquid chemical reagents, such as Ninhydrin, for fingerprints on wallpaper, Luminol, Leuco Crystal Violet (LCV) and Amido Black, for blood identification and bloodstained impression evidence enhancement. As stated earlier, the crime scene walk through is utilized to identify all of the plain view evidence and each item of evidence is assessed to determine the order that these items of evidence must be documented, collected, processed, and packaged. This assessment deals with classifying the primary forensic evidence types first. Next each identified, individual item of primary forensic evidence must be assessed for all other forms of forensic evidence that may be located on it and then these items must be assigned an order in which they will be thoroughly documented, collected, processed, and packaged. As an example, an open bottle of beer, with the beer partially consumed, is found to have the following types of forensic evidence on the bottle: hair and fiber, and a partial blood print. It is also suspected of having DNA and latent fingerprint evidence. This being the case, the first type of forensic evidence to be documented, collected, processed, and packaged would be the hair and fiber evidence. Next it would be best to swab the bottle's opening rim or mouth area for DNA. Since we are swabbing for DNA evidence, we should look at the partial blood print and if there is a portion of blood with no ridge detail then carefully swab it before proceeding with fingerprint processing. While fingerprint powders, in and of themselves, won't inhabit the processing of serological evidence for obtaining a DNA profile, it's always best to try and obtain evidence for DNA profiling without fingerprint powder contamination. Following this, process the bottle for latent fingerprints utilizing conventional fingerprint powders. If digits are identified with no ridge details, AKA smudges, then swab the smudge for DNA evidence. Since we are talking about processing items for latent fingerprints with conventional fingerprint powders, we know this requires the use of fingerprint powder application brushes. These brushes should be new, unused, disposable, and single use. A small amount of powder should be poured into a clean, DNA contaminate free, disposable container or tray and the brush should be dipped in it, as opposed to dipping the brush into the fingerprint powder bottle. Once completed the fingerprint powder application brush, the container/tray containing the used powder, and the used powder should be properly disposed of as waste. Never return the used remaining powder back into the original powder container to avoid contaminating the remaining powder and don't reuse the contaminated fingerprint powder application brush. Another methodology that may be utilized to process an item for fingerprints, which can assist in eliminating contamination and cross contamination via the fingerprint powder, is to utilize spray fingerprint powders. With practice CSIs may be able to develop quality fingerprints with these spray fingerprint powders, without ever having to use a fingerprint powder application brush. Returning to the beer bottle, we should now concentrate on the partial blood print, by processing the bottle with Ninhydrin, if the bottle is a dark colored glass, and we can follow this up with LCV, then Amido Black, if warranted. If the bottle is not dark glass, then start with LCV, followed up with Amido Black, if necessary. Remember to be wearing new gloves when processing this bottle and to process it in the designated work area. As you can see, great thought and planning must go into processing the crime scene and its evidence, to prevent and control scene/evidence, contamination and destruction.

For further information, recommendations, and standards on crime scene/evidence contamination and destruction controls, we urge the CSIs to review the various forensic discipline's technical and scientific working group reports: the US Department of Justice (US DOJ), Office of Justice Programs (OJP), National Institute of Justice (NIJ) publications: Crime Scene Investigation: A Guide to Law Enforcement, the Federal Bureau of Investigation's (FBI) Handbook of Forensic Services, American National Standards Institute (ANSI) the American Society for Testing and Materials (ASTM), National Institute of Standards and Technology (NIST), the American Society of Crime Lab Directors (ASCLD) and the International Organization of Standardization (ISO) standards for crime scene/evidence contamination and destruction controls.

5

CRIME SCENE UNIT/INVESTIGATOR, TRAINING, ACCREDITATION, AND CERTIFICATION

Whether we are civilian crime scene investigators (CSIs) with undergraduate or graduate degrees in forensics, or sworn CSIs, officers, investigators, or detectives, with or without degrees, our employers are responsible for training and or certifying us on every aspect of the tasks that we are expected to perform as a CSI. The crime scene unit must establish a written, detailed, validated and robust, training and certification program as a part of its overall quality assurance and quality control (QA/QC) program. Our agencies can't rely on our degree(s), previous training or experience obtained before employment or assignment to a crime scene investigative unit, to send us directly into the field to conduct crime scene investigations, as this is just our foundation for our employment or assignment. Our employers must train and certify us on the entire unit's, forensic protocols, procedures, processes, field tests, methodologies, equipment, and tools, as well as, reports, paperwork, and court room testimony requirements. And, we must be tested to show proficiency and competency in all the aforementioned areas. We must pass these tests to obtain our certifications and to proceed forward with our quest to be CSIs. If our units do not have the capabilities to provide the required CSI training in house, there are numerous CSI schools where our agencies can send us. Some of these CSI schools are free, such as those run by the Federal Bureau of Investigation (FBI), the Federal Law Enforcement Training Center (FLETC), US Department of Justice (US DOJ), Office of Justice Programs (OJP), National Institute of Justice (NIJ), grant funded forensic training programs from West Virginia University's (WVU) Forensic Science Initiative (FSI), the National Forensic Science Technology Center (NFSTC) and RTI International. Other CSI schools charge fees like, the National Forensic Academy (NFA) at the University of Tennessee's (UT) Law Enforcement Innovation Center (LEIC), various colleges/universities with forensic science programs, various law enforcement agencies, and numerous private vendors who list their courses with the various forensic/crime scene associations. Even after we complete and pass all of basic formal CSI training, we will still need additional on the job training in the form of field training. This is accomplished by being assigned to a CSI field training team (FTT), whose members' are certified by the International Association for Identification (IAI) in crime scene investigations, preferably to the highest level of certification. The new CSI will then ride along with this CSI FTT for a defined period, depending on the activity of the crime scene units' jurisdiction. The more crime scene investigation responses a jurisdiction has, the less time it will require to achieve this goal, and conversely, the fewer crime scene investigation responses a jurisdiction has, the more time it will require. Once the appropriate amount of responses has been achieved, then CSI FTT can allow the new CSI to start "catching cases," under the FTT's guidance. The CSI FTT will generate frequent progress reports on the new CSI and submit them to the appropriate supervisor for review and action. These reports must be placed in the new CSI's personnel folder. Upon the completion of the field training, the CSI FTT, will generate a CSI final field training evaluation report and submit this to the appropriate supervisor for review and action. Just as before, this report and any subsequent action by the reviewing supervisor will be placed in the new CSI's personnel folder. At this point the responsible crime scene unit supervisor will review the evaluation and will make one of several determinations. This supervisor can find the new CSI ready to conduct independent crime scene investigations and assign them to a field partner and a supervisor. The new CSI may require additional field training and be assigned to a new CSI FTT for specified period of time, or may not befit to be a CSI and termination or reassignment is recommended. If the CSI makes it out into the field all their work/reports will be reviewed by their supervisor as required. The new CSIs' training must be followed up with continuing education in all the forensic areas previously trained in. This training will take the form of annual in-service training and outsourced training, and followed up by proficiency and competency testing, announced and blind (where required), in order to maintain skills and certifications. We must also receive training and testing any time new protocols, procedures, processes, field tests, methodologies, equipment, tools, reports, or paperwork are introduced into our standard operating procedures. And, as stated previously, all of our training, testing, and certifications, must be documented and maintained in our personnel folders.

Once we have successfully made it through the crime scene unit's basic in-house training, including the field training, and as soon as we meet the International Association for Identification's (IAI) criteria for the various CSI certifications, then the crime scene unit should require us to obtain these certifications for crime scene investigations, and make them a condition of our employment or assignment. The IAI offers four levels of CSI certifications and they are:

1. Certified Crime Scene Investigator (CCSI)
2. Certified Crime Scene Analyst (CCSA)
3. Certified Crime Scene Reconstructionist (CCSR)
4. Certified Senior Crime Scene Analyst (CSCSA)

Our employer would then be responsible for our membership of the IAI, all associated fees for the certification exams and certification renewal exams, examination preparation courses and required reading materials. The following are the requirements for the various IAI CSI certifications as published by the IAI:

A. General Qualifications
    1. An applicant for certification must be of good moral character, high integrity, and good repute and must possess high ethical professional standing.
    2. An applicant must be employed full time in an occupation that includes crime scene related activities.
        a. "Crime scene related activities" is understood to mean responding to crime scenes, and

having a significant role in locating, documenting, recovering and analyzing physical evidence.

b. Processing or enhancing physical evidence solely in a laboratory or evidence warehouse environment does not meet this description.

c. "Crime scene related activities" will normally be conducted by personnel employed by law enforcement agencies, but may occasionally be performed by non-government personnel acting in an adjunct or advisory role.

B. Certification

Applicants may apply for any certification where the applicant meets the requirements as listed below. It should be noted that for initial certification, hours will be used to calculate the figures, and credits used to calculate the recertification figures.

1. Certified Crime Scene Investigator
   a. Must have a minimum of one (1) year in crime scene related activities.
   b. Must have completed a minimum of 48 hours of Crime Scene Certification Board approved instruction in crime scene related courses within the last five (5) years.

2. Certified Crime Scene Analyst
   a. Must have a minimum of three (3) years in crime scene related activities.
   b. Must have completed a minimum of 96 hours of Crime Scene Certification Board approved instruction in crime scene related courses within the last five (5) years.

3. Certified Crime Scene Reconstructionist
   a. Have a minimum of five (5) years experience as a crime scene investigator involved in crime scene reconstruction.
   b. Have completed a minimum of 120 hours of Crime Scene Certification Board approved instruction in crime scene and crime scene reconstruction related courses within the last five (5) years. NOTE:

   This training MUST include the following courses:
   1. The time frame on the acceptance of bloodstain analysis courses and shooting reconstruction courses for the CCSR has been changed from 5 years to 10 years. Training in these two courses can take place up to 10 years prior to application for certification. This only applies to the CCSR certification and it only applies to those specific courses of instruction.
   2. A Bloodstain Pattern Interpretation course that is a minimum of 40 hours in length.
   3. Shooting Incident Reconstruction courses that total 40 hours

   Additional elective courses must total a minimum of 40 hours. The topics that qualify in the area of crime scene approved training are:

   Alternate Light Source Training
   Arson Investigations*
   Blood Pattern Analysis*

Clandestine Lab Training
Collection & Preservation of Evidence*
Courtroom Testimony*
Crime Scene Documentation*
Crime Scene Investigations*
Crime Scene Photography and Evidence Photography*
Crime Scene Reconstruction*
Death Investigations*
Footwear and Tire Tread
Forensic Anthropology
Forensic Archeology
Forensic Odontology
Latent Print Detection/Comparison*
Post Blast Investigations
Report Writing
Rules of Evidence
Sex Crime Investigations*
Traffic Accident Investigations*
Underwater/Subsurface search and recovery
Wound Dynamics*

*Recommended for reconstruction training

The Crime Scene Certification Board, on request, will consider other topics.

c. AND one of the following;
   1. Must have authored or coauthored an article on some phase of crime scene reconstruction published in a professional journal OR;
   2. Made a presentation on some phase of crime scene reconstruction to a professional organization, OR;
   3. Be an active instructor in some phase of crime scene reconstruction who is currently teaching at least once a year, OR;
   4. Submit a court transcript from an actual crime scene reconstruction case in which the applicant gave testimony on the reconstruction.

4. Certified Senior Crime Scene Analyst
   a. Must have a minimum of six (6) years in crime scene related activities.
   b. Must have completed a minimum of 144 hours of Crime Scene Certification Board approved instruction in crime scene related courses within the last five (5) years. AND one of the following:
      1. Must have authored or coauthored an article on some phase of crime scene investigation published in a professional journal OR;
      2. Made a presentation on some phase of crime scene investigation to a professional organization, OR;

3. Be an active instructor in some phase of crime scene investigation who is currently teaching at least once a year, OR;
4. Submit a court transcript from an actual case in which the applicant gave testimony on some phase of crime scene investigation.

C. Initial In-house Training:
Upon approval by the Crime Scene Certification Board, an agency's structured training program hours may be reciprocated for portions of or for the amount of required hours of instruction for the appropriate crime scene certification.

D. Continuing Education/Professional Development Hours:
The topics that qualify in the area of crime scene approved training are as listed below. The Crime Scene Certification Board, on request, will consider other topics:

Alternate Light Source Training
Arson Investigations
Blood Pattern Analysis
Clandestine Lab Training
Collection & Preservation of Evidence
Courtroom Testimony
Crime Scene Documentation
Crime Scene Investigations
Crime Scene Photography
Crime Scene Reconstruction
Death Investigations
Evidence Photography
Footwear and Tire Tread
Forensic Anthropology
Forensic Archeology
Forensic Odontology
Latent Print Detection
Post Blast Investigations
Report Writing
Rules of Evidence
Sex Crime Investigations
Traffic Accident Investigations
Underwater/Subsurface search and recovery
Wound Dynamics

Please note: Certification exam book review courses do not count towards the number of required hours for the various crime scene certification programs.
Online courses and college and university curriculum courses are not accepted for certification/recertification purposes.

E. Testing
In addition to the listed requirements for each level the applicant must successfully pass a written test with a minimum score of 75%. All written tests are graded and recorded on a pass/fail basis only. (Numerical scores are not provided)

1. The tests will be taken from publications selected by the Crime Scene Certification Board. The titles will be published and the Board may not change them for a minimum of three (3) years.
2. These texts supersede any practice or agency directives for certification testing purposes.
3. Questions and time
    a. CCSI: 200 questions with a time limit of 3 hours
    b. CCSA: 300 questions with a time limit of 4 hours
    c. CCSR: 300 questions with a time limit 4½ hours
        1. Practical Questions

A. Practical questions will now be sent with the written portion of the test and will be taken at the same time

B. 3 additional hours are now added for the completion of the practical questions

2. Failures

A. If the applicant fails the comprehensive portion of the test the applicant may reapply after 60 days by submitting a new application and the appropriate fees.

B. If the applicant passes the comprehensive test and fails the practical test the applicant may request to take the practical portion again by submitting a letter to the Secretary of the CSCB within 30 days after notification of the failure without incurring additional fees.

C. If the applicant fails either portion of the certification test for a second time, the applicant must wait 12 months from the date of the failure to reapply.

d. CSCSA: 400 questions with a time limit of 5 hours

4. All crime scene certification tests are proctored.

5. Throughout the comprehensive written testing process you may not have/use any supporting/reference material/textbooks or have internet access.

I. TEST MATERIAL PUBLICATIONS

a. Certified Crime Scene Investigator (CCSI)

- *Crime Scene Photography, Edition II,* by Edward Robinson, 2010, Elsevier Science & Technology Books (All Chapters EXCEPT 1, 8 and 12)
- *Practical Crime Scene Processing and Investigation* by Ross M. Gardner, 2005, CRC Press Tests on all Crime Scene Certifications will be based on the 2nd Edition of "*Practical Crime Scene Processing and Investigation*" by Ross Gardner.

b. Certified Crime Scene Analyst (CCSA)

- *Crime Scene Photography, Edition II,* by Edward Robinson, 2010, Elsevier Science & Technology Books (All Chapters EXCEPT 1, 8 and 12)
- *Practical Crime Scene Processing and Investigation* by Ross M. Gardner, 2005, CRC Press Tests on all Crime Scene Certifications will be based on the 2nd Edition of "*Practical Crime Scene Processing and Investigation*" by Ross Gardner.
- *Techniques of Crime Scene Investigation, 8th ed.* by Fisher, Barry and Fisher, David 2012, CRC Press

c. Certified Crime Scene Reconstructionist (CSCR)

- Bloodstain Pattern Analysis: With an Introduction to Crime Scene Reconstruction, 3rd Edition by Tom Bevel, Ross M. Gardner, CRC Press 2008
- Cold Case Homicides: Practical Investigative Techniques, Richard H. Walton, CRC Press, 2006
- Shooting Incident Reconstruction: By Lucien C. Haag – Elsevier Academic Press (2006)

d. Certified Senior Crime Scene Analyst (CSCSA)

- *Crime Scene Photography, Edition II,* by Edward Robinson, 2010, Elsevier Science & Technology Books (All Chapters EXCEPT 1, 8 and 12)
- *Practical Crime Scene Processing and Investigation* by Ross M. Gardner, 2005, CRC Press Tests on all Crime Scene Certifications will be based on the 2nd Edition of "*Practical Crime Scene Processing and Investigation*" by Ross Gardner.

- *Criminalistics: An Introduction to Forensic Science (9th Edition)* by Richard Saferstein, 2007, Prentice Hall

II. APPLICATION PROCEDURES

a. Application forms may be obtained from:
International Association for Identification
2131 Hollywood Blvd., Suite 403
Hollywood, FL 33020

b. All applicants for certification must submit two letters of endorsement. Endorsements are required from the applicant's employer/supervisor and/or persons who have knowledge of the applicant's experience as a practitioner in the discipline for which they applied.

c. The completed application, with supporting documentation to include a recent photograph, and the application fee of $200.00 (not refundable) for IAI members or $300.00 (not refundable) for non-members, shall be forwarded to:
International Association for Identification
Crime Scene Certification Board
2131 Hollywood Blvd., Suite 403
Hollywood, FL 33020

d. Crime Scene Certification shall be issued for a period of five (5) years.

e. Applicant procedures for certification are subject to revision by the Crime Scene Certification Board (CSCB). The latest official version is always available from the CSCB Secretary.

III. RECERTIFICATION TESTING METHODOLOGIES

a. Applicants must meet the recertification requirements as of the date of the recertification application and pass the recertification examination.

b. Reconstruction recertification testing will be a "Complete Case Analysis" with a reconstruction opinion report submitted.

There are two (2) certifications under the crime scene certifications that require specialized training and they are CCSR and CSCSA. These two require bloodstain pattern analysis training and shooting reconstruction training, along with the additional training listed. Since we will be discussing bloodstain pattern analysis certification later in this the chapter, we would like to concentrate briefly on the shooting reconstruction training at this time. This is specialized forensic discipline and requires the CSI to have good foundation of physics, geometry, and trigonometry. There are basic, intermediate, and advanced courses in this discipline that range in length from 24 hours to 40 hours. Owing to the expense of developing and delivering courses on shooting reconstruction, most, if not all of these schools charge a fee for this training and if our units expect us to perform this type of analysis, then they will pay for the training, as well as their associated fees. CSIs can obtain these courses from various entities such as: WVU FSI, the NFSTC, RTI International, NFA at UT's LEIC, various colleges or universities with forensic science programs, law enforcement agencies and numerous private vendors who list their courses with the various forensic/crime scene associations. Upon completion of this type of training the CSIs should join the Association for Crime Scene Reconstruction (ACSR). Once we finish a specialty course like this, by no means are we now experts in this discipline. We must continue our training by going through a very similar field training process, as outlined previously for the basic CSI field training, but now the CSI FTT must be certified by IAI to the level of CCSR or CSCSA. Once the newly trained shooting reconstructionist completes this field training and evaluation the appropriate supervisor will make a determination on how to proceed with the newly trained shooting reconstructionist. This supervisor can find the new CSI ready to conduct independent shooting reconstruction investigations and assign them to a field partner and a supervisor. The supervisor may find that the new CSI requires additional field training and assigns them to a new CSI FTT for specified period of time, or decides that the new CSI is not fit to conduct shooting reconstruction investigation and recommends the CSIs exclusion from this assignment. All of the shooting reconstruction training and evaluations will be placed in the CSI's personnel folder. If this CSI is allowed to conduct shooting reconstruction analysis for their units, then as a condition of this assignment, they must obtain either the CCSR or CSCSA certification from the IAI. All analysis performed by this CSI will be reviewed by supervisor and a three-person panel who are all CCSR or CSCSA and authorized by the unit to conduct shooting reconstruction analysis. This panel shall review the CSI's analysis and findings for correctness and accuracy and report their findings to the CSI and the CSI's supervisor. The new shooting reconstructionist's training must be followed up with continuing education in shooting reconstruction analysis. This training will take the form of annual in-service training and out sourced training, and followed up by proficiency and competency testing, announced and blind (where required), in order to maintain their skills and certifications. Again, as stated previously, all of the CSIs' training, testing, and certifications, must be documented and maintained in their personnel folders.

The IAI also offers additional certifications for CSIs, which would beneficial for us and our crime scene units to have or require and they are:

1. Certified Forensic Photography (CFP)
2. Certified Latent Print Examiner (CLPE)
    A. If the CSIs also perform latent print examinations/comparisons/identifications

Besides our in-unit training in forensic photography and latent fingerprint, we should also seek additional outside training courses in this discipline. There are numerous free and fee based training courses for this discipline provided by the FBI, FLETC, US DOJ, OJP, NIJ grant funded forensic training programs from WVUs FSI, NFSTC and RTI International. Other CSI schools charge fees like, the NFA at UT's LEIC, Nikon Forensic School and numerous private vendors who list their courses with the various forensic/crime scene associations. We should note that it is always a best practice to receive training from the manufacturer of the equipment we are expected to use. So, if we are using a Nikon D700 digital single lens reflex (DSLR) camera, then it would be best to be trained by Nikon and the same would be true of a Canon DSLR, or any other electronic forensic equipment (e.g. automated fingerprint identification system (AFIS), alternate light source (ALS) or electrostatic dust lifter [EDL]) for that matter. And, just as stated previously, for CSI certifications, our employer would be responsible for our membership of the IAI, all associated fees for the certification exams and certification renewal exams, examination preparation courses and required reading materials. The following are the requirements for the various CFP and CLPE certifications as published by the IAI:

Certified Forensic Photography:

I. General Requirements
   A. An applicant for certification must possess a high ethical and professional standing.
   B. An applicant for certification must be primarily employed in the field of Forensic Science whose duties include forensic photography.

II. Education and Experience Requirements
An applicant must have a minimum of three (3) years of experience working in the area of photography and/or digital imaging.

III. Training Requirements
An applicant must have satisfactorily completed a minimum of forty (40) classroom hours of photography courses, either police academy, or college level. Examples of qualified training may include college photography, or digital imaging courses, IAI conference classes or workshops, training in photography, image analysis and/or digital imaging through the FBI, state and local academies, or other forensic imaging workshops.

IV. Endorsements
All applicants must submit two letters of endorsement, one of which must be from an individual actively working in the area of photography and/or digital imaging. One of which must be from the individual's immediate supervisor. These should be addressed to the Secretary of the Certification Board.

V. Examinations
   A. Certification shall be determined by testing and meeting the above qualifications. The certification test was developed and is maintained by the IAI Forensic Photography and Digital Imaging Certification Board. Applicants have three (3) hours to complete the written examination and forty-five (45) days from receipt of certified mail to work and return the practical test.
      1. The written test consists of 100 multiple choice, true/false and narrative questions, including, but not limited to, history of photography, cameras, lenses, film, exposure, depth of field, light and color theory, lighting, filters, close-up photography, presentation and digital imaging. Passing grade is 75%. The test questions are from the texts listed at the bottom of the requirements.
      2. The practical test shall consist of submission of ten (10) assignments prepared by the applicant, seven (7) of which are from a required list and three (3) from a list of optional assignments.
         a. Evaluation of the submitted images is based on a pass/fail basis, using the following factors:
            i. Compliance with requirements
            ii. Utilization of proper photographic techniques
            iii. Overall image quality
            iv. Compliance with SWGIT guidelines/best practices regarding photographic techniques.
         b. Images are to be submitted in a digital format. The image quality and resolution must be adequate to show the required detail for the assignment.

VI. General Provisions Concerning Certification

1. Violation of the IAI, or, Forensic Photography and Digital imaging Certification Board code of ethics.
2. A misstatement, misrepresentation, concealment, or omission of a material fact or facts in an application or any other communication related to certification.

A. Conviction of an applicant for IAI certification, or holder of an IAI certification, by a court of competent jurisdiction of a felony, or any crime involving The right to deny certification is reserved by the Forensic Photography Certification Board.

B. Applicants who are denied certification by the Forensic Photography and Digital Imaging Certification Board may appeal such action in writing to the IAI Board of Directors within sixty (60) days of such notification.

C. The certificate issued by the IAI are non-transferable. They remain the property of the IAI. However, every person to whom a certificate has been issued shall be entitled to its continued possession unless, or until, such certificate is revoked.

D. Certificates are issued for a period of five (5) years, subject to renewal upon application by a member. Such application for renewal shall be subject to standards in effect at the time of the request for renewal and payment of the established fee.

E. Membership in the IAI, or any of its state or regional divisions, is not mandatory for certification.

F. Certificates may be suspended or revoked by the Forensic Photography and Digital Imaging Certification Board for any of the following reasons:

1. moral turpitude.
2. Issuance of a certificate contrary to, or in violation of, any of the laws, standards, rules, or regulations, of the IAI; or determination that the person certified was not, in fact, eligible to receive such certificate at the time of its issuance.
3. Unethical conduct, or other conduct, by a holder of a certificate that brings the specialty of forensic photography and digital imaging into dispute.

VII. Certification - Grandfathering

- No waivers or Grandfather provisions are in this program.

VIII. Test questions are taken from the following publications:

- ★*A Short Course in Digital Photography (2nd Edition)* By Barbara London and Jim Stone
- ★*Crime Scene Photography, Second Edition* [Hardcover] By Edward M. Robinson
- ★All forensic photography appropriate SWIG Guideline
- ★These texts will apply to anyone who applies for Forensic Photography Certification after January 1, 2013.

IX. For further information; contact:

David T. Gamble, Secretary
Forensic Photography Certification Board
417 Jefferson Ave
Avon, NJ 07717
Phone: (732) 492–5436

Certified Latent Print Examiner:

A. Technical Training Required:
Minimum of 80 Hours of Certification Board approved training in latent print matters, along with criteria listed on the application form. It should be noted that for Certification, hours will be used to calculate figures and credits used to calculate recertification figures.

B. Basic Experience Required:
1. Minimum of two (2) years full-time experience in the comparison and identification of latent print material and related matters.
2. If less than full-time experience for the given time period is possessed, times must be accumulated to reach an acceptable minimum.

C. Education Requirements:
1. A Bachelor's Degree plus two (2) years full-time experience as prescribed by the LPCB.
or
a. An Associate Degree (or documentation of 60 semester hours or 90 quarter hours of college credits) plus 3 years full-time experience as a latent print examiner equals the Bachelor's Degree requirement.
or
b. Four (4) years full-time experience as a latent print examiner required by Section C, 1 equals the Bachelor's Degree requirement.
2. Educational requirements are not applicable to recertification.

D. Examinations:
Certification shall be determined by testing. The certification test was developed and is maintained by the IAI Latent Print Certification Board. The applicants have 8 hours to complete parts 1, 2, and 3 of the test. All written tests are graded and recorded on a pass/fail basis as follows:
1. Comparison of 15 latent prints with inked prints. The applicant must correctly identify a minimum of 12 of the latent prints without an erroneous identification.
2. Pattern Interpretation of 35 Inked Impressions. The applicant must correctly interpret a minimum of 32 prints.
3. True and false, multiple choice questions relative to the history of fingerprints, pattern interpretation and latent prints. Must successfully pass a written test with a minimum score 85%.

E. Either oral board testing and/or presentation of a case for review to include latent print, inked print, charted enlargements and court qualifying questions and answers.
1. If the applicant has already testified in a court of law as an expert, the applicant may submit a case for review, or may submit to the oral board testing.
2. If the applicant for certification indicated on the original application that he/she had previously testified in a court of law to a latent print identification, the letter will specify a 90 day time limit by which the applicant must submit to the Division Certification Committee a case for review and documentation of prior testimony.

3. The case for review shall include:
   a. A copy of the latent print
   b. A copy of the inked print
   c. Charted photographic enlargements of a and b, and include an explanation on how the conclusion is reached.
   d. Qualifying questions with answers to include the introduction and identification of the latent print.
4. Documentation of prior testimony may be one of the following or other similar documentation:
   a. Letter from judge in whose court he/she testified.
   b. Letter from prosecuting attorney of case in which he/she testified.
   c. Letter from defense attorney in case.
   d. Court transcript of his/her testimony.
   e. Letter from his/her immediate superior who has personal knowledge of applicant's prior testimony.
5. The Division Certification Committee will review the "Case for Review" and the documentation of prior testimony and if in order will forward same to the Secretary of the Latent Print Certification Board.
   a. If the applicant has not given testimony in a court of law as an expert, the applicant shall be required to undergo oral board testing as follows:
      1. If applicant on original application indicated that he/she had not previously furnished testimony, then a letter will be forwarded from the Secretary of the Latent Print Certification Board to the applicant, advising the applicant that he/she had achieved passing grades on the initial three portions of the test and is eligible for an oral board testing. The Chairman of the Division Certification Committee will be notified of the applicant passing the written test, no scores will be provided.
      2. The Chairperson of the Division Certification Committee will be requested to set a date within six months of passing of the written test for the oral board test and to advise the applicant and Secretary of the Latent Print Certification Board of the test date.
      3. The oral board test shall be administered by a minimum of two members of the Division Certification Committee and preferably by all three.
      4. The oral board should be approximately one hour in length and should include the following:
         a. A latent print and/or copy thereof.
         b. Inked print and/or copy thereof.
         c. Charted photographic enlargements depicting the identification.
         d. List of qualifying questions.
         e. Original notes, work sheets or report.
         (The above should be prepared and brought to the oral board test by the applicant and should be a hypothetical case as opposed to an actual case not yet adjudicated.)
6. The Division Certification Committee should put the applicant through a mock trial, as would be experienced in a regular court of law with judge, prosecutor and defense counsel.

   a. The prosecutor should go through qualifying questions with the applicant responding, through the evidence testimony, and an explanation by the applicant of the charted enlargements depicting the latent print and inked print, and should then be cross examined by the defense.
   b. The cross examination should proceed as dictated by the direct testimony and should include questions on the background of fingerprint identification, methodology and criteria used in effecting an identification, as well as questions relative to his/her background and experience.
7. A videotape recording shall be made of each applicant's mock trial proceeding and should include the date, name of the applicant and names of those participating in the oral board test.
   a. The videotape should be forwarded with comments of the Division Certification Committee as to the satisfactory or unsatisfactory participation by the applicant to the Secretary of the Latent Print Certification Board.
8. Anyone failing the test for any reason other than an erroneous identification must wait 6 months from the test date to reapply.
9. Anyone failing the test by making one or more erroneous identifications must wait 1 year before they can reapply to take the test.
10. Those reapplying must submit a new application with all attachments plus whatever fee may be in effect at that time.
11. An applicant failing any part of the test need only retake that part which he/she failed; unless an erroneous identification was made in which case the entire test must be retaken.

F. Recertification:
1. All applicants for recertification must accumulate 80 Continuing Education/Professional Development Credits since initial certification or recertification.
2. The certification program calls for recertification every five years. This is necessary to determine the activities of the examiner over the previous five years and provide for updating of records.
3. Applicants for recertification must prove continued competency by means of a comparison test. After approval of the Division Latent Print Certification Committee, the Secretary/designee of the Latent Print Certification Board will send the applicant a comparison test.
   a. Test will consist of five latent prints and five inked cards. The latent prints will all be identifiable with the inked prints provided.
   b. The applicant will have thirty days to complete the test and return it to the Secretary of the LPCB for grading. The applicant will provide a signed statement affirming that he/she took the test without assistance.
   c. All of the latent prints must be identified to pass the test.
   d. Failure to identify all of the latent prints will cause the suspension of their Certificate pending the applicant completing a new application for Certification and paying the applicable fee as stated on the IAI Website and taking the Certification test as stated. Failure to apply for testing prior to one year after the original expiration date of the Certificate will cause the suspension of the Certificate.
   e. An erroneous identification will cause the suspension of their Certificate for one year. After one year the applicant may apply for Certification and be tested as stated.

G. Final Review:
   1. The Secretary of the Latent Print Certification Board will review the application and all related material including all test material, case for review, documentation of prior testimony, tape of mock trial and recommendations of the Division Certification Committee. If everything is acceptable, a certificate and certification card will be issued to the applicant.
   2. The entire Latent Print Certification Board will review the application and all related material in the event there is a technical concern about the application or test results.

H. The following publications are the suggested reading materials for preparing for the Certification test. Answers to all questions appearing on the written portion of the test can be found in these books:
   1. The Fingerprint Sourcebook (U.S. Dept of Justice, National Institute of Justice) by I.A.I, Scientific Working Group on Friction Ridge Analysis, Study and Technology (SWGFAST) et al. Eric H. Holder, Laurie O. Robinson, John H. Laub
   2. Quantitative-Qualitative Friction Ridge Analysis: An Introduction to Basic and Advanced Ridgeology (Crc Series in Practical Aspects of Criminal and Forensic Investigations) (Hardcover) by David R. Ashbaugh (Author)
   3. The Science of Fingerprints: Classification and Uses (Paperback) by Federal Bureau of Investigation (U.S.)
   4. Scott's Fingerprint Mechanics (Hardcover) by Robert D. Olsen (Author), Walter R. Scott (Author)
   5. Advances in Fingerprint Technology, Second Edition (Forensic and Police Science Series) (Hardcover) by Henry C. Lee (Editor), R. E. Gaensslen (Editor)

I. Any further questions, please contact the Latent Print Certification Board Secretary at:
   1. James E. Bush, Secretary
      Latent Print Certification Board, I. A. I.
      Mississippi Crime Laboratory
      PO Box 4450
      Meridian, MS 39304
      Phone: (601) 483-5273
      Fax: (601) 483-5278
      E-mail: jbush@mcl.state.ms.us

Latent fingerprint examination, comparison, and identification is another specialized forensic discipline and requires the CSI to have good foundation in the science of fingerprints. There are basic, intermediate, and advanced courses in this discipline that range in length from 24 hours to 40 hours. There are both free and fee based schools for this training and if our units expect us to perform this type of analysis, then they will pay for the training, as well as their associated fees. CSIs can obtain these courses from various entities such as the FBI, WVU FSI, the NFSTC, RTI International, NFA at UT's LEIC, various colleges and universities with forensic science programs, and numerous private vendors who list their courses with the various forensic/crime scene associations. We highly recommended that the CSIs only obtain training from schools who teach and practice the "Analysis, Comparison, Evaluation, and Verification" standard known as ACE-V, developed by the Scientific

Working Group on Friction Ridge Analysis, Study and Technology (SWGFAST) and AFIS. It bears repeating, once we finish a specialty course like this, by no means are we now experts in this discipline. We must continue our training by going through a very similar field training process, as outlined previously for the shooting reconstruction analysis, but now the CSI Latent Examiner Trainer (LET) must be an IAI CLPE. Once the newly trained latent print examiner completes this field training and evaluation, the appropriate supervisor will make a determination on how to proceed with the newly trained examiner. This supervisor can find the new CSI ready to conduct independent latent print examinations and assign them to a supervisor. The new CSI examiner may require additional field training and the supervisor assigns them to a new CSI LET for specified period of time, or decides that the new CSI is not fit to conduct latent fingerprint examinations and recommends the CSI's exclusion from this assignment. All of the latent fingerprint examiner training and evaluations will be placed in the CSI's personnel folder. If this CSI is allowed to conduct latent fingerprint examinations for their units, then as a condition of this assignment, they must obtain the CLPE certification from the IAI. All analysis performed by this CSI/Examiner will be reviewed by another CLPE, who is authorized by the unit to conduct latent fingerprint examinations. This examiner shall review the CSI's examination, findings, and or identification for correctness, accuracy, and identification verification, and report their findings to the CSI and the CSI's supervisor. The new latent fingerprint examiner training must be followed up with continuing education in latent fingerprint examinations. This training will take the form of annual in-service training and outsourced training, and followed up by proficiency and competency testing, announced and blind (where required), in order to maintain their skills and certifications. Again, as stated previously, all of the CSIs' training, testing, and certifications, must be documented and maintained in their personnel folders.

If our crime scene units require us to conduct bloodstain pattern analysis, then we should attend a 40-hour basic bloodstain pattern analysis course, followed by a 40-hour advanced bloodstain pattern analysis course. Upon completion of the basic 40-hour course we should join the International Association of Bloodstain Pattern Analyst (IABPA), as well as the ACSR. The training and the association memberships cost should be incurred by our employer. There are some free basic bloodstain pattern analysis courses, provided by numerous forensic academic providers, paid for by training grants obtained from US DOJ, OJP, NIJ: WVU's FSI, NFSTC and the New York City, Office of Chief Medical Examiner (NYC OCME), Forensic Sciences Training Program (FSTP). Other courses are offered at the FLETC, the NFA at UT's LEIC, various colleges/universities with forensic science programs, law enforcement agencies, and numerous private vendors who list their courses with the various forensic/crime scene associations. Once we meet the requirements, as outlined below, we should seek certification in bloodstain pattern analysis from the IAI. Again, our employer would then be responsible for our membership of the IAI, all associated fees for the certification exams and certification renewal exams, examination preparation courses and required reading materials. Once we finish a bloodstain pattern analysis course, by no means are we now experts in this discipline. We must continue our training by going through a very similar field training process, as outlined previously for the shooting reconstruction analysis field training, but now the CSI FTT must be certified by IAI to the level of; CCSR, CSCSA or CBPA. Once the newly trained bloodstain pattern analyst completes this field training and evaluation, the appropriate supervisor will make a determination on how to proceed with the newly trained bloodstain pattern analyst. This supervisor can find the new CSI ready to conduct independent bloodstain pattern analysis and assign them to a field partner and a supervisor. The new CSI may require additional field training and the supervisor assigns them to a new CSI FTT for specified period of time, or decides that the new CSI is not fit to conduct bloodstain pattern analysis and recommends the CSI's exclusion from this assignment. All of the bloodstain pattern analysis training and evaluations will be placed in the CSI's personnel folder. If this CSI is allowed to conduct bloodstain pattern analysis for their units, then as a condition of this assignment, they must obtain either the CBPA certification from the IAI. All analysis performed by this CSI will be reviewed by supervisor and a three-person panel who have one or more of the following certifications; CCSR, CSCSA or CBPA, and authorized by the unit to conduct bloodstain pattern analysis. This panel shall review the CSI's analysis and findings for correctness and accuracy and report their findings to the CSI and the CSI's supervisor. The new bloodstain pattern analyst's training must be followed up with continuing education in bloodstain pattern analysis. This training will take the form of annual in-service training and outsourced training, and followed up by proficiency and competency testing, announced and blind (where required), in order to maintain their skills and certifications. Again, as stated previously, all of the CSIs': training, testing, and certifications, must be documented and maintained in their personnel folders.

The following are the requirements for the bloodstain pattern analyst certification as published by the IAI:

> General Qualifications:
>
> > An applicant for certification must be of good moral character, high integrity, good repute, and must possess a high ethical and professional standing (See Section III).
> >
> > All applicants for certification must submit two letters of endorsement. Endorsements are required from the applicant's employer/supervisor and/or persons who have knowledge of the applicant's experience as a practitioner in the discipline for which they applied.
>
> Training Requirements:
> Applicants for certification must provide documentation that evidences the required amount of certification credits (training certificates, etc.).
> A minimum of forty (40) hours of education in an approved workshop providing theory, study and practice as follows:
>
> a. Flight characteristics and stain patterns
> b. Examination and identification of bloodstain evidence
> c. Documentation of blood stains and patterns
>
> This forty (40) hour course must include the following:
>
> a. Oral and/or visual presentation of physical activity of blood droplets illustrating blood as fluid being acted upon by motion or force. Past research, treatise or other reference materials for the student.
> b. Laboratory exercises which document bloodstains and standards by previous research. Exercises must include – but not be limited to the following:
>
> Falling Blood:
>
> a. Spot size related to distance fallen and blood volume variations.

Surface Considerations:

a. Texture: smooth, rough, porous.
b. Flat or angular surfaces.
c. Drying time.

Impact Angle Determinations:

Blood in motion striking a horizontal surface or vertical target. Study of spot size, shape and spatter characteristics related to:

a. Distance fallen
b. Speed of travel
c. Direction of travel

Increased Blood Volumes:

a. Stain shape and satellite spatter related to volume and distance
b. Radial patterns
    1. Dripped
    2. Splashed

Flow Patterns (horizontal/vertical):

a. Accumulative/passive.
b. Secondary, altered.

Projected Patterns:

Cast-Off:

a. Arc of the swing, number of swings or patterns, weapon variations.

Impact Patterns:

a. Blunt force, explosive (gunshot).
b. Size, shape and distribution of spots related to degree of force and distance traveled.

Transfer Stains and Impression Patterns:

a. Secondary targets, intermediate or intervening objects, images and impressions, wipe and swipe patterns (hair, skin, cloth, etc.)

Laboratory manual and glossary of approved terms should be provided, describing exercises conducted – allowing space for written findings and observations of each exercise. Participants should be required to prepare individual standards of stain/pattern documentation for each exercise completed.

a. Preservation of evidence.
b. Documentation of evidence by measurement, sketch and properly oriented photograph.

The Student should be awarded a Certificate of Completion describing course dates and hours completed, instructor and sponsoring institution. This Certificate (copy) shall be submitted to meet the specified application requirements.

Other Topics Suggested (NOT required):

a. Correlation of stain and patterns to the scene surroundings and/or body trauma.
b. Serological/DNA considerations.
c. Chemical and light source absorption and enhancement.
d. Blood detection/collection techniques.
e. Stain pattern reconstruction.

The minimum requirement of this forty (40) hour course must be met, with NO exceptions as an entry for Certification requirement. Various course content and areas of study must be approved by the Board and a Certificate of Completion must be forwarded with application for Certification testing.

Documentation will be required of course outline or equivalents. Acceptance will be required to fit the specified guidelines or be at the discretion of the Certification Board.

Time Practicing within Discipline:

A minimum of three (3) years of practice within the discipline of bloodstain Pattern Identification, following the required forty (40) hour training course, must be documented.

a. Dates of training course must be provided.
b. Documentation required for time in discipline may be provided in the following manner:
    1. Transcripts of testimony.
    2. Published work.
    3. Articles published.
    4. Instructional activities (documented).
    5. Case submission/multiple cases.
    6. Case reviewed (by Board).
    7. Other analysis (documented).
    8. Other means of establishing time in discipline (to be approved by Board).
c. Documentation provided will be approved by review and at the discretion of the Board.

Training Courses/Study Required:

A minimum of 240 hours of instruction in fields of study relating to bloodstain pattern analysis is required. This 240 hour requirement includes the aforementioned 40 hour basic bloodstain pattern analysis course.

Additionally, completion of a 40 hour photography course is also required. A certificate of completion MUST be provided showing successful completion of the 40 hour photography course. A compilation of photography courses relating to crime scene photography totaling 40 hours or a Board approved college course in crime scene related photography may also meet this requirement.

- In the absence of 40 hours of photography training/education the Board will accept a letter signed by a supervisor relating the training, competency and experience of the applicant in crime scene photography. All certificates relating to photography training described in this letter must be included with the application.

Fields of study/courses qualifying for the remaining 160 hours of required training are:

- Crime scene investigation technology.

- Evidence recovery.
- Blood detection techniques/presumptives.
- Medico legal death investigation.
- Forensic science and technology.

The balance of the course hours required MUST also have some type of certificate of completion. Courses without certificates offered to meet the aforementioned training requirements will be evaluated by the Board.

Additional courses may be approved by the Board on an individual basis. Documentation must be provided. Or:

- Elective credit may be earned through research, published work, submission of a case investigative report worked by the applicant or transcript of testimony. Or:
- Elective credit will be considered on an individual basis at the discretion of the Board. Or:
- Applicant may apply credit for being certified as a Senior Crime Scene Analyst through the IAI.
- Documentation of the instruction of courses fitting the prescribed outline or hours of documented instruction may be substituted upon approval of the Board. Documentation must be submitted to the Board for their review and approval.
- However, the applicant MUST still meet the minimum requirements for a forty (40) hour Bloodstain Pattern Analysis Course and a (40) photography course, as well as the additional training and time in discipline requirements.

Certification Testing and Study Reference List

Effective of August 5th, 2011, the current study references are:

1 *Principles of Bloodstain Pattern Analysis: Theory and Practice*, S.H. James, P.E. Kish, T.P. Sutton; CRC Press; 2005.
2 *Practical Crime Scene Analysis and Reconstruction*, R. Gardner and T. Bevel; CRC Press; 2009.
3 *Handbook of Forensic Pathology, 2nd Ed.*, V.J. DiMaio and S.E. Dana; CRC Press; 2006.
4 SWGSTAIN Recommended Terminology

NOTE: Terminology for the updated test will come from the SWGSTAIN Recommended Terminology listed above.

The examination for Bloodstain Pattern Analysis Certification is divided into four (4) sections. Six (6) hours are allotted to complete the entire examination. Each part/section will be graded separately. All four sections must individually be passed with a 75% on each section to pass the certification test. The four (4) sections include:

Section 1. Written Examination: The written examination consists of 100 multiple choice and true-false questions. The section will include, but not be limited to:

- Bloodstain pattern analysis terminology.
- A holistic approach to documentation, photography, illustration and sketching of bloodstains and bloodstain patterns.
- Wound pathology.

- Investigative and scene reconstruction procedures.
- Crime Scene processing.
- History of bloodstain pattern analysis.
- Bloodstain pattern analysis theory and logic.
- Mathematics (Basic understanding pertaining to discipline applications).
- Stain and stain pattern recognition (Characteristics and visual recognition).

Section 2. Pattern Identification: Correctly identify and provide information regarding designated bloodstain patterns.

Section 3. Analysis Portion: Correctly answer questions regarding bloodstain patterns in crime scene images and provide information to support the conclusion/s offered.

Section 4. Area of Convergence and Area of Origin Calculation: Correctly determine the location of the area of convergence and correctly calculate the area of origin of a spatter pattern.

For further information, contact:
Grant D. Graham Sr., MFS, CBPA, CSCSA
Secretary, IAI BPA Certification Board
7308 Mariners Landing Drive
Fayetteville, NC 28306
228-918-0400

The next area of CSI training we wish to touch on deals with weapons of mass destruction (WMD) which consist of: chemical, biological, radiological, nuclear, and explosive (CBRNE) agents and hazmat. For the purpose of this chapter we will separate explosives from the CBRNE and discuss them first. Given that terrorist use explosives more than any other weapon, all CSIs should be trained in "post blast" investigations (PBI). There are numerous basic, advanced, large vehicle, and suicide bomber, PBI courses, ranging from twenty 24 hours to 80 hours. Many are free and others are fee based. CSIs can obtain PBI training from the following entities: FBI, ATF, US DHS, WVU FSI, the NFSTC, RTI International, NFA at UT's LEIC, various colleges or universities with forensic science programs, law enforcement agencies and numerous private vendors who list their courses with the various forensic/crime scene associations. Here is a short list of just some of the post blast training courses available to CSIs:

FBI:
1. Basic Post Blast School, 40 hours
2. Large Vehicle Post Blast School, 40 hours

The Bureau of Alcohol, Tobacco, Firearms and Explosives (ATF):
1. Post Blast Investigative Techniques I, 40 hours
2. Advanced Explosives Investigative Techniques Course, 80 Hours

US DHS/New Mexico Tech (NMT) Energetic Materials Research and Testing Center (EMRTC):
1. Incident Response to Terrorist Bombings (IRTB), 32 hours
2. Prevention of and Response to Suicide Bombing Incident (PRSBI) 40 hours

US DHS/National Fire Academy

Once the CSI completes a forty 40 hour post blast school, they should join, at their employer's' expense, the International Association of Bomb Technicians and Investigators (IABTI). Passing these training courses should be made a condition of our employment or assignment and our certification as a post blast investigator (PBI), can be obtained from the IABTI. The CSI/Post Blast Investigator's (PBI) training must be followed up with continuing education in post blast investigations. This training will take the form of annual in-service training and outsourced training, and followed up by proficiency and competency testing, announced and blind (where required), in order to maintain their skills and certifications. Again, as stated previously, all of the CSI's training, testing, and certifications, must be documented and maintained in their personnel folders. Once we meet the requirements, as outlined below, we should seek certification in PBI from the IABTI. Again, our employer would then be responsible for our membership in the IABTI, all associated fees for the certification exams and certification renewal exams, examination preparation courses and required reading materials. Once we finish a post blast investigation course, by no means are we now experts in this discipline. We must continue our training by going through a very similar field training process, as outlined previously for the basic CSI field training, but now the CSI FTT members' must be certified by IABTI as Certified International Post Blast Investigator (CIPBI). Once the newly trained PBI/CSI completes this field training and evaluation the appropriate supervisor will make a determination on how to proceed with the newly trained PBI/CSI. This supervisor can find: the new PBI/CSI ready to conduct Post Blast Investigations and assign them to a field partner and a supervisor; the new PBI/CSI requires additional field training and assigns them to a new CSI FTT for specified period of time, or the new PBI/CSI is not fit to conduct Post Blast Investigations and recommends the CSIs exclusion from this assignment. All of the Post Blast Investigation training and evaluations will be placed in the CSI's personnel folder. If this CSI is allowed to conduct Post Blast Investigations for their units', then as a condition of this assignment, they must obtain the CIPBI certification from the IABTI.

The following are the requirements for Certified International Post Blast Investigator as published by the IABTI

Applicants must:

1. Have a minimum of 3 years' experience in a position with responsibility to investigate, analyze, and/or reconstruct post blast explosive crime scenes, events or devices.
   a. An IABTI Regular member who has retired from active service and is currently working as an instructor for a government, state, local, or scholastic entity may apply. For those who have retired and are no longer working the application must be received prior to five years after their retirement date.
2. Have completed a minimum of 200 hours of post blast investigator certification committee approved training in post blast related courses.
   a. Have completed a minimum of one (1) 40 hour post blast investigations training course which includes at least one practical hands-on exorcise involving the documentation, collection and preservation of a post blast crime scene, reconstruction of a post blast device, and presentation of the event.
   b. Have completed a minimum of one (1) 40 hour course of training in criminal investigations.
   c. Additional elective courses must total a minimum of 120 hours. The topics that qualify in the area of post blast investigation approved training include but not limited to are:

Advanced Improvised Explosive Device and Terrorist Activities Conferences
Hazardous Devices Render Safe or Explosives Ordnance Disposal
Explosive Handling, Disposal and Effects
Arson or Fire and Explosion Investigations
Criminal Investigations
Advanced Post Blast Investigations
Interview and Interrogations
Collection & Preservation of Evidence
Expert Witness Courtroom Testimony
Device Electronics
Crime Scene Investigations
Crime Scene Documentation
Underwater Post Blast Investigations
Crime Scene Photography
Crime Scene Reconstruction
Death Investigations
Wound Dynamics
Evidence Analysis or Laboratory Analysis

The Post Blast Certification Committee, on request, will consider other topics.

3. Applicant will fill out the CIPBI application and sign ALL required signature lines. By submitting your payment, you acknowledge all requirements of the application to include the Code of Conduct and truthfulness of you application. Scan copies of all certificates, transcripts or letters and send to the International Business Office (IBO).
4. An application fee of $150.00 must be paid at the time of application.
5. Once your application has been reviewed and accepted, you will be given information on how and where to take the exam.
6. Comprehensive, Proctored Examination: A "closed book" examination that is based on the requisite skills and knowledge sets within the CIPBI guidelines. A passing score of 80% or above must be achieved to successfully pass the exam. The applicant will be allowed 3 hours to complete a 200 hour exam. The test will be created from the following publication.
   a. Practical Bomb Scene Investigations, 2nd edition by James T. Thurman, CRC Press 2011.
   b. Practical Crime Scene Processing and Investigation, 2nd edition by Ross M. Gardner, CRC Press 2012.
7. If the applicant fails the examination, the applicant will be allowed to retest after six (6) months and within twelve (12) months. If the twelve (12) months pass without retaking the exam then the applicant must start the process over to include the application fee.
8. When the applicant completes the process and passes the written examination, the certification will be good for five (5) years.
9. In order to recertify:
   a. The applicant must continue to be a member of IABTI in good standing.
   b. During the five (5) years the applicant must attend two hundred (200) hours (total) of post blast investigations related training.

c. Have authored or coauthored an article on some aspect of post blast investigations and submit it to the CIPBI committee for review. The committee will publish in the Detonator or request a presentation at an RTC or ITC.

Now we will move on to CBRN training for CSIs. As we discussed in Chapter 3, we feel that all CSIs must be trained and certified as hazardous material technicians, able work in confined spaces, able to work at excavations and as collapses technicians, and to ship hazardous materials, so we can conform to the US Department of Labor's (US DOL), Occupational Safety and Health Administration's (OSHA) regulations (law) as well as, US Department of Transportation (US DOT) and International Air Transportation Association regulations, and US Environmental Protection Agency (US EPA) regulations, to protect ourselves from the various forensic chemicals, reagents, and powders that we use at conventional crime scene investigations and so that we can process CBRNE (unconventional) crime scenes safely and to deal with shipping hazardous materials we may collect as evidence and finally, disposing/cleaning up hazardous waste we created at our crime scenes. Thus we need training and certifications on all the following:

1. OSHA Law, Blood Borne Pathogens 29 CFR 1910.1030
2. OSHA Law, Hazardous Waste Operations and Emergency Response (Hazwoper) 29 CFR 1910.120 for states who have OSHA approved occupational safety and health plans or US EPA law, 40 CFR Part 311, for states who do not. OSHA Law
3. Respiratory Protection 29 CFR 1910.134
4. OSHA Law, Confined Space 29 CFR 1910.146
5. OSHA Law, Lock Out/Tag Out 29 CFR 1910.147
6. OSHA Law, Trenches and Excavations 29 CFR 1926.650, 1926.651, 1926.652
7. Federal Emergency Management Agency's (FEMA) Structural Collapse Technician Course
8. US Department of Transportation (US DOT) Law, Hazardous Material Transportation Regulations, 49 CFR Subchapter C
9. International Air Transport Association (IATA) regulations
10. US EPA Law, Resource Conservation and Recovery Act (RCRA)
11. US DHS CBRNE/Collapse/Trench & Excavation/Confined Space, Training
12. US Drug Enforcement Administration (DEA), Clan Lab School

There are numerous schools, for hazardous material technician, confined space technician/operator, trenches/excavations, collapse, shipping/transporting hazardous materials, and hazardous materials waste cleanup and disposal. These courses range from two hours to 160 hours. Many are free and others are fee based. CSIs can undergo these trainings at the following entities: US EPA, US DHS, US DOT, the NFSTC, RTI International, NFA at UT's LEIC, various colleges or universities with forensic science programs, law enforcement agencies and numerous private vendors who list their courses with the various forensic/crime scene/hazardous materials/shipping/waste disposal associations. Here is a shortlist of just some of these courses available to CSIs:

1. US DHS Training Providers:
   a. Center for Domestic Preparedness (CDP), https://cdp.dhs.gov/
      i. WMD/Emergency Responder Hazardous Material Technician

    ii. WMD/Crime Scene Management for Emergency Responders
    iii. WMD/Hazmat Evidence Collection

b. Center for Radiological/Nuclear Training, Nevada National Security Site, www.ctosnnsa.org/
    i. AWR-140 WMD Rad/Nuc Awareness
    ii. AWR-140-1 WMD Rad/Nuc Awareness Train-the-Trainer
    iii. PER-240 WMD Rad/Nuc Responder Operations
    iv. PER-241 WMD Rad/Nuc Course for Hazardous Materials Technicians
    v. PER-243-1 Personal Radiation Detector Train-the-Trainer
    vi. Preventative Rad/Nuc Detection On-Site (PRNDOS) Program
    vii. PER-245 Secondary Screener Radiation Isotope Identifier Device (SS-RIID)
    viii. PER-246 Primary Screener Backpack Basic Course (PS/BB)
    ix. PER-247 Secondary Screener Radiation Detection Kit (SS-RDK)

c. Dougway Proving Grounds, Special Programs Division, www.acbirc.net/
    i. Advanced Chemical and Biological Integrated Response Course

d. FEMA Radiation Training, www.fema.gov/training-2
    i. PER-904 Radiological Emergency Response Operations (RERO) Course
    ii. PER-905 Advanced Radiological Incident Operations (ARIO) Course

e. National Center for Biomedical Research and Training (NCBRT) at Louisiana State University (LSU), www.ncbrt.lsu.edu
    i. PER-220 Emergency Response to Domestic Biological Incidents
    ii. PER-222 Public Safety WMD Response- Sampling Techniques and Guidelines
    iii. PER- 228 Advanced Forensics for Hazardous Environments

f. National Emergency Response and Training Center at Texas A&M Engineering Extension Service, www.teex.org/nerrtc/
    i. PER-212 Operational Level Response to HazMat/WMD Incidents
    ii. URO23A Structural Collapse Awareness
    iii. TNG23R Collapse Rescue Operations
    iv. TNG23T Structural Collapse Technician 2
    v. TNG25S Advanced Structural Collapse 3
    vi. TNG26S Advanced Structural Collapse 4
    vii. TNG27S Advanced Structural Collapse 5
    viii. RES500 Trench Rescue Awareness and Operations Training
    ix. SAF217 Excavation Safety
    x. OSH301 Excavation, Trenching and Soil Mechanics (OSHA 3015)
    xi. ASP122Rescue II Trench Rescue
    xii. WWW352 Confined Space Awareness
    xiii. URO22A Confined Space Rescue Awareness
    xiv. RES001 Confined Space Rescue Training
    xv. RES002 NFPA 1006 2008 Edition Confined Space Rescue Levels I & II Training
    xvi. ASP124 Rescue V Confined Space Rescue NFPA 1006
    xvii. WWW202 Confined Space Entry
    xviii. OSH226 Permit-Required Confined Space Entry (OSHA 2264)
    xix. WWW212 Applied Confined Space Safety

g. National Fire Academy, www.usfa.fema.gov/downloads/pdf/nfa/1314_nfa_catalog.pdf

2. US EPA Training, http://trainex.org/
   a. 165.5 Hazardous Materials Incident Response Operations
   b. 165.15 Emergency Response to Hazardous Material Incidents
   c. 165.9 Sampling for Hazardous Materials
   d. 165.4 Air Monitoring for Hazardous Materials
   e. 165.11 Radiation Safety at Superfund Sites
   f. 165.12 Radiation Overview, Practical and Advanced Course
   g. 165.21. Chemistry for Environmental Professionals – Fundamentals
   h. 165.21 Chemistry for Environmental Professionals – Applied
   i. Advanced Environmental Crimes Training Program

Once the CSI successfully completes these training courses our employers' will certify us as hazmat technicians, structural collapse technicians, excavation/trenching technicians, confined space technicians, shipping hazardous materials, and RCRA hazardous materials waste cleanup and disposal complainant. Passing these training courses and medical requirements should be made a condition of our employment or assignment. The CSI training listed above must be followed up with continuing education. This training will take the form of annual in-service training and outsourced training, and followed up by proficiency and competency testing, announced and blind (where required), in order to maintain their skills and certifications. Also the CSI's will be required to have annual base line medicals and fit testing of their respirators, as outlined in OSHA 1910.134. Again, as stated previously, all of the CSIs' training, testing, and certifications, must be documented and maintained in their personnel folders.

If our crime scene units require us to conduct fire investigations, then we should attend, at a minimum, a 40-hour basic cause and origin fire investigator course, followed by a 40-hour advanced cause and origin fire investigator course. Upon completion of the basic 40-hour course we should join the International Association of Arson Investigators (IAAI). The training and the association memberships cost should be incurred by our employer. ranging from 40-hours to 80-hours. Many are free and others are fee based. CSIs can obtain cause and origin fire investigator training from the following entities: FBI, ATF, US DHS (National Fire Academy), FLETC, WVU FSI, the NFSTC, RTI International, NFA at UT's LEIC, International Association of Arson Investigation's (IAAI) CFI Trainer.net, various colleges and universities with forensic science programs, law enforcement agencies, fire agencies, and numerous private vendors who list their courses with the various forensic/crime scene associations. Once we finish a cause and origin fire investigations course, by no means are we now experts in this discipline. We must continue our training by going through a very similar field training process, as outlined previously for the shooting reconstruction analysis field training, but now the CSI FTT members' must be certified by IAAI or the state as a certified fire investigator (CFI). Once the newly trained CSI/CFI completes this field training and evaluation the appropriate supervisor will make a determination on how to proceed with the newly trained CFI/CSI. This supervisor can find the new CSI/CFI ready to conduct independent cause and origin fire investigations and assign them to a field partner and a supervisor. The new CSI/CFI may require additional field training and the supervisor assigns them to a new CSI FTT for specified period of time, or decides that the new CSI is not fit to conduct cause and origin fire investigations and recommends the CSIs exclusion from this assignment. All of the fire investigation training and evaluations will be placed in the CSI's personnel folder. Once we have successfully made it through the cause and origin fire investigations training including the field training, and as soon as we meet the IAAI or state, criteria for the CFI certifications, then the crime scene unit should require us to obtain these certifications for crime scene investigations, and make them a condition of our employment or assignment. If this CSI is allowed to conduct fire investigations for their units, then as a condition of this assignment, they must obtain either the IAAI or state CFI certifications. All fire investigation analysis performed by this CSI will be reviewed by supervisor and a three-person panel consisting entirely of CSIs who are CFIs, and authorized by the unit to conduct cause and origin fire investigations. This panel shall review the CSIs' analysis and findings for correctness and accuracy and report their findings to the CSI and the CSI's supervisor. The new CSI/CFI's training must be followed up with continuing education in cause and origin fire investigations. This training will take the form of annual in-service training and outsourced training, and followed up by proficiency and competency testing, announced and blind (where required), in order to maintain their skills and certifications. Again, as stated previously, all of the CSI's training, testing, and certifications, must be documented and maintained in their personnel folders.

The following are the requirements for the CFI as published by the IAAI:

> Certification is based on attainment of at least 150 points through education, training and experience, as well as a passing grade on a comprehensive examination. Before you are permitted to sit for the examination, your application must be approved by a review committee. You must be able to document every point claimed on your application. Certificates, diplomas, testament letters and transcripts are examples of acceptable documentation. Once your application is approved, you will be sent the name of a proctor in your area.
>
> COMPREHENSIVE PROCTORED EXAMINATION: A "closed book" examination that is based upon every duty area within NFPA 1033. A score of 70% or above must be achieved to successfully pass the exam.
>
> IAAI-CFI APPLICATION FEES:
>
> IAAI MEMBERS: $ 150.00 USD (Effective 1/1/2014 – $195)
> Note: This rate applies to International members only. IAAI chapter members must belong to the International Association of Arson Investigators to be able to receive the member rate.
> NON-MEMBERS: $ 525.00 USD (Effective 1/1/2014 – $570)
>
> IAAI-CFI RECERTIFICATION FEES:
>
> All certified fire investigators must re-certify every five (5) years.
> IAAI MEMBERS: $ 95.00 USD (Effective 1/1/2014 – $140)
> NON-MEMBERS: $ 475.00 USD (Effective 1/1/2014 – $520)

EDUCATION

Highest Level of Education Achieved:

Check only one (1) of the following eleven (11) fields related to fire investigation including Fire Sciences, Engineering, Physical Sciences and Law Enforcement. The fields of Education, Mathematics and liberal Arts do not qualify as fire investigation related.

Courses taken in pursuit of a degree, when the degree has not been conferred, should be claimed in the training section of this application. However, if you claim points for a degree, do not claim points in the training section for those courses completed to attain the degree.

EDUCATION OR RECOGNIZED EQUIVALENT:

1.	High School Graduate, G.E.D. Certificate or Equivalent (Cegep-Quebec)	10 pts
2.	One Year Certificate in Fire Investigation	12 pts
3.	Associate Degree in field unrelated to Fire Investigation	12 pts
4.	Associate Degree in field related to Fire Investigation	20 pts
5.	Bachelors Degree in field unrelated to Fire Investigation	20 pts
6.	Bachelors Degree in field related to Fire Investigation	30 pts
7.	Masters Degree in field unrelated to Fire Investigation	25 pts
8.	Masters Degree in field related to Fire Investigation	40 pts
9.	Doctoral Degree in field unrelated to Fire Investigation	30 pts
10.	L.L.B. or J.D.	45 pts
11.	Doctoral Degree in field related Fire Investigation	50 pts

Attach diploma only for unrelated degrees.
Attach diploma and transcript for related degrees.

Total Education Points Claimed: _____
(Minimum of 10 pts. Required – Max. of 50 pts.)

EXPERIENCE – FULL/PART-TIME
Full and Part-time Investigator

12. Full-Time Fire Investigator — 10 pts per year
    Investigators working 52 weeks per year or a minimum of 1,500 hours per year including vacation, sick leave, etc.
13. Part-Time Fire Investigator — 8 pts per year
    Investigators working less than 1,500 hours per year in fire investigation and able to document (with letters from supervisors or employers) an average of twelve (12) fires worked or 250 hours (31 days) of active fire investigation duties per year.

Total Full/Part –Time Experience Points Claimed _____
(Minimum of 40 points required)

Other Experience

14. Direct active supervision of two (2) or more full-time fire investigators 8 pts per year
    (Do not claim credit here unless you were actively involved in fire investigation during that time period)
15. Direct active supervision of two (2) or more part-time fire investigators 4 pts per year
    (Do not claim credit here unless you were actively involved in fire investigation during that time period)
16. Non-fire, full-time Criminal Investigator 1 pt per year
17. Firefighter or Law Enforcement Officer (Patrolman/Constable) 1 pt per year
18. Fire Department Lieutenant, Police Department Sergeant or above 1 pt per year
19. Evidence Technician (Full-Time Only) ½ pt per year
20. Private Investigator (Non-Fire) ½ pt per year
21. Fire Insurance Adjuster ½ pt per year

List the employers' names, dates of employment, location and job description for all related employment. You must include letters attesting to your employment experience for the points you claim. Please list these items in reverse chronological order. Write the line number from above in the space on the left.

22. Book published on subject directly related to the investigation of fire or explosions. 25 pts per book

    List the title and publisher's name for all books authored and attach copy of copyright page, with Library of Congress Catalog Number.
23. Paper/Article published on a subject directly related to the investigation of fires or explosions. 1½ pts per each (Maximum of 10 pts)
    List the title and publisher's name for all authored materials and attach a copy of the article page which shows the journal name, date, article title and your name.
24. Lecture taught on fire investigation ½ pt per contact hour (Maximum of 20 pts)
    List the locations, dates and topic of each lecture taught. Attach attestment letters from program manager.
25. Membership in professional organizations directly related to fire investigations. ½ pt per year (Maximum of 10 pts)

List the organization, total years as a member and current status in the Description field.

26A. Per occasion testified as an expert witness regarding the point of origin or cause of fire or explosion. 5 pts per occasion

or

26B. If you have completed the IAAI, ATF, NFA or Canadian Testimony course, attach your diploma to this sheet and check the box. For points claimed, put 10 points in the space at the bottom for "Page 3 Experience Points Claimed."

Diploma attached

Please list the location, date and case identification number for each trial/deposition/hearing.

Attach a letter of attestment. (Usually, letters from prosecutors or attorneys are submitted on their letterhead.)

Training

27. Certified Firefighter I or substantially similar program (may be claimed only once) 10 Points
28. Certified Firefighter II or substantially similar program(may be claimed only once) 15 Points
29. IAAI-FIT Designation 15 Points

Courses claimed below CANNOT have been included in any of the above. This also includes courses taken towards a degree not yet received.

30. Certified Police Academy (240Hours) or substantially similar program 15 Points (may be claimed only once)

31. Tested Courses★ Fire Investigation Training programs, seminars or college level Courses conducted by a recognized agency or group. (IAAI, ATF, Police and Fire service, Dept. of Scientific & Industrial Research, etc.)
    ★A passing grade is required to claim credit here. ¼ point per hour

32. Untested Courses: fire Investigation training conducted by a recognized agency or group. 1/8 point per hour (1 point per 8 hours)

NOTE: for both tested and untested training, a maximum of ten percent (10%) of the total training points claimed are allowed for training courses which are not specifically described or titled as being fire investigation related (e.g. hazardous materials, police procedures, claims adjustment).

Please list the course sponsor, topic, total training contact hours and date. This is in addition to the requirement of attaching (in the order listed) copies of certificates/diplomas received for training. If the course was tested, the certificate should indicate such.

Total Training Points Claimed ______
(Minimum of 20 pts. Required – Maximum of 90 pts.)
Total Education Points Claimed (10 points Minimum/50 points Maximum) ______
Total Full/Part – Time Experience Claimed (40 points Minimum) ______
Total Other Experience Points Claimed (10 points must be from testimony) ______
If you requested the IAAI Testimony course, write "TCR" next to the space.
Total Training Points Claimed (20 points Minimum/90 points Maximum) ______
Total Points Claimed For This Application ______
(150 Points is the minimum to be eligible to challenge the examination)

References

List three (3) references who can attest to your background and experience as an investigator:

Required reading for the written examination:

Publication/Author

1. NFPA 921, *Guide for Fire and Explosion Investigation,* 2011 Edition, entire booklet.
2. NFPA 1033, *Professional Qualifications for Fire Investigator,* 2014 Edition, entire booklet.
3. Brady, *Kirk's Fire Investigation*, 7th Edition, (Chapters 4, 7, 8, 10, 15, 16, and 17)
4. IFSTA, *Essentials of Firefighting*, 5th Edition, (Chapters 1, 2, 8, 14, 15, 16 and 20)

5. NFPA, *Fire Protection Handbook,* 20th Edition (2008) (Sections 3, Chapter 8)
6. IFSTA, *Hazardous Materials for First Responders*, 4th Edition, (Chapters 1 and 2)
7. IFSTA, *Fire Inspection and Code Enforcement,* 7th Edition, (Chapters 8, 9 and 10)
8. Cole, Lee S., *Investigation of Motor Vehicle Fires,* 4th Edition, (Chapter 2)
9. Delmar, *Principles of Fire Behavior,* James G. Quintiere

For more information on the IAAI CFI, visit http://firearson.com/professional-credentialing-programs/certified-fire-investigator-(cfi).

For individual State CFI requirements, check with your state.

Throughout this chapter we have stated numerous times that if your employer requires these certifications issued by forensic associations, then they should pay the fees associated with membership in these organizations and their certifications. Many times our employers will only pay the fees associated with the certifications and not pay for our membership. If this is the case, it is in our best professional interest to join these organizations' and pay the fees ourselves, in order to network, stay current on these forensic disciplines and to obtain continuing education in these forensic areas. The fees associated with joining these associations and organizations are typically tax deductable. As true dedicated forensic professionals, we should seek these memberships and certification regardless if our employers' require them or not.

As you can see from the content of this chapter, to conduct professional crime scene investigations requires a considerable commitment, in time and money to properly train and certify our CSIs. This training must be ongoing and have a very strong QA/QC program. Unfortunately when our agency's finances get tight, the first thing to get reduced in the budget is training. However in order to maintain the professional standards for our crime scene units as required by ASCLAD and ISO accreditations, the best forensic scientific practices, and the trust of our communities, we must fight for the necessary monies to obtain training and certifications. Remember we are professionals, practicing forensics, just as doctors practice medicine. We are far more than "glorified garbage men," mindlessly picking up evidence at crime scenes. Unfortunately there are no licensing requirements for CSIs as there are for doctors. Without a license to practice crime scene investigations, the best we can currently do is to obtain good forensic training and certifications in the various forensic disciplines. And, just like doctors, obtain continuing education, to maintain our certifications, but unlike doctors, we must pass numerous proficiency tests, post certification, to demonstrate our competencies, to do anything less, is to do a disservice to our profession.

References

The International Association for Identification (http://theiai.org/certifications/)
The Association For Crime Scene Reconstruction (www.acsr.org/)
The International Association of Bloodstain Pattern Analyst (www.iabpa.org/)
The International Association of Bomb Technicians and Investigators (www.iabti.org/)
The International Association of Arson Investigators (http://firearson.com/home)
The United States Department of Labor, Occupational Safety and Health Administration (www.osha.gov/)
The United States Department of Justice, Federal Bureau of Investigation (www.fbi.gov/about-us/lab/handbook-of-forensic-services-pdf)

The United States Department of Justice,Federal Bureau of Investigation (www.fbi.gov/about-us/cjis/fingerprints_biometrics/fingerprint-criminal-history-record-training/catalog-of-courses)

Marshall University/The Federal Bureau of Investigation (http://forensics.marshall.edu/Training/Training-FBI.html)

The National Domestic Preparedness Consortium (www.ndpc.us/)

The United States Fire Academy/United States Department of Homeland Security, Federal Emergency Management Agency (www.usfa.fema.gov/nfa/)

The United States Department of Homeland Security, Federal Law Enforcement Training Center (www.fletc.gov/)

The United States Department of Justice, National Institute of Justice (www.nij.gov/training/forensic.htm)

The United Stated Department of Justice, Alcohol, Tobacco, Firearms, and Explosives (www.atf.gov/training/explosives-arson/index.html)

The University of Tennessee's (UT) Law Enforcement Innovation Center (LEIC) (www.leic.tennessee.edu/training/nfa/national-forensic-academy)

The WVU; West Virginia University, FSI; Forensic Science Initiative The National Forensic Science Technology Center (http://fsi.research.wvu.edu/)

The National Forensic Science Technology Center (www.nfstc.org/)

The RTI International, The New York City Office of Chief Medical Examiner, Forensic Science Training Program (www.rti.org/page.cfm/Forensic_Science_Education)

The United States Department of Justice, Drug Enforcement Administration (https://a913-mli.nyc.gov/fstp/) (www.justice.gov/dea/ops/Training/Clandestine.shtml)

6

DEVELOPING PROCEDURES

Introduction

The path forward for forensic science in the current climate will be one that mandates the adherence to a procedural guide or manual. This guide will proscribe how an organization conducts business and will touch on all aspects of the operation. Some parts of the procedural guide will be required if the unit seeks accreditation; however, it may be worthwhile to outline all the practices of the crime scene unit. Very often, crime scene units operate with what one might call business rules or traditions. These are often characterized by the fact that it has always been done this way and these rules are disseminated by oral tradition from one generation to the next. This can be problematic, especially when deviations are made for one reason or another. This can happen during a change of supervision when new supervisors come in to a unit and feel the need to "reinvent the wheel". This is not to say that people cannot contribute to the operations of the unit, but, when business rules change, or change for some and not others, confusion and inconsistency in work product are often created.

The development of procedures can seem like a daunting task. Just considering the undertaking will create confusion and apprehension. This is unnecessary. There are many crime scene units, both accredited and unaccredited, who have created protocols or SOPs. Obviously there have been different levels of success. Take heart in knowing that many have succeeded and as a result, there are many successful examples out in the world for one to look at for ideas on how to proceed and succeed. Rest assured that somebody was the first to succeed. Also take note that is not improper to look at other successful examples of protocols, procedures, and SOPs, for ideas on how to create protocols. Further, one should not be ashamed to seek help. Reaching out for help is a good way to learn and understand the concepts and to ensure getting the concept correct in as few attempts as possible.

Another resource that can be used are professional organizations and committees (e.g. OSACS). They are often a useful resource for content required to satisfy requirements.

There are some good reasons for creating a guide on one's own. Primarily, it affords the opportunity to learn and gain a deeper understanding of forensic science in general. It will be very difficult to sit and create a guide from memory. There will be research and consultation. The exercise will be a good instruction opportunity for the unit.

In the future, crime scene units will be judged on how they do things. The procedural guide will define how things are done. Anyone reading the guide will judge the way things are done vs. some other standard. The reader will look to see if the methods used by the unit equate to some "gold standard" or best practice. If the guide is followed, it will be very hard to attack the investigator in court with regard to how things were done. In this way, the community will be able to quickly assess the quality of the unit. If the guide shows that the unit is following best practices with regard to their tasks, and the guide really is followed, that will be an indication of the quality.

Overview

There are several ways to get started with the task of creating a guide. If the unit's ultimate goal is to seek accreditation, the first two steps should be to read the requirements of the accreditation body that the unit will seek accreditation from. The second will be to seek out examples of documents from other units that have received accreditation from the same body. There will be no reason to write a guide or manual if it will not aid the unit in achieving a goal that it is seeking.

If the unit has no desire or need to seek accreditation, then it should feel free to produce a document that suits its own needs. This chapter will explore the creation of a guide from this perspective. If the unit will not seek accreditation and proceed to create their own guide, it is possible to later modify the document to suit the requirements of an accrediting body.

Putting that aside for the time being, this chapter will seek to assist a crime scene unit in creating a manual that outlines how it will perform its tasks. Readers should pick and choose what to use, based upon what they do and do not do.

Another idea to keep in mind is to get people involved as much as practical. Obviously, this may not be easy. Investigators have investigative duties to handle and may not have the time to dedicate to writing any or all of a procedural manual. In fact, it may be advantageous that a small number of people actually pen the manual. This will help keep consistency of style. However, polling investigators for input on how to do things before they are codified in a guide is a useful exercise.

The actual steps and mechanics of creating a manual can be done many ways. Also, the manual can be one big document or several documents. There is no good or bad way to organize it but, however you do it, start from the beginning. Try to be systematic and methodical. In this way, nothing is missed along the way.

In order for a procedural guide to work (especially if it is being done to meet accreditation requirements) it must be a document of the organization or agency, not just the crime scene unit of that agency. This is especially true if the crime scene unit is part of a paramilitary organization. When the crime scene unit is part of a police department, there are many opportunities for the rank structure of that department to "interfere" with the work of the crime scene unit. Without regard to the intentions, this interference gives the image of partiality. One purpose of the procedural guide will be to protect the impartiality of the crime scene unit. Even if the crime scene unit works as part of the police department or other law enforcement agency, it ultimately works for the criminal justice system, the same organization that all of those involved in a criminal investigation work for. The agency will have to adopt the document as its own and follow the "rules" set forth in it when required as a means of maintaining this impartiality. If the agency that the crime scene unit is attached to does not accept the document as its own, this process will be very hard to accomplish. When the crime scene unit does not work for the same organization that employs it, this is much easier to accomplish.

The procedural guide should not be a training manual. It should be more about why we do things and less about how we do things. Keeping this in mind, tasks that have very specific steps that do not invite deviations will certainly be more about how to do certain things.

The Guide

Overview

One of the first things that many people think about when it comes to a procedural guide is:

- What should it look like?
- What should be in it?

What it should look like is the easier question to answer. If the unit is attempting to seek accreditation with a particular accrediting body, use the style they require if they have one. If not, choose what you feel makes the most sense to you. Here are three styles:

- Outline style
- Book style
- Hybrid style
- Combination style

If the visual style is not a mandated item, go with what feels best.

The guide can be organized in any number of ways. The two simplest ways to consider organizing it would start with the idea of having one document that covers everything in different sections or separate documents for different topics. One is neither better or worse than the other, and, in reality, when you punch holes in them and stick them into a binder, they become "one" document. For simplicity in getting the project off the ground and to keep it moving along, it may be easier to tackle different topics separately, one at a time. Main sections or topics could include:

- Administration
- Crime scene operation
- Quality assurance

Style

It may be useful to get some idea of the style options available and decide how to begin so that, when the unit does proceed to put pen to paper, it can get down to the brass tacks. Keep in mind that there are several styles that can be used and, frankly, the unit can use any number of combinations of styles. Not every style type will be amenable to each topic and some topics may be easier to write about with a certain style type.

For example, tasks that have a definite and unbending order to them may be easier to write about using an outline style that enumerates steps in order. For example, when guiding investigators in issues pertaining to crime scene management, several actions might be going on at the same time, or several conditions may need to be assessed constantly. It may be easier to discuss these topics in book style text so the issues can be explained and described. Finally, some topics may have a combination of the two so a hybrid approach may be indicated. This could also include bulleted lists instead of numbering.

Very often, a hybrid approach is used for most things so that some explanation about the reasons why something is done can be discussed. Asking investigators to do things without explanation is dangerous. Dealing in absolutes is also very often dangerous. Eliminating problem solving and thinking is dangerous. Try not to deal in absolutes but in information so that when a problem is encountered that is not enumerated in the guide, it can be solved in the field.

Outline Style

The outline style uses ordered lists to describe tasks that must be performed in a very detailed and ordered manner. This style is useful to describe a procedure where no deviation will be allowed. In reality, there are several times when this style lends itself very well. Chief among these is recipes. When the unit adopts a reagent recipe, its very easy to describe how to prepare it in a step-by-step manner. This style also lends itself well to some quality assurance methods. The outline style has the following physical characteristics:

1. Start
2. Perform Step 1
   A. If A occurs go to Step 2
   B. If B occurs go to Step 3
3. Step 2
4. Step 3
   C. If Step 3 yields the following then proceed
   D. If Step 3 does not yield the following then stop

As you might guess, this style and associated procedure would be fairly rigid and unyielding. Sometimes this is required, sometimes not. It can always be prefaced with an explanation of its purpose and the reasoning for the necessity of the rigidity.

Book Style

Book style is what it sounds like. It is a narrative of information. A narrative lends itself very well to information that does not need to be presented in a rigid format. Book style works well where the purpose of the procedure is to get one to think and be aware of something and to offer explanations. This allows the investigator to learn, so they they can think.

In some places, believe it or not, these are dirty words. Do not be afraid of learning and free thinking. Some may say that given the opportunity, people will do less work out of laziness and by giving people options in a document such as a procedural guide, this is what they will opt to do. Then, they will use the procedural guide to justify why they did not do some amount of work. If management has chosen a staff of good people for the crime scene unit, however, they will not need to worry about such things. If management is worried about these things, something is wrong, and no procedural manual, good or bad, will fix it.

Hybrid Style

Hybrid style is a very flexible way to create all kinds of individual procedures. This style combines the narrative style of a book with the outline style to create specific points of tasks. This style is an excellent way to give guidance. Text can be used to explain the reasons why something is done, then outline specific points of reinforcement. This can be done with the outline form shown previously or by using bulleted points.

- Point 1
- Point 2
- Point 3

Combination

The combination style takes advantage of all the styles and mixes and matches within the same guide as the authors see fit. It is probably best to consider adopting this free flowing style so as not to limit the ability to make the job of getting idea onto paper easier. The authors can produce some individual procedures or procedural guide areas in one style, some other areas in another style and combine styles when it is felt that information will be easier to convey and understand.

Topics

Administration

Administration will deal with all aspects of the day-to-day management and tasks of the unit (but not necessarily with the actual processing of crime scenes). The administration section should address some or all of the following topics:

- Chain of command and decision making
- Duties
- Security of the facility and documents
- Communications
- Administrative case review
- Publishing of reports

Chain of Command and Decision Making

Outlining the chain of command and decision-making responsibilities will allow for efficient operations of the unit both administratively and operationally when at scenes. Keep in mind, however, that in order to make certain decisions, for example decisions with regard to how a crime scene is processed or how specific tasks at a crime scene will be performed, the decision maker must have the requisite training. Without that training, they will be unable to contribute in this manner.

The chain of command really becomes important for "running interference" and maintaining the impartiality and independence of the crime scene unit. This will be especially true in organizations that adhere to a paramilitary structure. As previously mentioned, the agency for which the crime scene unit serves under will have to adopt the document agency wide and accept those parts of the document that limit the agencies involvement in actual crime scene investigations. In other words, the agency cannot dictate the crime scene investigation. Information, science and best practices will be the driving forces behind how and why things are done at a crime scene.

One way to begin to flesh this out is to create an organization chart (Figure 6.1). Within that chart, the positions will be enumerated. This should include the command positions, quality assurance positions and technical manager positions. At this point, the agency will have to give these positions the status necessary (position power) to perform their operations without interference from command structures outside of the unit.

Responsibilities for each job should be outlined in the guide. These descriptions do not have to be exact enumerations of their tasks, but a general description. For example, the general job description of the quality assurance manager would go here, however, the exact tasks that s/he is responsible for would be outlined in the quality assurance manual.

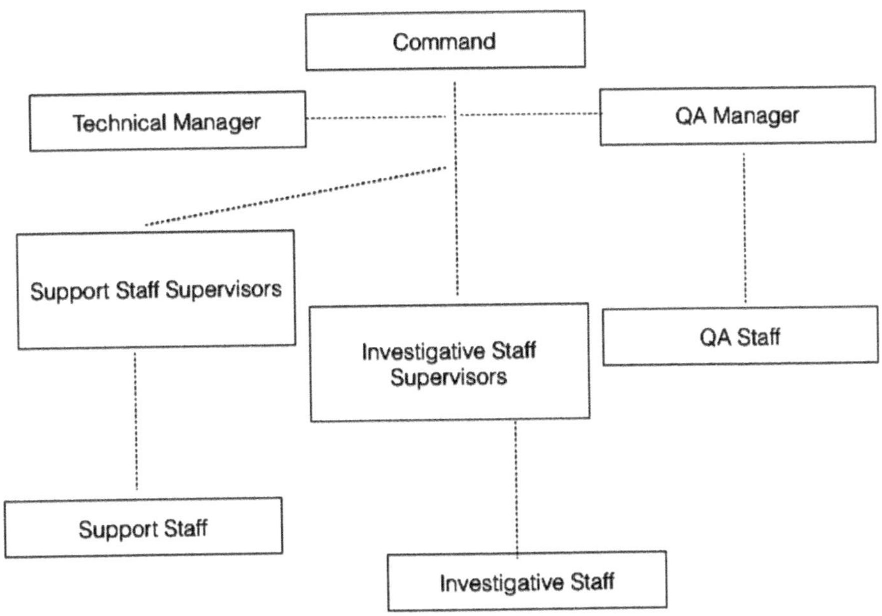

FIGURE 6.1 Basic crime scene organizational chart

Also in these descriptions, who has responsibility for general decisions or operations at particular times and/or for particular areas will be enumerated in these descriptions.

Duties

The duties of all positions should be outlined in the administrative section of the guide to a certain extent. Although no guide or manual can account for every scenario, the day-to-day responsibilities of each position can be. A good way to start is to codify the responsibilities of the current positions that the unit already has. Take the unwritten business rules or traditions and put them on paper. Using lists for this task is a natural way to proceed.

This is also a good time to make changes. If things have not been working or have not been working well, try something new. Do not be afraid of ideas. If what you have done traditionally works fine, then leave it alone.

Keep in mind that, if accreditation is on the horizon, the unit may need to create positions it does not currently have and this is a good opportunity to learn something. Many may not know what the job of a quality assurance manager will entail so an effort to learn will be required. Many crime labs will have a quality assurance manager and they would be a good place to start.

Aside from duties in that sense of the word, daily expectation of routine operations can be outlined in a section such as this. There may be aspects of the operation that should probably be done on a daily basis. Consider some of the following ideas:

- WHO
  - Vehicle inspection
  - Cleanliness
  - Equipment
- WHO
  - Sensitive materials (e.g. reagents)
  - Availability
  - Expiration
- WHO
  - Batteries
  - Charged
  - Availability

Any other ideas pertinent to current operations that might need to be implemented in a daily routine.

Security of the Facility

Security is an important aspect of any operation. Don't forget, photographs and documents are sensitive data that must be protected and how they will be protected should be outlined in the guide. Consider the following points when creating this section of the manual:

- Who will be allowed access to the facility?
- How will they access the facility?

- How will access to the facility be restricted?
- How will guests access the facility?
- How will access records be kept and who will keep them?
- Will areas within the facility be restricted?
- How will documents be protected?
- Who will have access to documents?
- Who will track access to documents?
- How will access to documents be tracked?

In the day and age of technology, this can be done easily, however technology costs money. Electronic access can restrict access on an individual basis as well as track persons. If money is no object, that is great. However, not every jurisdiction has a lot of money.

Be that as it may, rules outlining the above are needed and they can be devised without expensive electronics. Again, if you have business rules and traditions that work stick with them and memorialize them on paper in the guide. Bound, paper logs can also be used effectively as a tracking mechanism so long as everyone takes them seriously and completes them when they are supposed to.

Communications

The crime scene unit will need to decide how it will deal with the outside world and under what circumstances. Politics aside, the crime scene unit will need to decide on some or all of the following points:

- What services will the crime scene unit provide?
- Who will the crime scene unit provide the services to?
- Who can request the services?
- Who makes daily decisions on the provision of services?

Consider the first point in terms of what types of crimes the unit will respond to or what services the unit will provide. If the unit is full service, then it may be easier to outline the types of crimes it will respond to and enumerate the services later in the guide. If the unit performs only a few tasks, it may be easier to describe what it will respond for. In other words, if the crime scene unit only processes for latent prints and takes photographs, the guide might say that the unit will respond to any request where fingerprint processing and photographs are required.

The next issue to consider is who will the crime scene unit provide services too. This is probably something that is already decided for many jurisdictions. Since every eventuality cannot be considered in a guide, traditions, business rules or even local laws may already be in place that guide or mandate this.

Who can request services, and under what circumstances may follow along the same lines as who will the unit provide services to. A relatively simple issue that can be resolved as above.

The final area that should be considered is who has the authority to provision services. Someone has to have the authority (and knowledge) to be able to prioritize requests but to decide which requests will get services at all. Unfortunately, there is no endless supply of money, personnel and associated resources. It is easy to decide upon who can make decisions and what decisions they can make. Again, this is probably already going on in the unit so just codify it.

Administrative Case Review

Documents should not be published outside of the crime scene unit until they are complete. Documents cannot be complete until they are edited. Editing or, what we will call an administrative review, is simply having someone look over the report to ensure that commonplace types of errors are corrected. Some of the issues that might be reviewed are:

- All papers, reports, forms, etc., that are supposed to be there are there
- Completeness
- Spelling errors
- Correctness
- Omissions
- Grammar
- Consistency (for example, the photographs match the descriptions in the photo log)
- Readability

A form or checklist can be created for the guide that helps remind the reviewer of the basic items that should be reviewed and corrected. An example of an administrative review (as a form) can be found in Chapter 10, Figure 10.3. This won't be an all inclusive review of the paperwork because it is not meant as a technical review. Again, it's a guide to help catch administrative mistakes, not mistakes of conclusions that would be found during a technical review.

Aside from this, the procedure should also outline who will perform the administrative review, when, and/or under what circumstances. Generally, since people make typos and such all the time, reports should always be reviewed before they are published. Frankly, it can be embarrassing having to admit mistakes were made. This can often be cured with a fresh set of eyes reading a document critically.

Publishing of Reports

The crime scene unit will have clear guidelines covering the publishing of reports. This should include publishing reports to others within the agency and externally (for example to a prosecutor). It is suggested that a procedure be in place that specifies under what circumstances a report will be published and to whom. Please do not think this is a silly need. There have been times where well intentioned people have been taken advantage of. The press has even been known to try and pull a fast one, especially in high profile cases. It is unfortunate, but it happens. One would be amazed.

If the unit wants to keep out of trouble it will write clear guidelines covering the following:

- Who may request documents
- What method will be used to convey the request (e.g. subpoena, letter, etc.)?
- At what stage in its drafting will a report be sent?
- Who will track and fulfill the requests?
- How will they be transmitted?
- How will receipt be tracked?

It is very simple and very necessary. Reports really should be sent out to those who need to know, not those who want to know or need photographs for their lectures. Unfortunately, a written guide cannot plan for every eventuality. Someone will have to be empowered with the responsibility to review requests and decide if they will be fulfilled. Ninety nine percent of the time, there won't be an issue. Let one slip through the cracks and there will be trouble.

Crime Scene Operations

Introduction and Overview

By far, the largest section of a crime scene unit's procedural guide will be the sections that govern crime scene operations. This section will guide investigators in all aspects of crime scene management and processing. An easy way to get some ideas of the topics and their order is to perhaps take a look at a few of the more popular crime scene investigation textbooks. The topics in many of them, in a way, mimic the order of how one would approach planning and processing a crime scene. Another way to approach it is to just jot down simple keywords or phrases that outline how one's own crime scene unit operates. Here is one list of topics that one could consider using or expanding upon to fit their own needs:

- Crime scene management
- Documentation
- Collecting evidence
- Processing techniques
- Paperwork (very specific to the agency)

Once the unit decides on these main topics, they can begin to flesh out the subtopics that make these whole. They will be considered in these sections.

Crime Scene Management

Crime scene management would cover all the topics an investigator should be aware of that affect how the job will get done and what will affect their ability to perform the scene processing. It should also give guidance with regard to what to do when they are faced with a situation that will affect the ability to adequately process a scene efficiently in a way that the usefulness of the evidence is diminished as little as possible. Some topics worth considering are:

- Personnel safety
- Personal protective equipment
- Contamination prevention
- Establishing the scene
- Surveying the scene
- Special issues
- Conditions – environmental/ambient
- Planning

- Information gathering
- Search needs
- Crime scene release

Personal and Personnel Safety

The main consideration in this guide will be to outline situations in which the investigator should take extra care when approaching a scene. Aside from security concerns, these issues come from problems such as unstable structures due to fire or other structural issues, hazardous materials, and even operations on the side of a busy highway. In times like these, the crime scene investigator may need to turn to an expert who can advise them about the safety issues concerned. This might include a building inspector, firefighter, and the like. Crime scene investigators should know under what circumstances they should seek a professional opinion and who will provide that professional opinion.

Personal Protective Equipment

Some crime scene units may wish to establish minimum PPE requirements at a crime scene, not only to protect the evidence from contamination but more importantly to protect the investigator from blood borne pathogens that may harm them or others that they interact with. At scenes that are not typical (such as the hazmat or fire scene) the unit may wish to adopt the PPE requirements of the incident commander.

Contamination Prevention

Contamination, although sometimes unavoidable and even expected in certain cases, will always be portrayed as negligence. This will be the case even if the contamination occurs during life saving activities. That being the case, it can, at the least, be explained reasonably and to the satisfaction of many. Those who are not satisfied, risk looking callous and uncaring, even inhuman.

Contamination after that is hard to explain and will make the contaminator look irresponsible. So, this guide should outline the need for proper PPE as well as minimum requirements for general situation and/or types of evidence.

Another issue dealing with contamination prevention that is often forgotten is the reparation of responses to different parts of the same incident by either a physical barrier or time. It is a poor idea for an investigator to enter a victims apartment and then a suspect's apartment, even if PPE is worn. Even if we are very sure, and we are, that the probability of contaminating the apartment is akin to zero, there will always be a "possibility". These concepts should be explained in the guide with a few examples as illustrations.

Establishing the Scene

Writing a simple text guide on how to establish a crime scene, or how to assess and fix an already established scene is sufficient for this topic. There are a few concepts that might want to be covered in this guide. Include some or all of the following plus additional ones as is needed:

- Is the scene too big or to small?
- Are there layers of security?
- Are there established entry/exit routes (different from those used by suspects if possible)?
- Is there an entry/exit log

These are just some of the more basic topics that might be included in this guide. Fleshing them out to one's liking should be relatively easy. There may be directives already in place if a police department is involved. They can be adapted and improved upon if necessary this is not such a difficult task.

Surveying the Scene, Planning, Special Issues and Conditions (Environmental and Ambient)

Surveying the scene and planning is a simple discussion about taking a quick inventory of the scene and coming up with some basic idea of what is going to be involved in the processing of it from start to finish. The writers of the guide may want to talk about what to look for during a walk though that might make this crime scene particularly complicated or problematic to process. These things will vary from one crime scene unit to another. Only those involved in the operation can know what makes things difficult. There may be specific issues that make certain situations difficult for anyone such as evidence underwater, remote locations that need lighting or perhaps a hazardous location. Any out of the ordinary situation discovered during the survey must be factored into the overall plan. This means that whatever will be needed to mitigate the special issue will have to move through the crime scene processing chronology at the correct time. Guidance should be given about how to get assistance needed to complete this as well as examples of things that the unit may consider an out of the ordinary need.

Environmental and ambient conditions will generally require constant monitoring. Changes in weather may require a change in the processing plan in order to prevent damage to evidence.

Information Gathering

One of the keys to efficient crime scene processing is information. Knowledge about what happened will allow the investigators to focus their processing efforts in areas that would yield the best results. The guide should give instruction on information gathering activities. The guide should enumerate who the investigator should seek out and the information they should seek. Some information that will be useful to the investigators can be:

- Sights
- Smells
- Sounds
- Witness statements
- Changes to the scene by emergency services
- Points of entry and exit
- Video
- Audio
- Other

- Victim injuries
- Known or potential suspect injuries

These things should be documented in the notes and utilized to advantage.

Search Needs

Searching the crime scene may require processing techniques other than just systematic and methodical looking. This can include fingerprint processing, Luminol, alternate light source and other tools. The difference between these methods and just looking is that they can be destructive – destructive not only to the evidence that one is searching for with the particular method but to other evidence that may be latent. The best ways of ensuring that this task gets done properly is through good training and a firm understanding of what will be the best actions at any one particular crime scene.

With care, it is likely that more than one technique can be applied to the same area of a scene and, perhaps to the same item. Guidance should be included about the techniques available to the investigator as well as the order in which they are generally conducted.

Crime Scene Release

At the completion of crime scene activities, there must be some mechanism for the investigators to release the crime scene to another authority. This should only be done after the crime scene personnel have been able to confer with the other investigating authorities responsible. Guidance should be clear that this step is important for a few reasons. First, crime scene investigators must know if any further information has been obtained. Second, the investigative authorities should know what was accomplished. This will create a system of checks and balances so to speak so that all possible services have been rendered. Lastly, if further processing activities will be required at a later time, arraignments must be made for a responsible authority to safeguard that scene until processing activities reconvene. This exchange of information should be documented in case notes so that everyone is on the same page.

The guide should express who should be conferred with and the general topics that should be covered during the conferral. Again, no procedural guide can account for every eventuality but giving investigators a place to start will lead to further ideas when different situations are encountered.

Documentation

Documentation is one of the critical tasks performed at a crime scene. Memorializing the condition of the scene, the items recovered from the scene and the changes made to the scene by processing activities are expected by the criminal justice system. In addition, this recording will allow the scene to be revisited at later times. In some cases even more information can be gained by this virtual visitation when more questions need to be answered.

As a result, investigators must take care to do the best job possible with documentation. In reality, with the hectic nature of crime scene work and criminal investigations in general, things sometimes get missed. It is very easy to be pulled in many different directions at once. As soon as the systematic and methodical routine is broken, the probability of missing something increases. As part of regular crime scene operations part of the manual should be dedicated to documentation, the techniques and requirements.

The requirements for any particular crime scene unit will vary. This will depend on what the unit does (in terms of what services are performed), what the capabilities are (in terms of what equipment is available) and what the local jurisdiction requires.

A good way to start is to sit and consider what you do already. If the unit processes crime scene, the unit should at least document the scene with photographs, sketches, measurements, and notes. Keep in mind however, that there are other things that can be done (such as video) and different ways to do things. Once you have considered and decided upon the requirements for the unit, take a look at the way things are done already. If you use forms to capture some or all of your data, see if they are complete or if more can be added. If free style notes are the vehicle of choice, look at what the unit is capturing regularly in various cases. The desire is both to ensure you are capturing all that you should be but also to ensure that there will be a reference for people to go to as a check for themselves.

Documentation Styles

Two main ways to document information with notes are forms and free style notes. Forms are nice because they help to ensure that, at the very least, the minimum amount of information needed is captured. Forms also lead to complacency. It is one thing to tell someone to complete all the applicable captions on a form with information, however it's another thing to ensure that, in each and every case, those forms will capture all the the data required for that scene. So where those forms will capture the data that the unit must always capture (for example location, time and date, victim information, suspect information, and things like that), the forms cannot plan for every eventuality.

Free style notes are good because they are open for capturing whatever is needed, however, sometimes things get lost in the sauce. The crime scene is not like any other forensic discipline. It is just so dynamic that this will occur. The best that can be done is to guide personnel in such a way that they can do the best job possible.

This part of the guide should help the investigators with information about what information they should capture, at a minimum, without regard to the technique used to capture it.

Photography

Photography is a quintessential means of documenting crime scenes and evidence. The guide should describe the methods used to take photographs under common situations as well as the composition of various types of photographs.

Crime scene investigators will encounter scenes and evidence in various states. These include well lit indoor and outdoor scenes as well as poorly lit indoor and outdoor scene. In addition, investigators will need to take pictures of evidence under unusual circumstances such as with Luminol or an alternate light source. A guide should include information about when these techniques should be considered for use and also some information about the major points for performing them. This can include:

- Outdoor photography – both daylight and night (low light/existing light photography)
- Fill flash
- Flash photography – both indoor and outdoor

- Alternate light source photography
- Luminol
- Examination/scientific quality photography (comparison photography)

If desired, the crime scene unit can create a photo SOP that dictates the methods used for each of these techniques. The guide should not be a discussion about how to do these various techniques; that should be left for training.

In addition, the guide should describe the composure of photographs and should describe what photographs should be taken. This can include, at a minimum, overall view photographs, mid-range view photographs and close-up view photographs. Again, how to do this should be left to training.

Photo Log

The photo log is a document in list form that describes photographs taken with regard to crime scene processing. Some people may advocate that the photo log is no longer needed with the advent of digital photography and the inclusion of meta data in the file. This may be so. However be cautioned. The meta data cannot capture the subject of the photograph nor where the photographer was when the photograph was taken. On occasion, the position of the photographer has been an issue at trial. Don't rely on memory. At the very least, if the unit was capturing descriptions of photographs as well as camera settings, and it is comfortable with relying on meta data to capture camera settings, at least continue to capture descriptions at scenes.

Sketches and Diagrams

The sketch and diagram of the crime scene are very similar. One is done free hand at a scene, perhaps in pencil and one is done, perhaps at a later time, with a computer or a pen and ruler. Other than that, they should be consistent with each other in many ways. The sketch and diagram should not differ substantially in proportion, and, the information contained on both should be the same. As an aside, these documents should be checked during an administrative review.

It is difficult for a guide to enumerate exactly what should be on a sketch/diagram. However, there are some general ideas that can be included in a guide. This might include:

- A header with information about the location of the scene, dates, creator of the sketch/diagram, other identifying information the unit uses
- Boundaries such as wall, floor roads, curb lines and building lines
- Dimensions of boundaries
- Contents of room
- Windows
- Doors
- Lighting
- Location of evidence
- Visible conditions
- Notation section for non-visible conditions (temperature, humidity, etc.)
- Legend

In addition, the guide may explain the utility of different sketch/diagram styles such as bird's eye view, cross projection and elevation sketches/diagrams. In this way, the investigator can choose to use these different techniques if the circumstances present themselves.

Notes

For purposes of this section, notes is used to mean any written information made at the scene whether done on a form, free written style or a combination of the two. Written notes are, along with photographs, the most common way crime scenes are documented. The better the notes, the better the ability to come along later on and recover information when memory forgets. Some people will advocate that photographs are better than notes since a picture is worth a thousand words. This is true if the camera sees everything that the eye does. If the crime scene unit takes pictures of everything for all different angles, maybe it can forgo taking good notes. But, it is doubtful that this happens. Good photographs and good notes are not in competition with each other. They are complementary to each other.

What information a crime scene unit captures will be based on what they do. The more they do, the more notes they will have to take. This section will examine some common, main categories of notes (not including the photo log). It is not meant to be all inclusive. It is hoped that this will help get a crime scene unit off the ground with ideas of where to get started. Those crime scene units that find holes here can springboard from there.

Scene Notes

Notes describing the crime scene should be detailed. Again, it is very hard to enumerate every single item that one might need to put into notes at any one time. A guide outlining the basic information is a useful start in that it will get investigators moving at a scene and hopefully start them thinking about things that are not expressly written in the guide. This comes with training and experience and as such can be added later if left out. The guide is a living document and as such can be (and should be) modified over time. Notes can be either in the form of free style notes or some kind of captioned form. It will probably be easier to devise, if desired, some hybrid method. It is very easy to come up with captions for the data that the unit always needs to document based on their business rules or traditions. Sit at the table with people and brainstorm. The form does not have to be fancy. Don't waste time on fancy formatting; ideas on paper are more important. Some of these things can include:

- Times and dates
- Locations
- Temperature
- Humidity
- Investigators involved
- Requestor information
- Other information that a unit needs to capture all the time.

Once this is done there will be a need to describe the scene in detail and the information that was learned at the scene. This is a little harder to caption and lends itself to free style notes. Here is where a guide can help get things moving. Start with some main categories and drill down from there.

- Where is the scene: indoor or outdoor?
- What is the scene: second floor, basement, house, apartment, park, field, street, driveway, backyard?
- Describe the scene location: third floor rear apartment (south side of building)
- Describe the scene: room contents, locations in room, locations in apartment, what is visible, etc.
- Entry/exit points
- Views into and out of scene if applicable
- Results of information gathering

At the end of the processing, the investigator can then describe the steps taken to process the scene and results obtained from the various activities. This can include:

- What was documented
- What was collected
- What PPE was employed
- What processes were employed
- What were the results of the processes

None of this is earth shattering but it gets people going and leaves them room for independent thought to add more information as they see fit.

Evidence Notes

Evidence notes should describe in detail at least the following: what the item is, where was it recovered from, what was it recovered for, whether it was processed in the field in any way, and how was it packaged. Any further information that a crime scene unit normally notates based on business rules or tradition should also be included in the notes. Evidence notes lend themselves well to a captioned, free style hybrid note.

Documentation Charts

Sometimes, documenting the location of evidence on or in items can be difficult to do with words alone. That's why crime scene investigators draw diagrams and take photographs. Diagrams of scenes are required to be done at scenes because each scene is different. When documenting evidence in cars or on clothing however, a crime scene unit can take advantage of pre-made generic sheets that we will call documentation charts. These sheets can include generic outlines of bodies, clothing items and car types. They can be very useful as a demonstrative method of documenting damage or conditions to these types of evidence. Computer drafting programs such as Crime Zone have many symbols that can be made into forms for use at scenes. Unusual or substantial differences between symbol and the actual, encountered item can be noted on the symbol. This technique is especially useful for those who are less inclined to be artistic.

The guide can include copies of symbols or forms that the crime scene unit will use consistently with instruction on how to document different, common conditions on them such as bullet holes and other types of damage.

Measurements

The methods a crime scene unit uses to measure scenes and evidence should be enumerated in the guide with an explanation regarding the advantages and disadvantages of each as well as when each technique should be considered for use as opposed to other techniques.

If a particular technique requires a calibration step prior to use, the calibration method should be outlined and the documentation requirements should be enumerated in the guide as well.

Other

Certain activities that gather data for the purpose of drawing a conclusion will need special attention. These topics should not be done by a generalist. Topics such as blood stain pattern analysis and shooting reconstruction require specialized training and as such, those with specialized training can assist in preparing SOPs. Many working groups publish model SOPs for their particular disciplines. When creating a guide for these topics, those model SOPs should be consulted where available.

Evidence Collection and Packaging

As most already know, lots of things can be evidence. Some of it can be analyzed and some of it can't. Some of it will prove useful to the investigation and some of it won't. One of the main considerations in how useful evidence is can be the condition it is received in at the laboratory. Evidence that is not packaged well can be damaged and ruined. It is very important for a procedural guide to assist the investigator in the field with information about how to package different kinds of evidence. The contents of this area will be limited only by what the crime scene unit is prepared to or able to do. For purposes of this section, do not consider only what your submitting lab's capabilities are. A lab can always be found to analyze something if the affiliated lab cannot do it. For those items that you do submit to a lab, seek their input. Find out how they analyze the particular types of evidence and how they would like it packaged. Discuss with them best practices. If the lab is accredited, chances are they are using great practices already. If you collect evidence that is sent to other labs on occasion, follow best practices for that type of evidence. If a unit doesn't know what to do, seek advice.

In general, guides in this section should have, at least, some of the following information:

- Recognition: why is this evidence valuable
- What is it valuable for (class characteristics, individual characteristics, etc.) and why? What about the evidence gives it class or individual characteristics (e.g. patterns)?
- What can damage the evidence (not the self-evident means to damage evidence such as gross or negligent physical mishandling)? Is the evidence susceptible to not so common things (consider the effect of UV light on DNA as an example)?
- Does certain packaging lend itself to easier lab analysis?
- If necessary, explicit instructions on how to package or what to package certain types of evidence.

Much of this can be handled in a few paragraphs of text, but an outline style might be a more amenable way to convey information when giving some type of explicit instruction. This will be especially true of complicated types of evidence. What would a crime scene unit do if they had to collect unknown chemicals for identification? There are many situations where this could present itself, especially dealing with clandestine laboratories. There are books dealing with the topic. A crime scene unit that will have to deal with these things will need to come up with a guide that will not only recover evidence that will be analyzed but do it in a safe way.

When creating guides that describe the collection of evidence, try to keep in mind that documentation of evidence as it is found should be a function that always precedes any steps that alter the state of the crime scene unless some exigent circumstance exists. There really is no need to start every procedure with a statement that all evidence should be documented prior to collection. Having said that, create simple outlines, bullet lists or simple paragraphs of how evidence should be collected. Keep in mind that context of evidence is also of great importance. Context of evidence will be recorded in the crime scene documentation, however, attempting to maintain context of evidence for the laboratory scientist can increase efficiency and may lead to better analytical evidence and information. For example, consider the collection of fiber evidence. If an investigator recognizes that some fibers found on the clothing of a homicide victim are out of place or otherwise unusual, collecting just those fibers and submitting them to the laboratory for identification will be easier if just those fibers were collected and sent. The crime scene investigator could choose to tape lift or vacuum those fibers, but it would add extra complications to the analysis.

A few examples of more common types of evidence can be found below. Always keep in mind that not everyone will do everything the same way. Consult your laboratory and seek guidance from them so that the methods used by the crime scene unit are symbiotic to those techniques used by the laboratory.

Hair and/or Fiber Evidence

Hair evidence and fiber evidence are often treated similarly because they share similar overall macro characteristics. On the macro level, it is not easy to tell the difference between a hair and a fiber and it is most probably appropriate that one should not try. In any event, unusual fibers and/or hairs found at a crime scene should be collected by carefully picking them up with gloves and putting them in a paper envelope. If they are spread out over a large area or the evidence is not readily defined, one can opt to recover fibers by lifting them on clear lifting tape. When no clear evidence is defined and the area is sizable the investigator may consider using a trace evidence vacuum to recover any small items such as hair and fiber evidence from an area. If potential sources and elimination samples are present, they should be collected also and packaged separately from the evidence (unknown) samples.

Questioned Documents

Questioned documents can have usefulness for several reasons: handwriting, indented writing, ink, watermarks, mechanical markings from printers and copiers as well as latent fingerprints. These items can be damaged if they are not handled carefully. Adding creases and creating more indented writing can obscure evidence. Questioned documents can be packaged so that it is immobilized between material that will prevent this from occurring such as sheets of cardboard.

Fire Debris

Flammable liquids are volatile and can be lost to evaporation if not protected from the time they are collected in the field to the time they are analyzed in the laboratory. The best choices for packaging fire debris with flammable liquids will be in air-tight, non-reactive containers such as glass mason jars and clean metal paint cans with air-tight lids. Nylon bags specifically made for this purpose can be used for unusually shaped or large items.

Biological Evidence for DNA

Swabs of wet or dried biological evidence from surfaces or items that cannot be reasonably collected and submitted to the laboratory can be recovered in a manner of ways. If the sample is dry, rehydrate by adding a very small amount of sterile water to a swab to rehydrate the sample. If the sample is wet, collect the sample with a dry swab. In either case, allow the swab to air dry and package in a paper container.

If biological evidence can be submitted by collecting the item or surface that it is on, allow the evidence to air dry and package in a paper container.

Fingerprint Evidence

Evidence submitted to the laboratory for fingerprint analysis, other than questioned documents, should be immobilized in a container so that it does not move. Movement may mechanically damage fingerprints on the surface of the object. As much as possible, try to secure the object in the container by using surfaces on the object that are the least likely to yield fingerprints (e.g. the knurled surfaces of a firearm).

These are just a small sampling of types of evidence that one might encounter at a crime scene. The point is that the guide does not need to be a dissertation about evidence, just an idea of what is important about that evidence and some examples of how to deal with it. More knowledge is better than no knowledge. There will inevitably be situations where the process may not be clear cut but relying on guidance will allow people to get it right.

Processing Techniques

Guides pertaining to processing techniques will be more involved. Not only might they describe when the technique can be used but also guide the investigator somewhat through the process. As mentioned before, there is no substitute for good training, however, the investigator should have some guidance as some processing techniques can be complicated. These procedures lend themselves to a hybrid style combining text explanations with step instructions where applicable. Some of the topics that might be covered by this section of the guide include, but are not limited to fingerprint processing, footwear impressions and the use of reagents.

Fingerprint Processing

There are many ways to process different items for fingerprints. A crime scene unit can use one or all of these techniques depending upon circumstances. Some techniques that might be included are powders, cyanoacrylate fuming, and small particle reagent. Each of these techniques have their utility. The techniques are all generally straightforward and uncomplicated. Be aware, however, that in some cases certain circumstances may dictate that an order be followed. Further, the crime scene unit should be aware of what it is equipped to do. Generally, guidance can be offered to the investigator with regard to when these techniques should be used and any special considerations that should be accounted for when used.

Footwear Impressions and Tool Mark Impressions

Footwear impressions can be present at a crime scene in different ways. They can be presented as two dimensional created by wet and dry materials and three dimensional in many kinds of surfaces. These different situations will have to be dealt with according to both the resources of the unit and the type of impression presented. The guide should start off with a discussion of the different types of impressions and how to recognize them. Once this is covered, a list of the steps will be needed to document and collect the impression. This should include special photography methods that may be required as well as the options available for collection either by lifting or casting. Bodziak, *in Footwear Impression Evidence: Detection, Recovery and Examination* 2nd Edition CRC PRESS (2000), is a great resource for this topic. It is again worth mentioning that the crime scene unit may want to consult with the examiner who will receive this evidence in order to learn about their requirements. Generally, the steps one should consider following are:

- General documentation (demonstrative photographs, notes/descriptions and inclusion on sketches and diagrams)
- Examination quality photography (if the impression is visible)
- Treatment if needed (capability and impression type dependent)
- Examination quality photography
- Recovery (capability and impression type dependent)

Tool marks will be handled in a similar manner in that they might be photographed and recovered if the surface or item they are in will allow it. Sometimes, it may not be reasonable to recover the tool mark but this will be based upon the unit's traditions and business rules. A similar system for documentation and recovery can be followed for tool marks.

Reagents (Presumptive Tests and Enhancement Techniques)

The use of reagents will not be complicated, but will include more information. Guides pertaining to the use of reagents might necessarily include a discussion of when to use the reagent, how to prepare the reagent, quality assurance steps that will be required before use, how to apply the reagent and specialized documentation techniques that may be required. Reagents can be discussed either on their own or when discussing the type of evidence they are used for. It is simply a style choice. For example, leuco crystal violet can be discussed on its own or during a discussion of patent blood impressions.

If the unit uses these or similar tools (e.g. Amido Black), start creating a procedure from the traditional way you use it. Go through the steps and write them down.

- When do you use the reagent?
- Do you do anything before using the reagent (for example, do you conduct a visual search for blood in areas that are protected from cleanup before applying Luminol)?
- Do you do any special documentation before applying a reagent (for example, do you take examination quality photographs of patent blood impressions before you apply leuco crystal violet)?
- How do you mix the reagent (is it a commercial kit or will the reagents be mixed fresh before responding)?
- How will you verify if the reagent is working properly before you apply it to evidence or in a scene?
- How will you document this verification
- How will you apply the reagent (for example will it be sprayed, dipped, or washed on)?
- How will you document the evidence or scene after application to document results?
- What will you do with the evidence afterwards?

In general, when it comes to processing techniques, guidance on the why, the steps and the techniques could stand to be a bit more specific. Very often, processing is final. In other words, once it's done it cannot be undone. If one makes a mistake here, it's final and can be disastrous. Washing patent blood hand impressions down a wall because of over application of leuco crystal violet is a final action. Over application of Luminol can dilute and ruin a sample for DNA.

Work Expectations for Scene Types

Another area that might be included in a guide is simple explanation of what to look for at different types of scenes, even what work might be expected at different types of scenes. As one knows, no two scenes are ever the same, however generalized guidance on some of the steps one might take to process the scene can be offered. So, somewhat specific guidance with regard to individual crime scene types as well as general guidance about how one can approach a scene might be useful. Figure 6.2 is an outline of a general processing scheme that a crime scene unit can build from.

Quality Assurance

Quality assurance procedures will be a requirement for all in the near future. In reality, most, if not all laboratories, accredited or otherwise have quality assurance procedures. It is time for crime scene units to do the same. For a more intensive discussion of quality assurance, please see Chapter 10. This section will endeavor to give the reader an outline with regard to procedure creation.

The quality assurance manual can be a stand-alone document or be included in the the procedural manual. Either way, it ends up being the same really. Some of these procedures are not strictly quality assurance in the traditional sense of the word however, as has been proposed in several sections of this book, quality assurance can take a much wider role in the unit's operations than perhaps it already does. At any rate, some procedures that will definitely need to be in the quality manual will be:

- Reagents: including initial inspection and verification before use at scene
- Standards: traceability

1. Search
    a. Walk-through with pertinent personnel
    b. Focus of a crime scene search
    c. Types of probative evidence
    d. Methods and patterns of search
    e. Responsibilities of search personnel
    f. Types of search areas
        i. Points of entry or exit
        ii. Paths
        iii. Immediate area of incident
        iv. Accessible, obstructed and inaccessible areas
    g. Hazardous scene considerations
    h. Other resources for searching crime scenes
        i. Lighting
        ii. Surveillance
        iii. Chemical enhancement
        iv. Specialized equipment
2. Recognize and assess for evidentiary value
    a. Conferral at scene
        i. Investigators and other pertinent personnel
    b. Highly probative, probative or potentially probative
        i. Investigative leads
        ii. Include or exclude suspects
        iii. Describe people, places and things involved in the incident
        iv. Reconstruct the event
3. Secure and protect
    a. Safeguarding evidence
        i. Removal
        ii. Loss
        iii. Disturbance
        iv. Repositioning
    b. Protection of evidence
        i. Destruction
        ii. Alteration
        iii. Degradation
        iv. Contamination
        v. Diminution
    c. Other deleterious effects and/or hazardous conditions
        i. Determine required PPE
4. Document
    a Case notes (basic)
        i. Initial call out to the crime scene
        ii. Time and date of occurrence
        iii. Requestor information
        iv. Complainant/victim information
            1. Location
            2. Removal from scene (location if applicable)
            3. Pedigree
        v. Suspect or perpetrator information
            1. Pedigree
            2. Removal from scene (location if applicable)
        vi. Scene or location information and personnel
            1. Address of location
            2. Arrival time
            3. Personnel in scene at arrival

FIGURE 6.2 Basic crime scene investigation workflow

4. Narrative of incident
5. Scene appearance
   a. Weather
   b. Lighting
   c. Transient conditions and/or evidence
   d. Victim and/or decedent(s) location in scene

vii. Medical examiner information
viii. Hospital or morgue information
ix. Evidence recovered or removed from scene
x. Specialized equipment used
xi. Warrant or consent
xii. Additional support units' personnel information

b. Images and photographic log
   i. Type of camera
   ii. Format
   iii. Lens
   iv. Specialized photography
   v. Types of photograph views
   vi. Methods of measurements

c. Rough sketch
   i. Preparation
   ii. Types of rough sketches
   iii. Components and contents of rough sketch

d. Crime scene diagram
   i. Preparation
   ii. Types of crime scene diagrams
   iii. Components and contents of crime Scene diagram
   iv. Specialized
      1. 2D and 3D
      2. Animated
      3. Physical model

5. Process and visualize
   a. Latent fingerprints
      i. Powders
      ii. Cyanoacrylate
      iii. SPR
   b. Light
      i. Bright, white light
      ii. Bright, white, oblique light
      iii. Alternate light source
         1. Biological fluids
   c. Reagent
      i. Presumptive ID
         1. Blood
         2. Ballistic impact marks and bullet holes
      ii. Enhancement of blood for documentation
   d. Blood spatter patterns
      i. ID of probative blood utilizing blood spatter pattern indicators
      ii. ID of suspect blood utilizing blood spatter pattern indicators (e.g. continuous trail, dripping and directionality)
   e. Ballistic trajectory indicators
      i. Directionality
         1. Locating ballistic components (using trajectory and directionality determinations)
         2. Rods and lasers
   f. RUVIS

FIGURE 6.2 continued

6. Sample and collect
    a. Probative v. non-probative
        i. Conferrals
    b. Prioritization of collection – factors
        i. Fragile to sturdy
        ii. Environmental factors
        iii. Safety factors
        iv. Subject to damage
        v. Subject to disturbance
        vi. Subject to loss
    c. Monitoring of factors
        i. Prioritization must be flexible
        ii. Continuous monitoring
        iii. Adjust prioritization as factors change
        iv. Collection
        v. Disposable tools
        vi. Non-disposable tools
            1. Cleaning
        vii. Protect evidence from work surfaces
            1. Kraft paper
                a. For drying
                b. Processing
                c. Handling
                d. While packaging
            2. Custody of Kraft paper (for trace evidence)
    d. Control samples
        i. DNA
        ii. Elimination DNA samples
        iii. Victim DNA samples
        iv. Suspect DNA samples
        v. Prescription drugs
        vi. Foods
            1. Solids
            2. Liquids
        vii. Needed for comparisons and/or as physical evidence
            1. Paint
            2. Soil
            3. Hair
            4. Fiber
            5. Impressions and imprints
            6. Tool marks
            7. GSR
                a. Firearm for distance determination
            8. Glass
            9. Fingerprint eliminations
            10. Any evidence requiring identification and/or individualization
7. Marking
    a. Technique
        i. Write or inscribe
            1. Instrument
            2. Scribe, pen or marker
            3. Style
            4. Print
    b. Location
        i. Appropriate that it will not affect evidentiary value

FIGURE 6.2 continued

- ii. Techniques
  1. Textiles
  2. Ballistics
  3. Substrates

c. Manner
- i. Initials
- ii. Unique, consecutive number

d. Marking proximal container
- i. If marking evidence will effect evidentiary value
- ii. Information on container
  1. Name (in block letters)
  2. Unique consecutive ID number
  3. Accurate description of evidence and substrate
  4. Accurate description regarding
     a. Where the evidence (substrate) was found.
     b. Specific location on the substrate where the evidence was found e.g. left sleeve of the victim's shirt.

8. Preservation

a. Use appropriate methods, techniques, materials, etc. to preserve evidence.
- i. Chemical, e.g. blood and/or urine taken from person
- ii. Chemical, e.g. blood on a substrate
- iii. Physical, e.g. suspend, tie down
- iv. Fuming
- v. Environmental, e.g. temperature and humidity
- vi. Physical and environmental, e.g. soaking and drying
- vii. Packaging, e.g. paper, plastic, metal or glass
- viii. Transport and delivery
- ix. Chemical, e.g. acids, bases
- x. Chemical, e.g. hydrocarbons (arson evidence)

b. Conferral with laboratory if needed.

9. Package

a. Determine correct packaging material for type of evidence.
- i. Biological evidence
  1. Package in paper
  2. Dry to prevent degradation
- ii. Ballistic evidence
  1. Packaged safely and kept out of battery
  2. Wire tied into gun box
  3. Chamber round packaged separately
  4. Scene ballistics
- iii. Arson evidence
  1. Debris and liquids
  2. Other
- iv. Hair evidence
  1. Clothing
  2. Individual hairs
- v. Fiber evidence
  1. Clothing
  2. Individual fibers
- vi. Other physical evidence

b. Secure evidence to prevent damage.
- i. Cardboard boxes
- ii. Wire ties
- iii. Double or triple bag
- iv. Evidence tins

FIGURE 6.2 continued

   c. Secure evidence to ensure safety to yourself and others.
10. Seal
    a. Seal with evidence tape
    b. A proper seal is proof that an item was not accessible and, therefore, could not have been altered or contaminated during storage
    c. Secure evidence tape around openings
    d. Sign across the seal in the appropriate fashion
    e. In bold black lettering: rank, name, tax, date
    f. The writing will be visible on both the tape and the evidence container
11. Take evidence into custody
    a. Conferral
        i. Probative value
        ii. Priority
        iii. Testing needs
        iv. Case facts
    b. Unit paperwork
12. Chain of custody
    a. Should be no longer than necessary (shorter the better)
    b. Evidence should be documented from recovery, to invoicing officer, to transfer to the lab, to intake at lab, to analysis, to storage, and to the courtroom

FIGURE 6.2 continued

- Proficiency testing
- Technical review
- Measurements (including uncertainty)

Ideas for how to prepare guides for reagents and standards can be found in Chapter 10. For an understanding of the requirements for proficiency testing, technical review and measurements, it is worth taking a look at accreditation requirements as a guide even if the crime scene unit is not seeking accreditation. These documents are a good place to start.

Quality assurance procedures center around the use of reagents and standards. The goal is to ensure that reagents, which are very often presumptive tests of some kind, are functioning prior to using them in a crime scene on potential evidence. Three things can happen when reagents are used. First they can work as expected and a sample is potentially identified and collected. Second, they can react positively with something other than what you are looking for. This is called a false positive. A sample is collected and the laboratory discovers that it is not what it was thought to be. The third thing that can happen is that the reagent fails to work properly and a sample of evidence is missed. This is called a false negative and there are a few reasons why this would happen. If something is interfering with the reaction, either physically or chemically, the reagent may not work. The other reason is that the reagents are not working.

Sometimes, an investigator will understand the reasons for a false positive result when it occurs. For example, applying a catalytic presumptive test to a metal item or surface will often result in a positive reaction. If a single part solution is being used, it would be hard to distinguish this false positive from a positive reaction. If this is a two-part solution wherein the reagent is added and then the hydrogen peroxide is added, identifying the false positive would be easier.

When a negative reaction occurs, it is not easy to tell if this is false negative. One situation where it is somewhat easy to predict is when using sodium rhodizonate as a presumptive test for lead. If blood is present on the sample, it can prevent the lead from transferring to the filter paper when the transfer technique is used. So, when the sodium rhodizonate solution is added, no color change is observed. However, when using catalytic presumptive tests, predicting a false negative might be very difficult. The investigator would have to recognize the presence of something that would block the oxidation reaction. Some have postulated that strong reducing agents can do this but it may not be intuitive that a strong reducing agent is present at the scene.

What can absolutely be prevented is the occurrence of false negatives due to faulty reagents. Reagents are like any other delicate tool that a tradesman uses, they must be taken care of. They must be stored properly, mixed properly and have a shelf life both before and after mixing. Before using the reagent in the crime scene, it should be tested against a known standard to ensure that it is working.

Applying a reagent to evidence or a scene without knowledge of the fact that it works is problematic. Applying a non-working reagent to a scene, knowingly or unknowingly has the potential to cause evidence that has the ability to identify the guilty and exonerate the innocent to be missed.

Proprietary Guidance

Proprietary sections of the guide will deal with specific tasks associated with the crime scene units or, even the agencies, business rules and traditions. These can include any paperwork unique to the department or parent organization that is required for the taking of evidence into custody, tracking the chain of custody, submitting items for laboratory services, and so on. If the unit uses a computer based, proprietary report system, instruction on requirements for its use might also be included here. In short, this section of the manual might be used to codify any business rules or traditions unique to the unit and not used by the parent agency or those used by both. If the parent agency already uses a guide for some of this, inclusion of that into the crime scene unit's guide would suffice as well. Keep in mind that contradictory information from parent agency to crime scene unit would be problematic.

Conclusions

The preparation of a procedural guide will be a requirement in the future and it can seem a daunting task. Sometimes the hardest part is just getting started and once the unit gets past issues of style and content, it becomes easier. The procedural guide already exists to a certain extent. It is in the heads of the investigators. Just start by writing down how the crime scene unit does things. Again, remember, there are many guides out there for one to get started with and that is how many crime scene units have gotten started. Once the crime scene unit has parts of the guide written or scratched out, they should ensure that the way they do things amounts to best practices. If not, they should consider making changes so that they do. Remember to consult the laboratory that the unit will be working with. Evidence handling at the scene must be symbiotic with the needs of the laboratory or the ways in which they analyze evidence. Don't be afraid to mix and match styles in the guide. It is not about being beautiful it is about being useful. Don't say that the crime scene unit can or will do things that it cannot. If the guide is not a reasonable document, it will be unreasonable to follow it. Create a document that works for the unit in so far as capabilities, but, use best practices for what the unit will do. If the unit will do something but in a substandard manner just to say it is being done, they are better off just not doing it. Creating a guide is a good way for people to get involved and learn about topics. Creating the guide may force people to conduct research and learn new things and that is the best part of it.

7

INVESTIGATIVE EQUIPMENT

Overview

Twenty years ago crime scene investigation centered on photography and fingerprints, although these are still quite important today much has changed. Crime scene investigators through the 1980s were photographers and experts at latent print recovery. Most had a favorite fingerprint brush that was treasured for its unique qualities and was only used for special circumstances. I can still recall being given my first latent print kit in the late 1980s from a retiring NYPD Police Officer by the name of Bill Guido. It was a worn out old box with an array of brushes and powders inside and Bill was quite proud of its years of service. He made it quite clear that one of the brushes within, a red colored ostrich feather brush was special and should be handled with care. It was only to be used on the highest priority cases. I appreciated Bill's experience and advice and I took good care of his kit and his favorite brush for several years but eventually it was forced into retirement. In today's world of forensics we can see a contrast between an old treasured fingerprint brush and new disposable brushes that are designed for a single use before they are discarded or else risk cross contaminating DNA evidence. Bill was a great cop and mentor and a fine fingerprint technician but his generation had barely heard of DNA evidence and never benefited from its ability to solve crimes. Much has changed since those years before forensic DNA analysis and much more change is still likely to come.

Today a crime scene investigator uses a small arsenal of equipment to process a scene and complete casework. Upon arrival at the scene the CSI uses an array of tools to document the crime scene and then moves to a second set of tools to search for and recognize probative evidence. Once evidence is located a third set of tools may be required to process or enhance the evidence and then of course additional tools and supplies will be required to collect and package the evidence so it can be safely transported away from the scene for laboratory testing or secure storage. While all of this activity takes place additional tools and supplies are required to protect the scene from contamination as well as protect the investigative team from hazards. It must also be pointed out that accredited crime scene units will be required to validate, calibrate and regularly inspect this equipment which can be a full-time endeavor in itself.

Once back at the office the investigator uses computers connected to secure servers to write reports, process digital photos and store case files. Renderings of the scene may be created in 3D software and large format printers may be needed to generate court exhibits on demand. It requires a tremendous amount of effort to sustain such an investigative operation and to procure and maintain all of the required supplies and equipment.

Medium and large jurisdictions will require several sets of equipment since it is likely that they may have to process more than one scene simultaneously, in reality even the smaller jurisdictions that choose to operate a full service crime scene unit will need to have several sets of equipment ready to roll.

To oversee all of this an equipment manager will need to be designated to ensure all of the equipment is properly maintained, serviced, calibrated and repaired as needed. The equipment manager will have additional responsibilities as well. To ensure all of the necessary supplies are stocked and available as needed, contracts need to be procured with suppliers and orders and deliveries routinely handled. Inventory needs to be maintained and rotated and properly stored in its assigned locations. Malfunctioning equipment or items that have passed their shelf life need to be removed from service. Preventive and routine maintenance needs to be performed on the investigative equipment. While there may have been a time when a crime scene investigator was individually responsible to keep and maintain their equipment it is not practical with today's changing demands in crime scene investigation. In smaller jurisdictions that employ just a few CSIs the equipment manager may be a dual role shared by an active investigator so long as the person is afforded ample time for the workload, but in larger jurisdictions it must be someone's primary responsibility is to manage equipment and supplies.

All of the investigative equipment also needs to be able to be rapidly deployed to a scene along with the investigative team whenever an incident requiring crime scene investigation occurs. It is not practical or efficient to store all of the equipment inside a central office and then find a vehicle to transport it each time it is needed in the field. It is also not possible to predict which items will be needed at any particular scene prior to the arrival of CSIs. Therefore it is necessary to have dedicated pre-stocked crime scene response vehicles specifically designed to expeditiously transport the investigators and all of the equipment and supplies to a scene and to return all of the above along with the forensic evidence back to the crime lab after the processing is complete.

Forensic evidence can be in the form of tiny fiber samples or may take a much larger form, such as a rolled up carpet or bedroom mattress, so the availability of transport vehicles for evidence also requires consideration. Well-designed crime scene response vehicles should also be able to serve as shelter for the investigative team and a temporary secure evidence holding area during prolonged scene investigations. Features such as well-designed work space that can be easily decontaminated, communications, generator power, refrigeration and heating and air conditioning are just some of the important factors to consider.

Once the scene investigation has been carried out a significant amount of casework still remains to be done. This casework requires suitable office space with good quality computers and IT infrastructure along with photo processing, evidence processing and exhibit preparation capabilities. The CSI's office should be designed more closely with a laboratory layout then a typical police detective squad office.

This chapter will look at all of the equipment and supply considerations that a modern CSI unit must consider when establishing a well-planned operation and will provide lists of recommended equipment and supplies. Although the lists provided may seem extensive they are by no means exhaustive as each unit's operation may have some differences and since new products to improve operations become available as time passes.

Investigative equipment is broken down into the following categories:

- Computers and electronics
- Photography equipment
- Forensic mapping equipment
- Scene processing equipment and supplies
- Evidence collection and packing supplies
- Reagents and presumptive tests
- Administrative supplies

Computers and Electronics

Computer and electronic equipment presents a large expense for a crime scene unit's budget and as such needs to be planned, tracked and maintained. Many or the larger CSI units will have support from the agencies or municipalities' IT departments when it comes to computer systems, however small and medium sized units may be left to design and purchase computer systems on their own with only minimal support from IT professionals.

It is important to understand the demands that a CSI unit will place onto a computer and network systems when planning and designing systems. Workstations that may be very well suited to other case investigators within the agency may not serve very well in a CSI unit. This is due to the fact that CSI units utilized unique software applications and process large batches of high resolution images as part of their casework routines. New technologies such as 3D laser scanning at crime scenes is capable of capturing huge amounts of data and the demand for graphic intensive video and 3D renderings are becoming much more common. CAD and forensic mapping programs are also frequently utilized. Many of these applications require more powerful computers then what may be commonly used in typical police work. The third-party providers of the software products used by CSIs frequently provide updates to their software which will require administrative access to install.

Workstations

Good quality computers that have the capability to handle large image and data files are required. Up-to-date processor speed and memory will be required to keep pace with third-party software that is frequently used, such as CAD diagramming, and 3D reconstruction software. Since video, images and other graphically demanding data such as 3D point clouds is common to CSI work the computers should be also be equipped with good graphics cards with a sufficient amount of dedicated memory for graphics. Dual screen monitors will speed workflow when working with images, 3D design and CAD software and will reduce fatigue on investigators who are otherwise forced to work with several small windows open at one time on a single monitor screen.

Mobile Computers

Ruggedized laptops may not be needed at more routine crime scenes but they can be very helpful to have at a scene when large-scale investigations are involved and extended time is to be spent at the scene. Having a computer available at the scene allows for the preparation of reports, review of photos and video captured at the scene, review of surveillance video, sending and receiving email communication. Researching topics and reviewing electronic versions of standard operating procedures, and so on. Laptops are often permanently secured inside police vehicles but in the case of crime scene response vehicles they should be removable since a temporary work site may be set up inside the scene and the computer will need to be available in these remote locations.

Field PDA Devices and Communication

Electronic field data collection is a somewhat new but important consideration. Today's smart phones, tablets and PDAs can be leveraged to speed data collection while improving data quality. Many CSI units are currently using online case management software. Merging this process with data collection devices that can be used in the field reduces work and helps to eliminate repetition and minimizes errors. Currently many CSIs collect written notes in the field and then use those notes along with their observations to type written reports. This process typically involves a lot of duplication of effort. For instance typing the address of occurrence at the top of a report about DNA evidence and then repeatedly typing that same information at the top of several subsequent reports about other evidence in the case results in repetitive work and an increased risk of error each time the same information is typed. Data collection devices employed in the field and running software applications that can integrate with the case management system eliminates these issues. There are currently several off the shelf software apps available for this purpose. It is recommended that products be researched carefully to make sure they can be customized to fully fit the needs of the agency and to make sure the data will not be stored in a third-party server or held in some proprietary format that is controlled by someone other than the agency.

Saving the data and uploading it to the case management system in the office can be accomplished in several ways. While transmitting the data wirelessly from the field is a possibility, several issues arise including security and transfer of large file sizes. A more appropriate method at this point in time may be to have data collector with docking stations in the office. Once a device is returned from a field assignment and returned to its docking station the data transfer can be initiated. This method also allows an investigator to review entries prior to entering the information as part of casework.

Even with PDAs, verbal communication between an investigator at the scene, others involved in the investigation, and supervisory personnel is critical. A crime scene investigation can last many hours or even days and new information develops constantly during those early hours following an incident. A suspect may make statements during interrogation, witnesses may call police to report observations, developments may occur at related scenes such as the hospital where an injured person is being treated. As new facts develop the information must be relayed to the scene since they can have significant impact on how the scene is processed.

Equally important is outgoing communication from the CSI at the scene. Guidance on procedure may be needed from supervisors, or reach-back support may be needed from the crime laboratory. The CSI may also discover new facts during processing at the scene that have immediate value to others. For example, the discovery of a blood trail may indicate a suspect received injuries and conveying this information quickly may lead a patrol officer to locate a suspect seeking treatment at a local hospital.

Computer Infrastructure

Computer infrastructure such as secure servers for storage and retrieval of case data is required for a modern CSI operation. Since digital photography has taken hold in CSI work most agencies report a large increase in the number of photographs captured at a crime scene. It is not uncommon to have a homicide investigation contain well over 100 photos with each being captured in high resolution with file sizes up to about 15 megabyte each. New cameras are continuing be released to the market with increased resolution capabilities and consequently, larger file sizes. Also, as stated earlier laser scanning is also becoming a more routine procedure for documentation at crime scenes. While these technologies improve casework tremendously they also result is huge amounts of data that will need to be uploaded across communication lines and stored to servers. Wireless connections are still not practical for transferring such large amounts of data so wired infrastructure will be needed. If servers are stored off site then data will have to be transferred through utility provider communication lines and the utility company should be consulted to assure the required bandwidth is available. If servers are stored locally then data transfers will be easier to control however professional support should be sought in systems design to ensure there is minimal risk to data integrity.

Electronic Case Data Distribution

Case data requires frequent sharing with parties outside of the agency. Casework will be frequently requested by other investigative bodies and agencies and is routinely subpoenaed by prosecutors, defense attorneys, and civil litigants. While sharing data inter-agency is possible through servers, access is seldom granted to those outside of the agencies employment. Therefore equipment such as CD and DVD burners are required to accommodate the requests for information. Larger operations will handle hundreds of requests for information every year. Good quality disc burners and duplicators will be required and whenever possible standalone burners that have no internal memory are recommended for duplicating data rather than utilizing a computer which retains copies of data on the hard drive. Several manufacturers produce this type of equipment. Adams Evidence Grade technologies produces equipment and supplies exclusively for law enforcement use.

Printing

A goal of modern CSI units should be to become a paperless operation. Although this may not be fully achievable it is a goal worth striving for as cost savings and environmental benefits can be significant. Printing (especially photo printing) is very costly and may be largely unnecessary in today's technology rich society. An exception may be during a trial where reports or photos from the scene are often entered into evidence. It may be preferable to have a printed report or 8 × 10 photo so the physical item can be displayed and marked as evidence in the courtroom. But, of the hundreds of photos captured of the scene that process may be required for only a small amount since all of the photos are seldom needed as evidence. Developing a policy of printing only when necessary produces a cost savings of about one dollar per 8 × 10 photo in paper and ink costs. Another benefit of paperless operations is a reduction in the amount of physical file storage space needed to hold file archives.

When printing is required good quality laser printers are currently the best choice for report printing. Sharing the same printer for documents and photos is not practical for CSI operations.

Instead a separate good quality photo printer capable of printing enlargements of at least 8 ×10″ is recommended. Large format plotter printers are also required for a full-scale CSI office. Large format printers will allow for the production of enlarged diagrams and photos which are frequently used in testimony and briefings. Supplies for large format printers include specialty papers usually purchased in large rolls, adhesives, cutting mats and mounting boards. Printers and supplies can be expensive and should not be overlooked when calculating operating costs.

Photography Equipment

Photography equipment is perhaps one of the single most important aspects of the CSI's equipment. High quality photography equipment is a necessity in crime scene investigation work. The CSI utilizes camera equipment to create a visual record of the scene as it was discovered and to document the appearance and locations of evidence. It must also be remembered that the photography equipment may also be used to create the only record of some types of evidence such as a bloody fingerprint on an immovable object.

The Scientific Working Group on Imaging Technology (SWIGIT) has published some excellent resources to provide guidelines for crime scene photography using digital cameras. Their publications can be found on the internet at www.SWIGIT.org. As stated in SWIGIT Guidelines for the Forensic Practitioner Version 3.0 2009.01.15

> The agency should have a specific mechanism for determining whether a piece of hardware meets a requirement. Some applications, such as impression evidence, have specific quantitative requirements regarding equipment or resolution (see SWGIT documents "*General Guidelines for Capturing Latent Impressions Using a Digital Camera*," "*General Guidelines for Photographing Tire Impressions*" and "*General Guidelines for Photographing Footwear Impressions*.") Specification sheets may be used as a guide, but in most cases it will be necessary to test the equipment under operational conditions.

The photography equipment must be up to the task under all of the varying conditions where a crime scene may be encountered. The CSI personally, and the case overall, will be judged heavily by the quality and professionalism of the case photos. Failure to capture a particular image or capturing one with poor quality often results in someone establishing a poor regard for the CSI's work, even if the shortcoming is of no blame to the CSI themselves. A CSI must be equipped with high quality camera equipment and be trained as an expert in its use in order to be successful in the field. Professional camera equipment is not inexpensive and the cost of a well-designed crime scene photography kit can exceed US$5,000.

Camera Type

Crime scene photography demands the use of a camera system that can accommodate interchangeable lenses as well as an external flash system. The overwhelming majority of CSIs today utilize 35mm single lens reflex cameras with Nikon and Canon being the most popular brands. These cameras are workhorses and perform well in the field meeting all of the needs of crime scene investigation very well. Although other camera types, such as medium format cameras, may produce better quality photos the quality, versatility and affordability of the 35mm SLR makes it a very popular choice.

The choice of whether to go with digital or film format has all but been settled with digital having become the overwhelming format for crime scene investigation. Although this now seems rudimentary the switch from film format to digital was an arduous task and it took many years for the forensic community to accept digital photography as a viable alternative to film. Of course the end goal of crime scene photography is to record the scene and evidence so it may be analyzed and ultimately presented to the trier of fact during a criminal trial and digital photography has proven to be up to this task. Although digital photography began to gain popularity with the general public starting in 1999 after Nikon introduced the DSLR D1 camera it still took a lot of deliberation for the forensic community to become convinced that the format was a good fit and that digital photos would be accepted by the courts. During the time of the switch from film to digital I worked as a CSI in New York City at the nation's largest police department and was frequently involved in many meetings where we labored over this topic for what seemed like years. In the end the courts accepted digital photographs with barely a second thought and the court challenges to admissibility never really materialized.

Digital Camera Sensor

The type and size of the camera sensor is a very important consideration when choosing a digital camera for CSI work. Camera sensors are typically available in two types CMOS and CCD. Although CCD sensors were once known for lower noise capability than CMOS sensors, today's technology has progressed to a point where both sensor types are capable of producing high quality photos. Of more importance then the sensor type is the size of the sensor. Cameras with "full frame sensors" have a sensor that is 36mm by 24mm in size; this is the equivalent size of the negative for a 35mm film photograph, hence the term "Full frame." Larger sensors have the capability of producing higher resolution photos that are required in crime scene photography. Many digital cameras have sensors that are considerably smaller than the full frame sensor with the APS-C sensor being the most common when it comes to DSLR cameras. APS-C sensors vary slightly in size between different manufacturers. For example the APS-C sensor that is used on Nikon DX cameras is 23.6mm × 15.7mm and the APS-C sensor in Canon models measures 22.2 × 14.8mm in size. Cameras with smaller sensors have a crop factor of 1.5–1.6 compared to full frame sensors. To accommodate the crop factor of smaller sensor sizes camera manufacturers, including Nikon and Canon, produce different lenses for cameras with smaller sensors than their cameras with full frame sensors. The major impact of sensor size is the size of the individual pixels that make up the photograph. If two cameras are compared, each with the same megapixel rating but one has a full frame sensor and one has a smaller sensor then the pixels captured by the camera with the smaller sensor will be of smaller individual size. The end result is a picture of lower quality, particularly when viewed or printed in enlarged sizes as is often necessary with examination quality crime scene photos. For this reason full frame sensors are recommended for crime scene photography, particularly if the camera will be utilized to capture examination quality images of evidence such as fingerprints.

Mega Pixel Ratings

Mega pixel ratings are often used to gauge the quality of a camera. This is a mistake! Manufacturers are constantly one-upping each other by increasing the number of megapixels their cameras can capture and for most consumers this is the major factor used when purchasing a camera. Professional photographers term this misnomer "the megapixel myth." Crime scene managers cannot afford to behave the same as the general consumer or their unit's photographic capabilities will suffer.

At the time of this writing smart phone cameras are available with over 40 mega pixels. Does this mean that these cameras can produce better quality photos then a 12 megapixel 35mm full frame DSLR used by CSIs? Should we scrap the 35mm camera and photograph crime scenes with our cell phones? No, absolutely not. What is more important to the ultimate photo quality is the size of each of those thousands of pixels. In the end squeezing 41,000 pixels onto a sensor that is about 7mm × 5mm allows manufacturers to make bold claims about their products but it results in very small pixels with very little light gathering ability and when these photos are printed or viewed in enlarged formats the quality diminishes very quickly. The term for this poor quality is pixilation. Most readers are very familiar with viewing low quality photos on computers and in emails, when zooming in on the photos the quality just disappears, certainly an unacceptable situation for crime scene photos where enlargement to reveal details may be absolutely required. The 12 megapixel camera with a full frame sensor will produce much better results for crime scene photography then the 41 megapixel cell phone camera will. But what is an acceptable megapixel rating for crime scene photos?

Perhaps the most challenging photos in crime scene investigation work are those of latent prints and footwear impressions. The SWIGIT guidelines offer specific resolutions that must be achieved for these types of photographs. However, this is not a cut-and-dried topic as many variables are involved.

When addressing photos of footwear impressions SWIGIT recommends a professional camera, 35mm or digital SLR with a minimum eight megapixel native resolution, capable of interchangeable lenses, manual override for exposure and focus.

The following is from SWIGIT Guidelines for Capturing Latent Impressions Using a Digital Camera Version 1.3 2010.06.11.

Step 1: Prior to Initial Use

a) Determine the maximum field of view in which a minimum of 1,000 ppi may be achieved. Refer to the effective pixel dimensions of the camera's sensor as stated by the manufacturer (e.g. 3872 × 2592 pixels).
b) Divide each dimension by 1,000 ppi which, in this example equals 3.872 inches × 2.592 inches. This makes the maximum field of view approximately 3¾ inches × 2½ inches. To convert inches to millimeters, multiply inches by 25.4. To achieve maximum detail, it is best practice to fill the frame with the impression.
c) Not all camera viewfinders cover 100 percent of the capture area. Take a test image of scales across the vertical and horizontal axis to determine coverage of viewfinder.

According to the SWIGIT guides in order for latent prints to be acceptable for examination and for entry into an automated fingerprint identification system it must meet the required resolution of 1,000 ppi. To capture a digital image of this quality the user must first know the specifications of the camera and then calculate the maximum field of view that can be captured while still maintaining that resolution. We can follow the above step using a Nikon D700 DSLR with a full frame sensor as an example. The Nikon D700 has a pixel dimension of 4288 × 2848. If we divide these figures by 1,000 we get 4.288 × 2.848. Round off the figures and we get 4.3 × 2.9. This means if we are to use a

Nikon D700 to capture an image of a latent print for examination then the largest area we can photograph is 4.3 × 2.9 inches.

In the end each agency must look at the requirements of their work process and determine precisely what types of images will be captured in order to decide on resolution requirements. However, when utilized properly a digital SLR camera with a full frame sensor and a megapixel rating of 12mp can produce outstanding results and meet the resolution requirements for most examination quality photos as stated in the SWIGIT guides. That being said, as time marches on and manufacturers continue marketing higher resolution cameras there will certainly come a time to upgrade. In times gone by a good quality camera was something a photographer would treasure for life but in today's age of digital technology cameras fall into the category of electronics and most electronics have a useful life span of about 3–5 years before technology outpaces them.

Shutter System and Camera Body

Cameras, like all mechanical equipment, have wearable parts and are built by manufacturers to provide a predetermined service life. Consumer grade photography equipment may fail under the demands of crime scene investigation work. A consumer grade digital SLR camera may have a shutter life rating of 50,000–100,000 photos, meaning that the camera's mechanical systems are designed to provide that many photos over the useful life of the camera. In a busy crime scene investigation unit that might correlate to just a few year time period before the camera is nearing the end of its life cycle. A professional grade camera will have a much greater shutter life span (sometimes two to three times a consumer grade camera).

The camera body is also an important consideration. Consumer grade cameras do not have ruggedized bodies. They are made with the needs of the average user who takes the camera along on family vacation in mind. Rugged camera bodies with magnesium covers add significant weight to the camera; this is not a desirable feature for amateur photographers but it is a requirement for crime scene photographers who will expose the camera to the rigors of field work on a routine basis.

ISO Rating

ISO ratings on a digital camera are equivalent to film speed on older film cameras and refer to the sensitivity to light. Film speed is determined by a rating system known as ISO (International Standards Organization) and will typically range from a slow speed of ISO 25 up until ISO 25,000 and higher on some digital cameras. The higher the ISO rating the more light can be captured in the photograph. Generally speaking the lowest ISO rating suitable for the given photograph should be chosen to produce optimal results in crime scene photographs. To explain the reason for this a brief explanation of ISO and its correlation to film speed may be helpful. In conventional photography silver halide crystals, which are sensitive to light, are embedded in the film. The larger the size of the silver halide crystals that are used when manufacturing the film the faster the film can record light. Therefore, when a photographer uses a film camera to capture photos in low light a fast film speed can be used to help achieve a properly exposed photograph. Conversely when abundant light is present a slower film speed can be used. The problem with using fast film speeds is the larger that the silver halide crystals are the more graininess is introduced into the photo. Because grainy photos are not desirable in crime scene photos CSIs traditionally have used slow film speeds such as ISO 100 and even slower film when examination quality photographs were being captured. Although digital photos no longer use film coated with silver halide crystals they do use digital sensors and similar to the graininess caused by fast film speed digital photos suffer from noise with fast ISO speeds.

In film based cameras the photographer had to make a decision about what film speed to load into the camera and was then stuck with that choice until a new roll of film was loaded. Switching the film speed for individual photos would mean having to constantly change film before the roll was completely exposed; this process would be impractical and expensive. Digital cameras have now solved this dilemma. On digital cameras film speed can be adjusted as needed for each individual photograph. Digital cameras have also pushed the limits of fast film speeds much farther than film photography was ever able to achieve. Some digital cameras now have ISO speeds of over ISO 25,000 available. This means a photo can be captured in very low light without the need for a flash. This may be a very valuable feature for some types of photography, such as surveillance photography or taking photos at a symphony where flash use is not permitted; however, the problem of noise being introduced has not been completely solved so these high ISO speeds may be of little use to crime scene photographers.

Crime scene photos are still best produced with slow film speeds such as ISO 100. Although somewhat faster film speeds may be tolerable for overall scene photos during low light situations caution should be used when using speeds faster than ISO 1200 and these speeds should not be used when examination quality photos are being captured. Experimentation is required to determine the highest tolerable ISO settings for each camera model in use since each model will produce different results. The best practice will be to utilize the lowest possible ISO, up to the maximum, necessary to properly expose the scene photos. When faced with low light situations utilize a flash or other external light source to achieve proper exposure absent exigent circumstance which prevents their use. A maximum ISO should be established in the written protocol, at the very least for examination quality photos.

Video Capability

Video capability is now a common feature on digital SLRs however its usefulness may be limited at crime scenes. Digital cameras do not provide a stable platform to record crime scene video which is typically done while walking through the scene and shaky video produces un-professional results. Another problem is that the microphone usually cannot be disabled as is typical for crime scene video. Although video capability may be useful in a pinch it should not be a major factor in deciding which digital camera to purchase.

Camera Lenses

The choice of camera lens may be as important as the camera body itself. Poor quality lenses will produce sub-standard results regardless of how good the camera is that it is attached to. A professional photographer is always concerned about the quality of the lens (aka glass) and does not skimp on the lens choice. A CSI photographer will require several different lenses to properly record the various situations that will be encountered. A good quality variable zoom lens may serve well as a general purpose lens but will need to be supplemented by at least a macro lens for close up photography and a telephoto lens for special circumstances such as aerial photos. Lens quality is often judged, and rightfully so, by its speed or widest possible aperture. Lenses with wide apertures, such as f/1.4, are considered fast lenses and have more value than slower lenses.

A good quality variable zoom 28mm–70mm lens (for full frame sensor cameras) is recommended for overall scene photos. This lens limits the amount of distortion that can be introduced into photos by using too wide or too telephoto fields of view. A well trained CSI photographer will avoid wide angles and telephoto angles as much as possible when photographing a scene to avoid pin cushion and barrel distortion which can severely affect the depiction of a scene.

A high quality macro lens will also be required to properly record close up photos particularly examination quality photos such as latent print or impression evidence photos. The variable zoom lens will not be able to achieve proper focus at the very close lens to subject distances that are required for this type of close up photography. The macro lens must also have manual setting capability which will be necessary when capturing 1:1 photos.

Although a telephoto lens will not be required on routine scene investigations it can be very useful in certain situations when distance to the subject cannot be reduced. These situations include photos of evidence or features at high elevations from the ground, such as a bullet hole in the side of a building several stories high. Another common situation in crime scene photography is capturing aerial photos of exterior scenes from helicopters. In this situation a telephoto lens will be absolutely required.

Filters

A circular polarizing filter is recommended for reducing glare on surfaces such as glass or standing water. These filters can also be very useful for revealing tire marks on blacktop surfaces or blood stains on dark backgrounds.

Forensic light sources are frequently used to reveal evidence at the crime scene that is not otherwise seen in visible light. When these techniques are used it may be required to photograph fluorescence or absorption in various wavelengths of light including ultra-violet and infra-red. Special filters are needed in order to capture these photos. The most common filters will be a red barrier filter, orange barrier filter, yellow barrier filter, 18A UV filter and 80B IR filter.

Flash Systems

Although most all consumer grade digital cameras have internal pop-up flashes when it comes to professional photography a high powered external strobe flash is an absolute requirement. A professional crime scene photographer will rarely have use for the internal pop-up type flash instead choosing the external strobe flash through which subject lighting can be controlled to a much greater extent. The flash unit should have through the lens (TTL) capability and should be properly paired with the camera system. The flash will often need to be removed from the flash shoe on top of the camera in order to control the light so a flash sync cord (PC cord) or wireless controller will also be required.

For examination quality photographs a macro flash system can also be extremely helpful to produce high quality photos that reveal all of the details of the evidence being recorded. These flash systems come with adapters that allow small flash heads to be attached to the forward edge of the lens so light can be properly directed onto a subject when the camera lens is very close to the subject.

Studio Light Kits

The crime scene photographer does not have the luxury of working in a studio where good lighting is permanently installed. In contrast, more often than not, the crime scene photographer works in very poor lighting conditions. Criminals seem to enjoy carrying out their activities under cover of darkness and other incidents such as crash scenes more commonly occur at night. This being the case there is nothing that prevents the crime scene photographer from bringing their own lighting to the scene. Of course there are some practical considerations, including the availability of electrical outlets to power the lights, but even this can be overcome by using a portable generator. Many of the temporary lights that are used at an incident scene are sodium type vehicle mounted lights. These lights produce yellow hues in photos which are undesirable. Portable studio light kits are available and come in carry cases which can be transported to the scene as part of the standard equipment stocked on the crime scene response vehicle. These kits usually contain two or three individual lights and tripod stands which can be arranged at the scene and will produce daylight quality light and result in improved quality photos.

Tripods

A tripod will be a necessity for night time photography and a good quality lightweight tripod can become a CSI photographer's best friend as it holds the camera in a clean safe spot freeing up a the CSI's hands when needed. Tripods with quick release features can cost quite bit more than conventional tripods but will be well worth their cost in convenience and time savings at the crime scene. A rolling ball tripod head is also recommended to allow the photographer to quickly rotate the camera to any position needed without wasted effort.

In certain situations the CSI photographer will need to mount the camera in a stationary position over evidence on a surface. This is common when encountering footwear impressions in soil or dust. To properly record the impressions the camera must remain stationary and perfectly parallel to the surface bearing the impression. In order to accomplish this type of photo the tripod must be able to swivel to the underside of the tripod or it must have a head that can be removed and inverted. Special tripods are available for this purpose and can be well worth their weight when these types of evidence present themselves at a crime scene.

Photography Accessories

A shutter release cable will be required to capture low light photos when the camera is mounted on a tripod. These devices are available in wireless models on some digital cameras as well as wired plunger type cords.

Extra batteries for the camera and flash system as well as desktop and portable chargers are recommended. A portable charger that can be plugged into a cigarette lighter in a vehicle is recommended for those situations where outlets are not available in the field.

Photographic scales will be needed in several styles. The ABFO #2 scale designed by the American Board of Forensic Odontology has been frequently adopted as the standard when photographing small items of evidence and for recording examination quality photos. These scales should be high quality and should be validated as accurate prior to being used on casework. The National Institute of

Standards and Technology has published a study regarding the accuracy of scales used in forensic photography which provides useful information and illustrates the varying quality that may be found among manufacturers. The NIST study may be found on the NIST website at www.nist.gov/forensics/research/upload/Dimensional-Review-of-Scales-for-Forensic-Photography.pdf. Larger L shaped plastic scales will also be needed for documenting larger items of evidence and footwear impressions. Finally longer folding scales can be helpful when working with items of greater length such as tire tread impressions.

A complete set of 100 evidence markers will be required. Evidence markers are utilized as identifiers to indicate the position of the various items of evidence in photographs as well as in notes and a sketch. These markers are typically found as 3–4″ yellow colored tents which are sequentially numbered (sometimes letters are used in place of numbers). As evidence is discovered at the scene a numbered evidence marker is placed next to the item and a description of the item is sequentially recorded in the evidence list. This numbering system provides an organized method for recording each item of evidence in writing as well as depicting the location of the items on the crime scene sketch and in the scene photos. A couple of drawbacks to the common tent style design are that they are susceptible to being blown around in heavy wind and they need to be rotated when photos are taken from a side angle so that the numbered face is visible. Some of the forensic equipment suppliers now offer cone and pyramid shaped markers which have some additional wind resistance and are labeled with numbers on several different sides. Weighted evidence number sets are also available and may be useful for areas with frequently high winds. Another useful option is cardboard evidence markers which can be labeled with a permanent marker on scene.

For areas that cannot accommodate the placement of the evidence markers, such as a blood stain on a wall, adhesive labels are required. Forensic suppliers offer peel and stick evidence labels in binders making it convenient to carry full sets of adhesive labels and also making it easy to replace only the sheets that are used when re-stocking. Both the evidence markers and the adhesive labels are available with scales printed on the face making it easy to include a scale in close up photos (note that this scale should not be used in place of the ABFO scales in examination quality photos).

Miscellaneous accessories include a good quality carry case that will protect the equipment under harsh conditions and inclement weather, a gray card for determining exposure settings, white 12″ × 12× flash bounce card, a lens cleaning cloth and a large piece of black felt fabric for blocking shadows.

Forensic Mapping Equipment

The proper documentation of a crime scene is among the most demanding and critical tasks required of forensic investigators in the field. The need to thoroughly document the scene cannot be overstated. This work must be carried out by trained and qualified personnel in a well-planned methodical manner if it is to be done successfully. As part of the documentation process purposefully designed tools and equipment are required to measure the scene and to fix and record the positions of physical evidence and other important features. Once the appropriate data has been collected from the scene additional tools and equipment will be required to facilitate the preparation of diagrams, maps, 3D models and other exhibits.

The term "forensic mapping" is typically applied to the process of collecting measurement data from a crime scene using some type of electronic instrument rather than conventional tape measures. While some CSI units still utilize conventional tools such as generic tape measures and rolling distance measuring wheels to accomplish these tasks many units have turned toward technology as a way to improve these efforts. It should be anticipated that as we move along the path forward to improved forensic investigations that the use of electronic equipment which can be tested and validated will become more widespread. Equipment such as total stations and laser scanners that were once used exclusively for land surveying and engineering applications have proved to be very well suited for forensic applications. This type of equipment has the capability to produce highly accurate measurements faster than could be done before. The ability for electronic instrumentation to be calibrated will also benefit agencies who seek accreditation for their crime scene investigation operations. Calibration and validation are requirements for units that seek accreditation under ISO 17025 or ASCLAD LAB standards. The process of acquiring forensic mapping equipment and training investigators to a high level of proficiency in their use requires commitment, dedication, funding and time. It is not a process that can be left to the last minute and then be expected to be successfully implemented.

The publication released in 2013 titled "Crime Scene Investigation, A Guide for Law Enforcement" (available online at www.nist.gov/forensics/upload/Crime-Scene-Investigation.pdf) is the result of a partnership of the National Institute of Standards and Technology, National Institute of Justice, Bureau of Justice Assistance, and the National Forensic Science Technology Center. The 180-page guide was prepared and reviewed by noted experts and this edition has been significantly expanded since it was first published in 2000. The guide contains a wealth of information on processing techniques. Of particular importance to the task of forensic mapping is the guide's recommendation that crime scene measurements are accurate to within ¼″ and that the accuracy of all measuring devices should be ensured by comparison to a measure of certified accuracy, such as a NIST traceable ruler. Many crime scene units cannot currently state the accuracy of their scene measurements nor do they utilize NIST traceable standards to ensure accuracy. These are concepts new to CSI work but methods to achieve these standards will need to be adopted if the unit is to successfully operate in the future. Having the proper forensic mapping tools is the key to meeting these standards.

The following topics will be discussed as part of forensic mapping concerns:

- Conventional measuring tools
- Forensic mapping software
- Handheld electronic instruments
- Total stations
- Laser scanners

Conventional Measuring Tools

Although electronic instruments can improve accuracy and speed work flow there will likely always be a need for some hand held conventional measuring tools such as tape measures and calipers at a crime scene. Small items, such as a single drop of blood, may not be suitable for measuring with electronic devices and some areas will not allow line of sight for measuring with devices such as a total station or laser scanner. Tapes and rulers are also very helpful to include in photographs in order to show actual size of an object. However not all tape measures are created equal and some may have significant errors due to poor manufacturing processes. When tape measures or rulers are used they should be purchased from a manufacturer that implements high quality control standards in their manufacturing processes. One way to assure this is to purchase tape measures from manufacturers that are ISO 9000 certified. Manufacturers, just like forensic practitioners, have accreditation standards that they can utilize so that interested parties can be assured of good quality. Lufkin, Starrett, and Stanley are manufacturers that produce tape measures and rulers and are ISO 9000 certified. Decide on a single manufacturer to purchase the devices from and when purchasing the measuring tools ask the manufacturer for a certificate of tolerance. This certificate will describe the tolerance that they build the tape measure or ruler to conform to (typically +/- 1/64″). This certificate can then be filed with the unit's quality control documents. Prior to using the tape measure or ruler, and again at interim periods while it is in use, it may be necessary to validate the accuracy of the tools. Interim validations can be accomplished by using a reference standard to compare the measuring tools against. Several manufacturers (such as Lixar Tools) produce NIST traceable standards to validate the measuring tool's accuracy easily and quickly. Investigators must also be trained in a routine of inspecting the measuring tools before each use for damage, edge wear, or wear of numbers and to immediately replace any measuring tool that is not in good condition.

Another common measuring tool utilized by crime scene investigators (unfortunately) is the rolling measuring wheel. These devices are only useful for long distance measuring when a large tolerance for error is acceptable. Due to the lack of precision that the devices are handled with they cannot reliably produce the ¼″ accuracy that has been recommended by nationally recognized experts in the previously mentioned publication "Crime Scene Investigation, A Guide for Law Enforcement." For this reason rolling measuring wheels are not recommended for use to fix the position of evidence. They may not have application at a scene except when approximating measurements over very long distances, such as a route of travel, and in that case the distance should be very clearly stated as "Approximate."

Forensic Mapping Software

The following paragraphs cover the equipment used to collect positioning and measurement data at the crime scene but whichever tool is used at the scene to collect the data it will become necessary back in the office to utilize software to visualize the data and create final deliverable diagrams, maps and 3D models. Before a crime scene unit decides on purchasing forensic mapping hardware it is strongly advised to conduct research and determine which software best meets the needs of the unit and then make sure the hardware is compatible.

Diagramming software customized to forensics is offered by several different companies. Some of the software is made to quickly produce 2D diagrams from scratch using field measurements, rough sketches and notes from the scene while other products, such as Leica IMS 360 have full CADD engines similar to the robust CADD software used in the construction, architecture and engineering fields. Full CADD engines will ultimately provide more capabilities for project data. This software can import total station data and with proper code lists and symbol libraries a basic line drawing can be close to complete upon import.

With the rising popularity of laser scan point clouds several software CADD software companies have begun to offer point cloud plug-ins to their software. The plug-ins are often offered as separate purchase items and are sometimes more expensive than the basic software itself. Leica IMS 360 has a very powerful point cloud engine that can handle millions of points.

Leica IMS 360 software allows users to open point clouds within a project and create line work within the point cloud. Line work can then be exported to the 2D drawing and conversely line work in the 2D drawing can be loaded into the point cloud. The product allows point clouds collected by laser scanners to be used in animations.

Handheld Electronic Distance Measuring Tools

Handheld distance measuring devices have become very popular and can help speed up the process of collecting measurement data at a scene. But, similar to tape measures not all devices are created equal. Here again research into the quality standards that a manufacturer uses are required to ensure that the device that is purchased is capable of delivering the accuracy that is required. The Leica Disto device is a top of the line device in this category. Although the devices can be more costly than local hardware store models, they are built to much higher standards that meet ISO accreditation requirements. These devices are simple to operate but training is required to achieve high precision in the method that the devices are handled. Some of the newer devices on the market, including the Leica Disto, have the ability to capture images of the item being measured and can store measurement data in memory to be downloaded later on at the office or onsite to a tablet computer or PDA. These devices should be purchased with a factory calibration certificate and while in use can be subjected to interim validation using targets established at known distance measurements.

Total Stations

Total stations are electronic instruments used traditionally by land surveyors to record features such as topographic mapping or to layout features such as property boundaries, roads, infrastructure or buildings. More recently total station has been used by crime and crash scene investigators to record the location and positions of evidence and other important features at incident scenes. Total stations have brought a new level of accuracy to the crime scene documentation process and the availability of computer aided drafting (CAD) software designed specifically for forensics use has made it possible to quickly produce professional quality drawings.

The total station is a tripod mounted instrument which incorporates a transit (also known as a theodolite) with electronic distance measurements and typically has a built in computer for collecting data on board the instrument. Older total stations require the use of a prism to collect measurements. These instruments are aimed at a reflector prism mounted atop a rod which serves as the target for measuring. This method requires two persons; one is the operator who controls the station and the other is a rod person who moves through the scene to position the rod at the various points to be measured. Newer total stations have incorporated reflectorless technology in which the station is aimed directly at the target to be measured without the need for a reflector. This reflectorless technology brings tremendous advantage to the crime scene mapping process and it should be considered a necessity when purchasing a total station system. The most advanced total stations on the market now offer robotic models in which the robot controls the station and constantly tracks an operator who is free to move through a scene and collect measurements remotely through the use of a handheld computer and wireless communication. Robotic total stations are designed for speed and efficiency in the field and have proven to be very reliable. One drawback is that the tracking ability of the system may be negatively affected in densely wooded areas or busy urban environments where people or vehicles moving about may block the line of sight between the instrument and target. However this is easily overcome since all robotic instruments can also be used in reflector or reflectorless modes as well so when robotic tracking is not optimal the station is simply used in another mode.

Leica Geosystems recently introduced an instrument to the total station market called the Leica Multi Station which is a hybrid between a laser scanner and total station. This user friendly instrument incorporates a top of the line robotic total station with imaging capability of both a wide angle and telephoto camera and laser scanning capability. A GPS module is also available to geographically fix the position of the station set up point. The laser scanning capability allows for the collection of up to 60,000 points per minute as the station scans an area selected from an on screen video display. This technology, which has already been adopted by some units, should prove extremely useful in forensic mapping as the scene can be quickly and accurately mapped using the robotic total station features and then areas of significant importance can be scanned and recorded in high resolution. The high resolution scans will bring big benefits if reconstruction becomes necessary later on. The imaging capability can attach photos to the measurement points to show exactly what was measured and capture panoramic photos of wide areas.

There are many manufacturers who produce excellent quality total station equipment including Leica, Nikon, Top Con, Sokkia and Trimble. Perhaps the most important aspect to consider when choosing a total station is whether the manufacturer has software which is specifically designed for forensic use. Although there are many third-party software solutions available for forensics they may not all work equally well across different manufacturers brands. Another important consideration is whether the data files collected by the total station instrument can be easily shared and imported into the desktop CAD software which is to be used to assemble the data from the scene into a final finished diagram. Many different file formats are in use and not all are compatible with each other.

Training will be required no matter what instrument or software is chosen and for the training to be effective it must be specifically designed for forensic users. A training program may be well-designed for surveyors and engineers but it will not be very well suited to forensic mapping as there are many differences in the workflows and end uses of the information.

Laser Scanners

The most recently adopted technology for recording accurate measurements at a crime scene is the laser scanner. This instrument has several unique characteristics that seem to be perfectly matched to the tasks involved in documenting a crime scene. Unlike the other tools available for this purpose the laser scanner allows the scene to be *objectively* recorded in an extremely through manner. Typical scene documentation requires the investigator to subjectively photograph and measure various items within the scene but the laser scanner has the capability to measure everything in a 360 degree field of view and can supplement those measurements with high resolution panoramic photos. The result is a three dimensional depiction of the scene which allows highly accurate analysis at any time in the future.

A 3D laser scanner is a positioning system that projects a laser beam out to a target surface and then receives and records characteristics of the beam reflected from the surface back to the scanner to create a data point or "point." This point has a three dimensional coordinate position relative to the scanners position in space. The laser scanner automatically repeats the process of collecting points very rapidly until it has swept across an entire field of view. Within minutes literally tens of millions of measurable points can be captured. The points are assembled into a point cloud which is viewed similar to a 3D model.

Terrestrial laser scanners were first introduced in the field around 1997. Since that time they have become an efficient and reliable instrument in the land surveying and engineering fields. They are often relied upon for the most demanding measuring tasks in critical processes such as power plant and infrastructure design and construction. Today many law enforcement agencies have adopted laser scanning technology as a way to improve their scene documentation techniques with cutting edge technology. Many in the forensics field have recognized the unique usefulness and relative ease of operation of these systems and the tremendous advantage they bring to scene investigations. Literally hundreds of agencies now deploy scanners to their scene investigations as a routine.

Laser scanners combine the collection of 3D measurable point clouds with panoramic photos and collect data at the scene in a much more objective manner than any other method since everything within the 360 degree field of view is photographed and measured. All of the other measuring tools routinely used at crime scenes require an operator to make subjective decisions on what objects, surfaces, or features should be measured (and consequently, what will not be measured). The benefit of this objective documentation is realized when unanticipated questions arise after the scene investigation has been completed since it is possible to virtually return to the scene and answer the questions quickly and accurately. Additionally, since accurate measurements can be obtained in a virtual environment less contact with the scene is required of the scene investigators. Non-contact measurements result in reduced risk of evidence contamination and, with experience, can reduce the time spent on scene.

Another unique feature with laser scanning is the ability to repeat measurement results and determine the error rate in the measurements obtained. In this manner measurements that fall outside of a tolerable margin of error may be recognized and discarded. It is important that the crime scene technicians know the manufacturers' published 3D positional accuracy of their instrument and that the accuracy has been validated prior to its being used at the scene. Leica Geosystems produces a scanning artifact that is calibrated by the National Institute of Standards and Technology (NIST) and when included in scene scans can be used as a tool to perform interim validations of the scanning equipment at the scene and to check the accuracy of measurements within the software environment. This scanning artifact called a Leica Twin Target Pole is used in a similar fashion as a ABFO scale may be used in a photograph to prove true size.

There are several manufacturers of 3D laser scanners but only a few specifically market to the forensic user and currently only Leica Geosystems has a dedicated department to handle sales, training, software and service for forensic customers. Laser scanner technology is expensive and may exceed the normal budgets of crime scene units, particularly at smaller agencies. Grants may be available for equipment such as laser scanners depending on the location's need and intended use for the equipment. Regardless of the cost, the technology is too valuable to crime scene investigation to be overlooked.

Point cloud software is the power behind laser scanning. Similar to total station a laser scanner will require field software to run the scanner equipment and desktop software to visualize and analyze the data that is collected. Purchasing equipment from one manufacturer and software from another can lead to problems in the data management process so it is advisable to choose a manufacturer that provides a complete solution of hardware, software, training and support when making a decision on which laser scanner to purchase.

Scene Processing Equipment and Supplies

Once scene documentation has been completed the crime scene investigator searches and processes the crime scene. Special equipment is required to facilitate the crime scene search so the discovery of probative evidence can be maximized. Once items are discovered additional tools and supplies may be needed to recover, mark and package the evidence. During the processing time period additional equipment may be required to protect the evidence and shelter the investigative team.

Scene processing equipment includes the following items of equipment and hardware that are reusable in nature:

- Scene lighting and flashlights
- Forensic light sources
- Impression evidence equipment
- Fingerprint supplies
- Ballistic trajectory equipment
- Metal detection, sifting and digging equipment

Flashlights and Scene Lighting

A powerful and reliable flashlight is without question the most useful tool a crime scene investigator can bring to a scene. There is simply no substitute for a strong white light when working a scene. Even scenes that occur in daylight will still have areas of shadows that need illumination from time to time and a good light can be used as oblique light when searching for items such as footwear impressions. LED technology has allowed manufacturers to produce rechargeable flashlights in compact sizes but still output some very bright and intense light. Each crime scene investigator should be equipped with good quality flashlight and all crime scene response vehicles should be equipped with chargers for the lights. It will be an obvious advantage to select a single model for use by all investigative personnel to allow for sharing of common charging stations. Spare bulbs should also be stocked in the crime scene vehicles in the event replacement is needed onsite.

Poor lighting is a frequently encountered issue at crime scenes. Criminals seem to prefer to carry out their work in poorly lit areas benefiting from the cover of darkness. While working in the dark may provide substantial benefit to the criminal it is a serious hindrance to the crime scene investigators who are responsible to sift through the often chaotic scenes that they leave behind. Since many scenes exist in poorly lit indoor areas, or occur outside during the night hours, the only way to efficiently process the scenes is to bring along equipment to illuminate the scene while the processing is underway.

Scene lighting is provided in two ways: through electric powered lights which are set up to illuminate wide areas or rooms, and flashlights used for illuminating small areas where an investigator is focused or areas that the electric lights may not reach such as underneath a bed.

Specially made scene lights are available for public safety use from several different manufacturers. The lights chosen must be rated for use outdoors and in wet locations as they will be exposed to the weather at various points. They should also be rugged and have protected bulbs to prevent breakage and risk of injury. Models with a tripod support system are also recommended since there will not always be convenient areas to suspend lights from available at the scene. Halogen lights and LED lights produce very bright light that can flood an area very well and are available in specially made telescoping tripod models for public safety. Of course a main concern for the lighting system is having an electrical power supply and extension cords. A well-designed crime scene vehicle may include a generator which can power the lights and extension cords can be stored on reels in the vehicle. The extension cords must be rated for exterior use in wet locations similar to the lights themselves.

If a generator is not available in the response vehicle then a portable gas powered generator(s) will be required particularly when scene are found in remote locations. Portable generators come in many sizes and are rated according to their power output. Since the size and weight of the generator is directly proportionate to the power output a compromise needs to be struck so that the generator provides sufficient power for its purpose without being too large to be moved into remote areas. A minimum of 2,000 watts is recommended for most crime scene applications in order to power items commonly used at a scene including, several lights, fans, small power tools, a laptop and printer. A 2,000 watt generator will typically weigh less than 50 pounds and have a single handle for one person to carry. Larger units will typically require more than one person to move unless they are equipped with wheels and even with wheels they may be difficult to move into wooded areas.

Some generators use an inverter that allows the engine to run at slower RPMs increasing the efficiency and reducing the noise level. Inverter generators produce cleaner power and may be better suited to power some of the sensitive equipment utilized at a crime scene; however, they are considerably more expensive. Honda produces a line of inverter generators which have an optional 500 watt halogen flood light that can be permanently attached directly to the unit making it easier to provide portable light to an area. The Honda EU2000i is reliable unit that is available with the light kit for between US$1,500–2,000 dollars. The unit produces enough power to operate the light as well as to power some other small tools and accessories at the scene.

Forensic Light Sources

It is a recognized that many types of forensic evidence at a crime scene, such as stains from saliva or seminal fluid, can be invisible to the naked eye or may be located on items where the color of the surface obscures the presence of the evidence. Therefore, forensic light sources (also known as alternate light sources) are used to search for and reveal evidence that may not be readily visible to the crime scene investigator while using conventional lights such as flashlights. In many cases it is critically important that a good quality forensic light is deployed before determining whether or not all possible evidence has been discovered.

Forensic light sources allow the crime scene investigator to take advantage of the fluorescent properties which are inherent to many different types of forensic evidence. However since different items produce fluorescence at varying wavelengths a light source that has the capability to be tuned to various wavelengths is required.

Until recently shortwave ultra-violet (UV) lights were frequently used at crime scenes since many biological fluids will fluoresce when exposed to UV light. This is no longer recommended as shortwave UV is particularly harmful to DNA. Instead most modern forensic lights produce various wavelengths of light that are in the long wave UV and near UV range. Infra-red (IR) and near IR wavelengths also have some applications at crime scenes although they are limited and are more commonly used in laboratory applications such as questioned document examination.

Forensic Lights for CSI work can be broken down into two distinct categories; handheld models, and bench top models. Handheld models certainly are beneficial to the CSI since they are lightweight, portable, and do not require an external power source. Traditionally drawbacks to handheld lights were that they were usually not tunable to different wavelength settings and had they limited intensity. Recently manufacturers have worked to solve these issues by taking advantage of high quality optics, LEDs, and rechargeable lithium ion batteries. Many of the handheld units now come with interchangeable heads that can be quickly swapped at the scene to allow many different wavelength options. A white light setting can also be utilized as a very intense light for more routine searching and for using oblique lighting techniques when searching for items such as footwear impressions. Bench top models will still outperform the intensity of most handheld lights, and therefore will reveal more evidence (at least theoretically). However it may not be practical to utilize these larger heavier units in the field and a power source may not be readily available since they require line voltage as a power source.

There are many different manufacturers and suppliers for forensic light sources. Some very good quality units are available through Foster & Freeman, Rofin, and Spex Forensics. A good quality system from these manufacturers can be quite expensive and typically fall within the range of US$5,000 – 7,500. Some of the bench top light sources will exceed US$10,000. Good quality light sources are capable of high intensity light output within narrow bands of wavelengths. The light produced should be shadow free and be capable of covering wide areas during a search or be focused to a more intense beam when performing close up work.

Single wavelength flashlight type handheld lights can be found for fewer than US$100 but these will not suffice for searching a crime scene for forensic evidence as they do not have the required intensity to reveal many biological evidence stains. An inexperienced person may search a scene using an inferior light source and conclude there is no evidence present only to be followed by an experienced person with a good quality light who may discover troves of biological stains that would have been otherwise missed. Since the goal of processing a crime scene is to collect the maximum amount of probative evidence then the only way to ensure that this occurs when searching with a forensic light source is to rely on high quality products. The lower quality and inexpensive light sources should be reserved for tasks such as working with fluorescent fingerprint powders.

Impression Evidence Equipment and Supplies

Impression evidence left behind by tool marks, tire treads and footwear impressions is often encountered at the crime scene and once they are properly photographed they may require special equipment and supplies for recovery. Impression evidence is typically fragile in nature and may contain both class characteristics and individual characteristics. Class characteristics can help to identify the group which the item that made the impression belongs to (such as a size 9 right athletic shoe). In some cases individual characteristics are also present which allow for comparison of the questioned impression evidence to a known recovered item to analyze if an exact match can be made. Impressions are either two dimensional or three dimensional and recovery methods depend on the type. Two dimensional impressions are impressions created when some contaminate, such as grease or blood, is present on the surface of a shoe or tire and it is then transferred onto another surface. Three dimensional impressions include tool marks in soft wood or door jambs and footwear and tire treads impressed in dirt or snow. Two dimensional impressions on immovable surfaces are typically photographed and then lifted. Three dimensional impressions are photographed and then require casting to record the impression features.

Casting of tool mark impressions is typically accomplished by using a silicone based compound. These compounds are available from forensic suppliers and either come in squeeze tubes or plastic tubes that are inserted into extruder guns. The kits will typically consist of two separate compounds including the casting material and a hardener additive which causes the mixture to set. The plastic extruders provide convenience as the user simply depresses a plastic plunger to dispense the proper amount of each ingredient from the tubes. As the compounds move through the nozzle of the device they are automatically mixed together and can be easily spread across the surface to be cast with disposable spatulas.

Three dimensional impression of footwear or tire treads in soil or snow need to be cast with a plaster based material. Mixing spoons, stirrers, and bowls are required and special hardeners and sprays are also sometimes utilized. Once the plaster is mixed a casting frame may need to be placed around the impression to create small retaining walls to hold the plaster mix as it sets and dries. Pre-assembled casting kits are available and contain all of the materials needed to recover this type of evidence. After use the kit is cleaned and the mixing material can be replaced so the kit can be reused time and again.

Footwear impressions in dust are a two dimensional impression which can be an extremely delicate type of evidence that requires an electrostatic dust lifter for recovery. Electrostatic dust lifters produce a charge that is applied to a sheet of Mylar film that is gently placed on top of the dust impression. Static electricity is produced causing the dust impression to adhere to the Mylar film which can then be recovered and examined in a laboratory. Older electrostatic lifters came assembled in small suitcase sized boxes and required connection to an electric outlet for power. Newer models are handheld palm sized devices and work on 9 volt battery power. A word of caution on storage for these units: since they do not get daily use leaving batteries in the unit can lead to leakage and corrosion that can destroy the instrument. Always remove the batteries after using the device and returning it to its storage location. Electrostatic lifters are available in kits which contain the required accessories including a ground plate, rubber roller, and Mylar film.

Expendable supplies are also needed in the recovery of impression evidence. Spare plaster mixing compound is required to re-stock the casting kit after each use. An innovative product that is available from forensic suppliers is pre-packaged plaster mixes. These kits are made by enclosing a pre-measured amount of plaster compound in a plastic bag along with an inner sealed bladder containing water. To mix the casting compound the inner water bladder is ruptured by applying pressure to the bag and the bag is then vigorously shaken to mix the compound. Although the kits are very convenient some investigators have reported mixed results and report that the compound sets up too quickly. No matter the type of plaster mixture that is used the cast will generate heat as it cures. This presents a problem for casting impressions in snow. The solution for this problem is to coat the impression with an aerosol spray wax prior to pouring in the casting mixture. Snow wax is typically packaged with casting kits but can be purchased separately from forensic suppliers to re-stock as necessary.

Another single use item that will be required to recover two dimensional impressions is gel lifters. These gelatin based sheets are available in black and white and come with a protective acetate cover. To recover a two dimensional impression the acetate is peeled away from the gel lifter to expose an adhesive coating before the lifter is applied over the surface containing the impression. A rubber roller is then needed to smooth the gel lifter prior to peeling it away from the surface and replacing the protective acetate cover.

Trace Evidence Tools

Trace evidence in the form of hair, fiber or paint is frequently transferred between persons or objects at the crime scene and may be used to corroborate other facts of the case. Trace evidence often exhibits class characteristics that may not by themselves identify a suspect but when analyzed can be placed into a group which either includes or excludes a potential suspect. Perhaps the most common method used in searching for trace evidence is the forensic light or a powerful white light source which have been previously discussed. However other tools are sometimes of value when processing a scene for trace evidence including vacuums, tweezers, forceps, and scrapers. Tweezers and forceps can be either single use disposable items or stainless steel reusable models. If reusable tools are used to collect samples they must be decontaminated between and before each use.

Trace evidence vacuums are used to process larger areas of a scene where hair or fiber evidence is suspected to reside. They may also be used in certain instances to recover traces of residue from explosives or hazardous substances. The vacuum is a compact electrical device available from forensic suppliers with a detachable hose and a replaceable internal filter. The internal filter cartridges are available in HEPA filters when being used for residue type collections. When collecting evidence at a scene an external filter canister is attached to the end of the vacuum hose while the area to be processed is vacuumed. The filter canister serves as the primary filter and it allows air to pass through while trapping debris (including the suspected hair or fiber evidence) inside a clear plastic chamber. Any microscopic material or residue may pass through this filter and reside in the internal filter cartridge. After vacuuming is completed the canister is sealed and transported to the laboratory where its contents are examined. A word of caution is appropriate here. When using trace evidence vacuums a large amount of debris may be pulled from the surface and much of this debris may have been present for quite a long time prior to the incident under investigation. Sifting through all of this debris in a laboratory can take an enormous amount of time for the laboratory technician. To avoid over burdening the laboratory it is often preferred to process areas for hair or fiber evidence by tamping the area with adhesive coated tape which can then be applied to acetate sheets. Theoretically speaking, this method captures the top layer of debris which may be more likely to yield probative evidence than what may be embedded further down into a surface. Perhaps the most thorough approach may be to combine these two methods in sequence and then only proceeding to examine the vacuum filters if probative evidence is not first located in the adhesive lifts.

The recovery of hair or fiber by adhesive tamping requires some expendable supplies. Clear adhesive tape is needed to tamp the area in question. Four-inch wide rolls of tape should be used to cover a 3″ swath each time the tape is applied to the surface while allowing for a 1″ overlap to ensure complete coverage. Acetate sheets 8″ × 12″ in size are then needed so the adhesive tape can be applied to the acetate thereby sealing the samples between the tape and acetate sheet.

Paint transfers are common on hit and run incidents where paint from a vehicle is transferred from the vehicle to another vehicle or to the victim's clothing during the collision. However paint can also be transferred in many other incidents including forced entry and assaults. When suspected paint transfers are on clothing the preferred method for recovery would be for the laboratory to examine the clothing and take cuttings as appropriate but when the paint transfers are on large or immovable surfaces then the crime scene investigator will need to collect the samples by scraping. When collecting paint scrapings, be they evidence samples or known samples for comparison, it is important to collect all of the layers down to the bare surface rather than scraping off just the top layer of paint the way house painter's scraper might. To accomplish the task properly the use of a chisel shaped steel tool with a sharp flared end is recommended and should be included in each investigators kit.

Fingerprint Processing Supplies

One of the primary processing activities at most crime scenes is fingerprint processing. Although DNA has proven to be a tremendous tool for forensic identification, fingerprints are still the primary method to positively identify people within the criminal justice system. Although statistical studies recommended in the 2009 National Academy of Science Report on Forensics may be warranted in this field, fingerprints benefit from well-established processes and systems to produce reliable identifications in a timely cost efficient manner and without the privacy concerns that surround an individual's DNA profile. Fingerprint identifications from crime scene evidence also benefit by leveraging the large available database of known prints that is available in Automated Fingerprint Identification Systems. Therefore, it can be expected that fingerprint processing will remain a primary activity for the crime scene investigator for the foreseeable future.

An interesting development in fingerprint powders is the emergence of nano-engineered particles for use in processing powders. These products are still new to the market and will require additional research and development but if they are successfully implemented they add new dimensions to the value of latent print evidence. The powder is smaller than conventional powders and the manufacturer suggests it can more effectively define a latent print image which in itself offers a benefit. However, the more interesting aspect of the nanotechnology is that when the developed prints are examined with mass spectrometry it can identify metabolites excreted from the body that can indicate prescription or illicit drug use, nicotine from smoking, and it can detect bio markers to give indication of the donors age, sex, and ethnicity. This information can obviously be very beneficial to investigators and can help to identify or eliminate potential suspects. The powders are currently available from forensic suppliers in multiple colors as well as conventional and magnetic forms.

Fingerprint processing at a crime scene requires a well-stocked latent print processing kit. Conventional processing requires the application of fingerprint powders using a brush as an applicator. Powders are available in many different colors and are selected based on the need to create a contrast between the color of the surface being processed and any developed prints. Of course black and white powder are the standards but other colors can be equally or more effective depending on the scene conditions. Silver black is a useful color as the developed print appears silver against a dark background and black against a light colored background. When the background is confused by multiple colors or patterns it is sometimes preferable to utilize fluorescent powders to effectively eliminate the background from view while observing the fluorescence of any developed prints in a darkened area utilizing a forensic light source. Whichever color powder is used it needs to be applied to the surface with a brush. Fingerprint brushes are available in several types with feather brushes and fiberglass bristle brushes being the most popular. Brushes also come in various sizes and it may be good practice to have large brushes available when processing large areas and smaller brushes to handle more delicate items.

As DNA, and in particular "Touch DNA," continues to play an increasingly important role in forensics concerns have begun to arise regarding how fingerprint processing can be carried out at the scene without risking cross contamination via the application of powder using a single brush across multiple surfaces. Studies indicate that although the risk appears low it is possible to transfer DNA from a surface onto a fingerprint brush during processing and it is obviously not practical to decontaminate a fingerprint brush. One part of the solution is to sequence the scene processing so that all of the DNA samples are collected at the scene prior to commencing fingerprint processing and to use a new brush at each scene. But, this still leaves the question of how to treat DNA evidence that is inevitably discovered during or post latent print processing. We must also consider that the latent impressions themselves may contain touch DNA. To help address these issues, forensic suppliers are now offering disposable single use powders and brushes for latent print processing. Although it may be an expensive proposition to dispose of these every time a separate area is processed within the scene it may be the best option if we are to continue to benefit from DNA and its advances and produce evidence in as pristine a condition as possible.

Magnetic fingerprint powder is a separate type of processing powder for latent prints. Magnetic powder contains ferrous filings and it is applied through the use of a magnetic wand. The powder adheres in a clump to the tip of the wand which is then used to brush the material across a surface. While conventional powder does not adhere well to non-porous surfaces the magnetic powder is much more successful, especially if the item was recently handled. Magnetic powders can be utilized on any non-metallic surface except those that require the wand to be held upside down since the powder will not adhere to the wand if it inverted. Like conventional powders, magnetic powder is available in multiple colors including fluorescent ones. Applicator wands typically resemble a ball-point pen but they are available in wider sizes for processing larger surface areas. Since, unlike brushes, the magnetic wand can be decontaminated it may be cleaned and reused between scenes.

Once developed latent prints need to be recovered by lifting them from the surface usually with adhesive tape. Lifting tape is available in several widths between one and four inches. The wider rolls are useful for handling palm prints while the narrower rolls are easier to manage when dealing with single finger marks. Once the latent print is lifted the adhesive tape needs to be applied to a fingerprint backing card. Backing cards are available with black or white mounting surfaces and are chosen based on which color will contrast best with the lifted impression. A substitute for lifting tape and backing cards is a hinge lifter. Hinge lifters have a clear adhesive cover over a black or white backing. To lift the print the clear adhesive film is peeled away from one side of the backing and applied over the print as the backing is folded behind. The print is then lifted and the clear adhesive film applied back onto the card. Hinge lifters are convenient although somewhat more expensive.

Sometimes latent print images are developed on surfaces that are not very conducive to lifting with tape either because of contours or textures on the surface. The example of a print on a curved edge of a door knob presents the likelihood that the lifting tape will crease once it is applied and the crease might obscure an otherwise valuable print. To solve this issue a CSI can utilize either the same silicone casting material that is used to cast tool mark impressions or might choose a rubberized clear lifting tape (sometimes referred to as its brand name Diff Lift) that can conform to contours much better than typical adhesive tape.

In some instances chemically treating surfaces may produce improved results over utilizing powders. There are many different chemical processes that are effective for developing latent print impressions but only a few are suitable for use outside of the laboratory. CSIs frequently use two processes at the crime scene to chemically develop prints; they are cyanoacrylate (superglue) fuming and small particle reagent.

Cyanoacrylate is the same substance used in superglue and it is well-established that when heated the gases produced polymerizes with residues in latent print impressions. The result is a developed print that is fixed to the surface and can be further chemically enhanced and photographed or dusted and lifted. To use the super glue fuming method the superglue and the item to be processed for latent prints must be enclosed in a chamber. Moderate heat is then applied to the superglue to turn it to a gaseous state and the item is observed for several minutes to see if impressions can be visualized. Once the item has been adequately exposed to the superglue it is removed from the chamber and examined. To facilitate this process in the field forensic suppliers offer compact folding chambers constructed either of Plexiglas, or more recently, a snap up metal frame that supports a disposable plastic cover as well as pre-packaged superglue and chemicals to create an exothermic reaction to generate the required heat.

Small particle reagent (SPR) is a chemical process to develop prints and it is particularly useful on items that are, or were, wet when the prints were deposited. Small particle reagent consists of aqueous solution of water and detergent containing molybdenum sulfide. At a crime scene the solution is sprayed onto the item suspected to contain prints and allowed to flow over the surface before being washed away by a clean water spray leaving behind the developed prints. SPR can be mixed in a laboratory and is commercially available from forensic suppliers as pre-packaged kits that are mixed together on demand at the scene.

Some other items that will be required in a fingerprint kit include printer's ink, an ink slab, roller and ten print cards for recording inked impressions of persons who have legitimate access to the crime scene area so that their prints can be compared to the crime scene impressions and any matches can be eliminated from the investigation. Also useful to include will be a magnifying glass, a hands free flashlight, scissors and permanent markers.

Ballistic and Bloodstain Evidence Equipment

When blood has been shed at the scene of a crime bloodstain patterns may be present and require special documentation and analysis. Analysis of blood stain patterns by properly trained experts can reveal important facts regarding the sequence and location of certain events within the overall incident. Analysis may also lead to better decision making in the bloodstain sample collection process. Much of the equipment used for bloodstain pattern analysis can also be utilized for ballistic trajectory analysis therefore the equipment needs for these two specific functions have been combined.

Bloodstain analysis uses trigonometric calculations at the scene which require a scientific calculator to make the process efficient. Many smartphones now offer scientific calculators as a software application but it is still recommended to have a calculator on hand.

Shooting incidents are the most common type of violent scene investigated by crime scene units in the United States. Ballistic damage and firearm related evidence is often left behind at the scene and the analysis of these items can lead to many conclusions regarding the facts of the occurrence. Equipment needed for these types of investigations includes tools for determining trajectory and for the safe handling of firearms.

Trajectory determination requires the analysis of ballistic damage at the scene in an effort to determine the directionality of the projectile that caused the damage so one can infer the approximate point of origin from which the weapon was fired. Aluminum rods are used as penetration rods that are inserted into bullet holes. The protruding rod can then be used to measure horizontal and vertical angles from the surface struck. Laser trajectory kits are also available allowing a laser pointer device to be screwed onto threads in the end of the trajectory rod so the laser light can be projected to illustrate the path of the bullet. In the past investigators have been known to create their own trajectory kits with wood dowels or gun cleaning rods. And then attach a presentation type laser pointer to the end. Problems can occur with these methods, particularly if no validation is carried out prior to using the equipment. Wood dowels are prone to warping and gun cleaning rods are typically not co-aligned to ensure they are straight and accurate. Trajectory kits are available from several manufacturers and include the threaded rods, plastic cones that can be used for centering the rods in bullet holes when appropriate, colored string spools that can be used to visualize trajectories over short distances, and co-aligned laser pointers. It is important that the lasers are co-aligned to ensure they are straight and accurate and procedures should be put in place to conduct interim validations in the field to ensure they remain so before each use.

Lasers and string are very useful for visualizing bullet paths as well as bloodstain trajectory at the scene but other tools are required to determine the angle of impact on both the horizontal and vertical axis. A digital protractor, such as the "Pro 360" is recommended for measuring the angle relative to the horizontal plane. Good quality digital protractors are available with NIST certifications of accuracy for an added cost. To measure the vertical aspect of the impact angle a zero edge plastic protractor may be used. The NIST certified digital protractor can be used to validate the accuracy of the plastic protractor prior to its first use and at interim periods while it is in service. An additional measuring tool required for documenting ballistic damage as well as blood stains is a digital caliper. Digital calipers can measure the inside and outside dimensions of ballistic impact marks as well as the depth when necessary. Digital calipers are also available with NIST certification.

Gunshot residue testing can be carried out on samples collected from suspected shooters hands in an effort to determine if the person fired a gun. In this test samples are collected either by mild acid swabbing or sticky tape lifts from certain areas of the hands. The usefulness of the test is the subject of some debate since what can be said when positive results are obtained is typically that the person fired a gun, handled a gun, or was in close proximity of a gun when it was discharged. Since the conclusion is somewhat ambiguous the test is sometimes determined to be not worth the cost and effort. When the test is to be carried out a GSR collection kit will be required to process the subject's hands.

Another important piece of equipment that should be available at the scene to ensure safety is a firearm unloading station. Portable and bench mounted units are available and can be installed in response vehicles to provide a safe place to unload weapons that are recovered at the crime scene. Many of the firearms encountered at crime scenes are in poorly maintained condition and some may have been modified in an amateur fashion thereby presenting a potentially dangerous condition for the investigators that must handle and examine these weapons. A properly designed and installed unloading station can safely contain a bullet should one be accidentally discharged during unloading. These devices are manufactured to contain specific caliber and bullet type and should be chosen according to the needs. Many of the bench type models are designed to contain handgun rounds rather than high powered rifle ammunition. The devices once installed should be clearly labeled so the user can easily determine if it is appropriate for any particular weapon.

Metal Detectors, Sifting and Digging Equipment

The search for evidence at outdoor crime scenes often times centers around small ballistic evidence in the form of metal jacketed bullets and shell casings that are dispersed at the scene and may be concealed by grass, brush and soil. In addition other weapons, especially knives, are constructed of metal and may be concealed at outdoor scenes. These crime scene searches may be aided by the use of metal detectors which can locate metallic objects below the surface. Garrett is a popular brand of metal detectors and the manufacturer makes a CSI model. Although a specially designed model is not required for CSI work it is desirable to have a depth gauge and sensitivity adjustments built into the unit. The depth gauge will allow the operator to quickly determine if the object being detected is of interest or not and the sensitivity adjustment will allow users to exclude metal objects which are considerably smaller than what is being sought. For instance if the object of the search is to locate a knife then the operator can use a relatively low sensitivity setting to avoid having to stop and investigate much smaller objects such as a paperclip.

Crime scene investigation occasionally involves excavation of clandestine grave sites as well as a search for evidence which may have become buried below the ground surface either due to the passage of time or during an intentional act to conceal it and prevent its discovery. Arson and explosion scenes present additional types of crime scenes where evidence is often concealed and needs to be dug out and sifted. When these types of scenes are encountered backhoes and power tools risk disturbing or destroying the evidence therefore hand tools must be utilized to excavate the evidence in a manner that follows archeological dig methods.

Tools for excavation include digging shovels, soil scoops, trowels, rakes for clearing and combing a surface, brooms and brushes and a pick ax for chopping tree roots and clearing stones. Digging shovels are available in two types, round points and square blades. Several of each will be required during a clandestine grave excavation. Scoop shovels have a broad wide flare and a square tip; they are terrible for digging but are quite useful when moving loose debris. Shovels should be made of steel to ensure that they are durable and can be properly cleaned and decontaminated between and before each use. Once the excavation process encounters evidence then the larger tools are switched out for handheld trowels, brushes and soil scoops and several of each of these items are recommended. The brushes should be disposable types since they are often very difficult to decontaminate and reusing them may risk cross contamination between scenes.

While larger, readily visible, items of evidence may be discovered during an excavation many items of evidence will be very small and embedded in soil. These items will be easily missed unless the soil is properly sifted as it is removed from the dig site. Sifting screens are used for this purpose and they are available in several different styles and sizes and several different screens may be required on various crime scene investigations. Some sifters are made to mount on a stand and are operated by two persons while others are smaller and made for single person operation. As soil is loaded into the screens the investigator rocks them back and forth allowing the soil to pass through while any items larger than the screen openings are captured for visual examination. Sifting screens are available with different size openings. If the subject of the search was perhaps a shell casing then a screen size of ½″ would be appropriate but if the subject of the search was say a fired bullet which may have fragmented then ¼″ or even 1/16″ screen size may be more appropriate.

Evidence Collection Supplies

Evidence collection and packaging supplies are expendable items that are used at the crime scene to collect, label, package and seal evidence in a way that minimizes the potential for destruction, degradation or contamination of the evidence while it is transported to the laboratory or placed in storage. Much of this material will be used to collect and handle DNA evidence in an acceptable manner. Evidence collection supplies typically have a long shelf life and can be purchased in bulk quantities provided clean dry storage space is available for stocking. This category consumes a large portion of a unit's operating budget and adequate stock of supplies must always be maintained.

Evidence Packaging

With a few exceptions (which we will cover shortly) evidence that is in a solid physical state and is of a manageable size, should be packaged in paper envelopes, paper bags or cardboard boxes while evidence in a liquid state should be packaged in jars and cans. Large or irregularly shaped items may be wrapped in Kraft paper. Kraft paper is also used to cover work surfaces and to layer protective sheets between folds in clothing or other materials that contain suspected biological stains. Plastic bags are useful for some types of evidence so long as there is absolutely no potential necessity for DNA testing to be performed on the item, such as a soil sample. Evidence that may contain DNA requires that it be air dried and then placed inside paper packaging which allows the evidence to breathe and reduces the possibility that bacteria can form inside the package and damage or destroy the DNA. With advancements in touch DNA (also known as low copy number) the potential for the recovery of DNA, either now or in the future, is possible from many items that are recovered so it is incumbent on the CSI to ensure the evidence is packaged so that it can be stored and remain as pristine as possible.

Paper bags and boxes used for evidence are not sterile (neither are the crime scenes where CSIs operate) but these items must be as clean as possible and always be used to package a single item during a single use. Always remember the goal of collecting as much probative evidence as possible in as pristine condition as possible. Incidents have occurred where DNA profiles have been developed from evidence only to be eventually traced back to a manufacturer's employee or some other individual who had contact with the material prior to it being used to package evidence. In these cases the contamination of the evidence was set in motion before the crime was even committed. Records should be kept of purchase and supplier information so in the event of suspected packaging contamination the issue can be properly investigated. All packaging must also be of good quality and of sufficient strength to prevent rips and tears.

Evidence bags and boxes are available from forensic suppliers with pre-printed labels that can be useful so that the items are clearly recognized as evidence but it may be necessary to customize the label printing to avoid having irrelevant captions that are left blank only to be construed as an omission by others who view the evidence.

To avoid the loss of flammables and hydrocarbons, and prevent the breakdown of plastic packages from solvents in accelerants, arson evidence must be packaged in clean metal cans (unused paint cans) or in nylon bags. The metal cans have tight fitting lids which should be kept fitted on the cans until they are needed for use to prevent environmental contamination from occurring during storage in a vehicle. When needed the lids can be removed by prying and then replaced after the evidence is placed inside. The nylon bags should be heat sealed to create an airtight package and prevent evaporation.

Once the evidence has been packaged the packaging will require marking, sealing and labeling. Evidence labels should contain relative case information, a unique identifying number, the name of the person collecting the evidence and a concise description of the evidence contained within.

Evidence that is suspected to contain blood or any other biological material must be clearly labeled with a bio-hazard warning label. Any openings in the package must be securely sealed with a tamper evident seal. This is typically accomplished by sealing the package with evidence tape and then signing across the seal with a permanent ink marker. If the seal is broken it should be readily evident to anyone who examines the package.

Insect activity may also be present at a scene which contains a deceased body. Insects, in particular flies and their larvae, can also be useful in helping to determine the time of death as well as whether a body was moved between scenes. Collection of the insects and larvae require some special collections tools and chemicals for use as a preservative. Forensic entomology kits are available pre-packaged with the required tool for this type of evidence collection when warranted.

DNA Collection Supplies

Swabs are used to collect samples from non-porous surfaces where a visible stain is present or there was suspected contact. Traditionally a simple cotton swab was used for collecting DNA which after collection needed to be laid out to be air dried before being packaged in paper envelopes. Laboratories have now produced swab kits for use at crime scenes which are self-contained in their own housings. Bode Technology produces the SecurSwab DNA Collector line. These swabs are contained in a plastic tube which also contains an indicating desiccant to ensure the swab is properly dried and prevents bacteria growth. The kits are individually wrapped and are opened on demand at the scene. Barcoded labels are included to cross label the swab, outer package and documentation. Although the cost is more than using conventional swabs the risk of contamination is reduced and there are several published reports that laboratory results improve with the use of these types of devices. Dry samples will require a small amount of sterile water to be added to the swab prior to collection of the sample. Single use sterile water ampules are available from lab and forensic suppliers. After collection is completed the swabs are sealed in a paper envelope which is marked, labeled and sealed in the same manner as described in the previous paragraph.

When the sample to be collected is located on a porous surface it will be necessary to either collect the entire item if practical or to cut the sample from the surface. Cutting can be accomplished with a disposable scalpel. Plastic scalpels are available in individually sealed single use packs. After a sample is cut the scalpel is disposed of into a sharps container. Depending on size the sample may need to be secured by using clean filter paper folded into a druggists fold before it is placed into a larger outer package which should be a paper envelope for small cuttings or a paper bag for larger pieces.

Buccal swabs are required when collecting known DNA samples from persons who may be suspects, convicted criminals, victims, or persons who had legitimate access to the crime scene and need to be eliminated from the crime scene evidence samples. Buccal swabs are collected by swabbing the inside of the cheek in a prescribed fashion. This is sometimes accomplished by having the person being swabbed perform the task while being constantly observed by the investigator. The swab is then sealed in an inner envelope before the investigator assumes custody and seals the inner envelope inside an outer envelope and marks, labels and seals the package. Forensic suppliers offer kits designed for buccal swab collection which contain the swabs, instructions, and required accessories in a single kit.

Reagents and Field Tests

Reagents and field tests used in the field vary from unit to unit but nearly every crime scene unit has a need to utilize some reagents to search for and recognize evidence. As discussed under quality assurance in Chapter 10 of this book, these supplies require rigid management since they may have a known shelf life and special storage requirements.

Common reagents used at the crime scene include:

- Chemi-luminescent blood detection (Luminol or Bluestar)
- Presumptive blood tests (Phenolphthalein or OBTI)
- Blood stain enhancement (Amido Black and leuco crystal violet)
- Presumptive semen testing (acid phosphatase for)
- Presumptive test for lead (sodium rhodizonate) and copper (Dithiooximide)

Chemi-luminescent Blood Detection

These reagents are useful on scenes where it is believed that there was a blood shed event in a particular scene but no blood is currently visible. This may be due to the fact that the scene was cleaned prior to the arrival of authorities or weather and the passage of time have removed visible traces of blood. These reagents contain a Luminol-based formula which is an extremely sensitive test for the presence of blood. Luminol mixed with an oxidizing agent and an alkaline agent and placed in contact with blood, will emit light (chemi-luminescence). Bluestar is one Luminol-based formula that has become popular for use at crime scenes and is easier to use than earlier products that required mixing several ingredients at the scene. Bluestar has pre-formulated tablets which makes the mixing process easy. The tablets are added to a sealed bottle containing liquid reagent and allowed to dissolve. A spray pump is then attached to the bottle and the solution is ready for use. Bluestar will not alter DNA (repeated application may dilute DNA) and produces a stronger and longer lasting luminescence than other Luminol products.

Presumptive Blood Tests

When searching a crime scene for blood the CSI may discover visible reddish brown stains or may observe luminescence when applying Luminol-based formulas. The CSI will then need to decide whether or not the sample should be collected for submission to a laboratory. Since many substances can appear reddish brown, and false positives are sometimes encountered with Luminol applications, presumptive blood tests can add very helpful insight when deciding which samples have probative value. A positive reaction in itself is not evidence of the presence of blood but it does indicate a high probability of its presence.

A common presumptive blood test is the Kastle-Mayer test which utilizes a phenolphthalein reagent. This is a sensitive test but it is not specific to human blood. The test has the same reaction with human blood as it does with any other hemoglobin based blood. OBTI is another presumptive blood test which is a bit more specific to indicate human blood. Although OBTI does react with blood from primates it does not react to other types of blood which may be frequently encountered at crime scenes including cattle, pig, chicken, and cat and dog blood.

Blood Stain Enhancement

Blood shed at a crime scene may lead to evidence being left behind in the form of bloody impressions. These can be from footwear, patent prints, fabric pattern transfers, tire marks and other objects. The blood stains may require enhancement to develop the pattern details to a point where they can be visualized and documented and examined. The most practical reagent to use at the crime scene for this purpose is leuco crystal violet (LCV). This peroxide based reagent can be purchased as a kit and mixed at the scene on demand. The solution is then sprayed with a fine mist sprayer across the surface requiring enhancement and the LCV reacts with the hemoglobin in blood to produce a violet color. Another blood stain enhancement reagent, which is sometimes used in sequence if LCV produces poor results, is Amido Black. Amido Black is typically not applied using a spray but instead the item to be enhanced is bathed in the solution and then washed with clean water. While it is possible to accomplish this on a fixed surface at a crime scene it may be hard to contain the solution to a confined area resulting in the need for a substantial clean up. Amido Black is available in a methanol-based formula but it is highly flammable and toxic. Therefore the water based formula should be used whenever it is applied at a crime scene.

Presumptive Semen Testing

When investigating sexual assault scenes the search for DNA evidence in the form of semen is often an important aspect of the crime scene processing activities. Although there are presumptive reagent tests that can be performed on suspected stains that are located at the scene it is usually preferable to instead collect the item for submission for laboratory testing if at all possible. The acid phosphatase test requires a contact transfer of the stain which could lead to issues surrounding contamination or stain dilution. An alternative is to view the stain using a forensic light source. Semen stains typically fluoresce very well under UV and blue light and, although highly presumptive, fluorescence can be considered a presumptive positive test which also avoids the need to unnecessarily manipulate the stain.

Presumptive Test for Lead and Copper

Incidents involving the discharge of a firearm often times result in ballistic damage at the crime scene. Ballistic damage takes a few different forms. Bullet holes result from a fired bullet perforating a substrate. Impact marks can result from a bullet striking a surface without passing through it (perhaps penetrating or partially penetrating into the surface) and ricochet marks result from bullets impacting the surface on an angle and deflecting off of the surface in a different direction. Sometimes it may be readily apparent that the damage observed was indeed caused by a fired bullet, as in the case of a well formed hole in plate glass with concentric and radial fractures surrounding the hole. Other times it may not be quite so easy to conclusively state whether or not a particular defect resulted from a bullet strike. This is especially true when tracking through the damage does not lead to the discovery of the projectile. In these cases presumptively testing the margins around the ballistic damage to detect the presence of metals commonly used in bullet design can be helpful in reaching a conclusion. Sodium rhodizonate is a presumptive test for the presence of lead and it is the most commonly used reagent for this purpose. Even fully jacketed bullets will typically deposit lead around the margin of a bullet hole since the bullet picks up lead from primer residue and as it travels down the barrel of the firearm. In some cases it may be helpful to determine if a jacketed bullet struck a surface as opposed to a plain lead bullet. In this instance dithiooximide (DTO) is a reagent that can presumptively identify the presence of copper (the most commonly used metal for bullet jacketing). Both of these reagents can be purchased through forensic suppliers and mixed on demand at the crime scene. They should be part of every CSIs routine scene response kit.

Support Equipment, Tools and Supplies

There are some additional miscellaneous items of equipment and supplies that will be required in some incidents for effective scene processing.

Death Investigation Scene Supplies

There are some necessary supply items to have on hand for use when a decedent's body is present at a crime scene. The body of a decedent will fall within the jurisdiction of the medical examiner or county coroner's office and in most locations a medico-legal death investigator will respond to the scene to examine the body. However, there are some instances where the CSI should work with the medico-legal investigator to ensure that any forensic evidence located on the body is properly preserved. In incidents involving firearm discharge, or where contact is suspected to have occurred between the victim and a perpetrator, the hands of the decedent may contain valuable evidence. To preserve the evidence until any evidence is collected during autopsy the hands should be covered. Paper bags are sometimes used to cover the hands by securing them at the wrists with adhesive tape. One issue with this is that fluids can penetrate the bags and contaminate the hands anyway. This exact scenario occurred during a homicide investigation in New York City where a female victim was bound with hands behind the back. The hands were covered with paper bags but during transport fluids penetrated the bags. Later a suspects DNA was recovered from underneath the fingernails of the victim but the DNA contained in the fluids overwhelmed the evidence samples and reduced the value of the evidence. To prevent this from occurring Tyvek pouches with draw strings should be used in place of the paper bags.

Another issue that should be considered is how the body is wrapped. Some morgue teams use heavy duty transport bags which are cleaned and reused between scenes. It is imperative that the decedent be placed into a new disposable water resistant body bag prior to being placed into a transport bag. CSIs should have various size body bags available for this purpose.

A thermometer is also a useful tool to have at the crime scene especially at a scene where a deceased body is located. After death bodies cool at a predictable rate. Although there are many variables this information can be used to help in determining the time of death. The medico-legal investigator will record the body temperature as well as the ambient temperature but since they may not arrive until well after the CSI it is quite possible that the scene ambient temperature will change. This is especially true when the area is ventilated to relieve foul odors. It is good practice for a CSI to record the ambient temperature upon arrival at the scene.

The thermometer should also be able to record water temperature as this will be useful in child abuse investigations involving scalding incidents.

Portable Tents, Shelters, Privacy Screens

Since crimes occur in all types of locations and all weather conditions it will sometimes be necessary to provide shelter and water for the crime scene personnel, the evidence, or both. Pop-up canopies can be very helpful to provide temporary shelter from hot sun, moderate to heavy rains or a light snow. They can also be used to provide protection for evidence and prevent spoliation between the time the evidence is discovered and the time it is able to be collected. In some cases fragile evidence or a decedent's body may need to be protected from approaching rains or direct sunlight while it is photographed, examined and documented prior to collection. The canopies can also shield sensitive evidence from prying eyes from above or television news cameras when required. Privacy barriers are also available for this purpose. Privacy barriers consist of a solid fabric that is erected around a site using a foldable light weight metal frame.

During prolonged investigations or in the event that shelter is required from cold weather conditions then full tents may be utilized. Light duty tents are available in models similar to pop-up canopies but include sidewalls. Heavy duty tents for emergency response are also available. Some of these tents, like those manufactured by Zumro and others, are heavy duty pneumatic rapid deploy models which have options to add heating and cooling equipment. This type of equipment can be quite large requiring a separate vehicle for transport and will require several people to carry and set up. However if a particular crime scene unit is one that would participate in a critical incident response where the scene investigation can span several days or weeks it may be advisable to plan for shelter to accommodate unit personnel, temporary evidence and equipment storage and the crime scene command functions.

Power Tools, Hand Tools, Ladders

A few power tools and a good set of hand tools can be very helpful when recovering evidence at crime scenes. It is very common, particularly at shooting incidents, to have to cut into buildings and open up walls, floors and ceilings in order to recover fired bullets. It is also quite common to have to disassemble appliances, furniture or vehicles to recover probative evidence. Work gloves, safety goggles and a hard hat should be provided for use whenever required and whenever power tools are being utilized.

Useful power tools include a reciprocating saw and a circular saw with blades for cutting both metal and wood and a drill with an assortment of drill bits up to 1½″ in size and both Philips head and flat head screw attachments. These tools are available in rechargeable battery models but since they are likely to be stored in the response vehicle and only used sporadically it is unlikely that the batteries will be charged when needed so it may be more practical to use electric power tools. Hand tools should include a basic tool kit including an assortment of screwdrivers, pliers, large slip joint pliers (for disassembling sink drains), needle nose pliers, an adjustable wrench, a hammer, heavy duty wire cutters, a good quality utility knife and a drywall saw. Each crime scene investigator should also be equipped with a multi tool which can be worn in a case on the belt. The multi tool will be indispensable while processing scenes. It should be of high quality and constructed completely of stainless steel to accommodate de-contamination as required.

Ladders are often required at the crime scene to search overhead areas and to recover evidence located high up off the ground. It is not practical for a crime scene unit to carry large extension ladders that can reach several stories high. Most units will rely on the assistance of the fire department when such ladders are required. However most times the need is not so great and much smaller folding ladders will get the job done. Many folding ladders are available that will be useful at crime scenes. Quick Step manufactures tactical ladders up to 12 feet tall which collapse down into a flat pack case. These ladders can store easily in a response vehicle and are easily assembled at the scene when needed.

First aid supplies should be available in the form of a basic first aid kit designed for the number of people typically assigned to a scene investigation. Since crime scene investigators are not generally considered first responders this first aid kit is intentioned for use in case of an accident at the scene involving unit personnel rather than rendering aid to the public, although in an emergency it may be used for either. Since chemicals and tools are used at the crime scene a portable eye wash kit is also recommended to be on hand for use in emergency situations in the field.

Administrative supplies cover the basic office supplies such as clipboards, paper, pens, staplers, and so on. Also included are additional materials to be considered such as items more unique to a CSI operation such as printing supplies for photographs, large format paper and ink supplies, DVDs and CDs for copying images and case files, removable media disks and drives, area maps, and spare batteries for the various battery operated equipment.

Camera/Video Equipment

Digital SLR Camera
Camera lenses (60mm, 28–70mm variable, 70mm – 300mm variable telephoto)
  Macro lens 60mm
  Variable zoom lens 28–70mm
  Variable telephoto lens 70mm – 300mm
Protective UV filter
Circular polarizing filter for 60mm and 28–70mm variable lens
Electronic flash
Remote flash cable
Macro flash system
Adjustable tripod rails for macro work
Shutter release cable
Camera tripod
Waterproof camera housing
Photo flood light kits
ABFO photographic scales
L shaped bureau scales
Adhesive paper scales
Compact flash /SD cards
Flash card readers
DVD burners
DVD –R discs and cases
Video camera
Video camera light

Media for video camera
Lens cleaning brush and cloth
4' × 3' black fabric for blocking shadows
Evidence placard kits (yellow #s)
Camera equipment cases

Forensic Mapping and Sketching Equipment

Total Station or Multi Station
Laser scanner
GPS mapping equipment
Clipboard, graph paper, pencils, straight edge
Write in the rain pad and pen
Compass
30' pocket tape measure (certified)
100' Tape measure reel (certified)
Pocket rod compact elevation rods
Laptop with CAD software
Disto handheld laser measurement device
Plumb bob
Wood stakes
Mag nails
Marking spray paint
Nylon twine

Scene Lighting

Rechargeable flashlight with vehicle charger
Portable scene lights
Portable gas generator
Exterior grade extension cords on reels

Forensic Light Source

Portable tunable forensic light
Barrier filters and goggles
Black out paper for darkening rooms
Camera filters

Impression Evidence Supplies

Impression casting kit
- Dental stone casting material
- Mixing bowls
- Mixing spoons
- Adjustable metal frames
- Snow wax
- Spray hardener
- Plaster cast labels

Electro static dust print lifter
Metallic electrostatic lifting sheets
Gel lifters – black, white and clear
Silicone casting material
Wooden mixing sticks

Trace Evidence Supplies

Trace evidence vacuum
Trace vacuum filters
8½″ × 12″ acetate sheets
4" clear adhesive lifting tape
Paint scraper tool
Filter paper

Finger Print Supplies

Black fingerprint powder
White fingerprint powder
Fluorescent fingerprint powder
Feather brushes
Fiberglass brushes
Straight brushes (for clean out)
Silver/black magnetic powder
Magnetic fluorescent powder
Magna wand
2½″ lifting tape
4″ lifting tape
Rubberized lift tape
Hinge lifters

Lifting cards (black and white and acetate)
Thermal paper register tape
Small particle reagent kits
Superglue fuming kit
Super glue supplies
Elimination ten print cards
Printers ink with slab and roller or porelon pad
Card holder
Ink remover towelettes
Magnifying glass
Scissors
Tool box carry case

Ballistic/Bloodstain Evidence Equipment

Ballistic rods
Ballistic laser pointers (2)
String kit
Tripod adapter to align lasers
Tripod
Aerosol can of photographic fog
Zero edge protractor
Digital protractor
Gunshot residue collection kits
Digital caliper with depth gauge
Unloading station
Scientific calculator
Adhesive scales
Straight edge metal pocket ruler (metric)
36" Metal ruler

Chemical Reagents

Luminol/Blue Star (chemi-luminescent)
Blue Star Magnum
Leuco crystal violet (blood stain enhancement)
Presumptive blood tests
Acid phosphatase (presumptive test for semen)
Sodium rhodizonate (presumptive test for lead)
Dithiooximide (DTO presumptive test for copper)

Spray applicator bottles
Benchkote paper and filter paper
Portable cooler for transportation

DNA Collection Supplies

DNA evidence swab kits
Disposable scalpels
Disposable forceps
Filter paper
Sterile water ampules
Buccal swab kits
DNA evidence envelopes

Evidence Packing Supplies

Evidence tape
Bio-hazard labels
Evidence labels
Kraft paper rolls
2oz glass jars and covers
Plastic jars and covers
Wire ties
Scribe/etching pen
Plastic evidence bags
- 3″ × 5″ plastic bags
- 5″ × 8″ plastic bags
- 9″ × 12″ plastic bags
- 12″ × 15× plastic bags

Paper evidence bags
- 5 lbs 11″ W × 5″ H
- 10 lbs 13″ W × 6″ H
- 25 lbs 18″ W × 8″ H
- X Large 35″ W x 16" H

Cardboard evidence boxes
- Gun boxes 25″ × 22″
- Knife boxes 17″ × 20″
- Bottle boxes 19″ × 16″
- Rifle Boxes 12″ × 68″

Arson evidence packages

- 1 quart cans with lids
- 1 gallon cans with lids
- 5 gallon cans with lids
- 5 gal. lid sealer
- Nylon bags 12″ × 18″
- Nylon roll for custom size bags
- Heat sealer

Entomology kit

Personal Protective Equipment

Tyvek suits
Latex gloves
Nitrile gloves
Shoe covers
Dust masks
Respirator masks
Respirator filter cartridges
Antiseptic hand wipes
Hard hats
Work gloves
Safety goggles
Bio-hazard garbage bags

Support Equipment, Tools

Crime scene barrier tape
Metal detector
Hand tools

- Hammer
- Screwdrivers
- Pliers
- Large slip joint pliers
- Wire cutters
- Bolt cutters
- Pry bar
- Drywall saw
- Adjustable wrench
- Utility knife

Multi tool with belt carry case

Power drill with assorted bits up to 1 1/2″
Reciprocating saw with metal and wood blades
Circular saw with metal and wood blades
Quick Step folding ladder
Soil screen sifters
Hand shovels spade, square point, scoop)
Trowels and handheld soil scoops
Paint brushes and cleaning brushes
Pick axe
Rake
Push broom
Extension cords
Large magnet for evidence retrieval
100' cord
Plastic tarps 10' x 10'
Heavy duty tarp 20' x 20'
Body bags
Tyvek wraps for hands
Pocket thermometer
Electric fan for ventilation
Pop-up canopy
Privacy screen
Portable tent shelter
First aid kit
Eye wash station
Fire extinguisher
Portable drinking water cooler and paper cups
Permanent markers
Writing pads
Pens, pencils
Metal clip board
Duct tape
Printed forms
Spare batteries for: camera, video camera, camera flash, lights, electrostatic lifter, lasers, digital protractor, thermometer, calipers, laser measurer

8

THE CRIME SCENE

The Investigative Team

The CSI team for major incidents should be made-up of multiple qualified personnel, each with clearly defined duties and responsibilities. Each member of the team, whether the team is large or small, must have a clear understanding of what is expected of them and what is permitted and prohibited during the scene process. Responsibilities begin with preparation before receiving an assignment and continue until after the scene has been released and the administrative process of completing casework has been completed. In some respects the responsibilities of being a member of a CSI team will extend to the completion of follow-up work and appearance and testimony during court hearings well after the incident has been concluded.

To properly manage a crime scene investigation team the crime scene unit manager must first delineate the required team components and the roles and responsibilities that each component will encompass. Once all of roles that are required to properly process a crime scene have been identified and the responsibilities of each are delineated then a review of the unit's personnel may be conducted to identify which members are qualified to perform the various roles required in a proficient manner. Having a unit roster with individual qualifications listed will help supervisors to quickly and properly staff a CSI team when it is needed. This pre-screening process will also serve to identify the strengths and weaknesses of the unit as a whole and may reveal areas where additional training resources need to be committed.

Since there are many roles listed in the team's makeup, it may be necessary for a single qualified individual to assume several roles during the various stages of the process. For instance, the lead investigator may also serve as the photographer and latent print technician.

There are often cases where multiple related scenes involved in a single crime are discovered. When secondary or tertiary scenes occur at the same time it is usually not the best practice to have a single individual serve as a CSI between multiple scenes. In order to avoid confusion, expedite evidence gathering and, perhaps most importantly, to avoid inter-scene contamination it may become necessary to assign separate investigators to handle each location independently. An example would be a homicide in a suspect's home where the victim's body is simultaneously recovered at a dump site. Locard's Theory of the transfer of evidence tells us that it is possible for a person who comes into contact with both scenes to cause a transfer of evidence from one scene into the other. So if for instance the victim's hair were discovered in the suspect's home by an investigator who had earlier visited the dump site it may become questionable as to whether the hair was deposited by contact between the suspect and victim or by cross contamination. The real possibility of cross contamination alone can raise doubt and diminish the probative value of forensic evidence whether or not it actually does occur. If it is a necessity to have investigators respond to associated crime scenes extraordinary steps must be taken to prevent the possibility of cross contamination and those steps should be meticulously documented.

How the scene process is approached by the crime scene investigation team is another concern which is usually pre-determined by the unit's business practices. In his book "A Practical Guide to Crime Scene Processing" Gardner describes two differing approaches to processing a crime scene. The first is an area approach where individuals are assigned to perform all of the tasks required to process a specific section or area within a scene. The second approach is task based where each individual on the team performs a single task in the process of the entire scene.

Many local and state agencies may lack the manpower to form a truly task based team; instead the team members may be forced to wear several different hats to accomplish the process in a practical amount of time. Perhaps a third approach, and one that is used on major investigations in New York City, might be a combination of the two methods where some members of the team may handle several tasks such as, photos, sketching, mapping, measurements, physical searches, and collection of physical evidence that does not require on-scene processing, while other members concentrate on single tasks such as only processing for latent prints or DNA. Either method may be acceptable as long as it is properly executed but there is great benefit to determining what the appropriate approach is and describing it in the unit's standard operating procedures in advance.

Another important consideration for managing a CSI team is the availability and procurement of expertise from outside the crime scene unit. Too often in law enforcement work there is a reluctance to consult with others from outside the immediate agency regarding an investigation. Confidentiality concerns are an issue but there are many forensic experts who can bring a wealth of knowledge to an investigation and the team can leverage that knowledge to maximize the evidence gathering process and improve the likelihood of a successful investigative outcome. The crime scene unit managers should foster the development of professional relationships between the members of the crime scene unit and other areas of forensic expertise. This can be done through attending professional association meetings, coordinating multi discipline training events, and developing written memos of understanding between the CSI team and other experts.

CSI Team Roles and Responsibilities

Primary Investigator

The primary investigator must be an experienced and qualified crime scene investigator. The primary investigator may not necessarily have supervisory authority over other members of the crime scene team but must be given clear authority over the investigative process. The primary investigator participates in scene processing but also coordinates personnel, develops a processing plan that complies with the unit's protocols, reviews the processing plan with supervisors, and keeps all interested parties briefed on issues and progress during processing. After processing is completed the primary investigator ensures casework is completed. The primary investigator should also be prepared to offer testimony at subsequent hearings and trials regarding results of the conferrals and the walk-through, the crime scene processing plan, team makeup and responsibilities and all crime scene investigative activities taking place during the investigation.

1. Prior to assignment –
   a. Ensures all crime scene investigative equipment is accounted for, operating properly, charged, validated and calibrated if applicable.
      i. Camera and video equipment and accessories
      ii. Forensic mapping and measuring equipment
      iii. Electrostatic dust lifter
      iv. Fingerprint supplies
      v. Impression evidence supplies
      vi. DNA collection supplies
      vii. Trace evidence supplies
      viii. Chemicals and reagents
      ix. Administrative supplies (adequate supply of forms and paperwork)
   b. Reviews incoming request for service and communicates as necessary with personnel on the scene
2. Upon receiving an assignment
   a. Communicates with other team members and unit supervisors regarding the nature, location and details of the assignment and gives an estimated time of arrival on scene
   b. Ensures proper communication with other required responders
      i. Medical examiner or coroner
      ii. Crime laboratory
      iii. Prosecutor's office
      iv. Other investigators
3. Upon arrival
   a. Conducts conferrals to gain cognitive awareness at the scene
      i. First arriving officer
      ii. Investigators
      iii. Civilian witnesses
      iv. Other emergency personnel on scene
   b. Performs a walk-through of the crime scene
   c. Develops a processing plan for the crime scene
   d. Reviews processing plan with crime scene supervisor for approval
   e. Reviews processing plan with crime scene team members
4. During scene processing
   a. Ensures that the scene is thoroughly documented
   b. Oversees and participates in initial crime scene search
   c. Performs processing duties as appropriate
   d. Collects, packages, and marks crime scene evidence

   e. Maintains communication with other case investigators (situational awareness)
   f. Ensures evidence is securely and properly stored while at scene
   g. Conducts final search of crime scene
   h. Reviews results of processing with supervisor and case investigators
   i. Releases crime scene
5. After completion of on-scene processing
   a. Completes initial evaluation of probative value of forensic evidence
   b. Ensures all casework is completed in a timely manner
   c. Remains available to offer court testimony

Assisting Investigator(s)

Assisting investigators must be experienced crime scene personnel and must be properly trained and qualified to carry out their assigned duties at a particular scene. Assisting investigators comply with the directions of supervisors and the primary investigator to carry out crime scene processing tasks in compliance with the unit's protocols. Assisting investigators must not self-initiate crime scene processing tasks instead when unforeseen issues or differing opinions arise they must brief the primary investigator or supervisor and then follow appropriate instruction. Assisting investigators must be prepared to testify at any hearings or trials regarding their activities and observations during the investigation.

1. Prior to assignment
   a. Operates the crime scene response vehicle and ensures it is properly maintained, fueled, cleaned and ready for deployment to a crime scene
   b. Ensures all necessary scene supplies and evidence packaging equipment is properly stocked inside the response vehicle
      i. Scene lighting and flashlights
      ii. Forensic light sources
      iii. DNA collection supplies
      iv. Impression evidence equipment
      v. Trace evidence equipment
      vi. Fingerprint processing supplies
      vii. Ballistic trajectory and bloodstain equipment
      viii. Metal detection, sifting and digging equipment
      ix. Personal protective equipment and supplies
   c. Reviews request for service with primary investigator
2. Upon arrival
   a. Assists the primary investigator to conduct conferrals to gain cognitive awareness at the scene
   b. Reviews results of the walk-through of the crime scene with the primary investigator
   c. Assists the primary investigator to formulate the scene processing plan
3. During scene processing
   a. Carries out scene processing tasks assigned by primary investigator
      i. Latent print processing
      ii. Evidence development and enhancement techniques

iii. Presumptive testing and use of reagents
iv. DNA evidence processing
v. Scene analysis (bullet paths, blood stains, etc.)

b. Assists the primary investigator with recording observations and facts regarding the investigation
c. Assists in documenting the scene (photos, sketch, measurements, etc.)
d. Assists in the initial crime scene search
e. Assists in collecting, packaging, marking and securing crime scene evidence
f. Assists in the final search of the crime scene

4. After completion of on-scene processing
   a. Completes all casework as appropriate
   b. Remains available to offer court testimony

Crime Scene Search Team Member(s)

Crime scene search team members do not necessarily require special qualification as a crime scene investigator. The searchers should have training as members of law enforcement and a basic understanding of crime scene preservation and contamination prevention. Patrol officers normally possess very good skills for searching a crime scene while under the supervision of the primary crime scene investigator and/or crime scene supervisor. Prior to the commencement of the crime scene search these team members must be briefed as to what types of evidence are actively being sought and what may be present at the scene and also on what actions to take if suspected evidence is encountered (searchers are normally advised to mark the location of suspected evidence and avoid any other disturbance of the scene). The search team members will also need to be outfitted with personal protective equipment by the CSI team as most patrol officers will usually not possess such equipment (with the exception of rubber gloves).

1. During scene processing
   a. Assists in the initial crime scene search
   b. Assists in the final search of the crime scene (if applicable)
2. After completion of on-scene processing
   a. Remains available to offer court testimony

Crime Scene Supervisor

The crime scene supervisor should be an experienced manager with a thorough understanding of the practical aspects of crime scene processing. The supervisor typically will not personally perform processing tasks at the scene but instead will review the crime scene processing plan and oversee operations. The CSI supervisor assures that personnel are assigned roles which they are qualified to perform and that the work is being carried out in an acceptable manner in conformance with unit protocols. The supervisor is responsible to ensure that all of the resources required to properly process the crime scene are made available to the CSI team.

When manpower shortages arise at the scene the crime scene supervisor may perform some of the duties of an assisting investigator but should not become fully consumed in this role as it may distract from the larger supervision responsibilities. The CSI supervisor has responsibility for the health and safety of the unit's personnel and must ensure that contamination prevention measures are strictly adhered to. The CSI supervisor acts as an intermediary between the CSI team and other units and personnel at the scene and may conduct briefings during the process, in this manner the supervisor prevents the investigators from being unnecessarily distracted from their tasks.

Since it may be necessary for the supervisor to simultaneously oversee multiple CSI operations the crime scene supervisor may not be physically present at the scene for the duration of the investigation. However, when major incidents arise it is preferable to have the supervisor on scene at least until the crime scene plan has been formulated and the CSI team members receive their assignments. When the supervisor cannot be present at the scene then phone conference briefings should be scheduled at pre-determined points in the investigation such as after the crime scene search and prior to release of the scene.

After completion of on-scene processing the crime scene supervisor is responsible to administratively review all casework and ensure it is correct, free from omissions and in conformance with the unit's protocols. Where the supervisor possesses the required experience and training, technical reviews of casework may also be performed. All requests for information related to casework from persons outside the crime scene unit must be reviewed and approved by the crime scene supervisor prior to dissemination.

1. Prior to assignment
   a. Makes assignments and maintains unit roster
   b. Assigns and inspects units vehicles
   c. Ensures all unit equipment is accounted for and operating properly
   d. Approves all incoming requests for service
2. Upon receiving an assignment
   a. Reviews preliminary facts of case
   b. Dispatches appropriate personnel to scene
   c. Ensures appropriate notifications are made
   d. Responds to the scene if required
3. Upon arrival
   a. Ensures proper conferrals are carried out
   b. Ensures a walk-through of the crime scene is completed
   c. Reviews and approves a processing plan for the crime scene
   d. Reviews processing plan with CSI team members
4. During scene processing
   a. Assumes responsibility for the health and safety of CSI team
   b. Ensures any technical assistance from forensic subject matter experts, laboratories, medical professionals, and other experts is considered and obtained as required
   c. Briefs superiors
   d. Acts as liaison between CSI team and other units
   e. Supervises compliance with contamination prevention protocols
   f. Supervises initial crime scene search
   g. Supervises compliance with scene processing protocols
   h. Supervises final search of crime scene

    i. Reviews results of processing
    j. Authorizes the releases of the crime scene
5. After completion of on-scene processing
    a. Reviews all casework for approval
        i. Administrative review
        ii. Technical review (if applicable)

Technical Assistants

When processing a major incident scene the CSI team may require the assistance of subject matter experts in various forensic disciplines as well as other areas of expertise. Consulting with subject matter experts should be routine for the CSI team. Contacts at laboratories and with forensic experts should be pre-established and the CSI team should build professional relationships with these individuals who can lend assistance when needed. It is ultimately the responsibility of the crime scene supervisor to ensure that consideration is given to the possibility that technical assistance may improve the outcome of an investigation and that all appropriate assistance and guidance is sought and received by the CSI team.

Areas where technical assistants may become integral to the CSI team include:

1. Laboratory personnel
2. Forensic biologists
3. Medical examiners and coroners
4. Forensic anthropologists
5. Forensic dentist
6. Forensic entomologist
7. Forensic engineers
8. Bloodstain pattern experts
9. Ballistic experts
10. Arson experts
11. Explosive experts
12. Handwriting experts
13. Soil and botany experts
14. Digital forensic experts (IT, computer, video and electronics)
15. NTSB investigators

Crime Scene Case Coordinator

In major investigations that involve multiple scenes and extended periods of time it can be very helpful to the investigation to assign a crime scene case coordinator. The case coordinator may or may not participate in on-scene processing activities. Although the responsibilities of this role may be handled by the primary investigator during routine investigations, when investigations involve complexities such as secondary and tertiary scenes it may be best to utilize a separate individual to serve as the coordinator. In most instances CSIs process a scene, complete the casework and move on to the next case. Follow up on evidence testing and results are usually left to the criminal investigator assigned to the case. During major investigations when a large amount of evidence may be collected from different locations by different investigators over an extended period of time this may prove very challenging. The various items of evidence are like pieces of a puzzle but they must be analyzed and put together and doing so requires time intensive case management which when appropriate can be provided by the case coordinator.

1. During the investigation
   a. Maintain a chronological list of all related crime scene investigations
      i. Date and time of assignment
      ii. Location information
      iii. Facts and circumstance of scene
      iv. Assigned investigative team
   b. Prepare an annotated map showing the geographical locations of each crime scene processed during the investigation
2. After completion of on-scene processing
   a. Prepare a case folder with copies of all casework, diagrams, photos, etc., for each individual crime scene investigation related to the incident (may be digital copies)
   b. Ascertain a complete list of all recovered forensic evidence and make a notation of the unique identifier assigned by the CSI team
   c. Verify the current location of all items of evidence
   d. Prepare a spreadsheet report listing all forensic evidence for each crime scene
      i. Evidence type
         1. DNA evidence
         2. Firearms related evidence
         3. Trace/criminalistics evidence
         4. Fingerprint evidence
         5. Impression evidence
         6. Electronic/digital evidence
         7. Document/handwriting evidence
         8. Controlled substance evidence
         9. Weapons
         10. Other physical evidence
      ii. If evidence is in storage indicate storage location
      iii. If evidence has been forwarded to a laboratory for testing specify which laboratory and section
      iv. If testing is complete indicate results of analysis
   e. Conduct regular briefings with crime scene supervisors, primary investigators and criminal investigators assigned to the case
      i. Review all evidence and potential probative value
      ii. Request additional laboratory testing if applicable
      iii. Review results of crime scene processing and ascertain if additional processing work is required
   f. Confer with laboratory personnel regarding results of briefings and new developments in the case

g. Ensure all required casework is present in the case folder
h. Upon approval of the crime scene supervisor furnish copies of casework as requested by authorized parties to the investigation
i. Coordinate court appearances of unit personnel to ensure timely appearance and avoid unnecessary scheduling

Working the Scene

Scene Security and Contamination Prevention

Securing the crime scene and preventing contamination are of paramount importance to the CSI team. The goals of the team are to completely document the scene and maximize the recovery of probative evidence to enable conclusions to be reached and individuals to be identified. The team can only be successful however if the goals are accomplished in accordance with accepted practices of forensic science and in a manner that will allow the evidence to be introduced in a court of law. Maintaining the scene in as pristine condition as is reasonably possible affords the greatest opportunity for this to occur. When scene security is compromised and the possibility of contamination or degradation of evidence is introduced the likelihood of the evidence being acceptable to legal standards begins to rapidly diminish. Chapter 4 in this book covers scene security and contamination prevention measures in depth; the following is a brief list of those details.

Steps to protect the scene include:

- Establishing clearly marked barriers around the scene perimeter
  - Crime scene tape
  - Signage
- Uniformed police officer stationed at entrance(s)
- Permitting only essential personnel entry to the scene
- Maintaining a crime scene entry log
- Donning proper personal protective equipment (PPE) prior to entering
- Changing PPE when re-entering scene
- Changing gloves before and between handling items
- Take steps to protect evidence against environmental conditions

Threat Assessments, Safety First

The CSI team should be aware of threats that may be present at the scene and can result in compromised safety of the team. Threats can emanate from suspects still being present at or near the scene so a thorough search for suspects must be conducted by sworn police officers prior to declaring that the scene is safe to process. Other threats may seem more mundane but can result in injury to personnel if they are not properly addressed. These threats are a result of conditions at the scene itself and the need for the CSI team to spend a large amount of time working the scene.

Bio-hazards, chemical hazards and physical hazards all may be present at the scene and are often a routine part of a crime scene investigators work. These hazards should not be taken lightly however, and a good crime scene processing plan should always give consideration to dealing with such hazards.

Chapter 3 covered investigators' safety in depth, and that information should be used when approaching hazards at crime scenes.

Interviewing Involved Parties and Witnesses

The Primary CSI is responsible to confer with involved parties and witnesses at the crime scene in order to gain information surrounding the incident under investigation. CSIs must not conduct interrogations of suspects, victims or witnesses. Instead the purposes of the CSI's interviews are to gain cognitive information of what has occurred at the scene and to then use that information in developing and carrying out a crime scene processing plan. If questioning is believed to have a potential negative impact or may jeopardize the investigation then it should be postponed. However it, remains true that a CSI processing a scene from a base of knowledge gathered from information gleaned during interviews will be more likely to recover probative evidence then a CSI blindly approaching the scene. A word of caution is due here, In practice it is not always the case that when the CSI arrives at the scene that people with knowledge about the incident are available or willing to provide information. Suspects may be removed to detention facilities.Victims may have been removed to a hospital and medical treatment may prevent interviews. Police officers may have been dispatched to other locations, and civilian witnesses tend to disappear quickly. This being the case, the CSI must still take every appropriate step to gather information about the scene through interviews and, at the very least, take care to document those steps in the case documentation.

Suspects

When handling crime scene investigations a CSI may have occasion to interact with a suspect but it should only be done relative to a specified crime scene processing function and then only in the presence of criminal investigators and, if appropriate, the suspects attorney. Legal issues concerning search and seizure and interrogation must be given due consideration and a suspect's right to legal representation during questioning must be strictly observed when applicable. One instance where a CSI may pose questions to a suspect might be when the suspect's hands are being processed for gunshot residue. Whether the procedure is being done by court order or by consent of the suspect it usually requires some basic questions that might impact test results, such as: When was the last time you washed your hands? Or, what is your occupation? Another situation where a CSI interacts with a suspect is when collecting clothing items or buccal swabs for DNA from the suspect. Again any questions or conversation should be directly related to the procedures being carried out and not the facts or circumstances of the incident under investigation.

In a recent homicide investigation I encountered a perpetrator who had shot and killed an innocent victim while riding on a city bus. The suspect was later apprehended by police while fleeing the scene. He had been placed into a holding cell at the local station house and I was dispatched to collect his clothing as evidence with the permission of the assigned prosecutor. When I arrived I identified myself to the suspect and informed him that I would be seizing his outer clothing as evidence and would provide him a Tyvek suit as a replacement. I noticed a coat on the holding cell floor and I asked the suspect if the coat belonged to him. He confirmed it was his coat and he took it off while he was in the holding cell (the suspect had already been read Miranda Warnings). As I examined the coat I discovered what appeared to be a bullet hole through the front pocket and a discharged shell casing inside the pocket. It was later confirmed that the suspect had shot the victim without warning while the gun was secreted inside the coat pocket. I was careful to only pose the single question of his ownership of the coat since it was my intention to seize his clothing. But, I never questioned him about the presence of the bullet hole or the shell casing. If I had posed such questions I believe I would have crossed a line into interrogation, a role reserved for other criminal investigators.

Police Officers

The primary investigator should make every effort to confer with the first arriving police officer. This Officer can offer information relative to the condition of the scene upon arrival and whether anything was disturbed in the scene during the emergency response. Almost every seasoned crime scene investigator can tell stories about how emergency responders altered a scene and then failed to inform the CSI team processing the scene. This can result in confusion or skewed conclusions by the CSI team. I can recall a homicide scene where the victim had been shot through an open first floor window in his home. The information received indicated that the victim fell immediately to the floor when he was shot and the perpetrator never entered inside the home. I was puzzled however by a blood trail that led across the carpeted floor from the area of the body into an adjoining room. If the perpetrator never entered the home then who walked through the blood? It wasn't until later during a thorough search of the home that I discovered a bag of dog food in the kitchen and then re-questioned the first officer at the scene. He had forgotten to mention that the victim had a large dog that was protecting the decedent's body when they arrived and had to be removed from the scene to a neighbor's house. A trip over to the neighbor's house and a quick inspection of the dog's paws revealed the source of the blood trail.

Diligence in obtaining the necessary information is required on the part of the CSI during the conferral with the first arriving officer(s). This is very important for clearing up matters that can lead to issues later on in the scene investigation. A concise and chronological recounting of the steps the first officers took upon arrival and their observations must be sought. The CSI must understand that patrol officers arriving at a major crime scene are faced with a chaotic situation and need to carry out multiple tasks such as searching for a suspect, rendering aid to the injured, detaining witnesses and communicating with other responders during those initial chaotic moments. It is sometimes unavoidable that the scene is altered during the emergency where the first duty of the responders is life safety. What is not acceptable is failing to protect the scene once the emergency situation is stabilized and failing to inform others, including the CSI team, of any alterations that were necessary during the emergency.

Some questions that should be asked include:

- How were you notified to respond to the scene?
- What time did you arrive?
- Was anyone else present when you arrived?
- Do you have any suspect's description?
- Have any suspects been identified, or arrested?
- Have any victims been identified?
- How did you enter the location?
- What pathway did you walk?
- Did you move or touch anything?

- Was any medical aid rendered or attempted? If so, by whom?
- Has anyone been removed for medical treatment? If so, what hospital?
- Was the victim's position disturbed in any way (death investigation cases)?
- Who pronounced the victim's death and when (death investigation cases)?
- Did you notice any odors when you arrived?
- Have any windows or doors been opened since you first arrived?
- Has any evidence been moved or weapons safeguarded?
- Who were the other first responders?
- When was the crime scene established and how was it safeguarded?
- Has a crime scene log been maintained? (obtain copies)
- Do you know the identity of any witnesses?
- Do you know the identity of any other persons who have legitimate access to the crime scene (i.e. roommates or family members)?
- Are you aware of any surveillance images of the scene?

Civilian Witnesses

Conferrals with civilian witnesses can serve to add additional clarity to the incident and help in establishing a sequence to events that occurred during the incident, particularly in the time period prior to the arrival of police officers at the scene. When dealing with civilian witnesses the burden of legal issues is removed however care must still be taken to ensure the witnesses safety and avoid negatively impacting their willingness to cooperate with investigators.

Civilian witnesses are different from police personnel and are likely to be traumatized to some extent if they have witnessed a violent crime. Allow the witness to tell their story without attempting to correct them and apply a healthy dose of skepticism since the stress and confusion of the incident may cloud their version of events. Although it may be seldom there are also witnesses who intentionally will mislead the police, particularly if they, or someone they know, was involved in the commission of the crime. It is the responsibility of the criminal investigators at the scene to secure the witness statements and corroborate or disprove their statements but the primary CSI investigator should also have an opportunity to speak with any witnesses to gain information that can enhance the crime scene processing plan.

Perhaps one of the more important pieces of information that can be gained from a witness is the suspect's description, movements and positioning. Knowing a suspect's position can focus the search for latent prints, DNA and footwear impressions at the scene and can enhance the probability of recovering probative evidence.

When crimes occur in residences or business premises the witnesses frequently have legitimate access to the area where the crime occurred. Therefore the initial conferral with the witness also presents the opportunity to arrange for the witnesses fingerprints and DNA to be collected if applicable. These prints and DNA samples are to be used for elimination purposes and not to be submitted to searches in a database. The intention is so that any questioned samples collected from the crime scene can be compared against the elimination samples and if a match is found then the sample can be eliminated as having come from the suspect. Collecting elimination fingerprints and DNA prevents costly delays in the investigation and wasted manpower chasing down dead end leads.

Some questions that should be asked include:

- What time did you arrive at the scene?
- How did you arrive at the scene?
- Did you observe the suspect at the scene? If yes, exactly where?
- How did the suspect arrive at and leave the scene?
- What items were handled?
- What items were moved?
- Was anyone else present when you arrived?
- Do you have any suspect's description?
- Do you know the identity of the victim(s)?
- Did you enter the location? If so, how?
- What pathway did you walk?
- Did you move or touch anything?
- Did you render any first aid?
- Was the victim's position disturbed in any way (death investigation cases)?
- Did you notice any odors when you arrived?
- Have any windows or doors been opened since you first arrived?
- Do you know the identity of any other witnesses?
- Prior to the crime did you have legitimate access to the area of the crime scene?
- Do you know the identity of any other persons who have legitimate access to the crime scene?

The Walk-Through

The walk-through of the crime scene is the first opportunity for a member of the CSI team to acquire a first-hand look at the scene. This is a necessary step in order to gain the first-hand perspective to prepare a proper crime scene processing plan; however it should not be rushed into. Take notice that the walk-through only occurs after the conferrals have been completed. The primary investigator has already reviewed the assignment, communicated by phone with persons at the scene and now has arrived and conducted some cognitive conferral interviews. At this point a good deal of information has already been learned about the incident and now a walk-through will provide the clarity to begin to tie things together and formulate a plan. If the walk-through is rushed into and done without the benefit of cognitive conferrals then important considerations may be overlooked and left out of the processing plan.

The walk-through should be led by an officer or investigator already familiar with the scene and must include the primary investigator. Accompanying the primary investigator may be assisting investigators, but at this phase of the investigation, crime scene preservation is more important than giving the entire CSI team an opportunity to view the scene, so personnel attending the walk-through should be minimized as much as possible. It is a good practice to take notes regarding the walk-through including the time of occurrence, the names of those present, and some brief observations including a list of any items of evidence that are in plain view.

Since the walk-through is the first time trained forensic investigators will be entering the scene rigorous enforcement of crime scene contamination prevention measures are now required. This is true regardless of what occurred during the emergency phase of the incident prior to the arrival of the CSI team. It may be that many police officers and medics have already been in and out of the scene but that should be during the emergency phase of the incident and done to address lifesaving and safety issues such as a search for a suspect, rendering aid to a victim, or extinguishing a fire. Lifesaving and safety issues trump evidence collection but the emergency phase has ended once the CSI team is ready to go to work and there is no longer a legitimate reason to risk contamination of the scene or degradation of the evidence within. As the scene transitions from an emergency phase to an investigative phase the primary CSI is the trained forensic expert on-scene who must assume the responsibility to ensure that proper protocols are being followed to secure the scene and protect it from contamination. The crime scene supervisor should be immediately informed if issues or non-compliance with protocols arise and cannot be immediately rectified.

Crime Scene Documentation; Recording Details and Observations

Contemporaneous note taking should be an essential and routine part of the CSI teams' workflow. Notes should be taken by all personnel who are actively participating in the crime scene processing functions. Contemporaneous notes are notes that are taken at the time or very shortly after an incident or action. For the CSI team contemporaneous notes should include entries for each important observation that is made, each time important information pertaining to the crime scene is heard and who it is heard from, and each time a step in the crime scene process is carried out. Contemporaneous notes are recognized as the most accurate record of events since when entries are made at the time of an event they are more likely to be accurately recorded since the event is still fresh in the mind.

Contemporaneous notes should be taken on clean lined paper separate from other documentation. Each page should contain the case number, date and note taker's name and be consecutively numbered. Notes should also include the basic facts of the case and the identities of persons present at the scene as well as victims, suspects, and witnesses. The notes should be concise and factual in nature; the CSI should not write anything that they would not want to be read in the courtroom. The writing should be done in permanent ink. Erasures should be avoided and corrections and revisions should be initialized. The notes may be discoverable and should be maintained with the case file. In some jurisdictions it may still be part of the routine to destroy the contemporaneous notes after the notes have been incorporated into a final report. This would be considered unethical by any standard and must not be an acceptable practice. Some States, such as New Jersey, have expressly prohibited this practice.

Good quality notes will serve as a permanent record that the CSI can return to in order to check facts and recall the events at the scene. Contemporaneous notes are not expected to be perfect but they will often be more accurate and more detailed then a formal crime scene report where transcription errors may occur. The wheels of justice can sometimes turn slowly and years may pass before a case needs to be reviewed for court proceedings. Good notes will help the CSI recall the events and facts of the case and enable effective testimony. These notes also present the opportunity for the CSI to leave behind a record of their diligent work for the next generation of investigators who may be able to take advantage of new developments in science to solve old crimes. Anyone who has worked cold cases knows the frustration that is felt when incomplete notes and records are contained in an otherwise solvable case.

Photography

Photography is such a critical component to the crime scene investigation process that it demands special attention from the primary investigator. In most cases it will be best if the primary investigator serves as the photographer and directly decides which photographs are to be taken and how they are to be taken. In instances where an assistant investigator is assigned as the photographer then the primary investigator must direct and control the photographic process to ensure that all areas that require recording have been properly captured.

Crime scene photography requires a specially trained photographer and adherence to a methodical and systematic process in order for the scene, and the evidence within, to be successfully documented. All photography processes should be done in compliance with written standard operating procedures. Once a photograph is captured it must be considered evidence and as such its handling should also be fully described in written procedures that also must be followed. The photography work at the scene needs to be choreographed with the other aspects of scene processing. One aspect cannot move forward without being in proper step with any other. This systematic and methodical process takes advanced training and practical experience to master.

Let's look at an example of a homicide where a firearm is discovered at the scene. The firearm can present a treasure trove of evidence but it must be documented and processed in a methodical manner if the evidence is to be exploited to its full value. The firearm has much potential as evidence, including:

- Make, model, type and caliber
- Serial number (Who is the registered owner?)
- History (manufacturer, transfers, sales, theft reports, etc.)
- State of load and ammunition types (How many shots could have been fired?)
- Operability testing (Is the firearm capable of firing a shot?)
- Comparison to fired bullets (Does the barrel rifling match the fired bullets?)
- Comparison to discharged shell casings (Do ejection and primer marks match other scene evidence?)
- IBIS entry (Does the firearm match evidence from other crimes?)
- Touch DNA on grips, slide, hammer, trigger, magazine, ammunition (Who handled the firearm?)
- Latent prints on the firearm (Who handled the firearm?)
- Blood on muzzle or in the barrel (Evidence of contact or close contact?)
- DNA from muzzle or barrel (Whose blood is it?)
- GSR patterns (Muzzle to target distance determination?)

Obviously some of the most immediate questions regarding the firearm are: What is the serial number? Is it loaded? And, what caliber is it? This information may be very valuable to get the ball rolling in an investigation and it may be tempting for an inexperienced scene investigator to act out of order to gather that information quickly. However if the process is not handled methodically there is an absolute risk of evidence being diminished or lost. If we were to pick up the firearm to inspect the serial number prior to photographing the item we would be violating the basic rule of documenting the scene in an as-is condition and may run into problems when trying to introduce the item as evidence in criminal proceedings, so instead, we must first make observations, take measurements and photograph the firearm in place. After the photographs are completed we can begin to exploit the other aspects of the firearm but we must do that methodically as well. We must consider all of the evidence possibilities and capture the appropriate photos before we rush too far forward. Is there a print on the barrel? Is there a tiny spec of blood on the muzzle? Is there a stove piped shell casing in the ejection port? What is the position of the discharged casings in the cylinder? All of these issues and many more require photography and other actions before proceeding forward with the evidence.

The example above should make it clear that photography will often dictate the pace of the CSI teams' work. If several assistant investigators have been assigned to process for latent prints they will not be able to proceed until the photography of the area is completed. Once they begin processing and they develop latent prints they may not be able to lift the prints until an additional round of photographs is taken documenting the developed prints in place. This is simply the nature of crime scene processing. It is, and it must remain, a systematic and methodical process. Each team member must coordinate with the other team members throughout the entire process.

Crime scene unit management must ensure that the personnel assigned to the CSI team have received proper training and are highly competent crime scene photographers prior to their assignment to the CSI team. The unit management must also ensure that the team is properly equipped to accomplish the photography portion of the crime scene processing. A single improperly captured or omitted photo can compromise an investigation, cause misleading conclusions or deprive an accused individual of the right to an adequate defense. The scene photography is critical and must be addressed diligently.

Scene photography follows these general steps:

- Wide angle overview photos are taken to depict the overall appearance and layout of the scene and surrounding areas
  - These photos may be repeated after the introduction of evidence markers into the scene
- Mid-range photos are taken to show important areas and items of evidence as well as their immediate surroundings
- Close up photos that reveal the details of an item of evidence in situ are taken
- Additional close up photos of evidence after it is recovered to reveal additional detail are taken
- Victim and/or decedent photos that reveal positioning, clothing, injury, identification, etc.
- Scientific examination quality photos that reveal evidence in close up views and are suitable for analysis and comparison by laboratory analysts may need to be taken
- Scene processing results are photographed if appropriate including, colorimetric tests, forensic and oblique light, reagent results, etc.
- Exit photographs to show the appearance of the scene after processing and final searching is complete

The crime scene photography process is a cyclical process. The scene may be photographed in wide angle overview, mid-range, and close up photos prior to the crime scene search but if new evidence is discovered during the search then it may be required to repeat the process to be able to show the newly discovered evidence in all of the required views.

Since the pace of the scene processing is dependent on the scene photography the practice of the primary investigator controlling the scene photography serves a valuable role in keeping things organized and keeping the primary investigator aware of, and in charge of, all other activities taking place.

When dealing with most conventional crime scenes it is not recommended to have more than one photographer for a single scene unless the scene is being geographically divided into sub-scenes and each sub-scene is being handled independent of the other. Crime scene photos are evidence and must be treated with proper integrity and chain of custody. Having more than one photographer can cause confusion in sequence where one photographer photographs an area in situ and then something is moved. Later another photographer unwittingly photographs the same area not realizing it has already been documented. The case now has two photos of the same area that show conflicting appearance and although it may be explainable it can mislead others who were not at the scene but review the case documentation later. Multiple photographers also reduce control over both what has been photographed and what needs to be photographed at the scene. It may also lead to issues during photograph reporting and image processing after the scene investigation is completed. This practice may change when dealing with very large-scale or mass fatality incidents where photographers may be assigned specific duties such as photographing decedents, or photographing fragments from an exploded IED, and so on.

Crime Scene Sketch and Measurements

The CSI supervisor and primary investigator should collectively determine how the scene should be documented to best preserve accurate measurements and positions of all of the important features and evidence at the scene. At some conventional scenes it may be appropriate to use simple tape measures to collect measurements but at major incident scenes it may be more appropriate to collect measurement and positional information using a formal process known as forensic mapping where electronic equipment such as laser scanners or total stations are deployed.

Conventional methods for sketching and mapping involve simple hand drawn two dimensional sketches which are annotated and labeled with dimensions to document the scene and create a proper perspective. The CSI team uses basic tools such as tape measures to collect the required spatial measurements and generally does so from a two dimensional point of view while ignoring changes in elevation. The overwhelming majority of crime scene sketches depict a two dimensional floor plan or site plan view although other views including perspective views, elevation views and projection views are also possible.

- Floor plan/site plan – common two dimensional views which shows the layout of the scene and the positions of items of evidence from an overhead view.
- Perspective view – shows an area of the scene from a camera lens perspective. This is useful to depict items on vertical surfaces such as bloodstains on a wall or items inside closed areas such as a firearm inside an open safe.
- Projection view – shows an interior area in a floor plan type view with the walls projected down flat around each side of the room. Used in scenes where evidence is located on the walls and needs to be depicted.

When considering what tools to utilize at the scene consider that in the National Forensic Science Technology Center (NFSTC) publication "Crime Scene Investigation: A Guide for Law Enforcement" (revised 2014) the following is stated "The accuracy of all measuring devices should be ensured by comparison to a measure of certified accuracy, such as a NIST traceable ruler" (measuring devices and how to ensure accuracy were discussed in Chapter 7). However, one should always remember that even though the measuring tool may be accurate the precision (or lack of precision) in which it is used in the field can still result in a large error tolerance in the results obtained.

The error tolerance of measurements at the scene needs to be acknowledged and understood by all involved in the process as well as those that utilize the information in future proceedings. The crime scene notes and reports should describe the methods used to collect measurements and the accuracy of the measurements (The NFSTC Guide recommends that all measurements are accurate to within ¼″).

The conventional method of documenting a scene may still be appropriate to use depending on the scope of the scene. For instance at a residential burglary scene where latent prints at the point of entry on the front door knob and a suspect's jacket on the floor are the only items of evidence recovered, measurements may ultimately not be extremely critical to reaching conclusions in the case and the measurements may never be called into question. The exact opposite may be true at a scene where blood has been shed or gunshots have been fired. However, in the end it is the court that decides how important the measurements are, therefore the CSI always needs to collect them in an acceptable manner. To ensure this is properly accomplished, the unit needs a policy on how they must be collected.

If forensic mapping is determined to be needed at the scene then this process requires deployment of electronic equipment that must be operated by properly qualified personnel. This may be an additional task assigned to the primary investigator but will be more practical if it is assigned to an assisting investigator, or a technical assistant who can concentrate more intently on completing the forensic mapping process. Not all scenes require the maximum forensic mapping effort. Instead the scope of the scene and facts of the case should be considered when determining what amount of effort is warranted. This decision process can be guided by some basic observations.

- Is the incident a shooting incident where positional relationships are critical to reconstruction?
- Is a motor vehicle involved in the incident?
- Are blood stains present that may be analyzed now or at any point in the future?
- Are there any line of sight issues?
- Was a struggle over a weapon, or lunging for a weapon involved?
- Is a major transportation carrier involved?
- Is arson or an explosion involved?
- Has a death occurred or is it likely?
- Has a police officer discharged a firearm resulting in injury?
- Are elevations important to the case?

If the answer to any of these questions is yes then forensic mapping efforts may be warranted to properly document the scene.

Conventional Measuring Techniques

If a conventional crime scene sketch is deemed appropriate for the scene it is preferable from a case organization point of view that the primary investigator prepares the rough sketch. The physical process of moving through the scene and collecting measurements with a tape measure is somewhat invasive and may require things to be moved to clear a path or create access. This being the case, the initial photographs should be completed prior to sketching and measuring. After leaving the scene the rough sketch should not be altered. If revisions are needed then the original must first be copied to preserve its integrity. In the event that an assisting investigator prepares the sketch then it should be properly labeled to indicate who prepared it and then it should be reviewed and approved (and labeled as such) by the primary investigator. If the primary investigator needs to revise the sketch a copy of the original should first be archived to preserve its integrity (this may be done by capturing it in a digital photo) and then any revisions may be made along with an annotation indicting the date, time and person performing the revision. A finished sketch may be derived from the rough sketch at some point later in time. This finished sketch is often produced with the aid of software applications.

The primary investigator will need to decide which method for fixing the location of items will be most appropriate for the scene. The methods and the tools used should be recorded in the investigative notes. There are many methods that can be used and again the scope of the scene may play a large part in dictating which method will work best. Below we will outline three of the more common techniques utilized in the field. All CSI team members should be competent in each of these three methods as the skills will be needed on various scenes.

Rectangular Coordinates

This frequently used method is the simplest way to record measurements to fix the location of items at the scene. The CSI measures the distances between the evidence and fixed objects at right angles. This is very common in indoor scenes where the items of evidence are measured from two adjoining walls. Since it is difficult in the field to keep the measurement lines at exact right angles this method is not very precise and the measurements will have a large error tolerance.

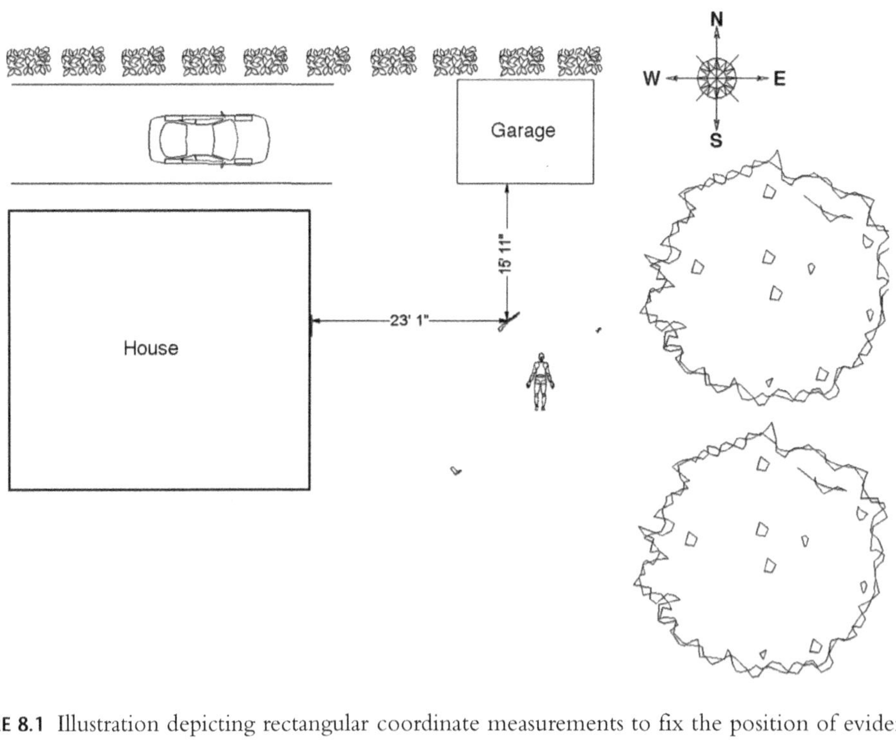

FIGURE 8.1 Illustration depicting rectangular coordinate measurements to fix the position of evidence at a crime scene

Triangulation

Triangulation is also a very common form of fixing the location of evidence at a scene. It is similar to rectangular coordinates in that it also uses two measurements from fixed points to the evidence but it is not as prone to error since it is not required to measure at right angles. With triangulation two fixed points are located within the scene that have line of sight to the evidence. The fixed points are labeled as point "A" and point "B." Distance measurements are then collected between the evidence and each of the fixed points. To complete the third side of the triangle the distance between points "A" and point "B" is also recorded. Triangulation is effective in both indoor and outdoor scenes.

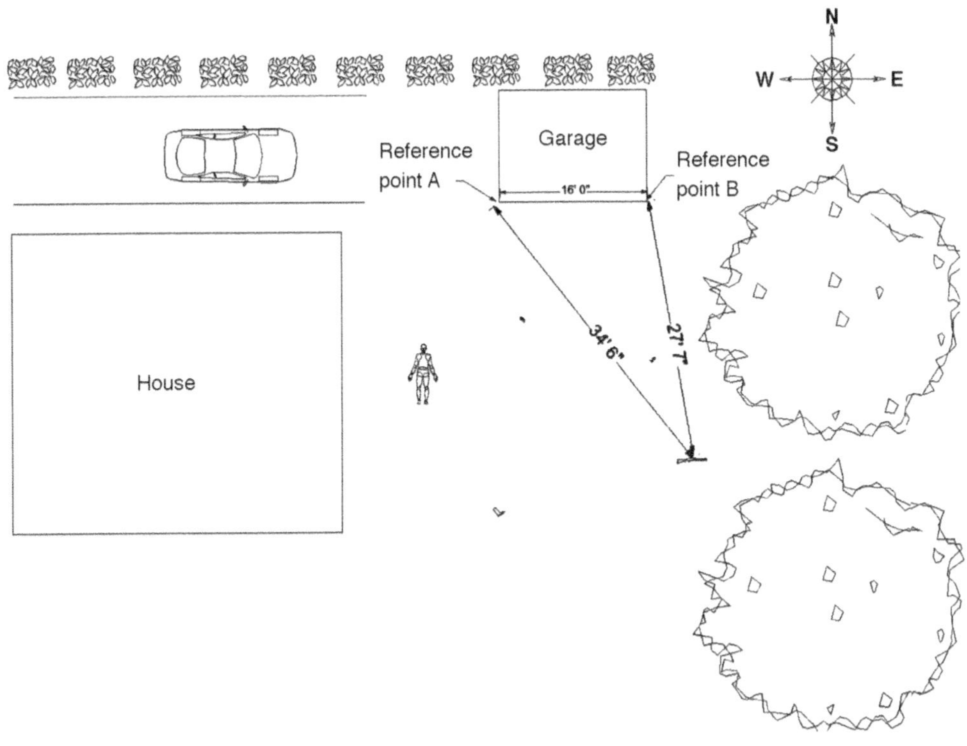

FIGURE 8.2 Illustration depicting triangulated measurements to fix the position of evidence at a crime scene

Baseline

Baseline measuring is a less common technique but can be very useful in large outdoor scenes, particularly in large open areas such as a park or in wooded areas where line of sight to any fixed objects is limited. When using this technique the starting point for the baseline is first located and the position is fixed using triangulation. If the scene is located in a remote area and there is no possibility to triangulate the starting point to fixed objects then the starting point is located simply by setting a large metal spike (steel rebar works well) in the ground. Later if there is a need to return to the scene the metal spike can be located with a metal detector to re-establish the position. Once the starting point is established the baseline is set out by stretching a tape measure in a cardinal direction with the assistance of a compass (the method may be easiest to utilize if the baseline is set up so it extends through the center of the scene in a north direction but any cardinal direction will work). Once the baseline is set up the measuring method is now similar to rectangular coordinates where the distance from the starting point along the length of the baseline to the evidence is recorded and the distance that the evidence is offset from either side of the baseline is recorded. These measurements should form right angles just like rectangular coordinates.

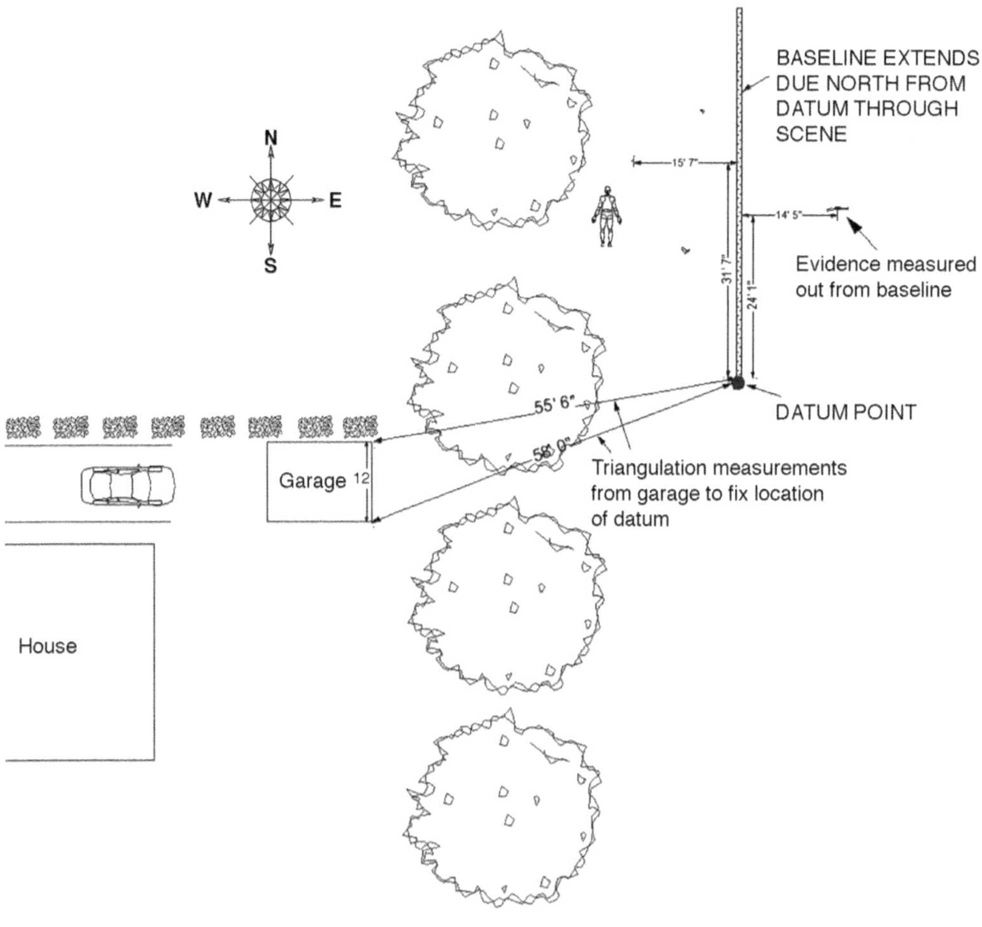

FIGURE 8.3 Illustration depicting baseline measurements to fix the position of evidence at a crime scene

Forensic mapping

The old process of using a pencil and paper to sketch out a crime scene with the assistance of a tape measure is continuing to evolve into a sub-discipline within crime scene investigation known as forensic mapping. Forensic mapping applies a more scientifically sound approach to the collection of positional data through the use of electronic instruments and methods once reserved for land surveyors. Once the data is collected the process then takes advantage of computer software to analyze the data, reach conclusions, and to create graphic presentations. The process allows for the use of calibrated equipment and produces results that are both repeatable and suitable for validation.

Utilizing forensic mapping techniques will improve the work product of the CSI team and create the possibility for other experts who may not have a first-hand opportunity to analyze the scene to conduct analyses and reach their own independent conclusions. Consider for example a shooting scene where the CSI team applies conventional sketching techniques to record the measurements of the angle of impact at several bullet holes. The CSI would utilize a tape measure and some other tools such as a protractor and inclinometer to record the measurements and then sketch it out on paper. These measurements may later be used to reach incriminating conclusions about a shooter's position. However since the crime scene will have been released it may be impossible for an independent expert to repeat the process and validate or refute the prosecutions account.

Repeatability of measurements can be very important when crime scene reconstruction is required. CSIs are very diligent professionals who work very hard to produce fair and accurate results; however, they are certainly not above the potential for error nor are the tools they use above the potential for defect. When a forensic mapping approach is applied to the same shooting scene the measurement and positional data is collected at the scene and archived. It can then be analyzed and interpreted by any number of qualified experts. The measurements can be validated and the accuracy of the electronic tools used to collect them can be determined. Individuals utilizing forensic mapping equipment should be specifically trained and certified for utilizing the equipment in a crime scene investigation capacity.

Forensic Mapping Techniques

Total Stations

Total stations are electronic optical instruments that are mounted on a tripod at the scene. An optical sight is used to focus the instrument on a point that needs to be recorded and then a light beam is emitted allowing the instrument to record the fixed position of the item in three dimensions. Descriptive data such as evidence item number and type of evidence can be attached to each point of measurement along with an image of what has been measured. These instruments were used traditionally by land surveyors to record features such as topographic mapping or to layout land features such as property boundaries. However the total station has now become an established tool used by crime and crash scene investigators to accurately and precisely record the location and positions of evidence and other important features at incident scenes. Some of the more advanced total stations such as Leica's Nova instruments now incorporate imaging, video, wireless communication, and robotics into easy to use instrument capable of capturing measurements, panoramic images and 3D scans making this type of equipment even more beneficial to the crime scene process. The advanced instruments also have greatly increased the speed in which a scene can be mapped.

At the crime scene the primary investigator and crime scene supervisor should decide if total station will enhance the scene investigation. If it is to be deployed it may be operated either by the primary investigator or an assisting investigator who is qualified to operate the instrument. If an assisting investigator is used to deploy the instrument then the primary investigator should confer with the assisting investigator to develop a plan on what is to be included in the total station mapping and how the work will be carried out including where the station will be set up. The crime scene notes should list the details of the total station mapping plan.

Once the data has been collected at the scene with a total station instrument it should be archived in its native format with a copy stored in the case folder. The data is then uploaded into a computer aided drafting and design (CADD) program where it is assembled into a finished product. The most common deliverable generated from total station data is a two dimensional scale diagram but there are many other possibilities including elevation diagrams, three dimensional diagrams and models and images. To produce these finished products a CSI typically utilizes CADD software which has been specifically designed for the forensics field. There are several different software products available and they range from those that are easy to use but have limited features to those that are built on full CADD platforms and offer very robust features but also have a higher learning curve. Some of the software products such as Leica IMS 360 also have forensics tools such as angle of impact and ballistic calculators built in.

Although an assistant investigator might have operated the total station in the field to collect data the responsibility to import the data into the diagramming software and produce final diagrams and graphics may remain with the assisting investigator or it may now fall back to the primary investigator who has more intimate knowledge of the scene and what is required from diagrams and graphics. This should be an established protocol since the field work and CADD work are two distinct phases to forensic mapping.

Laser Scanning

A 3D laser scanner is a positioning system that bears some similarities to the total station in that it is an optical instrument that sets up on a tripod at the scene and records positional data but laser scanners bring things to a new three dimensional level. A laser scanner projects a light beam out to a target surface and then receives and records characteristics of the beam reflected from the surface back to the scanner to create a data point or "point." This point has a three dimensional coordinate position relative to the scanners position in space. The laser scanner automatically repeats the process in an extremely rapid fashion until it has swept across an entire field of view. Within minutes tens of millions of measurable points can be captured. The points are assembled into a point cloud which is viewed similar to a 3D model but each of the millions of points in the model has their own coordinates allowing them to be precisely measured. Most laser scanning systems now incorporate digital imaging allowing high resolution panoramic images to be collected simultaneously with the scan data.

Laser scanners have been around for about two decades now but have gained their place in crime scene investigation only within the last 5–10 years. The technology and forensic specific software has now matured to the point where some progressive minded crime scene investigations units are actually operating their second generation of scanners. The technology has been accepted by local, state and federal courts as evidence in criminal proceedings and it has withstood the test of legal challenges.

Crime scene units engaged in scanning have now progressed with their laser scanning skills past the point where they were using scanning simply to record and preserve the scene to a point where they are now using the technology to increase efficiency by replacing nearly all sketching and measuring tasks that used to be done on the scene. Instead they scan the scene and then virtually measure it and prepare diagrams in the software environment back at the office. The process produces better accuracy and improved scale diagrams and it can be repeated, tested and validated as needed. Perhaps one of the biggest benefits to laser scanning though is that it is completely objective. Every other form of collecting measurements at a crime scene requires subjective decision making on the part of the CSI team about what is to be measured and, consequently, what is not going to be measured. With laser scanning everything in the field of view is not only measured but also photographed.

Laser scanning also presents a protective safety net against overlooking items of importance. The CSI team has many tools to effectively process a crime scene but a crystal ball is not one of them. As any experienced CSI can tell you, often things are overlooked during scene processing because they seem benign and un-important only to suddenly become important later on when new information becomes available. When this situation occurs it is nice to have that 360 degree objective scan data to enable you to virtually return to the scene.

When laser scanning is to be used at the scene the primary investigator, assisting investigator, or technical assistant may operate the instrument. Regardless of who will operate the instrument the primary investigator must work with the team prior to any scanning taking place to developed a written "Scan Plan" to describe the process being used, layout the scene, and decide how many scans should be collected and from what scanner positions. Once the plan has been finalized the scene can be scanned. Since the instrument will rapidly scan and image the scene in 360 degree panoramic views it will be necessary to clear the scene once the scanner is operational. The optimal point in the process to introduce laser scanning is after the scene has been photographed and evidence markers have been placed at items in plain view but before anything has been disturbed either by processing or invasive search.

To maximize the potential of laser scanning in forensics and help ensure admissibility of data in judicial proceedings measurement validation and traceability to national standards should be incorporated into laser scanning activities. Leica Geosystems manufactures a twin target validation system that consists of a high quality steel pole with scanning targets affixed at either end. It is possible for The National Institute of Standards and Technology (NIST) to issue calibration certificates for the target pole system so that a precise known (and NIST traceable) distance is established between the two targets. In the field the target pole is inserted into areas that are scanned in a similar manner that a scale ruler might be placed into a scientific quality photo. When accuracy needs to be validated the accuracy of the scan data can be compared against the known NIST traceable measurements of the twin target system.

After the scene scanning has been completed it is necessary to create an archive copy of the scan data and then to import the data into software where it can be visualized, analyzed and the desired measurements can be extracted. Finalized products from laser scan data include panoramic viewers, three dimensional point cloud models, and scale diagrams. The data can also be used to facilitate high quality three dimensional models of the scene but this work will require an additional commitment of time and expertise.

Similar to total station mapping, laser scanning has two distinct phases. The first phase is operating the instrument and collecting data at the scene. The second phase is data processing and analysis in a software application. The laser scan data may be processed by the CSI team members who captured it at the scene or it may be done by a technician who specializes in the area.

Laser scan data processing varies depending on case needs but typically includes the following steps:

- Create archive copies and working copies of electronic data
- Import project into point cloud software
- Stitch the various scans from the scene together to create a single model
- Visualize data and extract any required distance measurements
- Analyze trajectories and extract angle of impact measurements
- Create graphic presentations
    - Scale diagrams
    - Fly thru video
    - Witness viewpoints
    - Snapshot images
    - 360 panoramic images
    - Link scan points to close up photos from the scene
- Export presentations to disc to share information

Aerial Photos and Maps

Forensic mapping techniques can be combined with aerial photos and digital maps to create some very high quality graphic representations of the scene and they are fairly easy to produce. Measuring crime scenes from online aerial images and maps such as Google Earth may not produce the accuracy required for crime scene investigation. However when using total stations, survey grade GPS systems or laser scanners it is possible to create overlays of the forensic maps onto the aerial images. This technique produces high quality visual maps of exterior scenes. The process is made easy by crime scene specific CADD programs such as Leica IMS 360 (available from Micro Survey). Using these software applications allows imagery to easily be imported and the forensic map data to be correctly aligned on top of the image.

Another possibility, particularly for metropolitan regions, is access to a county, city or state governments geographic information systems (GIS). Most major areas employ these systems as a way to geographically manage various works of government such as infrastructure, roadways, land usage, and tax maps. These systems often include high resolution orthographic photos which are corrected for elevations and are the equivalent of a scaled map. Access to these maps can be extremely useful to crime scene investigations. For instance, in New York City, the Department of Information and Technology maintains the city GIS system. It graphically shows the locations and details of infrastructure, city buildings, roadways, parks and many other map features. It also holds in its database information such as property types, year built, property owner's information and much more which can be extremely useful during scene investigations. Perhaps one of the more intriguing aspects of these systems is the ability to see historic maps that reveal a locations history. The NYC GIS system allows users to view aerial photos from current images or at various points in time all the way back to the 1920s. This can be incredibly useful when investigating scenes such as suspected burial sites. Most of this information can be accessed by government agencies if they can justify a legitimate use for the information. In New York City certain aspects of the GIS map data were made available to the crime scene unit and the information was extremely beneficial to improving mapping of crime scenes. CSI teams are encouraged to work with their government officials to ascertain if this type of information exists in their jurisdictions and if it can be made available to CSI teams investigating crime scenes.

Executing the Crime Scene Search

Once the scene has been properly documented in an as-is condition the crime scene search can proceed. It is likely that items of evidence have already been discovered in plain view and that those items have been marked and documented but an invasive search will now be required to ascertain if additional items of evidence are present at the scene but concealed from view. Crime scene searches are invasive and during the process of the search the scene will be altered so it is absolutely critical that all areas have been properly documented in photos, notes, sketches, measurements and mapping prior to proceeding. It also may be necessary to collect some items of evidence that have already been discovered to prevent loss or diminution of the evidence prior to people moving through the scene during the search. Evidence such as hairs, fibers footwear impressions, patent prints or blood drops may be fragile or fleeting and need to be immediately addressed before proceeding. The crime scene notes should record the facts of any fleeting or fragile evidence or if none exists then noting the lack thereof indicates that all appropriate actions were considered prior to the search.

If decedents are present at the scene, the body should be attended to prior the crime scene search. Information gained during the examination of the body may be of great benefit to a successful crime scene search. A hypothetical example would be at a homicide scene where the victim appeared to have been bludgeoned the examination reveals apparent stab wounds which are visible on the back of the victim. The search would now be expanded to include a knife.

The crime scene search should be carefully planned by the primary investigator so that it is all inclusive, methodical and systematic. If the CSI team acts in a manner that is systematic and methodical the results will be a thorough search. The search plan should be based on the information that was gained during interviews, the scene walk-through, and the initial scene observations made during documentation work. The context of the search should be identified: there are two possibilities for the search context but most searches will actually be carried out with a combination of the two.

- Actively searching
    - Searchers proceed with knowledge of what they are searching for
        - Examples
            - The victim has a perforating bullet wound so the searchers are attempting to locate a fired bullet that passed through the victim.
            - The witnesses state the suspect was wearing a red baseball cap when he entered but not when he exited so the searchers are attempting to locate a red baseball cap.

A list of items that should be actively searched for should be compiled and included in the crime scene notes. Prior to the search all CSI team members should be briefed on what is being actively searched for at the crime scene.

- Passively searching

- Searchers proceed with only general knowledge about the incident and are looking for any items of forensic evidence that may exist at the scene

A checklist of items that should be passively searched for should be included in the crime scene notes (pre-printed checklists are helpful). Although the list may be broad it still provides some focus for the search team. Prior to the search all CSI team members should be briefed on what is being passively searched for at the crime scene. Items that may be part of a passive search list include:

- Firearms evidence
- Firearms related evidence (ammunition or components)
- Ballistic damage evidence
- Knives or other edged weapons
- Blunt instruments or other weapons
- Controlled substance evidence
- Medications or poisonous substances
- Footwear impression evidence
- Tire mark impression evidence
- Tool mark impression evidence
- Fingerprint impression evidence
- Patent prints
- DNA Evidence – blood
- DNA Evidence – other biological fluids
- DNA Evidence – touch
- Hair evidence
- Fiber evidence
- Glass evidence
- Documents and handwriting evidence
- Electronic evidence
- Arson or explosive evidence
- Clothing items
- Sexual assault evidence
- Ligature evidence
- Adhesive tape evidence
- Tools
- Other physical evidence

Once the context of the search focus is determined it is necessary for the primary investigator to identify the search method that will be utilized to carry out the search. There are several accepted search methods used in crime scene investigation and choosing to employ one of them will help to ensure a successful search is completed. Search methods include:

- Point to point search
  - Search of narrowly defined pathways
  - May be used to clear an initial path into a crime scene prior to carrying out a larger search

(for example a point to point search may be conducted to search a path from the entry point to the point where the body is located)

- Line search
    - Good for exterior scenes
        - Large open areas
        - Streets
    - Line broken up into multiple lanes. The searches stand shoulder to shoulder and proceed forward searching the width of their lane.
- Grid search
    - Variation of line search
    - Search of same location covered from two directions
- Zone search
    - Good in small confined spaces
    - Can break an apartment into zones and individual rooms (zones) into quadrants
- Spiral search
    - Spiral search is recommended for searches where evidence radiates out from a center point (e.g. post blast scenes or open areas of water). Search method has limited application but is useful when boundaries are not obvious such as in very large open areas or in open bodies of water. The spiral search is situated around a center point and moves inward or outward in circular patterns.

Once the crime scene search team has been briefed by the primary investigator on the context and scope of the search and the search pattern has been decided then the search is ready to begin. Each member of the search team must be equipped with the necessary personal protective equipment and the proper tools such as lights, metal detectors, rakes, and so on. The primary investigator must control the pace of the search. If the search is being conducted with knowledge of what is being sought out and those items are relatively large in size then the search may proceed fairly quickly but if the search is a passive search or very small (or latent) items may be present then the search must proceed much slower.

Any items discovered at the crime scene must be observed and assessed for potential value. If the item is deemed potentially valuable to the investigation it should be marked to allow it to be easily located for documentation, processing and recovery. Depending on the item type the assessment process may be very easy or may require some careful thought and reasoning. If a shell casing were located during the search of a shooting scene then it obviously has probative value to the investigation and would be quickly assessed and marked, but, the value of other items, such as an empty sports drink bottle on the ground at a crime scene which happens to be in a ball field, may not be so obvious. In the latter scenario the search team will have to assess if the sports drink bottle is simply trash that was present prior to the crime or if it is potentially probative forensic evidence. Once an item is deemed to have value to the investigation additional evaluation is required to determine if laboratory analysis needs to be requested.

Evaluating Potential Evidence

Since it is not practical to routinely collect every single piece of matter that happens to exist at a crime scene (that would amount to garbage collection) the CSI team will have to use investigative reasoning to make decisions about the value of any potential evidence. It must be understood by all interested parties that things like biological stains, latent print impressions, hairs and fibers are present in abundance throughout our entire environment. They are only considered crime scene evidence when they have value to answering questions related to the issue at hand, which is the investigation of a crime.

Physical evidence at the scene can be considered to have probative value to the investigation if:

- It may establish that a crime was committed
- It may establish how a crime was committed
- It may establish when a crime was committed
- It may identify a person (victim or suspect) involved in the crime
- It may link a person involved in the crime (victim or suspect) to the scene
- It may link a scene to a person involved
- It may link a victim and a suspect
- It may help establish motive
- An item that may be exculpatory in nature

Decisions regarding probative value of evidence should be made only with strong knowledge of the established facts surrounding the incident and a comprehensive awareness of the context of the crime scene. These decisions cannot be made in a vacuum and can only be said to be based on valid reasoning after conferrals with other case investigators and supervisors have been made and all available information about the case has been considered. When an item is in question but its probative value cannot be currently determined it is typically the best approach to consider it potentially probative and collect it but perhaps delay requesting laboratory analysis until additional information on its value is received. The only other option requires leaving a potentially valuable item behind and that would certainly not be acceptable.

Evidence collected by the CSI team should fit into one of the following descriptions:

- Probative to forensic investigation (laboratory analysis is warranted)
- Potentially probative to forensic investigation (laboratory analysis may become warranted in the future)
- Demonstrative (not subject to laboratory analysis but has value as an aid in explaining or understanding facts of the case)

The mere fact that at the time of the crime scene investigation the CSI team reasoned that an item had probative value and should be forwarded to a laboratory for testing should not be construed as a mandate, or demand, that actual testing be carried out by the laboratory. These decisions are made early on in an investigation and are intended to initiate an efficient handling and routing process for the evidence rather than dictate whether it will be ultimately analyzed or tested. Once evidence is received at the laboratory additional evaluation and decision making will take place prior to analysis. Crime laboratories simply do not have the resources to blindly analyze everything that happens to be present at a crime scene or even everything that is physically delivered for testing. Even if they did have unlimited resources blindly testing everything at a crime scene would only lead to confusion and raise unending legal issues. If forensic science is to be truly valuable to the criminal justice system then reasoning must be applied at each step in the process. Without reason the system will grind to a halt.

Marking Evidence and Unique Identifiers

Every item of physical evidence discovered at the crime scene which is designated for collection needs to be itemized with a unique identifier so it can be invoiced and effectively cross referenced in reports, diagrams and photos. The unique identifier is also used to physically mark the evidence (when appropriate) and the evidence packaging for future recognition. Consider that at the scene of a shooting incident ten ejected 9mm shell casings are recovered. Each shell casing has identical shape size markings, and color but they need to be located, individualized and analyzed separately. The only way to distinguish these items is by assigning them a unique identifier and individually marking them and/or the packaging that contains them. This process requires a system for assigning unique identifiers to each item of evidence at the scene. A standardized system of assigning unique identifiers should be adhered to by all forensic personnel involved in the collection and handling of evidence. When individual CSIs employ their own system of unique identifiers confusion will result and casework may suffer.

A simple but effective system of assigning unique identifiers consists of utilizing the initials of the first and last name of the person who physically recovers the evidence (typically this should be the primary investigator) followed by a number. The numbers should start at 1 and continue sequentially with numbers never being reused at a single crime scene. It is certainly possible that two CSIs in the unit share common initials so there may be instances where middle initials or symbols are needed to distinguish between personnel. A record should be maintained at the crime scene unit office of the markings utilized by each member assigned to the crime scene unit when marking evidence.

Numbered evidence markers, which correspond to the same number used in the unique identifier, should be placed near the various items of evidence at a crime scene (when appropriate) to provide a visual reference in photographs of the physical locations of the evidence. These markers are placed after the initial documentation of the scene in as-is condition has been completed and then the overall view photographs are repeated. This is a very helpful practice which provides viewers of the photos who were not present at the scene with an intuitive method to understand the context of the scene. The sequence of the numbers is not critical and requires flexibility due to the myriad of differing conditions that may be presented at scenes. The sequence may follow the order that items were discovered or there may be an effort to group numbers by evidence types. For example at a shooting incident where there are several ejected shell casings present along with several items of clothing removed from the victim, it may be logical to assign the ballistics related evidence the first group of numbers followed sequentially by the clothing items. However, it is not possible to rigidly conform to this system since it will fail when additional items of ballistic evidence are inevitably discovered later in the process and the original number assignments have already been recorded in the case documentation and cannot be rearranged.

Other than physical evidence items there are other artifacts and features that may require itemization and marking at the scene. Bullet damage, tire marks, footwear impressions, and patent prints can all fall into this category when they exist on surfaces that cannot be collected. Examples of this type of evidence include a bullet hole in a storefront window or a bloody footwear impression on a concrete surface. These items are certainly considered evidence and will require documentation at the scene but they may not be physically collected. Just like the physical evidence that is being collected this type of evidence will also need to be uniquely identified so that the accompanying photos and reports can be easily cross referenced in casework. To avoid gaps in number sequences and confusion later on in the investigation and court proceedings it is not recommended to utilize the same system of unique identifiers for items that are documented but cannot be collected as the unique identifiers being employed for the items of evidence that are being collected. Instead these items may be identified by a pre-established code followed by a sequential number. The following list shows items that may fall into this category along with a suggested code list.

- Bullet hole (perforating hole) – BHP
- Bullet impact mark (penetration/termination of bullet path) – BIM
- Bullet ricochet mark (linear defect/bullet struck and then left surface in new direction) – BRM
- Footwear impression – FWI
- Tool mark impression – TMI
- Tire mark – TRM
- Patent print – PTP
- Plastic print – PLP

Processing the Scene

Once the crime scene has been thoroughly documented and searched and all evidence has been located and marked then any necessary on-scene processing tasks can begin. Many types of evidence will not require processing at the scene and can simply be collected, packaged and transported to a storage facility or to the laboratory but others require additional processing before being collected. A good example may be a footwear impression in soil at the crime scene. This type of evidence cannot simply be collected without first going through the process of casting with a plaster based material.

On-scene processing may be required to develop, locate, visualize, fix or enhance evidence. When processing tasks are carried out at the scene another round of photographic documentation becomes required upon completion to either record the newly developed/enhanced evidence or to at least document the attempts that were made during processing.

Processing requires skill and expertise as well as a thorough understanding of forensic science in general. Processing tasks must be carried out in sequence and one step cannot be completed without consideration for the other necessary and available steps in the process. Failing to understand the various processes involved with crime scene investigation and their required sequences can lead to irreversible mistakes. For instance if Luminol were applied to a vehicle interior to search for latent bloodstains without first considering the need to search for hair and fibers, dust for prints or swab for touch DNA then these potential items of evidence would be at risk. Since such a mistake in sequence would be irreversible so it would be impossible to conclude that evidence was not lost or diminished in the process. The end result is that doubt is introduced and the quality of the investigation is compromised.

Processing tasks may be carried out by the primary investigator, assisting investigators, or a technical assistant who has been called to the scene. The crime scene unit management must ensure that a CSI team member carrying out any specific processing task is trained and proficient at completing that specific task and has a thorough understanding of forensic science as it relates to crime scene processing. In accredited units, and other progressive minded agencies, the person performing the task may need to be competency tested before they are allowed to perform the task at a crime scene. This is a policy that should be embraced by those involved in crime scene investigation whether the agency is accredited or not. Competency testing allows an individual to demonstrate that they have the ability to independently complete the task in a proper manner and according to established procedure and allows an agency to ensure quality is maintained in casework. When this is done prior to performing the task at the crime scene, credibility in the individual and reliability in the system is improved. Other than the effort required to maintain the testing program there is very little downside to proficiency testing.

Tasks which may require completion by the CSI team during scene processing and may be subjected to competency testing include the following:

- Latent print
    - Development techniques
        - Dusting with powders
        - Applying magnetic powders
        - Fluorescent powders
        - Super glue fuming
        - Small particle reagent application
        - Chemical treatment (typically reserved for laboratory use)
        - Dye staining (typically reserved for laboratory use)
        - Recovering prints from human skin
        - Sticky side tape
    - Fingerprint impression recovery techniques
        - Adhesive tape
        - Hinge lifters
        - Gel lifters
        - Transfer methods
        - Macro (1 × 1) photography
- Casting and lifting impressions
    - Casting three dimensional impressions
        - Plaster/dent stone
        - Silicone casting materials
    - Lifting two dimensional impressions
        - Gel lifters
        - Adhesive lifters
        - Electrostatic lifting
    - Collecting known exemplars
        - Footwear
        - Tire tread
        - Tool marks
- Ballistics applications
    - Presumptive tests to confirm bullet damage
        - Sodium rhodizonate (lead)
        - Dithiooxamide DTO/2NN (copper)
    - Analyzing bullet paths (vertical/azimuth angle measurements)
        - Lasers

        - String
        - Use of probes and trajectory rods
- Application of blood/biological reagents
    - Presumptive testing
        - Presumptive tests
            - Phenolphtalein
            - Leucomalachite green (McPhails reagent)
            - Hexagon OBTI
            - Acid phosphatase
        - Chemi-luminescent reagents
            - Luminol
            - Blue Star
            - Fluorescin
        - Dyes and stains
            - Amido Black
            - Leuco-crystal violet
- Blood stain pattern analysis
    - Stain recognition/classification/pattern characteristics
    - Determining directionality, sequence and motion
    - Determining point of convergence and the area or origin
    - Analyzing clothing bearing bloodstains
- Forensic light source techniques
    - Fluorescence
    - Absorption
- DNA evidence processing
    - Scene collection techniques
        - Swabbing
        - Cutting
        - Scraping
    - Suspect sample collection
        - Ruse samples from suspects in custody
        - Discarded samples from suspects under observation
    - Exemplars sample collection
        - Buccal swabs
        - Fingernail scraping and cutting
        - Hair samples
- Trace Evidence techniques
    - Adhesive tamping
    - Trace vacuum collection
    - Paint sample collection (known and questioned)
    - Collecting known exemplars
- Evidence collection and documentation during coroner or ME post mortem exams
    - Documenting decedents at the scene
        - Identification

        - Clothing and property
        - Wounds and injuries
        - Changes during the post mortem interval
    - Searching decedents and clothing
    - Securing evidence
        - Securing fleeting evidence
        - Protecting the hands
        - Securing the body in a body bag
- Entomology evidence
    - Collection of insects
    - Preservation techniques and solutions
- Excavation techniques
    - Controlled excavations
    - Digging
    - Sifting
    - Soil sampling
- Computers, electronics and digital evidence recovery
    - Surveillance recordings (video, still images, audio)
    - Computers
    - Personal devices (PDA, smart devices, cell phones, tablets, etc.)
    - Vehicle computer data recorders

Collecting Evidence

Once the crime scene processing tasks are completed then evidence can be collected by the primary or assistant investigators. A written record should be kept detailing the time, date and person collecting the evidence. In large-scale investigations where there are multiple assistant investigators then collection activities for some items of evidence and processing activities for other items of evidence may proceed simultaneously so long as activities are tightly coordinated by the primary investigator.

Although evidence collection may seem to the layperson like a simple task (easy as picking things up and bagging them) it is not. Crime scene evidence can be severely diminished if it is not collected, marked and packaged in an appropriate manner. With advancements in DNA analysis, including low copy number testing and touch DNA, forensics is continuing to become an increasingly important asset to criminal investigations. But the sensitivity of these tests demands that evidence is handled and packaged according to strict requirement. When DNA was first introduced into crime scene investigation it was limited to biological stains, but now with touch DNA becoming reliable for identification, any surface that can be touched by persons involved in a crime might be considered DNA evidence. Even surfaces such as fabrics that are not capable of bearing latent prints can be useful for touch DNA in certain instances. This being the case the collection of evidence at the scene must be carried out by trained personnel with approved materials.

Most evidence is packaged in paper and cardboard packaging materials due to their ability to breathe and then labeling information is applied to the exterior of the packages. Paper is the general preferred material for evidence packaging due to the potential for DNA to reside on the items. In order to prevent bacteria and mold from breaking down the DNA evidence, the items must be allowed to breathe. Packaging materials include various sized paper bags, cardboard boxes and rolled Kraft paper. There are several types of evidence that should not be packaged in paper goods including arson and explosive evidence, chemical unknowns and liquids. Instead these materials are packaged in cans, jars, and plastic or nylon bags as appropriate. Crime scene unit managers should ensure that the unit's procedures clearly describe the appropriate packaging materials for each evidence type that may be encountered.

Whatever the packaging material that is used, it is important that it is clean and single use. Packaging material, with the exception of certain swabs, is usually not sterile or certified as DNA free. This is also true of the environments where CSI teams carry out their work including the crime scene, CSI vehicles and CSI offices. This being the case the possibility of cross contamination of evidence from packaging material is impossible to eliminate. This fact has to be acknowledged and understood and steps to limit the possibilities needed to be taken. Steps to limit cross contamination from packaging include using trusted suppliers, only using single use items (not recycled material) in collection and packaging, having stringent cleaning procedures in place for crime scene vehicles, facilities and offices, having designated clean storage areas for packing materials and using PPE when stocking and handling packaging materials.

Evidence should be allowed to dry prior to it being packaged. When this is impossible, due to time constraints and drying times for soaking wet items such as clothing, the items should be packaged wet and immediately transported to a facility where they can be placed into approved drying cabinets. The initial temporary packaging should always be retained since it will likely contain transfer evidence.

Items being collected at the scene must be marked, either on the item itself or on the proximal package, with unique identifiers, the collector's information and case information for identification. Items that may bear fingerprint impressions, tool marks or touch DNA should not be marked directly but instead should be sealed and marked on the proximal packaging. Marking on these items directly will cause unnecessary risk of degradation or obliteration of the evidence. A crime scene unit should have established procedures on how and where the various categories of evidence are to be marked.

All packaging requires the application of a tamper evident seal. The intention is not to create an impenetrable barrier to the evidence but instead to seal the package so that another person cannot open it without it being clearly evident that the package has been opened. This is typically done by applying an adhesive tape over the opening and writing the collector's signature across the seal with indelible ink. When an evidence package is received at the laboratory the technician will typically make notes about the condition of the packaging upon receipt including the presence or absence of a taper evident seal. When a package is opened in the laboratory it is often done so by cutting the package open from an opposite end thereby maintaining the original seal for inspection by interested parties later on. After the evidence is examined it is typically repackaged either in its original package with a new tamper evident seal added, or, in new packaging with the original packaging secured along with the evidence inside.

Requesting Guidance and Assistance

As a collective entity an experienced CSI team will likely possess a wealth of valuable forensics experience and knowledge. That being said they should not be left as if on an island to fend for themselves. They should not be expected to single handedly have all the answers to the myriad of problems and issues that could arise at a crime scene. They should also not be expected to have all of the policies, procedures and methods for crime scene processing committed to memory and available for instant recall. Instead an established system for reach back support should exist and the CSI team members should be encouraged to use it without any potential for ridicule to occur for seeking a second opinion or clarification of a method, policy or procedure. A CSI team member must have self-confidence and be able to independently complete certain tasks but when he or she reaches out for clarification or advice before completing a difficult or seldom used task they must be hailed as a consummate professional much like the surgeon who seeks a second opinion before taking a patient to the operating room.

With today's smart phones and mobile computing applications, support can be easily delivered to the scene. With the exception of remote regions the CSI team can instantaneously talk and share texts with multiple parties, send and receive images or video, receive documents, and search the internet. Unit policies and procedures can be made available online for review while at the scene. The crime scene unit managers must ensure that technology is used to gain advantage and that an adequate reach back support system is in place. This would include contacts that are available to lend support 24/7 including:

- Crime laboratories
- DNA laboratory
- Public health laboratory
- Medical examiner's or Coroner's office
- Law enforcement agencies
- Fire department
- Fire investigators
- Explosive investigators
- Hazardous materials units
- FBI evidence response teams
- Equipment manufacturers

Personnel Issues at the Crime Scene

CSI work is long and demanding both physically and mentally. In order for a unit to continually operate successfully, policies and procedures must be developed by unit managers and put in place to systematically monitor and addresses the needs of the CSI team members.

The CSI team at a major incident crime scene will likely be expected to work extended hours in order to carry out all of the required tasks associated with processing a scene. Most scenes will exceed the normal work day hours with some spanning several days. Many occur during the late night and early hours of the morning requiring the CSI team to be on call to respond at a moment's notice. Criminals do not work a nine-to-five schedule with weekends off and therefore neither do CSIs. Criminals also do not have the courtesy to commit their crimes when the lighting is good or the weather is clear. The crime scenes they leave behind need to be tended to immediately and the CSI team does not have the luxury of waiting for morning, or for better weather, or for the weekend to be over. When the call comes in it is time to roll and everything else in life needs to take a back seat for a while.

This 24/7 aspect of CSI work is among the most undesirable features of the job description, seconded only by the fact that you are constantly exposed to violence, death and destruction. When one realizes that the glitz and glamour created by television CSI shows is purely fiction it might seem a wonder that anyone is really willing to do the job. However any experienced CSI can tell of the satisfaction of helping to solve a difficult case and bringing some measure of closure to victims and their families.

Whatever the case, CSI work is certainly arduous and it can be quite stressful. The crime scene supervisor and unit managers must have policies for looking after the wellbeing of the CSI team out at the scene. Since crime scenes occur in irregular places which typically do not provide many comforts or provide for personal necessities it will be required to schedule breaks and meal times. Even if the crime scene happened to be in a beautiful mansion it would not be possible for the CSI team to avail themselves of the amenities since they would risk contaminating or disturbing the scene by doing so.

In order for the CSI team to leave the scene for a break, or a meal, certain matters must be tended to. Who will safeguard the scene during the CSI team's absence? Where will evidence that has been collected thus far be secured? How will the team be transported to and from a break location? What decontamination procedures are in place to leave and then re-enter the scene? These are issues that require policy development and which the crime scene supervisor should make sure are properly addressed.

Another concern has to do with fatigue and the fact that the propensity for errors increases greatly as fatigue builds. The CSI supervisor must recognize that fatigue will eventually set in and that the risk for errors and omissions will inevitably increase as it does. How long should the CSI team be allowed to work the scene before being sent home for rest? The answer is it depends on the scene. This will vary depending on the assignment type, environmental conditions, expected time for completion, amount of rest the CSI team got prior to the assignment, and so on. Ignoring the fact that fatigue affects the decision-making process and then blaming the CSI team for errors made under fatigue should not be an acceptable form of crime scene management. This type of approach definitely will not help ensure successful investigations are carried out.

When appropriate, the CSI supervisor may have to send the CSI team for rest. A decision will then need to be made as to whether the operation will be temporarily halted or if a fresh team will be sent to continue the processing. If time allows it would usually be preferable to maintain continuity and suspend processing until the original CSI team returns. There are instances though (particularly at outdoor scenes in public areas) where it is not feasible and instead a new team must continue the work. If a new team is being dispatched then a thorough formal briefing must take place between the original CSI team and the replacement team during the scene handoff.

Conducting the Final Search

Once all of the evidence has been collected and all processing and documentation is complete a final search should be conducted. This search is the final safeguard to ensure that all evidence has been recognized and collected. Areas that might have been obstructed or inaccessible during the initial search should now be thoroughly searched to make sure nothing has been missed. During this search all tools, equipment and debris generated from processing activities should be secured for removal from the scene. If any additional evidence is located then documentation, processing and collection will be required. If there is no additional evidence discovered then exit photos to depict the scene conditions upon the CSI teams exit should be taken.

Releasing the Scene

After concluding all investigative activities and exiting the scene, the primary investigator should conduct a briefing with the CSI team supervisor and the other case investigators. The briefing should cover all aspects of the scene investigation and the evidence recovered. If any biohazards or other hazards exist at the scene or if any damage was necessitated to the property during processing the details should be discussed so appropriate action can be taken. If there is no additional scene processing requested by the case investigator then control of the scene should be returned to the case investigators for eventual release to proper custodians.

9

SCENE DOCUMENTATION

Overview

Over the last 50 years forensic science has become increasingly relied on and intertwined with criminal investigations and the criminal justice system. As the use of forensic science expanded in criminal investigations the field split into distinct bodies of practitioners. The three major groups of people providing forensic services for criminal investigations include medical professionals employed by coroners and medical examiners, scientists employed by laboratories, and the field technicians known as crime scene investigators (CSIs).

When it comes to CSIs perhaps the most critical aspect of the work that is performed involves documenting the crime scene. The work that is done by medical professionals and laboratories relies on the documentation collected at the crime scene. If meaningful value is to be placed on the discoveries made during autopsy then the context of how the body relates to the crime scene must first be considered. For instance, if a pathologist utilizes body temperature to help determine time of death the physician will first endeavor to determine the environment in which the body was discovered. Was the body in a warm room with the heat turned high or out in the cold? If a scientist in the DNA laboratory is to analyze a DNA swab it must first be understood where the swab was obtained from. Was the DNA deposited during the crime or at some earlier time? Similarly, if a latent print is identified as belonging to an individual it must be understood where the impression was located before that person can be ruled in, or out, as a suspect. All of these decisions and conclusions rely on good documentation from the scene.

Once a suspect is charged, the work of the forensic service providers is turned over to the justice system. It is here that the true weight of the evidence will be decided. The judge acts as a gatekeeper and must decide what evidence is admissible and the jurors must weigh the evidence that is presented to them to reach a determination of guilt or innocence. Again reliance on the scene documentation becomes critically important to explain the findings so the judge and jury may understand, in a comprehensive manner, its true meaning and significance.

The methods that have been developed for scene documentation at the crime scene involve recording the scene in an as in condition using visual, written, and metrological methods. Visually recording the scene centers on photography and is sometimes supplemented with video and other imaging technologies. The written form involves note taking and report writing, and metrology (metrology is the science of measurement) involves utilization of measuring tools to gather spatial information and fix locations which are reported and depicted on exhibits such as sketches and diagrams.

Photography

Crime scene photography involves both science and art. The crime scene photographer must have good knowledge of the science involved with light and optical systems incorporated into cameras and understand the principles of recording light to capture a moment in time in a photograph. Today's digital systems also require a thorough understanding of computers, electronics, and digital media. The CSI must also be able to practice the art required to properly frame a photograph and decide how to best capture it with the light that is available. Since the crime scene photos form a critical component of the case they must be captured properly and this requires substantial training and experience. There will be no second chances to capture the scene in its undisturbed condition; it is indeed a one shot deal.

Training for a crime scene photographer is a lengthy endeavor that will take time to complete. It cannot be sufficiently accomplished with a couple of hours or even a couple of days of training embedded into a basic crime scene investigation course. Perhaps the best approach to a training program for crime scene photographers is to structure a tiered program where the CSI is expected to become competent in basic photography tasks and then after gaining experience and being evaluated more advanced tasks are added to the repertoire through additional training and testing.

The Scientific Working Group on Imaging Technology (SWIGIT) recommends the following regarding photography training in their guide titled Standard operating procedures (SOPs) and Training Version 2.1 2010.06.11

- Staff should be trained to competency in photography, all imaging equipment, hardware, software, and processes to include SOPs.
- Continuing training in imaging technology and processing is required.

Basic Crime Scene Photographer Training

A formal basic photography training program should exist and be included within the basic crime scene investigation curriculum that is delivered to newly assigned CSIs. The program should contain a minimum of 40 hours of instructional time with 80 hours being preferred. The lessons learned during the initial basic photography training should then be utilized and practiced during any related subsequent training. For example, if training on evidence collection techniques follows the photography portion of the course then photography should be used to document the evidence during that portion of training.

The following covers a recommended outline for basic crime scene photography training. Upon completion of the training and successfully completing the appropriate practical or written testing the CSI may be approved to capture general demonstrative photographs at crime scenes.

1. Crime scene photography overview
    a. Cameras and equipment
    b. Composition
        i. Overall, mid-range and close-up photos
        ii. Framing the primary subject
        iii. Viewpoint and depicting spatial relationships
        iv. Controlling shadows
    c. Cardinal rules of crime scene photography
        i. Fill the frame
        ii. Maximize depth of field
        iii. Keep the film plane parallel
2. Legal issues regarding crime scene photographs
    a. Admissibility issues
    b. Privacy issues
    c. Chain of custody issues
    d. Maintenance of records
3. Focus topics
    a. Important issues regarding focus
        i. Resolution
        ii. Acutance
        iii. Sharpness
    b. Focus modes
    c. Focus with zoom lens
    d. Pre-focus 1:1 photos
    e. Hyper focal focusing
    f. Zone focusing
    g. Rule of thirds
4. Exposure
    a. Exposure variables
    b. Shutter speed
    c. Apertures (f/stop)
    d. Film speed (ISO equivalent)
    e. Electronic flash or light source
    f. White balance
    g. Determining proper exposure
    h. Reciprocal exposures
    i. Reciprocity failure and black noise
    j. Bracketing
    k. Metering
    l. 18 percent Gray
    m. Normal and non-normal scenes
    n. f/16 Sunny day rule
5. Exposure modes
    a. Manual exposure

   b. Aperture priority
   c. Shutter priority
   d. Programmed auto
6. Controlling motion
   a. Tripod use
   b. Shutter speed
7. Depth of field
   a. Factors effecting depth of field
      i. f/stop choice
      ii. Lens choice
      iii. Camera to subject distance
   b. Methods to maximize depth of field
8. Lenses and filters
   a. Focal length
   b. Fast and slow lenses
   c. Normal lens
   d. Wide angle and telephoto lenses
   e. Macro lens
   f. DX or EF-S lenses
   g. Lens optical problems
      i. Aberrations
      ii. Diffraction
      iii. Distortion
   h. Common filters
      i. Polarizing filters
      ii. UV filters
      iii. IR filters
      iv. Color correction filters (film)
9. Electronic flash
   a. Sync speeds
   b. Guide numbers
   c. Inverse square law
   d. Flash exposure modes and TTL
   e. On camera vs. off camera flash
   f. Photographing light objects and dark objects
   g. Fill flash techniques
   h. Oblique light techniques
   i. Bounce flash
   j. Painting with light with an electronic flash
10. Digital imaging technology
   a. APS-C sensor lenses
   b. Components of a digital image
   c. Image quality and resolution
   d. Image file formats

   e. Compression
11. Recording mediums and printing
    a. Silver halide film
    b. Digital media
    c. Printing images
12. Image integrity
    a. Authentication
    b. Archiving images
    c. Storing image media and prints
    d. Copying images
    e. Authorization for releasing images
13. Introduction to evidence photography (80-hour programs only)
    a. Footwear photography
       i. Two dimensional impressions
       ii. Three dimensional impressions
    b. Introduction to tire tread photography
    c. Introduction to bite mark and bruising photography
    d. Introduction to oblique light photography
14. Level 1 enhancements (80-hour programs only)
    a. Archiving original image
    b. Creating a working copy
    c. Using Photoshop and recording keystrokes
    d. Cropping
    e. Adjusting brightness levels
    f. Dodging and burning

Advanced Crime Scene Photographer Training

At predetermined intervals as an entry-level crime scene photographer gains experience the quality assurance manager should review the photographic work (or order another qualified person to review the photographs) to ensure that the photographs are acceptable, conform to standards, and meet the unit's requirements. If the work product meets standards, additional photography training should be designated. If the work product does not meet standards, additional training should be administered and casework should be temporarily suspended. In this manner quality casework is maintained and additional photography training to cover advanced photography topics, such as examination quality photography and alternate light photography is delivered only when appropriate. The time frame for an entry-level CSI to gain the necessary experience to move forward will vary depending on the volume of cases the unit receives and the amount of time that is allowed to practice and develop photography skills.

Advanced photography training covers various topics but should be designed to build the skills required to capture examination quality photographs that are suitable for scientific analysis. These types of photographs require great skill and diligence to be correctly recorded. When it comes to impression evidence it is often the case that examination quality photographs become the only record of the evidence available for examination.

Examination quality photos are required when the evidence itself cannot be recovered (such as a bloody print on a concrete wall) or when the recovery process itself presents the risk that the evidence may be lost or diminished during the process. Impressions in sand or soil cannot be collected so they must be cast with plaster based materials. It is recognized that during the casting process some of the fine detail of the impression may be obscured or lost. Therefore examination quality photos are taken prior to the casting and these photos, if taken properly, will often reveal additional detail not found in the cast. Capturing these photos correctly is absolutely critical and requires advanced training.

The following covers a recommended outline for advanced crime scene photography training topics that may be part of the unit's continuing education activities. Advanced photography training should be conducted as an independent training course(s). The training for topics listed below would likely require 40 hours to 80 hours of instruction; these topics can be broken down into several individual training modules. Upon completion of each portion of the training and successfully completing the appropriate practical or written testing the CSI may be deemed competent to capture advanced photographs at crime scenes.

1. Examination quality photography
    a. Developed latent prints
    b. Patent prints
    c. Two dimensional footwear impressions
    d. Three dimensional footwear impressions
    e. Two dimensional tire tread impressions
    f. Three dimensional tire tread impressions
    g. Tool mark impressions
    h. Plastic prints
    i. Bite marks
    j. Wounds and bruising
2. Chemi-luminescent photography
        i. Luminol
        ii. Fluorescein
        iii. Blue Star
3. Forensic light source photography
    a. Electromagnetic spectrum
    b. Ultraviolet photography
    c. Infrared photography
    d. Visible light florescence photography
4. Photographing deceased victims
    a. Photographing decedents at the scene
        i. Facial identification
        ii. Front, rear, left side, right side
        iii. Clothing and footwear
            (1) Stains and transfers
            (2) Tears and damage
        iv. Positioning
        v. Wounds and injuries

        (1) Hands
        (2) Decedent's property
   b. Photographing decedents and evidence at autopsy
5. Photographing surviving crime victims
      i. Consent and privacy issues
      ii. Facial identification
      iii. Clothing
         (1) Stains and transfers
         (2) Tears and damage
      iv. Wounds and injuries
         (1) Hands
      v. Ultra violet and infrared lighting techniques for revealing bruising
6. Photographing arrestees
      i. Legal issues
      ii. Facial identification
      iii. Front, rear, left side, right side
      iv. Clothing and footwear
         (1) Stains and transfers
         (2) Tears and damage
      v. Property and belongings
      vi. Wounds, injuries and marks
         (1) Hands
      vii. Identifying marks and tattoos
7. Macro-photography
   a. Close-up photos
   b. 1 × 1 photography
   c. Utilizing a copy stand
   d. Utilizing a ring flash

Once training has been completed and the CSI has been tested for competency and approved to capture images at a crime scene the unit's managers must consider the need for continuing education. Continuing education is needed to keep skills sharp and to keep up to date with technology. Since most progressive crime scene units now rely on digital imaging technologies to carry out their scene documentation, as well as for archiving, sharing and printing images, there must be a serious effort to keep up to date with technology and train the staff accordingly.

Continuing education courses should be scheduled at least annually. These courses may be short in duration depending on the need but should also include proficiency testing. Proficiency testing differs from competency testing conducted during the initial training. The competency testing incorporated into the training program is designed to verify that an individual is able to conduct a specific photography task prior to its use in independent casework. Proficiency testing is the continual evaluation of agency personnel in the performance of tasks relating to their discipline. Both competency testing and proficiency testing are recommended by the Scientific Working Group on Imaging Technology (SWIGIT).

Standard Operating Procedures for Photography

Developing the knowledge, skill and ability to utilize the photography equipment to capture good quality photographs at the scene is the goal of the unit's training program. Given the proper training, equipment and practice CSIs should be able to achieve good competency in these tasks. However, once these skills are mastered then guidance is needed to ensure that the skills are used appropriately at the right time and that all of the required photos are captured in the correct manner and sequence. Once photos are captured at the scene they are considered evidence and additional guidance must be provided on how this evidence is to be handled. This guidance takes the form of photography standard operating procedures (SOPs).

There has been quite a bit of valuable research and reporting done by many within the forensic science field on developing photography SOPs for crime scene investigation. Much of this work was completed as digital photography began to come of age and the field needed guidance on integrating this new technology into the forensics field. The Scientific Working Group on Imaging Technology (SWIGIT) has been at the forefront of this work and has provided many reports and documents regarding their work and recommendations to the great benefit of the forensic community.

Scientific Working Groups (SWGs) have existed for more than 20 years; The Federal Bureau of Investigation along with several other federal agencies support the efforts of various scientific working groups for the advancement of forensic standards and techniques. These multidisciplinary groups, who have assisted in developing standards and guidelines and improving communications throughout their respective disciplines, are now being replaced by NIST administered committees being formed under the Organization for Scientific Area Committees (OSAC). These OSAC committees will inherit, and build on, the good work that has been done by the SWGs.

Since the material produced by SWIGIT is comprehensive and has been well received and adopted by so many involved in the field it is unlikely that their recommendations for developing SOPs will require extensive revision. Instead what is likely is that the recommendations become a mandate for units which use photography techniques to record crime scenes.

Recommended Guidelines for Developing Standard Operating Procedures for Imaging

Standard operating procedures (SOPs) are agency unique documents describing the methods and procedures to be followed in performing routine operations such as crime scene photography. SOPs are essential to improve the quality and to implement uniform processes for conducting forensic tasks in a precise, accurate manner. SOPs should be task-based and written for each procedure conducted.

The SOP must be in line with acceptable standards but it also should reasonably reflect what the unit actually does in the field. It may be well intentioned to write an impressive policy with strict rules but if the rules cannot be practically accomplished in the field then the only thing the SOP will do is set the unit up for failure since they will not be able to abide by their own dictates. The rule for writing SOPs is to "say what you do" and then make sure "you do what you said."

According to SWIGIT Guidelines photography SOPs may include but are not limited to:

- **SOP Name, effective date and version number.**

Crime Scene Imaging
SOP Effective (specify date of original SOP)
Version # (specify date of revision if applicable)
The SOP will be a living document and will need to be reviewed at least annually and updated regularly. Since most agencies are utilizing digital technologies if not at the scene then at some point in the process like archiving and printing it should be expected that technology will advance and changes in equipment and operation will need to follow. As changes are made to the SOP it will become required to archive the existing versions. It is common for court cases to take place many years after images are captured and it may become necessary to determine what the requirements were at any past moment in time.

- **The purpose and scope of the SOP**

The purpose of a crime scene unit photography SOP is to provide guidance through documented policies and procedures to unit personnel engaged in the capture, storage, processing, transmission, and output of images captured at crime scenes.

- **Definitions and abbreviations**

Definitions and abbreviations that are commonly used by unit personnel in the field or training or have a special connotation in the SOP should be listed. The source of these definitions should also be cited.

Many definitions and abbreviations will be unit specific but examples include:

- SLR – single lens reflex camera
- D-SLR – digital single lens reflex camera
- f/# – (F/Stop) refers to the numeric aperture setting on the lens of the camera which controls the diameter of the lens opening while capturing an image
- APS-C – refers to the image sensor contained inside certain digital cameras. An APS-C sensor measures approximately 23mm × 15mm depending on manufacturer
- Full frame – refers to the sensor size inside a digital camera which measures the equivalent to a 35mm film negative 36mm × 24mm
- CCD – (charged couple device) a type of camera sensor common in D-SLR cameras
- CMOS – (complementary metal oxide semiconductor) a type of sensor common in D-SLR cameras
- SS – (shutter speed) setting for the camera that controls how long the shutter remains open while capturing a image
- DOF – (depth of field) the distance between two points where the subject is in sharp focus between the foreground and background of an image
- FOV – (field of view) a camera lens angle of view
- MM – (millimeter) a measurement typically used to describe a lens field of view

- TTL – (through the lens) a metering system built into the camera which measures light through the camera lens and may have capability of adjusting for proper exposure
- VR – (vibration reduction)
- Zoom – (zoom lens) refers to a camera lens with variable focal lengths
- JPG – (joint photographic experts group) most common type of compressed image file format used in modern digital cameras; there is lossy compression used to minimize its size
- TIFF – (tagged image file format) an uncompressed image file that is lossless and produces no artefacts as is common with other image formats such as JPEG
- RAW – native file format that stores the unprocessed image data at 12 bits per channel directly from the camera's imaging chip to its memory storage device. RAW image files must be processed with special software before they can be viewed or printed; often considered a digital negative
- NEF – Nikon file format for RAW un-compressed image data
- CRW – Canon file format for RAW un-compressed image data
- CF – (compact flash) a digital media storage card that is inserted into certain cameras to record image data
- SD – (secure digital) a digital media storage card that is inserted into certain cameras to record image data
- MB – (megabyte) memory term meaning 1024 kilobytes
- GB – (gigabyte) a gigabyte is a measure of computer memory or disk space consisting of about one billion bytes
- IR – (infrared) used to describe infrared light or filters designed to control the flow of infrared light
- UV – (ultraviolet) used to describe ultraviolet light or filters designed to control the flow of ultraviolet light
- ND – (neutral density) a lens filter used to reduce the amount of light entering the lens
- RGB – (red, green and blue) the primary colors from which all other colors are derived

Image Capture

Capture is the process of recording an image. The taking of photographs with a digital, film, or video camera is an example of capture. Digitizing images with a scanner is another example of capture but it is not part of the photography SOP.

The SOP should include the following items regarding image capture:

- Indication of what methods the unit utilizes to capture images at a crime scene
    - Digital photography
    - Film photography
    - Supplemental imaging
        - Videography
        - Imaging devices such as laser scanners and panoramic imaging systems
- It should include a listing of what type of incidents require image data to be captured
    - Homicides
    - Death investigations
    - Officer involved shootings

    - Serious assaults
    - Serious sexual offences
    - Robbery
    - Burglary
    - Vehicular crimes
    - Other
- Who will be authorized to complete the different imaging tasks?
- What types of photographs are captured by the crime scene unit and what are the parameters for capturing the images?
    - General crime scene photos
        - Overall view photos are used to depict the overall scene and adjoining areas
            - May be taken with wide angle lenses (specify FOV limits to avoid distortion)
            - Should be taken prior to the introduction of evidence markers and be repeated after the introduction of markers
        - Mid-range view photos are used to depict spatial relationships of items at the scene. They depict areas within the scene which contain an item of significance or an item of evidence
            - Should be taken with a normal lens
            - Should be taken with a normal perspective
            - The photographer should be positioned an equilateral distance between the evidence and a fixed object
            - The frame should be filled with the item and fixed object in the field of view
        - Close-up photos are used to record the details of an item of significance or an item of evidence
            - Should be taken with a normal lens or a macro lens
            - The camera should be held parallel to the surface of the evidence
            - The frame should be filled with the item of evidence
    - Photographing decedents may seem a routine task for a crime scene photographer. However there are some specific issues that should be addressed in the SOP including the following
        - Facial identification photos
        - Photographing all sides of the body before and during the scene examination
        - Photographing overhead views
        - Photographing injuries, wounds and marks
        - Photographing decedent's property
    - Photographing surviving crime victims can be difficult since the CSI may be faced with a traumatized individual and depending on the nature of the crime there may be privacy issues to be concerned with. The SOP should be clear on when a photographing a crime victim is appropriate and who has the authority to authorize these photos to be taken. These photos should be taken in controlled environments such as a hospital with hospital staff and witnesses present. Victims of sexual assaults should not be photographed and should be tended to only by trained medical personnel such as a sexual assault nurse examiner or a physician.

The SOP should include details regarding the following concerns;

- Consent from the crime victim or other consenting party
- Crime victim privacy issues
    - Properly framing photos to protect identity as needed
- Photographing clothing
    - Stains and transfers
    - Tears and damage
- Wounds and injuries
    - Hands
- Ultra violet and infrared lighting techniques for revealing bruising

- Photographing arrestees is fairly common and may be very beneficial to an investigation. Once an arrestee is booked into a holding facility and arraigned access may be limited. Photographs of the arrestee, particularly if there was a struggle involved in the incident can be helpful in these situations. Crime scene photographs are different from identification photos taken at booking.

  There are also instances when a suspect or an arrestee has what is known as fleeting evidence on his person or clothing. This evidence can be lost if it is not quickly documented and collected and the courts have recognized this and allowed evidence that was seized under such circumstance to be admitted. This type of evidence includes things like blood stains, gunshot residue or soot marks on the hands and clothes.

  The SOP should include details regarding the following concerns;

    - Legal issues including consent and search warrants
    - Facial identification
    - Front, rear, left side, right side
    - Clothing and footwear
        - Stains and transfers
        - Tears and damage
    - Property and belongings
    - Wounds, injuries and marks
    - Identifying marks and tattoos

- Examination quality photos are close-up photographs taken with laboratory analysis and comparison as the intended use of the image. These images require experience and skill to be correctly captured. The process is different depending on the evidence types being photographed. It may be desirable to separate these procedures from the general photography SOP. Procedures for the photographing the following evidence types will be required:

    - Footwear impression
        - Two dimensional
        - Three dimensional
    - Tire tread impressions
        - Two dimensional
        - Three dimensional
    - Fingerprint impressions
        - Latent impressions
        - Patent impressions

        - Plastic impressions
    - Tool marks
- Forensic light source photography is utilized in conjunction with forensic lights which can be tuned to specific wavelengths of the visible spectrum as well as ultraviolet (UV) and in some cases infrared (IR). These lights are utilized to reveal evidence that is not visible to the naked eye under normal white light or to enhance evidence that is only partially visible under white light. This type of photography requires the use of special equipment and filters.
    - Ultraviolet photos
        - UV light, particularly short wave, can damage the structure of DNA. The SOP should specify what evidence can be examined with UV light and what wavelengths of the UV spectrum are permitted
        - Many lenses have a UV coating applied to the lens surface to block UV light from entering. The SOP should specify which lens is appropriate for UV photography
    - Infrared photos
        - IR light can cause interference with digital sensors therefore many digital cameras have a IR filter installed inside the camera to prevent IR light from striking the sensor
        - Specially made cameras such as the Fuji IR Pro are designed specifically for IR photography. The SOP should describe the appropriate capture device for IR photography
    - Fluorescence photography
- Chemi-luminescent photography is used to capture the light emitted from chemical reactions when Luminol type reagents are used to search for latent blood stains. This is a unique type of photography that is accomplished by using elapsed shutter release times required in very dark conditions. The SOP should describe the process and a range of settings to be used for these photos.

- Camera settings
    - Focus – many agencies will prefer to use auto focus settings for all images with the possible exceptions of alternate light photography and macro-photography
    - Exposure
        - Exposure modes
            - Although for general demonstrative photos taken in adequately lit scenes programmed auto exposure may be acceptable, however caution should be used since these settings tend to compromise good depth of field
            - Aperture priority mode is often a very useful setting for crime scene photography since the photographer can control depth of field and allow the camera system to choose an appropriate shutter speed to produce a well exposed photo
            - Manual exposure mode will be required for many crime scene situations especially those in very low light
        - Aperture settings (f/stop) should be used to maximize depth of field. A minimum recommended f/stop for most crime scene photography should be f/8 but that may be described as a suggestion rather than an absolute rule
        - Shutter speeds should be set to freeze motion of items within the crime. In many crime scenes there is very little motion but in outdoor scenes there may be activities taking

place in surrounding areas. Scenes with busy adjoining areas such as roadways may require faster shutter speeds to avoid blur in the background of some images

- ISO refers to the film, or digital sensors sensitivity to light. Higher ISO indicates an ability to absorb and record light faster which can be a benefit in low light situations. However higher ISO settings will also introduce noise and graininess into the photos which is very undesirable for crime scene photos. Each camera will produce different results so experimentation should be done to see what settings are acceptable for general crime scene photography. When it comes to capturing examination quality images that are intended for analysis and comparison then ISO settings should be limited to very low settings such as ISO 100

- Electronic flash can be very helpful to add light to a scene and to control shadows however these devices do have limitations such as limited distance and field of view. The SOP should indicate when it is appropriate to utilize an electronic flash and when it should be specifically avoided.
- Tripod use
  - When shutter speeds fall below certain limits a tripod should be required to avoid blur in photos. This setting should be described in the SOP. This is typically one full shutter speed faster than the focal length of the camera lens (e.g. if using a 50mm lens the minimum shutter speed to hand hold the camera is 1/60)

- How image data will be recorded in the capture device
  - Media refers to the recording medium used to store the primary image captured by the device. Historically this was done by producing a negative on to film. Now this is usually done by the use of flash media. Flash media is a term used to describe a solid-state removable storage device that utilizes a non-volatile chip to retain data. This includes Compact Flash, Smart Media, Secure Digital (SD), and Memory Stick. These cards come in various capacities, depending on your need.
  - Once data is captured how will the recorded media be safeguarded and handled.

Image Capture Equipment

When it comes to camera equipment, digital single lens reflex cameras (D-SLR) have become the preferred format although there are some crime scene units still using film cameras. The arguments over admissibility of digital have been put to rest and it is accepted that digital formats can provide a fair and accurate record of the scene as equally as film can and both can be subjected to manipulation if one has bad intentions. In the near future it is likely that those still using film will be forced to make the switch to digital. This is not so much because film will no longer be available as some believe (it will be available for a very long time) but because the fast pace of today's tech savvy world does not like to wait for photos to be processed in a darkroom only to be copied to digital devices anyway.

The SWIGIT guide titled "The Use of Imaging Technology in the Criminal Justice System" Version 3.3 2010.06.11 states the following regarding the admissibility of digital images:

> Digital imaging is an accepted practice in forensic science, law enforcement, and the courts. Relevant, properly authenticated digital images that accurately portray a scene or object are admissible in court. Digital images that have been enhanced are admissible when the enhancement can be explained by qualified personnel.

In any event digital provides the CSI with a means to instantly evaluate their results at the scene and make adjustments as needed. That fact alone should improve casework such that it makes the process of switching worthwhile. Switching from film to digital however is no simple task and there is significant cost to also be considered and funds must be appropriated to build a system from start to finish. When developing policies and training, unit managers need to consider not only what types of imaging equipment are currently being used but also what is likely to be used in the future. Each may have distinct differences and the focus of the work should be on the future.

A complete description of the camera equipment and the accessories and peripheral devices that are approved for use at a crime scene should be listed in the section for equipment. See Chapter 7 of this book for a comprehensive list of photography equipment that may be suitable for use at crime scenes. Also included should be a list of items that are explicitly unauthorized for use at a scene (such as personal cell phone cameras). An agency may wish to prohibit the use of personally owned equipment or smart devices from use at a crime scene since use of the equipment is not included in the training program and the practice poses a risk to the integrity of scene images. Although there may be some legitimate use for cell phone images, there have been too many instances where unauthorized images are captured by personnel at the scene for their own morbid use and then shared with someone via email or text messaging. Once the image is sent the agency no longer has control and before long it winds up going viral on the internet. This causes embarrassment (and potential liability) for the agency and demeans the crime victim and it cannot be tolerated.

Since crime scene investigation is a time limited activity that does not take place in a controlled environment it is important to consider the possibility of exigent circumstances occurring that may require personnel to improvise to complete a task. For example, if camera equipment malfunctions during an investigation in a remote area would the CSI team have leeway under the SOPs to utilize another camera of similar quality that is borrowed from a local police officer or does the investigation need to be halted till a replacement is transported from the office? Some flexibility should be incorporated into the SOPs to allow for exigencies.

- Image capture devices should be capable of rendering an accurate representation of the item or items of interest.
- Different applications will dictate different standards of accuracy. At a minimum, the following should be considered when selecting appropriate devices:
  - Resolution requirements which are in turn driven by the intended use of the image (first responder, crime scene work, preserve impressions, etc.)
  - Characteristics (size, movement, location, etc.) of the scene, item, or items of interest
  - Lighting of the items of interest
  - Dynamic range of the scene
  - Time constraints
  - Required end product(s)

Image Compression

The SOP should dictate what file format is to be used for capturing, archiving, processing and outputting images and what level of compression is acceptable. As stated in SWIGIT Guidelines, compression is the process of reducing a digital file's size. Compression may be lossy or lossless. The decision to use lossy or lossless compression will be dictated by the intended use of the image. Although lossy compression may be acceptable for demonstrative photos, when it is used critical image information can be lost and unwanted artefacts introduced as a result.

Most new digital cameras allow the user to save dual files for each image that is captured: one in a RAW or TIFF format with lossless or no compression applied and one in JPG format which applies lossy compression but gives the photographer an instantly usable image file. In this manner the RAW image can serve as the digital negative and the JPG image can be used as a working copy.

Repeatedly saving a file using lossy compression may exacerbate the loss of image information. Therefore, if an image is to be subjected to scientific analysis and compression is necessary, lossless compression is strongly recommended. Likewise, due to the fact that the end use of an image cannot always be predicted, it is recommended that original images be recorded using no compression or lossless compression. If lossy compression must be used, then the lowest level of compression should be used.

Image Integrity

As per SWIGIT Guidelines, a legal prerequisite to the admissibility of any evidence is that the evidence being offered in court can be authenticated. An exhibit is authenticated when there is sufficient evidence that the exhibit is what the proponent claims it to be. In the case of images the authentication requirement is usually satisfied when a witness can testify that the image accurately portrays the scene or objects that were captured. If authenticity is challenged, the proponent must be prepared to show that the image (or data) has not been altered.

In order to show that the image has not been altered the CSI must be able to produce the "Original Image" as well as the image being offered. These images can then be compared to see if any alteration has been made. In the case of digital files, software is available to detect alterations to the files but this should be accomplished only by persons with expertise in the field. Another way to do this is to utilize a camera that allows images to be saved in dual file formats. When an image is captured, one set of data is saved as a RAW file (this is destined for the archive) and a second is simultaneously saved as a JPG file that can also be archived and then used for processing, printing and sharing.

The RAW file by its very nature is a read-only file that contains all of the un-compressed and unprocessed data recorded by the camera sensor and it cannot be easily altered in its native state. This is not to say that it is absolutely impossible to alter the data in a RAW file; it is not, but it would take expertise and would be detectable. When a RAW data file is opened it must be processed in order to be displayed as an image. Once the image is opened it cannot be re-saved in the RAW format but instead needs to be saved as some other image file type such as TIFF or JPG thereby protecting the original RAW file. Some image processing software allows the user to add a sidecar file to the original RAW file. This sidecar contains image processing instructions that are applied when RAW files are converted.

RAW files are often considered a digital negative and Adobe has introduced a non-proprietary version of the file type .DNG (digital negative). There are some drawbacks to RAW files including the fact that camera manufacturers use their own proprietary versions of this file type (Nikon often uses .nef files and Canon uses .crw files). When the file formats are proprietary special software may be required to open the files. Software such as Photoshop negotiates special licensing in order to be able to process these file types. This raises the possibility that as time progresses and camera manufacturers change their equipment, file formats may become obsolete. Therefore to ensure accessibility to images in the future it may be necessary to also archive software along with the images.

There are software products available to authenticate images through encryption technologies either when they are originally captured on the device or upon import into the photo management software. Some of these products can be very helpful not only in authenticating and protecting the integrity of images but also in managing the digital archives and image output.

In the case of images processed using advanced enhancement techniques, qualified witnesses must be able to testify concerning the process used. The expert would need to produce the enhanced image as well as the original image and need to show the steps taken to enhance the image. An independent expert should be able to repeat the process stated and achieve similar results.

Identifying and Handling the Original Image

A primary image refers to the first instance in which an image is recorded onto any media that is a separate identifiable object. This would include the flash card inserted into the camera at a crime scene. An original image is an accurate and complete replica of the primary image, irrespective of media. Therefore when archiving images captured from the scene the primary image from the camera is used to create an exact copy known as an "original" which needs to be preserved. Primary images do not need to be preserved once the original has been produced thereby making it possible to reformat the flash media and reuse it at later scenes. Once an original image has been created it should never be altered. Instead the original image may be copied to create additional working copies of the image.

The flash media should be reformatted prior to use at a preceding crime scene investigation to avoid the possibility of images from being intermingled between cases. Reformatting a flash card inside the capture device may delete images but it often will leave traces of the files that can be restored using rescue software. For this reason even formatted media must be safeguarded against loss or inappropriate use once it has been used to capture crime scene images.

Preserving Original Images

As per SWIGIT Guidelines, the original image should be stored and maintained in an unaltered state. This includes maintaining original digital images in their native file format. To preserve the original image when processing is required SWGIT states that film-based media originals may be processed if the processing is non-destructive. With analog video, minimal playback of the original is recommended to avoid degradation of signal. Original digital images should not be altered. Processing should be performed on working images only.

Archiving

Archiving is the process of storing data in a manner suitable to ensure that it will be available when it is needed. Crime scene investigation images may be needed many years in the future. Cases can go cold for many years only to be revived again if a suspect is identified. This has become more common recently due to the advent and growing use of the Combined DNA Index System (CODIS).

Additionally court cases take years to wind their way through our justice system and even once they are concluded the possibility of appeals continues for many more years. Care must be taken to ensure that archival media that holds digital images is maintained in such a manner that the information contained thereon may be retrieved many years into the future. There are also statutory guidelines that may apply such as statutes of limitations which vary by jurisdiction and must be considered.

SWIGITS guide for Best Practices for Archiving Digital and Multimedia Evidence (DME) in the Criminal Justice System Version 1.1 2012.01.13 describes many issues regarding archiving image data including the following;

- Physical plant
  Physical plant concerns are multi-faceted. One of the biggest issues is environmental factors that can have an adverse effect to the archive. Some of these factors include temperature and humidity control, electrical surge protection, fire suppression, natural disaster preparation and electro-magnetic field mitigation. The use of a secondary off-site storage facility is encouraged to provide a backup to the primary archive facility.
- Security
  To ensure the integrity of the archive, security policies and procedures must be addressed by the agency. Security policies should address issues such as physical and electronic access tracking, limitation of access, virus detection and data suitability. In the event of an archive containing DME requiring a chain of custody, this issue should be addressed as part of agency policy and procedures.
- Hardware/software
  As technology progresses, and hardware and software are upgraded or changed, it is possible the original hardware and software used to create/access the DME may need to be retained in functional condition to ensure accessibility. This is especially true in the case of proprietary systems.
- Media
  In the field of imaging technology, photographic plates, films, and photographic prints have been shown to be appropriate media for archiving purposes, provided they are developed and stored according to industry standards. Videotape has also demonstrated the ability to be stored for long periods of time without degradation when stored correctly. There are many types of media to which DME data can be written for the purposes of archiving. These include optical media (including CDs and DVDs), magnetic tape, and servers which may or may not include redundant arrays of independent Disks (RAIDs). Serious consideration should be given to the type of media chosen for this purpose.

  Many law enforcement agencies have chosen to use optical media as an interim solution for the storage of DME. Concerns about the actual versus theoretical lifespan of optical media have been raised. The lifespan of optical media begins at the time of manufacture, not at the time it is first placed into service. While optical media has been shown through common experience to be sufficient for short to moderate-term storage, it is inadequate for archiving. However, optical media used for any length of storage should be specifically designed for archival purposes and multiple copies should be maintained. Rewritable optical media should never be used for archiving as it has the shortest lifespan. Steps should be taken to ensure the serviceability of the optical media used by periodically testing and refreshing as required. (In the refreshment process, data from the original media is copied onto new media.) When media is refreshed multiple copies still need to be maintained. This process should continue until the DME is placed onto different media, as technology advances, or the data is to be purged.

Some types of magnetic tape have been shown to be a reliable option in the long-term storage of data provided the media is refreshed as required per manufacturers' guidelines. At the time the archive is being planned and the use of magnetic tape archiving equipment has been determined, consideration should be given to the utilization of a magnetic tape format that is designed specifically for long-term archiving purposes. Many of these devices make use of hardware and/or software compression in their storage of data.

RAIDs can be implemented using different configurations, which have varying levels of redundancy and fault tolerance. For example RAID Level 0 provides for no redundancy or fault tolerance, whereas other levels of RAID provide for excellent redundancy and fault tolerance. When RAIDs are used, agencies should determine their long-term needs and resources and choose the appropriate RAID configuration for their archives.

Image Processing and Analysis

Image processing is any activity that transforms an input image to an output image. Crime scene units may have legitimate use for image processing activities but those should be restricted to basic enhancement techniques of category 1 photos only which are general crime scene photos used for demonstrative purposes and do not include examination quality photographs which should only be enhanced by the laboratory technician conducting an analysis. The possibility and conditions for enhancements and any prohibitions against enhancement must be addressed in the SOPs.

Image analysis, on the other hand, involves the application of image science and domain expertise to examine and interpret the content of an image and/or the image itself in legal matters. Image analysis is not a service that is typically conducted by crime scene units. If the unit does offer image analysis services it is strongly recommended to separate those activities out to a separate SOP document.

SWIGITS guide for Best Practices for Documenting Image Enhancement Version 1.3 2010.01.15 states the following regarding image enhancement:

- Image enhancement

  Image enhancement has been used in forensic applications since the 1840s and is an accepted practice in forensic science, regardless of whether it is performed in a traditional wet chemistry darkroom or in a laboratory equipped only with electronic devices, such as computers, scanners, and/or video capture systems.
- Image categories

  The degree to which procedures used in image enhancement should be documented will depend on the intended end use of the image. Furthermore, the nature of such documentation will depend on the procedures used.

  The Scientific Working Group on Imaging Technology recognizes two fundamental end uses for images encountered in the legal system.
- Category 1

  Category 1 images are used to demonstrate what the photographer or recording device witnessed but are not analyzed by subject matter experts. These can include, but are not limited, to the following:

  - General crime scene or investigative images
  - Surveillance images
  - Autopsy images
  - Documentation of items of evidence in a laboratory
  - Arrest photographs, such as mug shots
- Category 2

  Subject matter experts use Category 2 images for scientific analysis. These can include, but are not limited, to the following:
  - Latent prints
  - Questioned documents
  - Impression evidence
  - Patterned evidence
  - Category 1 images to be subjected to analysis
- Enhancement techniques
  - Basic techniques

    Basic image enhancement techniques are those used to improve the overall appearance of the image. When one visually compares an original image to that same image after basic enhancement, a trained professional should be able to produce comparable results even in the absence of documentation of specific parameterization or software settings. These techniques can be applied over an entire image and in localized areas in an image. They include, but are not limited to, the following:
    - Brightness and contrast adjustment, including dodging and burning
    - Resizing (file interpolation)
    - Cropping
    - Positive to negative inversion
    - Image rotation/inversion
    - Conversion to grayscale
    - White balance
    - Color balancing and/or color correction
    - Basic image sharpening and blurring (pixel averaging)
    - De-interlacing
  - Advanced techniques

    While advanced image enhancement techniques may also be applied to improve the overall appearance, they are often also used to extract specific information contained in the image. These techniques which are not easily approximated by a trained professional without documentation of specific parameterization or software settings. The techniques include, but are not limited, to the following:
    - Frame averaging
    - Fourier analysis (including the use of FFT)
    - Deblur
    - Noise reduction
    - Image restoration
    - Color channel selection and subtraction

- Perspective control and/or geometric correction
- Advanced sharpening tools, such as unsharp mask

Documenting Image Enhancement

The intended use of the image dictates the level to which the enhancements are documented. Any processed image subjected to image analysis should be documented with an image processing log. An image not subjected to image analysis does not need an image processing log.

- Enhancement documentation
  - Category 1 images
    When enhancing Category 1 images, one need only document the techniques with a standard operating procedure that describes the typical enhancement processes. If an original image previously treated as a Category 1 image is to be subjected to scientific analysis, it becomes a Category 2 image.
  - Category 2 images
    The use and sequence of any enhancement techniques in Category 2 images should be documented in every case. Documenting image enhancement steps should be sufficient to permit a comparably trained person to understand the steps taken, the techniques used, and to extract comparable information from the image. Documenting every change in every pixel value is discouraged because it adds nothing of value to the analysis.

    Exploratory enhancement operations not incorporated in the final image do not need to be documented. Test prints and/or intermediate images resulting from a variety of techniques not incorporated into the final image should be discarded.

    Minimum requirements for documentation of advanced techniques include identifying the software application and/or techniques as well as the settings and parameters used. Automated processes, such as running user-defined macros, require only documenting usage if the process is defined in the agency documentation.

Software

Software used in processing and analyzing digital images should produce consistent results, permitting comparably trained personnel to achieve comparable analytical results.

Outputting Images

In a crime scene unit outputting images usually refers to printing. If the unit is using a digital photography platform then printing needs may be significantly reduced but will not be eliminated. Photo printing is typically accomplished with two main types of photo printers, dye sublimation and inkjet. Consumer grade printers will not preform very well or meet the demands of a crime scene unit. The unit may need to print hundreds of case photos at a time and complete the printing in a short amount of time. Of course this needs to be done while still outputting high quality images and often in large size prints such as 8″ × 10.″ To accomplish these tasks a crime scene unit will require one or more professional grade, dedicated photo printers.

Dye sublimation (dye sub) printers use heat to transfer dyes stored on a rolled ribbon inside the printer to specially coated paper which is also often stored on a roll inside the printer. After the dyes are applied a clear coating is applied over the surface of the prints. These prints are dry and ready to use as soon as they exit the printer. Dye sub printers are used in many professional photo labs. After printing the roll of dye ribbon will contain a negative image of the prints. This ribbon should be shredded when they are disposed of to prevent unauthorized viewing of images.

Inkjet printers spray droplets of ink onto the surface of the photo paper. Originally inkjet printers were considered inferior to other printer types due to the large size of the ink droplets but newer technology produces microscopic droplets and the availability of supplementary ink colors can produce superior color prints. Inkjet printers are also available in wide format printers capable of printing high quality images on wide paper rolls of up to 60″ widths. These prints can be very useful for producing courtroom exhibits.

The following should be considered in the selection of printers:

- Final intended use of image
- Time constraints for printing operations
- Longevity/permanence of printed image
- Print resolution required
- Range of colors and brightness to be produced

Distributing Images

Crime scene unit managers need to establish an authorization process for the distribution of crime scene images. Images that are captured or received by the crime scene unit should be considered evidence and sensitive in nature. These images should not be distributed without first receiving a written request and verifying that the person requesting the images has a valid need for them and is authorized to receive them. Simply being in a position of authority should not by itself avail an individual to crime scene records.

All requests for distribution of images should be logged at the time they are received. Once the request is reviewed and approved by an appropriate crime scene unit manager the request should be accommodated and a record of exactly what records were distributed should be added to the log.

Images approved for distribution can be disseminated in multiple ways and a record of the method used should be added to the log. Images may be picked up by the person requesting them or by some other authorized individual, delivered by courier or US Mail, or electronically transmitted as digital files. When images are transmitted as digital files, it must only be done through secure and approved channels such as an agency intranet, server, or secure mail system.

All distributed images should accurately reflect the original image that was captured with the exception of enhanced copies of images. When enhanced copies are distributed they should be sent under separate cover or transmitted in a manner so that it is clearly understood by the person receiving the image that the image received is an enhanced copy.

The following should be considered in the selection of distribution methods and transmission devices:

- Final intended use of image

- Time constraints of the distribution
- File size if image is being electronically transmitted
- Security of transmission method and system
- Integrity of transmission
- Hardware and software compatibility of transmitters and receivers
- File format compatibility between the transmitter and receiver

Quality Assurance

Personnel utilizing images and imaging technology in the criminal justice system should implement quality assurance programs to ensure that results achieved are repeatable and valid. As part of these programs, performance checks and corrective actions should be documented on an ongoing basis. The SOP should include the required quality assurance measures and list who is responsible for completing them.

1. Equipment maintenance
   Where applicable, equipment utilized in imaging should be checked regularly for proper performance and calibration, and the findings should be documented. Cameras have a predictable life which is enumerated as shutter releases. Many cameras have internal tracking capability to count the number of shutter releases over its life.

   An annual inspection of the camera equipment might include checking and cleaning of any dust or dirt particles on the image sensor or lenses: checking the shutter release count to see if it is near the end of its predicted life cycle and inspecting electronic connections for peripherals and electronic flash. Check that all controls and all moving parts are operating properly and check that the electronic flash and flash shoe contacts are operating properly, flash media is in good condition and able to record data.

   Where applicable, an end-to-end system check from the capture device to the output device for consistency within specified system parameters should be performed on a regular basis and whenever modifications are made to the system. All equipment should always be maintained according to the manufacturer's specifications and recommendations as contained in the operating manuals.

   When a piece of equipment or a system falls outside the specifications and recommendations, the equipment or system should be taken out of service until it has been corrected. Evaluation of equipment and system checks should be documented in electronic or written logs and entries should include any corrective actions taken.
2. Software quality assurance
   Software applications may be used for various purposes within the crime scene unit imaging system including:

   - Converting images
   - Archiving images
   - Copying images
   - Burning images to optical media
   - Transmitting images

- Enhancing images
- Printing images

The SOP should specify the software that is authorized for each activity as well as the version of the software product currently in use. Software manufacturers regularly update their products and when updates are significant may release new versions of software. If software errors that significantly affect the results of a processing step are detected, then corrective actions should be taken. If the manufacturer identifies software errors and provides corrective remedies for them, the remedies should be implemented before the software is used again. Once corrective actions have been taken, an end-to-end system check should be performed prior to putting the system back into operation.

3. Personnel and Training quality assurance
All personnel utilizing imaging technologies shall be trained in accordance with the unit's photography training manual and be tested for competency in crime scene photography operations prior to being authorized to capture images at crime scenes.
Personnel authorized to capture images at crime scenes must receive continuing education in crime scene photography and related topics and may be proficiency tested on an annual basis in order to maintain their authorization to capture images at crime scenes.
4. Maintaining standard operation procedures (SOPs) quality assurance
Personnel engaged in the capture, storage, processing, analysis, transmission, or output of imagery in the criminal justice system should ensure that their use of images and imaging technology are governed by current documented policies and procedures.

Measurements, Sketch and Diagrams

After the initial photographs have been captured at the scene then the process of collecting measurement data can begin so that the scene can be depicted graphically in sketches, diagrams, and models. This process is often described simply by the term "sketching" but in reality it is a multi-step process. The process involves collecting and recording measurements, drawing a rough sketch, and the preparation of a finished diagram.

A sketch is a rough drawing representing the chief features of a scene and is made as a preliminary study. The rough sketch prepared at a scene may later be utilized along with the measurement data recorded at the scene to prepare a finished diagram. Webster dictionary defines a diagram as "a line drawing made for mathematical or scientific purposes." A rough sketch is intended for use by the CSI who prepared it while a finished diagram is intended for use by others (including forensic scientists, investigators, attorneys, witnesses, and juries).

Some texts suggest the sketch that is prepared at the scene should be a scale diagram but this is impractical. Scale diagram preparation is a time-consuming process that requires advanced skills and special equipment to prepare. Hand-drawn scale diagrams require drawing tools such as a parallel rule, plan wheel, scale, protractor, compass and French curve, for preparation and these are better used at a drawing table then in the field at a hectic crime scene.

In today's world most of the hand drawing of scale diagrams has been replaced by the use of computers and computer aided design and drafting (CADD) software but again in is not practical for a CSI to complete this work in the field. Instead a rough sketch should be drawn to illustrate the scene while maintaining good proportion of size and perspective of spatial relationship without the requirement of it being "to scale." Later the CSI uses the rough sketch along with the recorded dimensions and measurements to prepare a finished diagram.

Crime Scene Measurements

Training

A formal basic crime scene measurement training program should exist and be included within the basic crime scene investigation curriculum that is delivered to newly assigned CSIs. Although the tasks of measuring, sketching and diagramming go hand in hand the instructional content for each should be able to stand on their own. Basic crime scene measurement training involves instruction on techniques to record accurate dimensions of the scene layout and to record measurements to fix the position of items of evidence within the scene layout.

The following covers a recommended outline for basic crime scene measurement training. Upon completion of this training and the related areas of training (sketching and diagramming) and successfully completing the appropriate practical or written testing the CSI may be approved to collect basic measurements at crime scenes.

1. Types of basic measuring equipment
   a. Hand tools
      i. Rulers
      ii. Tapes
      iii. Measuring wheels
   b. Electronic tools
      i. Laser distance measure devices
      ii. Ultrasonic distance measuring device
   c. Surveyor grade equipment (introduction only)
      i. Total station
      ii. Laser scanner
      iii. Photogrammetry
2. Measurement uncertainty
   a. Accuracy
      i. Factors affecting accuracy of measurements
   b. Precision
      i. Factors effecting precision of measurements
      ii. Repeatability
   c. Significant digits in measurements
      i. Recording measurements
3. Dimension measurements at the crime scene
   a. Recording dimensions on the rough sketch
   b. Required precision of dimension measurements
4. Evidence measurements at the crime scene
   a. Methods of fixing positions at the crime scene

        i. Rectangular coordinates
        ii. Triangulation
        iii. Baseline coordinates
        iv. Polar coordinates
    b. Required precision of evidence measurements
    c. Recording fixed positions of evidence in the scene notes
5. Other measurements (introduction only)
    a. Surface area
    b. Volume
    c. Angle
    d. Elevation
    e. Clearance
6. Measurement quality control
    a. NIST traceability
    b. Certification of accuracy
    c. Interim validation of accuracy
    d. Confirming field measurements

Advanced Measurement Training

Just like in the case of photography the quality assurance manager should periodically review the measurement work to ensure that the measurements being collected at crime scenes are acceptable and conform to standards. If the work product meets standards additional measurement training may be designated. If the work product does not meet standards, remedial training should be administered and casework should be temporarily suspended. In this manner quality casework is maintained and additional training to cover advanced topics is delivered only when appropriate during the unit's continuing education activities. It is not realistic to expect that all of the skills and all of the equipment, particularly electronic equipment, can be mastered during a single basic crime scene investigation course.

Advanced measurement training may cover topics including ballistic trajectory and angle of impact measurements, areas of convergence and elevation determinations along with instruction in the forensic applications of surveyor grade equipment (total stations, GPS and laser scanners).

1. Ballistic damage analysis (may be part of basic training if training is of sufficient length)
    a. Fixing the three dimensional positions of ballistic damage
    b. Measuring the angle of impact
        i. Azimuth angle
        ii. Vertical angle
        iii. Use strings and rods
        iv. Use of lasers
    c. Angle of departure of ricochet bullets
    d. Area of convergence of bullet paths
2. Elevations
    a. Elevation plan views
    b. Determining elevation differences

3. Forensic mapping
    a. Laser scanners
        i. Collecting images and point cloud data at crime scenes
        ii. Accuracy and validation of point cloud data
        iii. Processing and analyzing point clouds
        iv. Virtual crime scene processing techniques in Cyclone
    b. Total station
        i. Collecting 3D point data with total stations
        ii. Creating line work
        iii. Reflectorless operation
        iv. Robotic operation
        v. Imaging total stations
    c. Global positioning systems
        i. Suitability and accuracy of GPS
        ii. Collecting 3D point data with GPS
        iii. Creating line work
    d. Photogrammetry
        i. Accuracy of photogrammetry
        ii. Photo modeler
    e. Basics of GIS systems
        i. Orthographic photos vs. aerial photos
        ii. Reliability of data
        iii. Verifying data

Crime Scene Measurement

Standard Operating Procedure

The SOP for crime scene measurements should delineate when taking physical measurements at a crime scene is required, what measurement information is to be captured and by what methods. The SOP should also describe the measurement system that is to be used to record any particular measurements at a scene. For example, dimensions of the scene layout may be recorded in feet and inches (US customary system) but the width of a blood stain may be recorded in millimeters (metric system).

The crime scene measurement SOP may include the following sections:

- SOP Name, effective date and version number
  Crime Scene Measurements
  SOP Effective (specify date or original procedure)
  Version 1.0 (specify last revision date)

- **SOP Purpose**
  The purpose of a crime scene unit measurement SOP is to go provide guidance through documented policies and procedures to unit personnel engaged in the collection of physical measurement data recorded at crime scenes.

Definitions and Abbreviations

Definitions and abbreviations that are commonly used by unit personnel in the field or training or have a special connotation in the SOP should be listed. The source of these definitions should also be cited.

Many definitions and abbreviations will be unit specific but examples include:

in. – onch, a standard US Customary System unit of length: 1/36th of a yard
ft – foot, a standard US Customary System unit of length: 12 inches equal 1 foot
yd – yard, a standard US Customary System unit of length: 3 feet equal 1 yard
mi – mile, a standard US Customary System unit of length: 5,280 feet equal 1 mile
oz – ounce, a standard US Customary System unit of weight: 1/16th of a pound
lb – pound, a standard US Customary System unit of weight: 16 ounces equal one pound
fl oz – fluid ounce, a standard US Customary System unit of capacity: 16 ounces equal one pint
pt – pint, a standard US Customary System unit of capacity: one pint equals 16 ounces
qt – quart, a standard US Customary System unit of capacity: one quart equals two pints
gal – gallon, a standard US Customary System unit of capacity: one gallon equals 2 quarts
F – Fahrenheit, a standard measurement unit of temperature

Measuring Methods

Measuring is the process of using tools to ascertain distances, volumes, areas or angles between two or more positions within the crime scene and recording the results. The crime scene SOP should describe when measuring is required at a crime scene and the method and system that is to be employed to carry out the measuring tasks.

Measuring is typically required in the following situations:

1. Whenever physical evidence is present and its position needs to be fixed and recorded
2. Whenever a firearm has been discharged at the scene
3. Whenever bloodstain patterns are present at a scene
4. When distances are required to record line of sight for victims, witnesses or others
5. When the incident involves a motor vehicle (other than parked and unoccupied vehicles)
6. Incidents involving transportation modes including crash scenes
7. When dimensions at the crime scene may be relevant to corroborating or disproving a witness or theory

There are situations where a CSI may be requested to process a scene but there is no need for measurements to be collected. These types of scene may include simple burglaries or assaults where there is no evidence discovered at the scene.

When measurements are required the SOP should specify what measurements are to be collected and what method is to be used for recording the fixed positions of evidence.

Measurement methods for evidence include the following:

Rectangular coordinates

Rectangular coordinates present an easy to understand method of measuring evidence that is acceptable when working in interior spaces with walls that meet at right angles. In this method the distance to the item of evidence is measured from two perpendicular walls at 90-degree angles. The accuracy of the method suffers from inherent difficulty in maintaining 90-degree angles over longer distances when measuring.

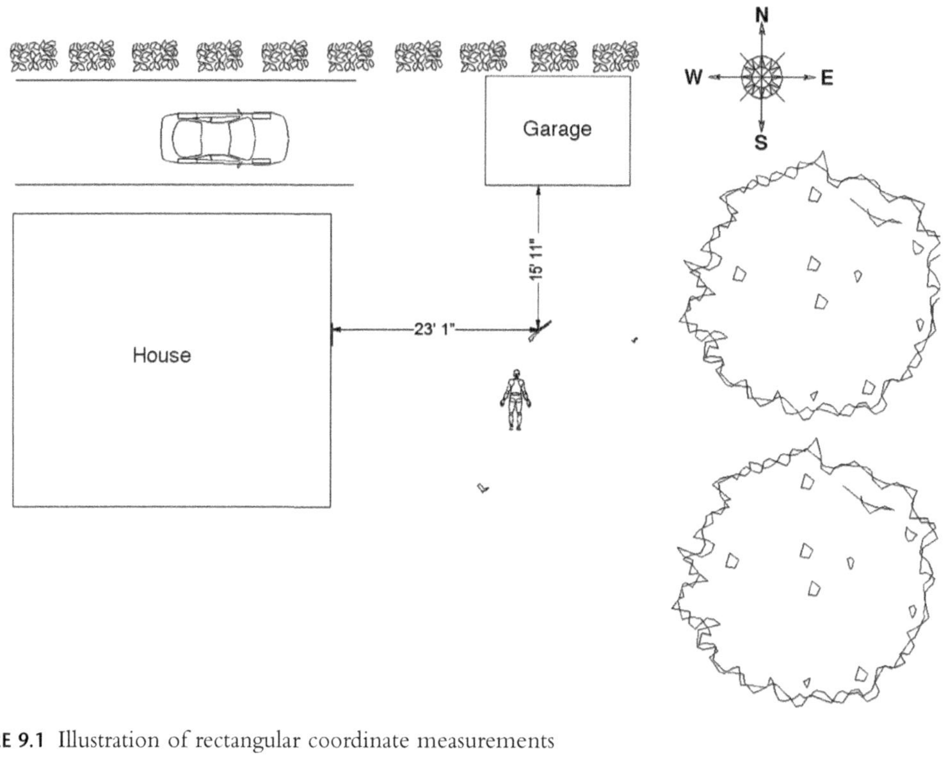

FIGURE 9.1 Illustration of rectangular coordinate measurements

Triangulation

Triangulation presents an accurate method for measuring evidence and is recommended at exterior scenes where rectangular coordinates may prove inaccurate. The method can also be used equally well at indoor scenes although obstructions from furnishings can present an issue. In this method, two fixed positions are chosen as reference points and all items of evidence in the vicinity are measured from each fixed point. A measurement is also taken to record the distance between the two fixed points to establish the third side of the triangular measurement.

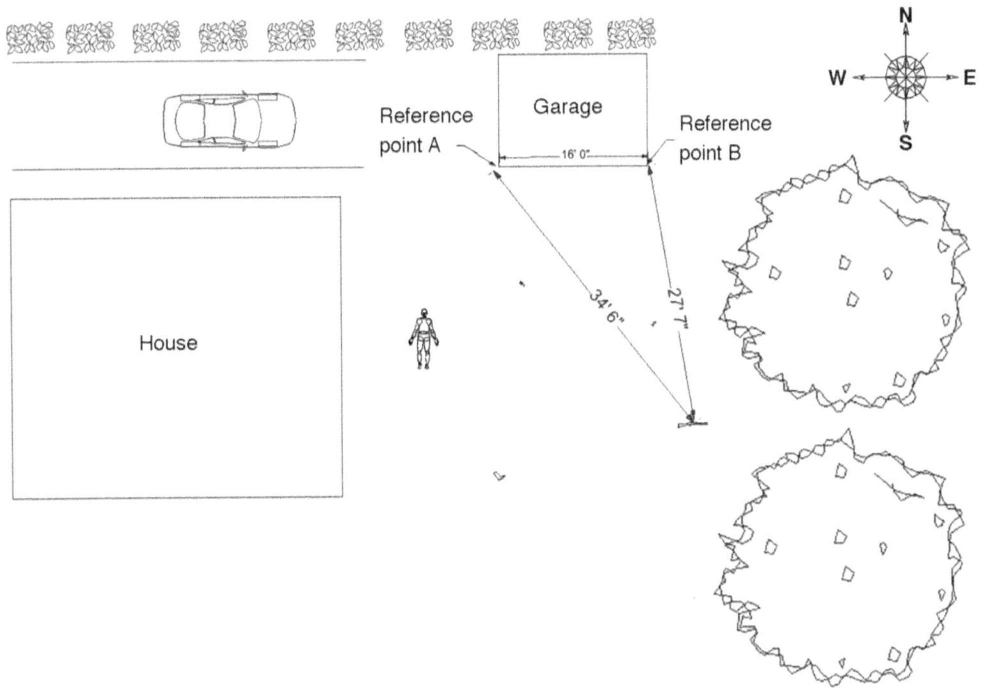

FIGURE 9.2 Illustration of triangulation measurements

Baseline coordinates

Baseline coordinates are a similar method to rectangular coordinates but can be applied in open areas where there are no perpendicular walls to measure from, or in indoor areas where there are too many obstructions to permit the use of other methods. To establish a baseline, a tape measured is laid out lengthwise from end to end through the entire crime scene (in a cardinal direction if possible). A second tape measure is then pulled at a 90-degree angle from either side of the baseline to the items of evidence and the measurements from the two tapes are recorded (Figure 9.3).

Polar coordinates

Polar coordinates are a useful in large remote areas that offer little or no fixed objects to reference measurements. With this method a datum point may be established by staking out a point in the ground and then from that point north is sited with a compass to establish zero degrees. Measurements of both distance from the datum point to the evidence and the degree of direction are then recorded (Figure 9.4).

The system used to record measurements should also be specified in the SOP. In the US most measurements typically should be reported using the US Customary System and read in feet and

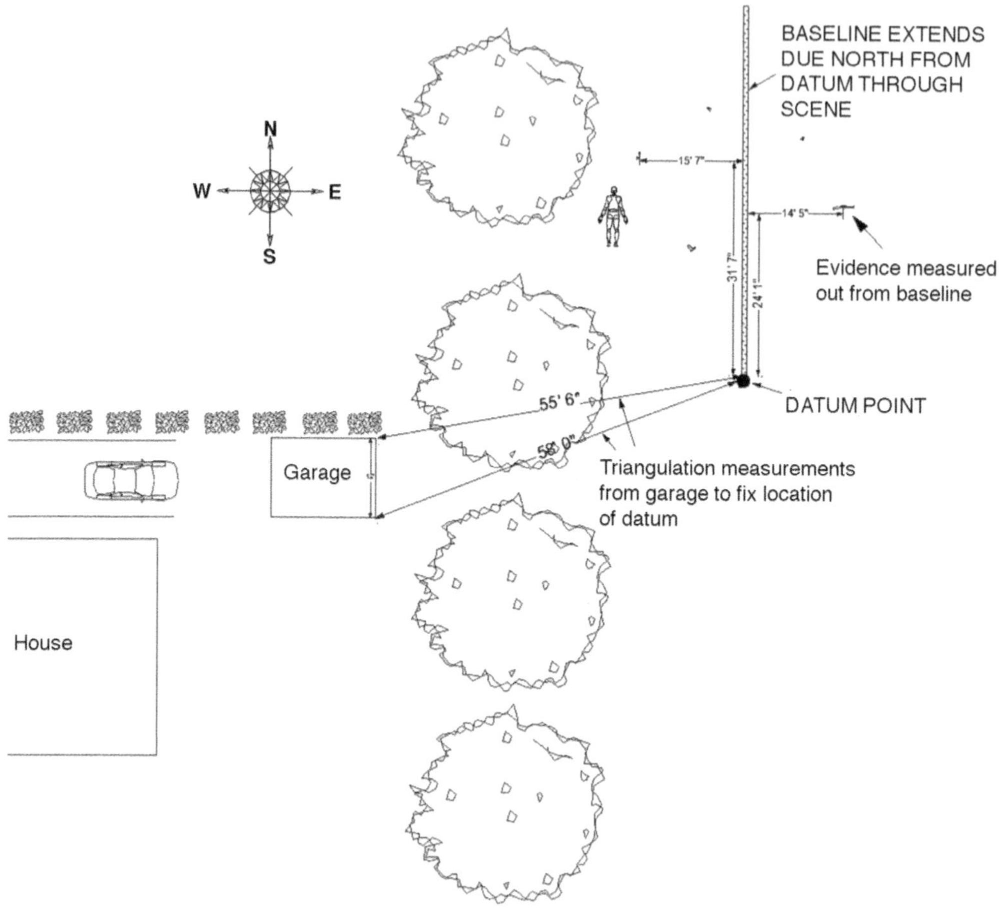

FIGURE 9.3 Illustration of baseline measurements. Note that baseline is fixed through triangulation

inches as most people will be most familiar with this system. Another possibility is to use the metric system but many who read the information later on may not relate easily and will need to do conversions. An exception to this may be when measuring bloodstains where the trigonometric formulas used for calculating impact angles require measurements in millimeters so here the metric system is used.

Equipment

Measuring equipment for the various tasks that may be carried out at the scene should be listed and described in the SOP. Measuring equipment may vary from conventional tools such as tapes and rulers to electronic equipment such as total stations and laser scanners. Each should be delineated along with a statement on when it is appropriate for use and by whom.

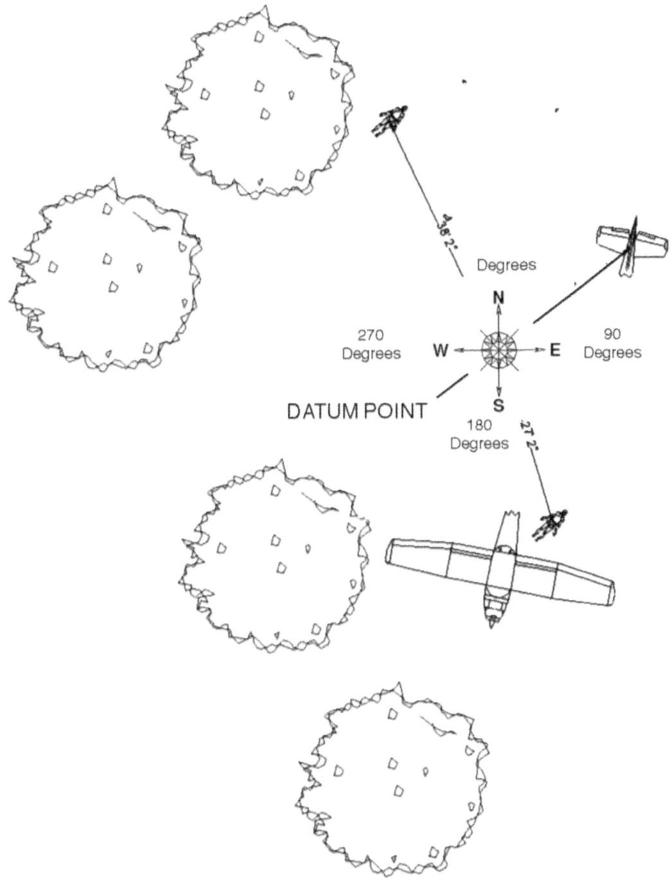

FIGURE 9.4 Illustration of polar coordinate measurements

Measuring equipment may also require calibration or interim validation prior to use in the field. These processes should also be clearly stated in the SOP.

Measuring tapes

These conventional measuring devices are available from different manufacturers and in both US Customary and metric system markings. When purchased with US Customary markings they are available with various graduations such as feet and inches and different precisions such as 1/16th″. Most tasks at the crime scene will require measurements to be recorded to the nearest ½ inch thus implying ¼″ accuracy. So the tape measure utilized should contain graduated marking for each ½″.

Tape measures should be purchased from a reputable manufacturer and should have a certificate of accuracy that meets or exceeds ¼″ supplied by the manufacturer. Tape measurers cannot be calibrated in the field but should be subjected to periodic interim validation where the tape measure is used against a known measure of distance.

Tape measurers are appropriate for collecting dimensions, distances and fixed position coordinates at crime scenes. Tape measures should not be used to collect measurements that are less than ¼″ in length.

Measuring wheels

Measuring wheels are not precision measuring instruments. They are susceptible to imprecise results due to the nature in which they are used at a crime scene. These devices are hard to use in a straight line and can skip when uneven surfaces are encountered. These devices are available in both the US Customary and metric systems but are typically graduated only to the foot, meter or inch and are not suited to measure to ¼″ accuracy as recommended by NIST and DOJ in their Guide for Crime Scene processing.

Measuring wheels may be appropriate to measure dimensions and distances at an exterior crime scene which exceed the length of other devices, including tape measures, and do not require any stated accuracy. When measurements are obtained through use of the measuring wheel they should be reported as "approximate" numbers.

A measuring wheel cannot be calibrated in the field but can be subjected to interim validation where they are compared against a known measure of length. However, if the instrument is recognized as being potentially imprecise anyway and the results are reported as approximate then this may not be required.

Rulers

Steel rules are available with both US Customary and metric system markings (sometimes both are available on a single rule). Rules will be required when measuring lengths of less than ¼″ and when measuring length and width of bloodstains which will be recorded in millimeters. Rules can also be effective when measuring lengths exceeding ¼″ up to the length of the rule. Useful lengths include 6″, 12″ and 1 yard. Rules are available in metal, wood and plastic but steel rules are recommended as they will hold up to the rigors of crime scene work and they can be subjected to decontamination without damage.

These devices are also very useful for inclusion in the scene photographs as a reference of size. For this reason multiple rules should be available for use at the scene.

Rules cannot be calibrated but are available with a manufacturer's certificate of accuracy and they can be subjected to interim validation by comparison to a known unit of length.

Ultra-sonic distance measuring devices

Ultra-sonic distance measuring tools are handheld devices that are aimed at a target (sometimes with the aid of a built-in laser pointer) and then a ultra-sonic sound wave is emitted. The ultrasound wave reflects off the surface and returns to the device. The device measures the time of flight of the pulse and calculates a distance. These devices are known to have a limited accuracy since sound is inherently difficult to focus (particularly over longer distances). The sound waves can be obstructed from objects near to the line of measurement and produce false results and marginalizing their usefulness for crime scene measurements.

Laser distance measuring devices

Laser distance measuring devices are similar to ultra-sonic devices except that instead of ultrasound they emit a tightly collimated beam of laser light which can be focused with very good accuracy. They are handheld and they send out a signal which reflects off a target surface and returns to the device which then calculates a distance either by measuring time of flight or the phase shift of the light. The laser has much better specifications for measuring than ultrasound and accordingly they can be quite a bit more costly but the benefits may be well worth the cost. Laser distance measuring devices are available with certificates of accuracy and can easily comply with ¼″ accuracy requirements. The Leica Disto line of devices offer accuracies of +/- 1mm and meet ISO Standard 16331-1 which describes how information concerning accuracy must be presented. These devices can be calibrated periodically by manufacturers in ISO certified facilities. In the field the units can be validated by comparing them against a unit of known measure.

Laser distance measuring devices are appropriate for use at the crime scene to measure distances up to their specified range which may be from about .05 meters up to 200 meters. They are not appropriate for very short distance measurements (as specified). The devices bring many benefits including allowing for non-contact measurements thereby helping to prevent crime scene contamination, allowing for measurement to areas that are out of reach without the need for climbing improving safety, the potential to reduce errors by reading measurements from a digital display instead of a graduated tape, and the ability to download a record of those measurements for review.

These devices are capable of advanced tasks such as using the Pythagorean Theorem to determine wall heights when the unit is placed on a tripod or measuring angles with an inclinometer. Some can also capture digital images. If these imaging functions are to be used they should be specifically stated in the SOP and should be included in training, certification and validation programs.

Total station

A total station is an electronic instrument most often associated with the land surveying profession. The instrument combines a transit with an electronic distance meter and it reads distances from the instrument to a target. The distances are stored in an integrated computer called a data collector. Measuring historically required a prism rod to be held by an assistant at the point to be measured but newer instruments have reflectorless capability which eliminates the need (in some conditions) for the prism.

Robotic total station instruments are also available and can be used by a single operator who carries a prism pole which is tracked by the station allowing the operator to remotely move about an area while capturing measurements with a wireless handheld data collector.

Total stations have extremely long-range measuring capabilities at very high accuracies. These instruments are relied upon to accomplish the most critical measurements in the surveying and engineering professions and their reliability has been well established for many years. More recently they have been applied to measuring for crime scene applications. Equipment and software manufacturers have recognized the forensics field as a viable market and have customized and tailored their products for these users making the instruments much more user friendly for forensics.

Total stations are appropriate for all crime scene measurements except distance measurements of points less than several feet away from the station's setup position. Different instruments have varying manufacturers' specifications for accuracy and can be calibrated in manufacturer's facilities. Prisms can be arranged at known distances to allow for interim validation of the instruments accuracy.

Laser scanner

A 3D laser scanner has many similarities to total stations. Both instruments had their roots in surveying and engineering before becoming adopted for forensics and the instruments are both set on a tripod at the scene and use light to measure points within the scene. However, a laser scanner takes this process to a different level. A laser scanner, just like a total station, projects a laser beam out to a target surface and then receives and records characteristics of the beam reflected from the surface back to the scanner to create a data point or "point." This point has a three dimensional coordinate position relative to the scanner's position in space. The laser scanner however automatically repeats the process extremely rapidly (up to a million times per second) until it has swept across an entire 360 degree field of view. Within minutes literally tens of millions of measurable points can be captured. The points are assembled into a point cloud which is viewed similar to a 3D model.

Laser scanners have been proven accurate and are well established within engineering and surveying applications. They are very well suited for capturing crime scenes and doing so in a very objective manner since everything in the field of view is captured. The information collected can be used to measure, repeat, validate and analyze the scene in ways not available prior to this technology being available.

Manufacturers offer various instruments with different specifications for speed and accuracy. The instrument must have the capability to produce single point accuracy of less than ¼″ in order to meet DOJ and NIST recommendations for crime scene measurements. The instrument must also be able to be used in various environmental conditions including heat, cold, rain and snow.

Since these instruments collect both measurement information, images and case related meta data the SOP will also need to specify how this data is recorded in the field and managed. Laser scan data is typically imported in point cloud software where it is enhanced, analyzed, and made into 3D presentations which can be very compelling. Similar to a digital photo SOP, the primary copy of laser scan data must be archived and maintained in an unaltered condition so that an original copy of the data can be presented along with any enhanced versions, a record of what was enhanced and the steps that were taken. On board scanner processing of data prior to archiving should be avoided. In this manner the presentations that are created from laser scan data can be proven to be fair, accurate and valid.

Some laser scanners have high definition target systems that can be placed in the vicinity of the scene and included in the scene scans as they are captures. These targets consist of steel poles with targets affixed at the top and bottom with a known distance between them. These target systems are available with calibration certificates from NIST to bring traceability to the process. The use of these target systems allows for interim validation of accuracy when collecting measurements in the virtual environment and should be included in all crime scene scans.

Laser scanning involves two phases: collecting data at the crime scene and, managing the electronic data with computers and software. The SOP should distinguish field work from computer processing work. In the field the SOP should specify when scanning is to be used, what the appropriate resolutions are, what steps are required for interim validation and how the electronic data is to be recorded, managed and archived. Weather images should be captured along with scans,The computer processing aspect of the SOP must specify what software is to be used to process and analyze point cloud data and what processes are acceptable and expected at various stages of the investigation. To improve efficiency the computer processing of data may be done incrementally as the need is presented through various stages of an investigation.

Evidence Integrity

Verification

When using hand tools for recording measurements repeatability is not possible. To ensure precision and to prevent errors have an assistant observe the process to verify the correct measurement is taken and recorded. Electronic devices are capable of recording the measurement and repeating for verification.

Maintaining Original Measurements

Measurements whether they are collected in written form or electronic form should be maintained in their originally recorded state.

Written measurements should be collected in a list type format and each entry should include a description of the points that were measured, the method and tool used and the quantity and units.

Electronic records may include instrument data from handheld laser distance measuring tools, total stations and laser scanners. This data must be archived properly and analysis and enhancements should only be done to working copies of the data.

Archiving of Electronic Measurement Data

Archiving is the process of storing data in a manner suitable to ensure that it will be available when it is needed. Crime scene investigation measurement data may be needed many years in the future. Care must be taken to ensure that archival media that holds measurement data is maintained in such a manner that the information contained thereon may be retrieved many years into the future. There are also statutory guidelines that may apply such as statute of limitations which vary by jurisdiction and must be considered.

SWIGITS guide for Best Practices for Archiving Digital and Multimedia Evidence (DME) in the Criminal Justice System Version 1.1 2012.01.13 describes many issues regarding archiving data. These procedures are not only appropriate for images but also for data recorded with electronic measurement devices.

- Physical plant
  Physical plant concerns are multi-faceted. One of the biggest issues is environmental factors that can have an adverse effect to the archive. Some of these factors include temperature and humidity control, electrical surge protection, fire suppression, natural disaster preparation and electromagnetic field mitigation. The use of a secondary off-site storage facility is encouraged to provide a backup to the primary archive facility.

- Security
  To ensure the integrity of the archive, security policies and procedures must be addressed by the agency. Security policies should address issues such as physical and electronic access tracking, limitation of access, virus detection and data suitability. In the event of an archive containing DME requiring a chain of custody, this issue should be addressed as part of agency policy and procedures.
- Hardware/software
  As technology progresses, and hardware and software are upgraded or changed, it is possible the original hardware and software used to create/access the DME may need to be retained in functional condition to ensure accessibility. This is especially true in the case of proprietary systems.

Software

Software used in processing and analyzing measurements should produce consistent results, permitting comparably trained personnel to achieve comparable analytical results.

Distributing Measurement Data

Crime scene unit managers need to establish an authorization process for the distribution of crime scene measurements. Measurements that are recorded by the crime scene unit should be considered evidence. These measurements should not be distributed without first receiving a written request and verifying that the person requesting the information has a valid need for them and is authorized to receive them.

All requests for distribution should be logged at the time they are received. Once the request is reviewed and approved by an appropriate crime scene unit manager the request should be accommodated and a record of exactly what records were distributed should be added to the log.

All distributed measurement data should accurately reflect the original that was recorded. When enhanced redacted or revised copies are distributed they should be sent under separate cover or transmitted in a manner so that it is clearly understood by the person receiving the data that it is an enhanced, redacted or revised copy. When electronic data is distributed in proprietary formats an indication of the file types and required proprietary software to utilize the file should be included.

The following should be considered in the selection of distribution methods and transmission devices:

- Final intended use of measurement data
- Time constraints of the distribution
- File size if data is being electronically transmitted
- Security of transmission method and system
- Integrity of transmission
- Hardware and software compatibility of transmitters and receivers
- File format compatibility between the transmitter and receiver

Quality Assurance

Crime scene unit managers should implement quality assurance programs to ensure that results achieved are repeatable and valid. As part of these programs, performance checks and corrective actions should be documented on an ongoing basis. The SOP should include the required quality assurance measures and list who is responsible for completing them.

1. Equipment maintenance
   Where applicable, equipment utilized in measurements should be checked regularly for proper performance and interim calibration, and the findings should be documented. All equipment should always be maintained according to the manufacturers' specifications and recommendations as contained in the operating manuals.
   When a piece of equipment or a system falls outside the specifications and recommendations, the equipment or system should be taken out of service until it has been corrected. Evaluation of equipment and system checks should be documented in electronic or written logs and entries should include any corrective actions taken.
2. Software quality assurance
   Software applications may be used for various purposes within the crime scene unit measuring systems including:
   - Recording measurements at the scene
   - Archiving measurement data
   - Burning data to optical media
   - Transmitting data
   - Enhancing measurement data
   - Printing measurement data and graphics

   The SOP should specify the software that is authorized for each activity as well as the version of the software product currently in use. Software manufacturers regularly update their products and when updates are significant may release new versions of software. If software errors that significantly affect the results of a processing step are detected, then corrective actions should be taken. If the manufacturer identifies software errors and provides corrective remedies for them, the remedies should be implemented before the software is used again. Once corrective actions have been taken, an end-to-end system check should be performed prior to putting the system back into operation.
3. Personnel and training quality assurance
   All personnel utilizing measurement tools at the crime scene shall be trained in accordance with the unit's crime scene measurement training manual and be tested for competency in crime scene measurement operations prior to being authorized to record measurements at crime scenes.
   Personnel authorized to record measurements at crime scenes must receive continuing education and may be proficiency tested on an annual basis in order to maintain their authorization to record measurements at crime scenes.
4. Maintaining standard operation procedures (SOPs) quality assurance
   Personnel engaged in the recording or use of crime scene measurements should ensure that their use of measurements is governed by current documented policies and procedures.

Crime Scene Sketch and Diagrams

Training

A formal basic crime scene sketching training program should exist and be included within the basic crime scene investigation curriculum that is delivered to newly assigned CSIs. Basic sketch training involves instruction on techniques and concepts that are similar to mechanical drafting. The participant does not require advanced artistic skills but will benefit from the ability to be neat and patient and to accurately estimate sizes.

The following covers a recommended outline for basic crime scene sketch training. Practice time is critical during training to help begin to master basic drafting skills. Several days should be allowed for completion of training. Upon completion of this and the related areas of training and successfully completing the appropriate practical or written testing the CSI may be approved to produce basic sketches of crime scenes.

1. Overview of crime scene sketching
   a. The nature of a sketch
   b. The purpose of a crime scene sketch
   c. Sketch orientation
   d. Sketch types
      i. 2D plan view
         1. Exploded
      ii. Detailed sketch (close-up of discrete area sown in larger sketch)
      iii. Elevation
      iv. Cross section
2. Tools for sketching
   a. Pencils
   b. Papers
      i. Graph paper scales
      ii. Non-reproducing lines
   c. Writing surfaces
   d. Rulers, scales, plan wheels
   e. Protractors, compass, T-square, triangles, rules, straight edges
3. Lettering
   a. Lettering styles
      i. Single stroke gothic lettering
   b. Lettering guides and templates
   c. Applications for using upper- and lower-case letters
   d. Numbering
   e. Spacing techniques
4. Line work
   a. Identify types of lines
   b. Freehand sketch straight lines, circles and curves.

5. Proportional sketching
    a. Importance to sketching
    b. Estimating lengths, sizes and proportions
6. Symbols
    a. Standard symbols
    b. Symbol templates
    c. Evidence symbols
7. Annotating the sketch
    a. Leaders and arrowheads
8. Dimensions
    a. Dimensions
        i. Interior
        ii. Exterior
    b. Dimension lines
    c. Extension lines
9. Title blocks
    a. Title block content
    b. Title block placement
    c. Revisions
10. Legends
    a. Creating a legend
    b. Descriptions
    c. Scales
    d. Indicating compass direction
11. Borders
    a. Using borders
    b. Inset area of detail
12. Mock scenes
    a. Indoor scene sketching
    b. Outdoor scene sketching
    c. Scenes involving vehicles

Advanced Crime Scene Diagram Training

The quality assurance manager should periodically review crime scene sketches and diagrams to ensure that the measurements being collected at crime scene are properly depicted in the sketches and diagrams and that the exhibits produced are of good quality and conform to standards. If the sketches and diagram work produced by a CSI meets standards, additional advanced training in the topic may be designated. If the work product does not meet standards remedial training should be administered and casework should be temporarily suspended.

Advanced diagramming training may cover topics including CADD software, 3D modeling and the forensic applications of data collected with total stations, GPS systems and laser scanners. This type of work requires advanced computer operation skills and may only be suited to a small number of personnel within a unit.

1. Introduction to CADD software
    a. CADD use in crime scene investigation
2. Preparing diagrams
    a. Preparing finished diagrams
    b. Preparing 2D diagrams with CADD
    c. Preparing court exhibits CADD software
        i. Importing scene data into CADD
        ii. Creating 2D drawings
        iii. Using CADD symbols
        iv. 3D CADD features
4. 3D modeling
    a. 3D modeling in CADD
    b. 3D point cloud data in Cyclone
        i. Cyclone forensic tools
            1. Trajectory
            2. Witness viewpoints
            3. Snapshots
            4. Fly thru
            5. TruView panoramic views
    c. 3D pody poser
    d. Texturing
        i. Basic textures
        ii. Photo textures

Standard Operating Procedure

The SOP for crime scene sketch and diagrams should specify when the preparation of a rough sketch is required at a crime scene and when a finished diagram is required to be prepared. A rough sketch is a hand-drawn document prepared at the crime scene during the investigation. A finished diagram is prepared from the rough sketch typically sometime following the conclusion of the on-scene portion of the investigation.

The crime scene sketch and diagram SOP may include the following sections:

- The name of the SOP, the effective date and version number.
  The purpose of a crime scene unit measurement SOP is to go provide guidance through documented policies and procedures to unit personnel engaged in the preparation of rough sketches at crime scenes and the preparation of finished diagrams for court exhibits.
- Definitions and abbreviations
  Definitions and abbreviations that are commonly used by unit personnel in the field or training or have a special connotation in the SOP should be listed. The source of these definitions should also be cited.

Many definitions and abbreviations will be unit specific but examples include:

Rough sketch – hand-drawn document prepared at the crime scene during the investigation to depict dimensions and spatial relationships
Finished diagram – CADD generated or professionally drafted diagram created with the aid of the rough sketch as a graphic exhibit of the scene for court presentation
CADD – computer aided drafting and design software
N. – North compass direction
S. – South compass direction
E. – East compass direction
W. – West compass direction
′ – symbol to denote feet
″ – symbol used to denote inches

- Sketch and Diagram
  A rough sketch is required whenever measurements need to be recorded at the scene. A finished diagram may not be required in all instances. For instance if a death investigation is confirmed to be a suicide then there will be no potential for a criminal trial to occur and the effort to produce a finished diagram may not be warranted. Also for lesser crimes that often do not result in trials it may be more efficient to prepare a rough sketch at the scene but not produce the finished diagram until there is a need for the material. If the need does arise then a finished diagram can always be prepared on demand so long as the information in the rough sketch is thorough and concise. If this approach is used then the SOP must specify when a diagram is automatically required and when it may be deferred.
  Whenever a rough sketch or diagram is prepared it should contain the following information as it applies to each individual crime scene case:

- The rough sketch includes the outline and boundaries of the scene and the locations of all important objects.
- Prepare the rough sketch with North facing the top of the page. Use landscape or portrait layout appropriately to create a best fit of the sketch to the paper.
- For indoor scenes include room use labels (bedroom, hallway, etc.).
- Indicate postal addresses, street names, place names, etc.
- For outdoor roadway scenes include pavement markings.
- Multiple sketches may be required to depict a single scene.
- The sketch must be drawn prior to disturbing items at the scene.
- General dimension measurements must be included on the sketch:
  - Indicate overall dimensions of interior rooms for indoor scenes
  - Indicate dimensions of streets walkways building lines, etc., for outdoor scenes
  - When applicable indicate dimensions of objects and furnishings
  - Indicate dimensions and locations of doors and windows
  - Indicate positions of involved vehicle (if applicable)
- Indicate the position of all items of evidence using unique identifiers:
- Physical evidence items being collected

- Impressions, marks, scuffs, tracks, trails, etc.
- Ballistic damage
- Blood stains
- Fixed measurements of evidence may be included on the rough sketch if adequate writing space is available on the paper. When the quantity of measurements exceeds available writing space or inclusion would result in illegible work, then fixed position measurements of the evidence should be recorded on a separate document in list format.
- Include the location of all persons (if known):
  - Victims
  - Decedents
  - Witnesses
  - Suspects
- Indicate points of entry and exit and flight paths if known.
- Indicate open windows or doors ajar.
- Indicate location of lighting, operational status, and type.
- For outdoor scene indicate vegetation and ground cover (i.e. grass, soil, sand, trees).
- Include a title block on the rough sketch:
  - Case number
  - Location
  - Date prepared
  - Crime type
  - Name of person preparing sketch
- Include a legend on the rough sketch:
  - Indicate North
  - Define unique identifiers and include evidence descriptions
  - Define symbols used in the sketch
  - Indicate the drawing scale used or write "not to scale"

Sketch and Diagram Types

- 2D Plan view
  Bird's eye type view of the scene depicting a floor plan for indoor scenes and a site plan for outdoor scenes. This sketch/diagram type is appropriate for all crime scenes requiring documentation through crime scene sketching. Additional types may be required as a supplement to this view to properly depict the scene.
- Exploded view
  An exploded view is useful for interior scenes where evidence including blood stains and bullet damage is located on the vertical surfaces of the interior side of the walls. This view shows a 2D plan view but also includes the walls folded down flat along each side of the floor plan.
- Detailed sketch (close-up of discrete area sown in larger sketch)
  A detailed sketch may be required to show small areas of important detail that cannot be depicted in the larger sketch due to drawing space limitations. In this case a second sketch is prepared as a separate document to show the area of detail and supplement the original sketch. This may be required to show congested areas of evidence, body positions, and details of impressions and blood stains.

- Elevation
  Elevation views show vertical surfaces such as a facing of a building or the side of a vehicle. These types of sketches are important to show heights of objects and evidence including bullet holes, bloodstains, tool marks, latent prints, and vehicle body damage.
- Cross section
  Cross sections require more artistic ability since they show a perspective view of a scene and give reference to distance and depth. Cross sections may be used to depict objects of evidence that are concealed from view such as a firearm inside a safe.

Equipment

Drafting equipment is needed for preparing a good quality rough sketch at the scene. The sketch should be prepared on quality paper that is designed for drawing with pencil. Graph paper is available with non-reproducing lines and it should be used when sketching at a crime scene. This gives the CSI the benefit of guidelines to keep the work neat but allows the sketch to be photocopied without the grids being reproduced. Good quality mechanical pencils are needed and are available in various widths. Several widths should be available to the CSI at the scene to allow for visual changes in line weights. Straight edges, protractors, erasers and rulers are also needed along with a magnetic compass and sturdy writing surface such as a metal clipboard with interior storage compartment for the supplies.

Evidence Integrity

Maintaining Original Sketches

The original hand-drawn rough sketch must be maintained as evidence. Upon completion of the rough sketch at the crime scene the CSI preparing the document should mark it "Original prepared by: Name/date." The rough sketch should not be altered after leaving the crime scene. If revisions are to be made they must be made to a reproduced copy of the original document rather than the original itself. When revisions are necessary to a reproduced copy of the sketch the newly revised copy should be marked "Revised by: Name/date/version #." Each time revisions are required the pre-existing document must first be reproduced and the revisions made to the copy and properly labeled.

Archiving of Electronic Diagram Data

Archiving is the process of storing data in a manner suitable to ensure that it will be available when it is needed. Crime scene investigation diagrams may be needed many years in the future. Just like with the other forms of documentation diagrams created by the crime scene unit require care to ensure that archival media that holds measurement data is maintained in such a manner that the information contained thereon may be retrieved many years into the future.

There are various CADD software products that may be used for creating crime scene diagrams. Many of these applications have proprietary file formats which require specific software to be installed on the computer to open the files. Once a CADD diagram has been completed it must be archived in its proprietary format so that if needed it can be opened and revised but it must also be archived in secondary format to memorialize its content and make it suitable for sharing. Since most of the intended receivers of the diagrams (such as investigators and prosecutors) will not possess the CADD software applications that the document was created in, it will be necessary to save the diagrams in the broadly adopted Portable Document Format.

The Portable Document Format (PDF), originally developed by Adobe Systems, is an open standard for electronic document exchange which is now maintained by the International Organization for Standardization (ISO). When you convert documents, forms, graphics, and web pages to PDF, they look just like they would if printed. When you share a PDF file, virtually anyone can read it using free Adobe Reader® software or the Adobe Reader mobile app. The integrity and longevity of these documents is ensured by the ISO 32000 open standard

Software

CADD software has become widely used in the preparation of crime scene diagrams. Several software applications that have been customized or specifically designed for crime scene diagramming are now available. These applications range from simple electronic line sketching to full feature design software based on robust CADD platforms. While the simpler versions may have an easier learning curve the programs designed around a full CADD platform will produce better results as far as accuracy and presentation are concerned. If software is utilized for diagramming purposes it must be described in the SOP along with the version number currently in use. If updates or changes are made to diagramming software then the previous versions must be archived to allow pre-existing files to be retrieved as needed. When software is utilized for diagramming it must be officially licensed by the crime scene unit and utilized on approved computers only.

Distributing Sketches and Diagrams

Consistent with other the forms of documentation crime scene unit managers must establish an authorization process for the distribution of crime scene sketches and diagrams. Sketches and diagrams that are created by the crime scene unit should be considered evidence. These sketches and diagrams should not be distributed without first receiving a written request and verifying that the person requesting the information has a valid need for them and is authorized to receive them. The policy outline in the prior sections on distributing crime scene images should be followed for sketches and diagrams as well.

Quality Assurance

As with all forms of crime scene documentation the crime scene unit managers should implement quality assurance programs to ensure that results achieved are repeatable and valid. Performance checks and corrective actions should be documented on an ongoing basis.

1. Software quality assurance
   When CADD or sketching software is intended for use by the crime scene unit the software application should first be validated. This can be accomplished by creating a sample diagram of a known location such as a floor plan of the crime scene unit office. Dimensions are then applied and the diagram is printed to a specific scale. A plan wheel or engineering scale is then used to

compare a series of known measurements from the location to the scale measurements produced by the software program. If software errors that significantly affect the results are detected, then corrective actions should be taken. If the manufacturer identifies software errors and provides corrective remedies for them, the remedies should be implemented before the software is used.

2. Personnel and rraining quality assurance
   All personnel preparing rough sketches and/or finished diagrams shall be trained in accordance with the unit's crime scene sketch and diagram training manual and be tested for competency in sketch and diagram preparation prior to being authorized to prepare sketches and diagrams of crime scenes.
   Personnel authorized to prepare sketches and diagrams of crime scenes must receive continuing education and may be proficiency tested on an annual basis in order to maintain their authorization to prepare sketches and diagrams.
3. Maintaining standard operation procedures (SOPs) quality assurance

Personnel engaged in the preparation of sketches and diagrams should ensure that their use of measurements is governed by current documented policies.

Investigative Scene Notes

A critical step in documenting crime scenes is the taking of notes while completing the tasks associated with the crime scene process. This task requires less training and equipment than the other forms of crime scene documentation but is no less important. Good quality notes will serve as a permanent record that the CSI and others can return to in order to check facts and recall the events at the scene. The notes must be contemporaneous meaning that they are recorded during the same time period as the event or observation. Contemporaneous notes are recognized as the most accurate record of events since when entries are made at the time of an event they are more likely to be accurately recorded.

Training

Note taking is an acquired skill that can be learned and improved and should not be overlooked during training. Time does not allow for lengthy or verbatim note taking so the CSI must select key facts and record them in an abbreviated form. Abbreviations and symbols used during shorthand should be standardized throughout the crime scene investigation unit to allow others to understand their meanings. Personnel must be discouraged from developing their own shorthand styles. The notes must also be legible to be of real value at later dates to different users.

The training program should cover the following topics:

1. Overview of contemporaneous notes
   a. What are contemporaneous notes
   b. Require notes for CSI
2. Effective note taking methods
   a. Format and style
      i. Headings

   b. Abbreviations
   c. Symbols
   d. Complete ideas
   e. Quantity
   f. Numbering and indexing
3. Archiving and memorializing notes
   a. Maintaining original copies
   b. Archiving methods
4. Admissibility of contemporaneous notes
   a. Authenticating
   b. Subpoena of notes
   c. Referring to notes during testimony
   d. Freedom of information
5. Effective report writing
   a. Using notes for report writing

Standard Operating Procedure

The SOP for crime scene notes should specify when notes are required to be recorded by the CSI which is likely to be for each and every crime scene investigation that is assigned to the individual. This must be decided not only for the primary crime scene investigator but also for any assisting investigators, supervisors and technical assistants who also participate in scene activities. If note taking is required for these personnel it should also describe how those notes are to be memorialized within the case folder. The format, style, method and required minimum content must also be stated in the SOP.

The Crime scene notes SOP may include the following sections:

- **SOP Name, effective date and version number**
  Crime scene notes
  SOP Effective (specify date or original procedure)
  Version 1.0 (specify last revision date)
- **Purpose**
  The purpose of a crime scene notes SOP is to go provide guidance through documented policies and procedures to unit personnel engaged in the taking of notes at crime scenes.
- **Definitions and Abbreviations**
  Include a list of standard abbreviations that the unit uses during note taking. Personnel should only be permitted to use abbreviations that are listed. A streamlined method for CSIs to request approval for use of new abbreviations should also be included.

Note Methods

Contemporaneous notes are required in the following instances:

- By a primary crime scene investigator when carrying out assigned investigative activities
- By an assisting investigator when performing scene processing tasks independent of the primary CSI

    - Notes are limited to the specific tasks performed
- By a technical assistant whenever responding to a crime scene
    - Notes are limited to specific tasks where the person has technical expertise
- By a supervisor when performing scene processing tasks independent of the primary CSI
    - Notes are limited to the specific tasks performed and do not include supervisory functions

Notes should be kept separate from other written material on clean lined paper and writing should be restricted to one side of the paper. Each page should be consecutively numbered (page 1 of 00) and include a heading stating the name of the preparer, case number, and date. The page should have a left side margin where times are recorded and a main writing area where details are written. Pre-printed forms may be helpful to capture notes in force captioned fields but freehand note taking will still be required in most cases.

Contemporaneous notes should begin at the time the assignment is received and continue until the scene processing has concluded. Additional notes may be taken in the period after scene processing has concluded in order to record facts including evidence transmittal and analysis or conferrals with investigators and lab personnel.

Entries should be made at the following steps:

- Upon receipt of assignment
    - Date/time
    - Assignment type
    - Location
    - CSI Team Members
    - Method of travel to scene (i.e. vehicle number)
- Upon arrival at scene
    - Persons present
        - Police personnel
            - Officer safeguarding scene
            - First responding officer
            - Investigators
            - Supervisors
        - Public safety personnel
        - Civilians
    - Environmental conditions
        - Outdoor weather and temperature
        - Temperature of indoor scenes
        - Lighting
        - Concerns for evidence due to environmental conditions
    - Scene description
        - General description
        - Boundaries
        - Points of entry or exit
    - Observations
        - General observations

        - Potential for secondary crime scenes
    - Contamination prevention
        - Scene security and safeguarding
        - Steps taken to prevent contamination
        - Personal protective equipment
- Upon completion of initial on-scene conferrals
    - Details of conferral
- Whenever learning of critical facts
    - Victim identity
    - Witness names
    - Details surrounding incident
    - Other important facts
- Upon making any notifications or requests
    - Person notified and reason for notification
- Upon completion of crime scene walk -
    - Who participated in walk-through
    - Observations made during the walk thru
    - Details of evidence in plain view
    - Details of state of victim
- Prior to beginning photos, sketch and measurements
    - Time photography or sketch initiated
    - Any details not being recorded in a photo log
- During crime scene search activities
    - Search warrant or consent issues
    - Search team members
    - Areas searched
    - Search method used
    - Search tools used
        - Forensic light source, filters and wavelengths
    - Results of search
- When carrying out scene processing tasks
    - Details of all processing activities (i.e. dusting for prints)
        - Persons performing task
        - Methods and equipment
        - Results including positive and negative findings
- When processing evidence
    - Details of processing activities (i.e. casting impressions)
        - Persons performing task
        - Methods and equipment
        - Results
- During use of reagents and testing
    - Details of reagents
        - Lot numbers and expirations
        - Control tests

        - Details of testing
        - Results of testing
- Upon collection and packaging of evidence
    - Item description
    - Unique identifier
    - Time collected
    - Packaging methods and materials
    - Evidence and package marking
    - Method used to seal package
- Upon examination of decedent(s)
    - Name and DOB
    - Method of confirming identity (if applicable)
    - Physical description
    - Clothing description
    - List of personal property
    - Location and position of body
    - Injury and wound description
    - Name of medical examiner representative at scene
    - Method used to secure evidence on body or hands
    - Method used to wrap body for transport and tag number
- Upon examination of vehicle(s)
    - Vehicles relationship to scene
        - Used during commission of crime
        - Used to travel to or from the crime scene
        - Victim's vehicle
        - Suspect's vehicle
        - Parked at scene or other
    - Make, model, color and year of vehicle
    - VIN plate number
    - Condition of vehicle exterior and interior
    - Location and position of vehicle
    - Details of examination and processing
- Upon completion of final search of scene
    - Search team members
    - Areas searched
    - Results
- Upon completion of on-scene activities

Equipment

Only basic supplies are required for note taking at the scene. Supplies include black permanent ink pens, lined writing pads and a clip board. If pre-printed forms are used to force caption notes at the scene then a supply of forms is also required.

Evidence Integrity

Maintaining Original Notes

The original hand written notes must be maintained as evidence and not be destroyed. Upon completion of each page of notes at the crime scene the CSI preparing the notes should initial and date the page. The notes should not be altered after leaving the crime scene.

Notes should only be made with permanent ink and any corrections should be made by striking through the word(s) with a single line and initialing the strike through. Erasures or white-out corrections should be prohibited. Extra spacing should not be left between lines. When extra spacing is left at the bottom of a page it should be cancelled out by drawing a diagonal line from the top left of the first blank line to the bottom right of the last blank line.

Software

Mobile devices are now being used in the field for various professions to capture contemporaneous information. This is a promising development for CSI work as it has the potential to streamline work at the scene and electronically record and archive data. It can also greatly improve efficiency and reduce errors by eliminating the need to enter redundant data.

If software is used on mobile devices to record the contemporaneous notes then the software application and the device must be tested for reliability and integrity of data. Wireless devices will also need a secure method to transmit the data collected to computer systems at the office.

Distributing Notes

Consistent with other the forms of documentation crime scene unit managers must establish an authorization process for the distribution of crime scene notes. Since notes may require interpretation by the person who prepared them, the policy may be that notes are not routinely distributed with generic requests for case records unless they are specifically requested. However when receiving a written request specifically requesting case notes and verifying that the person requesting the information is authorized to receive them, they should be made available.

Quality Assurance

As with all forms of crime scene documentation the crime scene unit managers should implement quality assurance programs to ensure that note taking is consistent, concise and in conformance with the SOP. Performance checks and corrective actions should be documented on an ongoing basis.

Personnel and Training Quality Assurance

All personnel recording notes at crime scenes shall be trained in accordance with the unit's training program prior to being authorized to prepare notes at crime scenes.

10

ENSURING QUALITY

Introduction

The need for a comprehensive quality control program with effective quality assurance procedures cannot be overstated. Although quality control programs are generally developed for, and mainly used by the laboratory, the need to ensure a quality product does not belong in the laboratory alone. In the report issued by the National Academy of Science (Strengthening Forensic Sciences in the United States, A Path Forward) the "subspecialty" of crime scene investigation is neither criticized nor complimented in the area of quality control and quality assurance; however it clearly indicates that the forensic sciences in general must have appropriate quality control programs.

The National Academy of Sciences report gives specific reasons or goals that quality assurance programs in the laboratory should strive to meet.[1] Some of them are:

- To ensure accuracy (of the analyses and practitioners' work)
- To identify issues such as mistakes, fraud and bias
- To ensure that best practices are followed
- To improve and/or correct

These goals must also be directed towards crime scene investigators and the crime scene investigation unit as a whole.

So, if the NAS Report does not specifically recommend that crime scene units create and implement quality control programs, they should be self-initiated. Just as the laboratory serves its customers by ensuring quality through its quality control program, so must the crime scene unit. The laboratory's customers (e.g. the criminal justice system) must be able to rely upon the results of analyses and the interpretation of those results. The criminal justice system must be assured that the laboratory used best practices, that the analysis was free of errors and that the testimony will be accurate and free of bias and fraud. Quality however should not start here; it should start at the crime scene. The question that needs to be resolved from a crime scene unit point of view is how can the lab ensure that the products it produces are quality if it cannot be assured of the product produced by the crime scene unit? How can a laboratory successfully build upon something that is already garbage? The laboratory must be able to trust that the evidence is cared for appropriately and was not diminished or damaged in any way especially a way that it would affect their analysis or interpretation. If it was, the lab needs to know that also.

Since the whole enterprise starts at the crime scene, so must the assurance of quality, and so the first persons that must ensure that the quality control program is effectively implemented is the crime scene unit.

Crime scene investigations have their own, unique issues and complications that are not found in the laboratory. As such, the quality control program will have to be reflective of those issues. Even if a crime scene unit incorporates elements of a quality assurance program from a laboratory, it will have to have elements unique and separate from the laboratory.

An appropriate quality control program should include measures that are tailored to ensure any issue can be rectified before it happens. Although not all quality control measures taken by any one discipline will be useful for another discipline, the goals remain the same. Contamination prevention will be discussed at length elsewhere in this text, but it is worth briefly mentioning as a function of quality at this time.

Quality and the Crime Scene Unit – Overview

Overall, quality assurance is achieved through different controls and systems of controls. Think of it as a series of checks and proactive maintenance steps. A crime scene unit will have to seek out new, novel and/or unique ways to ensure quality. Quality control programs designed for a crime scene unit will look different from one designed for and used in a laboratory.

Crime scene investigation differs from many other forensic subspecialties in that it occurs in the field. In other words, it occurs outside of the safe, stable and controllable environment of the laboratory. For this reason, some of the quality controls must be geared towards being able to, among other things, rapidly handle exigencies that most likely will not occur in a laboratory. These procedures should work to ensure that:

- The proper and needed equipment arrives at the crime scene in an expeditious manner
- The equipment that arrives at the crime scene is functioning properly and contains all peripherals, etc., necessary to do a good job

It is important that any action an investigator needs to take to document and secure items of fragile evidence (or evidence subject to environmental factors) can be taken at a moment's notice with the confidence of knowing that the equipment and materials needed will be there and the tools will work as they should.

If lab equipment breaks down, the lab can likely wait until the instrument is repaired or use another instrument, without any ill effects to the evidence. A laboratory can protect evidence in the interim. This may not be true for the crime scene unit, especially if long distances are involved.

Those tasked with the quality assurance assignment must devise methods that work for the tasks and equipment unique to a crime scene unit.

In addition, the quality assurance program will take on the more traditional tasks that would be seen in a laboratory, such as reagent verification, standard verification and tracking, instrument calibration and contamination prevention. The prevention of false negative results when using reagents to search for evidence is an undesirable outcome that a quality assurance program should seek to prevent. A negative result, when in fact a positive result should have been obtained will result in evidence not being identified and recovered, potentially allowing the guilty to go free. In consideration of the potential issues from reagents and contamination, some other specific areas that may require the attention of a quality control program are:

- Keeping investigators and the equipment used at a scene from contaminating the crime scene
- Keeping vehicles from contaminating the crime scene through contamination of an investigator or equipment stored in the vehicle
- Ensuring equipment in need of calibration, maintenance and/or repair receive the appropriate attention
- Reagent verification
- Tracking standards

As demonstrated, the quality control program will need to touch all aspects of a crime scene unit's operations. There are many times during a scene investigation where something can go wrong. There are, however, differences between that which might be preventable or foreseeable and those things that are just simply bad luck. Even the simplest or smallest of breakdowns can lead to undesirable results.

For the purposes of managing a crime scene unit quality control program, a simple breakdown could be defined as a preventable issue or complication arising from a breakdown of equipment, a lack of maintenance, or other issue of a similar theme that results in an undesirable result, especially where an action by a responsible person prior to the occurrence might have prevented it. That is not to say that the unforeseeable will never occur or equipment will not ever just spontaneously break. However, when responsible management knows that simple actions could prevent breakdowns and still, proactive measures are not taken, a different situation is described. These simple breakdowns can take many different forms. No matter what form these breakdowns take, the result will be the same. Something very simple such as dead batteries can have the same catastrophic results for fragile evidence at a scene and for an investigation overall, than any other conceivable breakdown could.

An undesirable result can include many different outcomes. They might range from a diminishment of the value of evidence to a complete loss of evidence.

Whenever possible, quality assurance should strive to be proactive in nature. It would be better if investigators and management alike could foresee any issues that might arise during the day-to-day operations of the crime scene unit and implement systems to prevent the undesirable ones before they happen. Whenever possible, it is better to prevent an undesirable outcome altogether then have to attempt to mitigate it in some way after it has happened. If the integrity of some part of an investigation is diminished or damaged, it is very hard to undo this.

The quality assurance program can and should interact with all aspects of the unit's operations in a number of different ways. Aside from proactive measures, those that one hopes to implement prior to problems arising in the hopes of preventing them, management and staff must be ready to react to situations encountered, not only in order to mitigate any adverse effects but also to conceive of measures in order to prevent the issue from arising again if possible. In this way, a unit's quality assurance plan can react quickly to any situation and remain as proactive as possible.

Because quality involves all aspects of the operation, the quality control program should be involved in all aspects of the operation. The quality control program should be prepared to involve itself in at least the following areas of the crime scene unit's operations:

- Expendable equipment
- Non-expendable equipment (maintenance, cleaning and calibration)
- Contamination prevention
- Reagents and standards
- Vehicles
- Work product

This list is not exhaustive. There are many things that can affect quality. Management should be flexible and inventive when needed. Methods can be found to help the unit achieve its mandate. The list presented represents just some areas that can cause problems for a crime scene unit.

Equipment – General

Crime scene units use many types of equipment and materials. We can classify these items into a few categories such as:

- Single-use or expendable items
    - Swabs
    - Bags
    - Tape
    - Personal protective equipment
    - Fingerprinting materials
    - Arson cans
    - Glass jars
    - Bloodstain pattern analysis materials
    - Impression materials (e.g. casting)
    - Reagents
- Non-expendable equipment
    - Tripods
    - Evidence markers
    - Tools
    - Measurement devices
    - Scales and rulers
    - Shovels
    - Rakes
- Technical equipment
    - Cameras
    - Alternate light sources
    - Video equipment
    - Metal detectors

- Total station
- Computer and connectivity devices

This list is not exhaustive by any stretch of the imagination. It is illustrative of just some of the items that a crime scene unit may have. The equipment used by any crime scene unit would be dependent on what that particular unit's investigators do and how they do it.

Equipment, expendable, non-expendable and technical is a very important area that quality assurance should be involved in. This must include inventory control of expendable equipment and the maintenance of non-expendable equipment (both for operability and for cleaning as a contamination preventative). This will including any vehicles and work surfaces. Quality assurance will also be responsible for the tracking of perishable materials such as reagents used by the unit and the monitoring of case work by investigators.

The failure to be able to recover evidence at a scene because investigators are out of some item or tool is a quality control issue. This will become a problem most often when external factors or uncontrollable factors such as weather cause an exigency. Under good conditions, evidence can be protected while someone brings the missing items to the scene. Even so this is not an optimal way to operate.

This should not be taken lightly. Delay in recovering evidence, especially evidence that is fragile or subject to a loss of usefulness because of environmental factors, can quickly lead to failure of the mission. As we know, once evidence is damaged or lost, the information it contains may be damaged or lost and may not be recoverable. This issue is the same when we discuss tools and technical equipment as well, and for some of the same reasons. Investigators should not spend time cleaning tools or calibrating equipment when there is pressure to complete tasks due to external forces, especially if these things can be done before.

Budgeting

One very important consideration that is often overlooked is budgeting. The crime scene unit must be able to maintain control over when or how often it replenishes the materials it uses. Although not a direct function of quality control, in order for quality to be maintained, this function must be free from interference. The budget must also be adequate to ensure that the needs of the crime scene unit are met at all times.

Expendable Materials – Single-use Items

Single-use items, where available, are probably the best choice to use at crime scenes for collecting evidence. Single-use items can be opened, used at the scene and discarded. This eliminates the need to clean tools before reuse, which saves time and effort.

It may not be readily apparent why a quality control program should be involved in this issue. There are two reasons. First, the quality control program should be involved in inventory control. Second, the quality control program should ensure that equipment gets to the scene when it is needed. Evidence recovered at a scene that is diminished in quality or degraded because the investigators ran out of or didn't have the proper equipment or materials is a quality control issue. To this end, creative systems should be employed in order to ensure that the unit as a whole never runs out of the items it needs and that the correct equipment always arrives at the scene.

Every crime scene investigation unit should have a master inventory list of the equipment used to carry out the tasks that are required of it based on what services the crimes scene unit performs. For ease, the inventory list might capture the following information:

- Item (general category such as evidence sealing tape)
- Brand
- Make
- Model
- Size
- Case quantity or standard package quantity
- Physical storage location within the crime scene unit
- Approximate or average time between orders
- Special considerations or storage requirements
- Notes
- Unit specific information (other information that a particular crime scene unit feels is important to them)

As important as knowing what you use is knowing how much is used during any given period of time and knowing how much time it takes to replenish unit supplies. How quickly it takes to replenish supplies can be affected by factors outside of the unit's control. Some questions that inventory control may want to have answers to are:

- About how much is used?
- About how long do we take to use this amount?
- At what amount will I need to initiate an order?
- How much time will it take to navigate the internal bureaucracy?
- What is the shipping time?

So, in other words, the quality control support staff must be assigned to manage equipment and to monitor and control inventory. Inventory control is an essential requirement of any good business, and this applies to crime scene investigation units as well.

The complexity of the task will increase with the amount of and types of items the unit requires to perform services. Simply, the more there is to track, the more complex the tracking becomes. The larger the span of control becomes, the harder it is to control. If a particular crime scene unit handles all types of physical evidence and/or has a high volume, the task becomes more difficult, and good control systems are even more essential. Being able to continuously measure usage and replenishment is essential.

A crime scene unit that is not particularly busy should not be complacent. If the crime scene unit is not busy it may tend to store smaller amounts of materials and order less often. Unfortunately, one bad day or a string of bad days can cause a crime scene unit to run out of items. So, the tendency may be to feel that since a crime scene unit may not be overly busy, anyone in the unit will know when things are running low. The quality assurance program team members should not leave things to chance.

There is some good news regarding these non-perishable materials. Generally, these types of materials (for example packaging materials, fingerprinting supplies, swabs and the like) do not have expiration dates or lose efficacy over time, as long as the items are stored in a dry location without any wild temperature swings. This allows a crime scene unit to buy some extra, creating a buffer. Without much concern for loss due to time or storage conditions, the extra inventory can be achieved without any waste of money.

Quality control program functions relating to inventory of expendable single-use items should be carried out on a regular basis, in a systematic and methodical manner. The task is made much easier when all of the expendable, single-use items are stored in the same location.

A storage system should include location awareness. A locating system can easily be derived to describe the location equipment is stored at by capturing the following:

- Room number or name
- Shelving unit location within room or shelving unit designation
- Shelf equipment or item is located on

Of course, any similar system will work just as well, as long as it makes sense to the crime scene unit using it.

Commercial inventory control systems are always a choice for inventory control. Bar-code type scanning based systems can lessen the work needed to devise a custom system on one's own. How much time is saved in the long run might depend on more than one factor. It may be a little cumbersome in some ways. Having to put things into the inventory stream as well as take things out of the inventory stream might add extra, unneeded steps. Also having to scan partial lots or loose items in opened cases or units might add more work than is needed. The question a manager would have to ask is how precise does inventory need to be. Commercial systems can be very precise but the expense and effort to maintain such a system in person-hours may not add anything to the operation. Perhaps one need not know how many bottles of black fingerprint powder are in the closet to the exact bottle. Maybe the information can be less precise and achieve the same goal.

An idea that might work with less effort than maintaining a complicated computer based inventory system is simply displaying stores of materials on storage shelves. First, putting everything in one room or area saves effort by simple economy of movement. Not having to move from one place to another and not having equipment stored all over the place increases efficiency. Also, putting equipment on plain, bare storage shelves allows people to see what is there by nature of not having walls and sides to block the view. In this way, boxes or cases of equipment can be placed on the shelves and will be easy to see.

Quality control program staff can now count cases or boxes of equipment. Opened cases can be counted as a half case, a quarter case or some consistent system that is amenable to the crime scene unit.

The crime scene unit can also choose to store open cases of materials in bins marked with graduations (like a measuring cup). In this way these graduations can be used to estimate approximate quantities of items. Whether this systems works any better remains to be seen. It may be more amenable for items that do not ship with a standard quantity amount per case or box.

Another work-saving step that might be employed is an equipment removal log. A pad of paper on a clip board hung from the door can capture basic information that would help whenever materials and equipment are removed from storage. In a best- case scenario, those removing the equipment will be part of the quality control program team, which might ensure the task is carried out properly. If not, ensure that all members of the crime scene unit who remove materials understand how to comply with the need to maintain these records. This technique can also be used in the same manner; however, a log is assigned to each item in the store room. A simple notation of the quantity of pieces removed from each item by those who take items can speed up the whole process. A form capturing the item, storage location and quantity removed or some derivation that captures similar information will suffice. This information will help direct staff to areas directly and quickly. In this way, not only will staff be on top of regular or normal usage situations during regular inspections but also the attention of staff will be drawn to areas that may become problematic before they occur.

There should be a regular schedule for inventory inspection. How often this needs to occur will depend upon a few factors such as:

- How often teams respond to requests for service
- How often materials and equipment are removed from storage to staging (for example staging could be placed on a vehicle for response)
- How busy a crime scene unit is (service wise)
- How often a particular task or group of tasks are performed (e.g., recovering latent fingerprints at burglaries)

Regularly and/or periodically inspecting inventory coupled with focusing on the areas that may become problematic will help to ward off issues of not having equipment and materials at a scene. In reality, any system that serves the purpose of quick and approximately accurate inventory measurement will suffice.

As noted, it is important to have some understanding of how quickly the various items are used. Based upon the amount of time it takes from order to delivery, it would be worthwhile to have a trigger point where, when a certain amount is left in storage, an order is placed and storage is replenished. Management should ensure that there is a clear system in place to facilitate this task.

Laying out a physical location for the crime scene unit's home base must include adequate storage for all materials. Consideration should be given to having adequate space where materials can be stored and in such a manner that it can be easily accessed and counted. This pre-planning will facilitate inventory tracking. Storage should also be amenable to the sensitivities of materials such as reagents used by the unit for things like blood detection and electronics like cameras, batteries, computers, total stations, and alternate light sources. Support staff should be intimately involved, understanding the layout and knowing where all items are.

Expendable Materials – Perishable Single-use Items

For purposes of this discussion, perishable items will include all materials that can lose or will lose efficacy over time for any reason. This loss of efficacy can occur on its own as an inherent property of the item, or it can occur over time because of improper storage. Many crime scene units will, at some point, need to deal with perishable materials. Depending upon the types of services that the unit performs, this could include, at the very minimum, reagents for the presumptive identification of biological materials such as blood and semen and non-biological materials such as lead and copper.

Investigators and managers may also be aware that there are many other materials that might be used during a crime scene investigation which can lose efficacy over time so it is important to note that some of these items can be perishable.

The quality control program must be concerned with both the conditions that these reagents are stored under as well as how the efficacy of the reagents are affected over time. Some reagents will have a *definite* shelf life or expiration date prescribed by the manufacturer and others will have a *recommended* shelf life prescribed by the manufacturer and some will have an *unlimited* shelf life. These recommendations hold so long as the storage conditions follow the manufacturer's recommendations. Experience has shown, anecdotally, that subjecting many materials to extremes of temperature, especially over time, is generally bad. Reagents not stored under proper conditions can lose their efficacy at any time, one will never know when they are going to stop working. Reagents that require storage at room temperature are damaged if left outside in a vehicle or other storage facility where the environment is not controlled.

Even if the reagent has no manufacturer expiration date or recommended shelf life, investigators must keep in mind that there will likely be a loss of efficacy with time, even if the reagents are properly stored.

This situation presents additional problems for the crime scene unit and additional responsibilities for the quality control program. At the most basic level, the quality control program must deal with these types of materials in the same way as regular expendable items. Additional tracking will be required, however, in order to deal with turnover due to expiration. Further, the quality control program will also need to be ready to deal with verifying the operability of reagents before they are used in the scene. Additionally, the reagents will require verification when they arrive at the unit and before use at a scene so as to rule out any problems due to malfunctioning reagents. An overview of the scheme might look like this:

- Arrival of reagent
- Logging of pertinent information
- Verification of shipment including the standard used
- Unpacking shipment into storage
- Distribution for deployment at scene

An additional topic that will also be part of the reagent discussion is the subject of standards. Traceable standards are going to be an important part of a quality control program, especially when it comes to reagents and verification. A traceable standard can be described at its simplest as a known item. Traceable means that it should come to the unit with some testament that it is what it is purported to be. Its origin can be traced to the company that created it. The company attests to that it is what they say it is. A certificate, letter or some other document is supplied by the company and, ideally supplied to the consumer. Standards will be used to verify that reagents are functioning properly.

Some perishable materials may not have expiration dates prescribed by the manufacturer but may have a recommended shelf life. These items may have a loss of efficacy with time or become unusable all together. In cases such as this, the crime scene unit may choose to leave the items on the shelf beyond the recommendation and see how it goes or can pull the materials upon the limit of the recommended shelf life.

If the unit chooses to pull these items upon the recommended time limit, quality control will need to devise a system to track these things. They might consider creating a serial number or lot number system based on the date it arrives at the unit. This devised number can be marked on each individual item. Once some kind of system such as this is devised, tracking the items can be done in the same manner as other, perishable items.

Personnel assigned to quality control tasks will need to become familiar with the items and materials used by the crime scene unit in order to know if an item has a recommended shelf life. One place to start should be the manufacturer's product literature. Sometimes the product literature of items commonly used during a crime scene investigation recommend a shelf life.

Quality Assurance Tasks at Arrival

As has been mentioned previously, the failure to recognize and recover evidence at a scene is problematic. If this happens because of a non-functioning reagent, a false negative has the potential to allow the guilty to go free or the innocent to be wrongly accused.

When reagents arrive at the crime scene unit, there will need to be a mechanism to check that at least something is working. This can be done a number of ways, so as to create confidence that the shipment is not compromised for some reason or occurrence during shipping. When a shipment of a reagent arrives at a crime scene unit, aside from logging information previously described such as the brand, quantity, storage location and so on, the quality assurance program should also note the date of arrival, the lot number and the expiration date. At the very minimum, this will allow the crime scene unit to categorize and differentiate one shipment from another. If there is no lot number or equivalent, then the quality control team can create one easily based on the date of arrival or some other simple methodology.

Once logged in, the reagent should be verified. Again, some percentage of the shipment received (for example one from every lot number or one from every shipment received) can suffice. This verification should be performed using a traceable standard. By using a known, traceable standard, the quality assurance program team can be sure that the reagent is functioning as it should be. The verification should be documented and the records should be stored. Only after this step occurs should the shipment be considered ready to be put in storage for response to crime scenes. This will not be the only time a reagent will be verified. A verification of the reagent immediately prior to use will also be advisable.

Standards

Standards are used, in this application, to verify the functionality of reagents. When they are purchased and received by the crime scene unit, they are generally not tested in any way, because the vendor is certifying that the standard is what it is claimed to be. Depending on what the standard is and the purpose it is serving, it may or may not have an expiration or shelf life. Generally, standards like blood which will be used for the verification of presumptive tests do not go bad. But, just in case, a unique labeling system will allow for easy tracking. Often, a standard will be purchased in bulk and will need to be broken down onto individual units. These also require unique labeling for tracking purposes.

Any documents or certificates accompanying the standards should be stored for access later. If there is ever a question about how reagents are verified (how an investigator knows the reagent is working properly) these documents will aid in explaining the details of this particular part of the quality assurance program.

Before choosing what standards to use, the crime scene unit should consider using, when possible, standards that will be detectable if they somehow contaminate the scene. For example, in the case of blood standards, it might be worth using animal blood where possible as opposed to human blood. When using presumptive tests for blood that work on the properties of hemoglobin, it doesn't matter whether the hemoglobin is animal or human.

At any rate, where this is not possible, care should be taken to prevent any contamination from the standard to the scene. Perform the verification step outside of the scene, taking all contamination prevention steps that would normally be taken.

Tracking

Purchasing and tracking of perishable items will have the same issues and requirements as non-perishable, single-use equipment, but with an added field capturing the expiration date. When the expiration date is reached, the material is no longer considered usable for casework and should be removed from both storage and staging and discarded or, perhaps, used for training and practice.

Quality assurance personnel will need to take steps to ensure that ample time exists prior to expiration in order to replenish storage before the perishable items will need to be removed from use. At the minimum, shelves should be labeled and dates inspected on a regularly scheduled basis, at the same time as scheduled inspections are performed. Another simple solution can be to set alarms in computer based, calendar applications that can email or alert at a set date. This can be used to both alert personnel to begin the order process as well as the process to reclaim materials set to expire.

An additional complication for the tracking task is knowing where these perishable items are staged and the expiration date of those items not in storage. Once equipment leaves the storage area, the amount of energy and effort in keeping track of them increases. If the items are distributed to teams, kits or into vehicles someone will need to know where it goes. If the crime scene unit is lucky enough to be able to park vehicles indoors where there is some amount of environmental control, the quality assurance personnel will need to know which truck it is on (if there is more than one). Because we know that expired reagents may not work or may not have the same efficacy as unexpired reagents, taking a chance with them at a scene would be a mistake. As such, there should be a plan in place to keep them out of the scene completely. The same issues present themselves with items that do not have an expiration date but have a recommended shelf life instead.

A crime scene unit can have various plans to achieve this goal. One viable idea is the use of response bags for perishable materials like reagents. A large cooler bag, duffle bag or the like can be stocked with all of the items that fit this description. Also, the bag can contain the ancillary items such as spray bottles and instruction sheets. The crime scene unit might put some of the following into the bag (note that the specific contents will be based upon the services the unit provides):

- Blood presumptive identification reagent
- Blood enhancement reagent
- Latent blood detection reagent
- Lead presumptive identification reagent
- Casting material
- Gel lifters
- Cyanoacrylate fuming materials

- Swabs
- Sterile water
- Spray bottles
- Blood standard
- Lead standard
- Batteries – equipment-specific

A content document that lists each item and pertinent information about it might also be included. The document can include expiration dates, preparation dates, and lot numbers. This information can be transcribed into case notes by the investigator who uses it (see Figure 10.1).

Sodium Rhodizonate Field Kit
Sodium Rhodizonate lot number:
15% acetic acid lot number:
Water lot number:
Lead standard lot number:
Expiration date:

Latent Blood Detection Kit
Lot number:
Expiration date:
Blood standard lot number:

Presumptive Blood Identification Kit
Lot number:
Expiration date:
Blood standard lot number:

Blood Enhancement Kit
Lot number:
Expiration date:
Blood standard lot number

Gel Lifter
Lot number:
Shelf life expiration:

Cyanoacrylate Fuming Kit
Lot number:
Shelf lift expiration:

Casting Material
Lot number:
Shelf life expiration:

Ancillary contents

FIGURE 10.1 Reagent response bag content document ("sample"). Use this document as a starting point for the types of information that a field investigator might find useful when preparing or using reagents

Once something from the response bag is used, it can be taken out of service, at which time quality control personnel will be required to inspect the contents, replenish used items and update the content document. A system such as this will serve several purposes:

- Decrease the span of control needed to track perishable materials
- Provide a method to store staged equipment under proper conditions yet have it readily available for response
- Decrease the amount of time investigators will need to spend on administrative tasks

A master list should be controlled by the quality control personnel so that, when materials expire, shelf life is reached or a problem is identified with a reagent or other equipment, the items that share its characteristics can be rapidly and efficiently recovered and replaced as necessary.

Verification at the Scene

Prior to using a reagent at any scene, it should be tested to ensure that it is working properly and this verification step should be documented. This can be easily done with a worksheet that assists the investigator in capturing all the data and results of each verification used. Also, it can be used to aid in proper interpretation of results (see Figure 10.2 field verification sheet). Even if the reagent is tested upon receipt at the unit, and is stored according to the manufacturer's recommendations, there is always the possibility that something has gone wrong in the interim. Again, false negatives lead to missed evidence and are not acceptable. A simple and quick verification step can prevent this from occurring.

Any reagent used for detection, enhancement or presumptive identification must be accompanied by some method that verifies it is working properly. Standards or controls will serve this purpose. Reagents that require preparation should be prepared according to procedure or manufacturer's recommendations and verified immediately prior to use.

The verification step is performed using a standard. It is a known quantity so one should be confident that, if everything is working as it should be, the reagent will behave as expected. If not, one should be confident that there is something wrong with the reagent. Reagents should be paired with the appropriate standard for this reason.

At the scene, the verification should be performed with a standard as the positive control. A reagent blank should also be run as a negative control. Since the purpose here is to identify non-functioning reagents, if the reagent reacts appropriately with the standard (the positive control) and also reacts with the negative control, a malfunctioning reagent is indicated. Once a reagent is verified as functioning properly, use in the scene should be done with proper background controls contemporaneously where appropriate.

This is a part of the quality control program that everyone will be required to know and be able to perform. In addition to training on how the reagents work and what false positives and negatives they are susceptible to, members will need to understand interpretation issues for each reagent or test used and why the step is necessary.

Field Verification Worksheet

DATE OF REPORT:	DATE OF OCCURRENCE:	
INVESTIGATOR ASSIGNED:		CRIME:
NUMBER:	PREPARED BY (PRINT NAME):	
LOCATION OF OCCURRENCE:	INITIALS:	

SODIUM RHODIZONATE

Sodium Rhodizonate Lot Number & Expiration Date	15% Acetic Acid Lot Number & Expiration Date	Lead Acetate Standard ID Number& Expiration Date	Positive Control Description of Result	Negative Control Description of Result
			Immediate color change to purple? Y__N__	Immediate color change to purple? Y__N__

Conclusion/Interpretation: Presumptive Presence of Lead:___y/____n

CHEMILUMINESCENT PRESUMPTIVE BLOOD

Lot Number & Expiration Date	Positive Control/ Standard ID Number & Expiration Date	Positive Control Description of Result	Negative Control Description of Result
		Immediate glow?Y__N__	Immediate glow?Y__N__

Conclusion/Interpretation: Presumptive Presence of blood:___y/____n

LEUCO CRYSTAL VIOLET

Lot Number& Expiration Date	Positive Control/ Standard ID Number & Expiration Date	Positive Control Description of Result	Negative Control Description of Result
		Immediate color change to purple? Y__N__	Immediate color change to purple? Y__N__

Conclusion/Interpretation: Presumptive Presence of blood:___y/____n

SMALL PARTICLE REAGENT

Lot Number& Expiration Date	Positive Control/ Standard ID Number & Expiration Date	Positive Control Description of Result	Negative Control Description of Result
		Build up of black or white at test print?Y__N__	Build up of black or white at test print?Y__N__

Conclusion/Interpretation: Presumptive Presence of Lanolin:___y/____n

FIGURE 10.2 Reagent verification worksheet ("sample"). Use this document to prompt the field investigator for important information regarding reagents used

Non-expendable Items

There will be items and equipment used by the crime scene unit that will not be expendable or perishable. Either because of their nature or expense, they will create issues for the quality control program. They can be broken down into a few categories:

- Non-expendable equipment
- Technical equipment
- Technical equipment requiring calibration or recalibration by qualified technical persons

Other Non-expendable Items

Items such as tripods, evidence markers, and tools can be categorized as non-expendable items. Their use at many scenes, and the fact that the item is in the scene, make them especially susceptible to contamination. This is a quality control issue. One of the issues that quality control must be concerned with is contamination prevention. Even if the actual cleaning of equipment is performed by *any* member of the unit, quality control should verify and assist in the task.

All items should be cleaned after use in a crime scene without regard to whether they were visibly contaminated or not. There are many sources of contamination which can occur on the macro as well as the micro scale. It is safe to always assume that equipment brought into a crime scene is contaminated from biological materials as well as other trace items. As a result, equipment must be cleaned after use and before returning it to either storage or staging. In other words, things like evidence markers and tripods cannot go back into the truck until they are cleaned.

The crime scene unit must consider how thoroughly it can perform this task in the field. The reality is they must do the best possible job they can. As a preventative measure and to back up the efforts of those working in the field, quality control should consider periodical complete overhaul of vehicles and equipment as a method to catch anything that might slip through the cracks. This may require scheduling a day where a vehicle and its equipment are out of service during which all items, surfaces and storage areas within are thoroughly cleaned. This should include all passenger areas as well.

Other issues that should be considered by quality control is ensuring that non-expendable equipment is in good working order. Inspections can coincide with cleaning duties. If not, there should be some periodical inspection. In addition, there needs to be a store of spare parts or backups that can be used to keep the equipment in service. Heavy use items such as lighting, tripods and evidence markers will become worn or damaged over time and will need to be replaced or maintained at some point.

Items that require batteries, especially specialized rechargeable batteries, present another area of concern. The equipment can't work if it doesn't have power, so someone should be in charge of ensuring that there are always charged batteries ready to go. It is not advisable to leave batteries out in the environment long-term, so storage on a vehicle in the heat of the summer and cold of the winter would diminish the batteries' life span and usefulness. However, they must be ready and available at all times. Crime scene units might consider a charging station for *all* batteries used. This can include batteries for total stations, portable alternate light sources, cameras, computers, and whatever else the unit considers necessary. The batteries of regularly used equipment can be staged in the reagent response bags. This method keeps them readily available to investigators in the field, allows for them to be rotated in and out of service for conditioning and recharging, and allows them to be stored in an appropriate environment.

Technical Equipment

Aside from issues already mentioned, technical equipment, specifically, those items that require calibration, may present another issue for the quality control program. Scheduled calibration of technical equipment should be carried out according to the manufacturer's recommendations or as needed. Rough handling or constant use might necessitate increased servicing by the manufacturer. Records of calibration should be kept in a log. If the item is calibrated by members of the unit, those members should be qualified to do so. If not, the job should be given to the appropriate, qualified entity. If the items require calibration in the field prior to use, anyone in the unit who will be required to use the item must be able to calibrate it. Members should be trained to proficiency and the training documented. Any tests associated with the training demonstrating proficiency should be retained. Results of calibration in the field prior to use should be documented in the case notes.

A crime scene unit may want to periodically test the equipment on its own. Equipment inspections can be scheduled and performed with the results documented in a log of some kind. Ultimately, it will be the responsibility of quality control to ensure that any mandatory calibration or servicing is scheduled and performed according to procedure or manufacturer's specification.

To help ensure that technical equipment is working as expected, service should only be performed by qualified persons.

Vehicles

Vehicles should be an area of concern for quality control for a few reasons. First, the vehicles must be serviceable and ready to go at any time from a mechanical standpoint. Second, the vehicles should have the proper equipment, in the proper amounts at all times. Third, vehicles must be clean at all times.

Although one can never predict a breakdown, the crime scene unit has a responsibility to ensure that the vehicles it relies upon to deliver investigators and materials to a scene are properly serviced. According to a schedule or between responses, vehicles should be maintained according to manufacturer's recommendations or, at least reasonable tradition. This should also include any built in, on board generators, refrigerators and the like.

Although mentioned in other sections of this text, maintaining the cleanliness of the vehicle is of paramount importance to the whole of the operation. As such, the cleaning of the vehicles should be monitored by quality control personnel and any deficiencies remedied immediately. There will be many opportunities for both the equipment stored in the vehicle and the vehicle itself to become contaminated. This can occur in many ways:

- Dirty, contaminated equipment placed or stored in the vehicle
- Contaminated PPE brought into or worn in the vehicle
- Evidence exposed and/or examined in the vehicle
- Materials packaged in bulk (for example single-use items) contaminated by investigators
- Materials stored in the vehicle that are left exposed to the occupants or evidence
- Vehicle surfaces contaminated by investigators

As a result of any of these actions, or any combination of these actions, contamination may occur. We might expect this to occur more often as DNA testing techniques become more sensitive.

In any event, the vehicle must be cleaned as a preventive measure when it has become knowingly or possibly contaminated, and as part of a routine maintenance schedule. This routine maintenance schedule should include cleaning of all surfaces as well as all equipment brought into and out of a scene. This might include items like evidence markers, tripods and other non-expendable equipment. Routine inspection by quality assurance and remediation of any issues observed might also be part of an overall quality assurance plan.

Investigative Work Product

Overview

Part of a quality assurance program should include the review of the investigative work product. This can take many forms; however a few ideas are presented here. The purpose of these reviews is twofold: first, to ensure that reports leaving the crime scene unit are proofread or edited for things such as completeness, accuracy, spelling and the like which might be termed the administrative review and second, to ensure that any conclusions given by the investigator are established by analyses performed at the scene. This is a technical review.

Every report should be subject to an administrative review and a technical review, when required, at its completion.

Administrative Review

An administrative review might be considered a proofreading of all reports before they are released to any entity outside of the crime scene unit. Whatever form reports take, there will always be a time between the investigation and publication, perhaps a working stage. During this working stage, the report will be in various stages of completeness and correctness. While being drafted, it would be unfair to presume or expect perfection during this working stage. Anyone looking at the report during this time must do so with the knowledge that it is still incomplete.

Once complete, however, there is an obligation to do everything possible to ensure it is correct. It is unrealistic to think that every report will be perfect. Mistakes will slip through. The crime scene unit must use all reasonable methods and take all reasonable steps to prevent this from occurring.

An administrative review can be, perhaps should be, at least a two-step process. The first review should be done by the investigator of record him/herself. There is no one better to ensure that the case file and report is complete than the person with the most intimate knowledge of the case. To this end, the investigator producing the report, whenever possible, should be someone with this intimate knowledge. If not the primary investigator, then the person with the next-most extensive knowledge base. If multiple people are responsible for various parts of the investigation, each should be responsible for his/her area.

Some things cannot be done at the time of administrative review. For example, any deficiencies in the case notes cannot be recreated after the scene is complete, unless the investigator has an independent recollection of some fact.

At the time of the administrative review, the investigator should proofread the case. The investigator might check the following:

- All notes are in the case notes
- Any reports, forms, etc., are contained in the file
- Any reports, forms, etc. are completed in compliance with procedure
- Spelling on all reports is correct
- Any required captions are correctly completed
- Written portions are clear and concise
- Photo logs correspond to photographs
- Final diagrams correctly reflect sketches completed at the scene
- Any areas the investigator, the unit or the agency deems an area requiring review

It may be beneficial for the crime scene unit to create an administrative review checklist or guide that will help the investigator work though these various things in a systematic and methodical way. This administrative review or checklist should be a guide based upon the crime scene unit's procedures. It could reflect all of the forms or captions required for particular situations. If reports are free form, the guide could be a bulleted list of information required for particular situations. Figure 10.3 is a simple guide to the information that an administrative review sheet might contain.

So, once the investigator completes writing and review, an independent review must be completed. This does not have to be a peer review. This review is being done for compliance with administrative requirements and to correct spelling, grammar and things like that, if possible. Choose someone with intimate knowledge of the crime scene unit's report requirement and an ability to read and edit with a critical eye. No report should be distributed until it has been edited. If, for some reason draft reports are distributed, they should be labeled clearly as such.

Technical Review

Technical reviews performed for crime scene activities might be considered whenever a conclusion is drawn with regard to some examination or analysis at the scene, in order to ensure best practices are used and correct assessments are made.

Generally, a technical review is done when a conclusion is drawn with regard to an analysis. A peer, or someone trained and proficient in the task (at the same level as the investigator) reviews the case in order to determine if the observations, documentation and tasks performed support the conclusion.

For example, if a presumptive blood test is performed at the scene, the investigator should describe the steps taken to perform the test and the observations made at the various stages. So, positive or negative color changes for positive controls, negative controls and samples from the scene should all be described in the case notes. This will also be necessary for other tasks such as bloodstain pattern analysis and ballistic trajectory analysis. If the unit has only one examiner in an area, a technical reviewer from outside the unit will need to be engaged, perhaps from a neighboring jurisdiction where assistance can be reciprocated. Under circumstances such as these, the crime scene unit should strive for 100 percent technical review. Under these circumstances, not every case will require a technical review and only the specific portions of a case that require it, will receive a technical review.

ADMINISTRATIVE CASE REVIEW
CHECKLIST

CRIME ____________________

INVESTIGATOR ____________________

Documents Reviewed

☐ Scene	☐ Additional Scene	☐ Person	☐ Evidence
☐ Latent Print	☐ Electronic Photo	☐ Film Photo	☐ Rough Sketch / Notes
☐ Body Exam	☐ Documentation Charts	☐ Vehicle Report	☐ Ballistic Damage
☐ Impression Evidence	☐ Blood Stain Pattern	☐ Presumptive Blood	☐ Chemical use/verification
☐ Finished Diagram	☐ Dept Investigation	☐ Case closing	☐ Panoscan

DIGITAL IMAGES/ VIDEO/ PANOSCAN

Case contains digital images? ☐Yes ☐No # ☐ VIDEO ☐ Yes ☐No

All images uploaded to ECMS? ☐Yes ☐No PANOSCAN ☐ Yes ☐No

Working copy of digital image DVD/ Panoscan DVD/ video tape stored in case folder? ☐Yes ☐No

EXAMINATION QUALITY PHOTOS

Case contains examination quality photos? ☐Yes ☐No # ☐

☐Footwear ☐Tire tread ☐Patent Print ☐Blood spatter ☐Other ____________________

Scale utilized at scene stored in case folder? ☐ABFO#2 ☐L shaped Bureau Scale

COMPUTER GENERATED FINISHED DIAGRAM

Finished diagram required? ☐Yes ☐No

Original in case folder? ☐Yes ☐No ____________________ ____________________

Case Folder Captions completed? ☐Yes ☐No D.A. copy of disk and paperwork enclosed? ☐Yes ☐No

REQUIRED PAPER DOCUMENTS PRESENT IN THE CASE FOLDER?

☐Run sheet	☐Case notes	☐Rough Sketch	☐Finished Diagram
☐Property Invoices	☐Request for Lab Report(s)	☐Evidence Transmittals	☐M/V Boat Invoices
☐Body wound chart	☐Vehicle chart	☐Clothing chart	☐Search consent/ warrant

☐ Other ____________________

DO ALL DOCUMENTS HAVE CORRECT # ☐Yes ☐No

DOES ACCURATELY DESCRIBE CONTENT AND NUMBER OF PHOTOS? ☐Yes ☐No

ARE THE MEASUREMENTS CONSISTENT ON THE ROUGH SKETCH AND FINISHED DIAGRAM? ☐Yes ☐No ☐NA

IS NOT TO SCALE AND NORTH INDICATED ON THE SKETCH AND DIAGRAM? ☐Yes ☐No ☐NA

ANY ADMINISTRATIVE ERRORS NOTED? ____________________

TOOLS/ EQUIPMENT UTILIZED

Forensic Light Source Used ☐Yes ☐No ____________________ ☐RUVIS Used ☐Yes ☐No

☐Hand Scope ☐Crime Scope Proper setting(s) documented ☐Yes ☐No

Chemicals, Re-agents and Tests ☐Sodium rhodizonate ☐Bluestar ☐LCV ☐SPR ☐Mikrosil ☐GSR Test Kit ☐CBTI Required DDs complete? ☐Yes ☐No

Footwear Impressions Scene searched for impressions? ☐Yes ☐No ____________________

Impressions discovered? ☐Yes ☐No ☐Electrostatic lifter ☐Gel Lifter ☐Casting ☐Photos

Ballistic Trajectory ☐Trajectory Rods ☐Angle of impact determined ☐Laser

Comments:

Administrative Review By: ____________________ Signature ____________________ Date ________

FIGURE 10.3 Administrative review list ("sample"). This list can be expanded or contracted for specific agency needs. It should be used as a tool to prompt reviewers while they are reading reports but should include critical reading and thinking. A checklist cannot replace one's critical eye

Proficiency Testing

Part of maintaining the quality of crime scene activities will be ensuring the quality of the investigators. This will be accomplished in many ways. Investigators will receive continuing education and their work will be judged or critiqued by a quality assurance program.

Which examination or analysis activities are subject to proficiency testing is not codified in any text or document, but guidance can be found in various documents that discuss accreditation for crime scene units. It would be safe to say that, in the end, all tasks, examinations and analyses performed or conducted by investigators should be subject to proficiency testing. How the actual proficiency testing is conducted will be determined by the activity in question.

However the testing is performed the biggest issue that will be encountered is the need for a disinterested party to evaluate the testing and results. This is easiest where a commercial entity can provide the testing and grading for the unit. There will also be tasks for which no commercial assessments exist. Where this is the case, the crime scene unit will have to create some method for conducting testing. Finally, certain tasks will not be subject to traditional proficiency testing. Consider general crime scene operations, documentation and similar tasks. In this case, work will have to be assessed or individual investigators observed while conducting investigations or examinations.

Perhaps one of the most important issues to keep in mind here is that any proficiency testing or grading should be conducted by a disinterested party, such as a quality assurance manager from outside the crime scene unit who holds no allegiance to those in the unit. In this way, everyone is above reproach.

Whether or not a formal program for non-accredited crime scene units will ever be a requirement is unknown. Be aware that whenever someone fails a proficiency test, some action to fix the problem (usually called a corrective action) must be taken. Generally, this takes the form of retraining and retesting.

In the end, continuous training and refresher training is something that should be done even if the crime scene unit has no formal proficiency testing program. The advantage of having a program from this perspective is that it can help identify deficiencies not only with investigators but with the training program itself. It helps identify more issues then one might expect.

Proficiency testing should take the form of performing specific tasks as well as observing the investigators to ensure they are following the procedures used by the unit. Deviation from procedure will cause a failure in the same way an incorrect answer on the actual specific task would. In other words misidentifying a sample as blood with a presumptive test will merit a failing grade in the same way as conducting the test incorrectly will. Conducting the test incorrectly will merit a failing grade even if the investigator gets the correct answer with respect to the sample.

Finally, if the crime scene unit decides to implement a proficiency testing program, it should structure the program to meet testing requirements of an accreditation program. In this way, if at some point later down the road the unit decides it would like to achieve accreditation, the unit will already be that one step closer without having to reinvent the wheel.

Maintenance of Records

Compliance with the procedures of the crime scene unit will be the purview of the quality assurance program. As such, quality assurance will need to monitor compliance with procedures dealing with maintenance of records, specifically reports, photos and other report-based evidence created by the crime scene unit's investigations.

The physical security of these reports will be a paramount concern. The reports must be kept from loss or damage from accidental circumstances. All reasonable measures should be taken in this regard. Further, storage of computer files and other digital media must be appropriate. In reality, these issues should be tackled from the beginning, and periodically reviewed depending upon a unit's particular circumstances. Once implemented, quality assurance should periodically inspect and review the situation for compliance. Additionally, the unit should have plans for tracking of case location before it goes to "storage" once completed. During the case preparation process, the security of the case and its location must be known. When investigators step away from their desks, the case should be secured. When work on the case is completed for the time being, the case should be stored in a location that is secure yet can be accessed by others who may need to be informed of its contents. Whatever systems are used, compliance will be verified by the quality assurance team.

Quality Assurance Procedures

Overview

The development of quality assurance procedures can be part of the crime scene unit's operations manual or can be a separate document or section within the manual. In reality, there will be quality assurance procedures that will concern just quality assurance personnel as well as other quality assurance procedures that investigators operating in the field will be required to perform.

The quality assurance manual will need to cover a broad area of topics that concern the operations of the unit. This might include technical review procedures, reagents or other presumptive testing methods, and general compliance with the unit's procedures. Although creating procedures will be discussed in detail in other chapters of this book, specific details pertaining to quality assurance will be discussed here.

The Quality Assurance Manual

The quality assurance manual will be a collection of procedures outlining or guiding the crime scene unit in tasks that work to assure the product of the unit adheres to some standard. This standard should be high but not impossible to reach.

Reagent Procedures

Reagents such as those that will be used for presumptive testing will be subject to regular quality assurance checks. Reagents can be either purchased commercially as pre-mixed kits or prepared from stock chemicals according to recipe. Either way, sources, lot numbers, preparation dates and expiration dates will need to be recorded. Additionally, reagents will need to be verified upon receipt and/or before use, according to the crime scene unit's schedule and procedures. If the crime scene unit has an operations manual, it should have procedures detailing how this all should be done.

There are two ways to create procedures for reagents. The unit can have one procedure that outlines what steps will be taken when a kit is received or reagent is prepared or a specific procedure for each reagent. One is neither better nor worse than the other.

Some might find it easier to have a specific protocol for each reagent. Sometimes it is easier to follow specific instructions. This is especially true if someone performing the task does not have a grasp of underlying quality assurance concepts. So, when a reagent or kit enters the unit's possession, there are step-by-step instructions on what to do. This makes it easy to get it right each and every time. If the unit has more than one person performing this task, or this is a part time task for an investigator, this might be a good approach.

Any particular procedure for the receipt of a reagent should generally describe the following steps:

- Person recording information
- Date of receipt
- Lot numbers received
- Expiration dates
- Date of verification for a batch received (either by date or lot number) or at time of mixing from stock chemicals
- Standard used to verify reagent upon receipt or at time of mixing from stock chemicals
- Observations of control tests made during verification
- Conclusion of verification

With regard to the last three points, the persons performing the verification would record what they observed with regard to the reagent's performance when it was tested with a positive control standard and a blank. The conclusion that the reagent was performing properly must be backed up by the correct observations and this must all be documented.

If the reagent is purchased as a commercially available kit, the amount of work is less. The reagent will arrive at the unit and should be inspected for shipping damage. Like reagents should be separated based on lot number, expiration dates or both. All lot numbers and expiration dates should be recorded in a log (electronic or paper). Finally, one kit from the shipment should be tested (verified) as a means of being confident that the shipment has been handled properly. A basic outline may look like this:

> Upon receipt of a reagent, perform the following tasks:
>
> 1. Examine each kit and observe the lot numbers and expiration dates.
> 2. Record lot number and expiration date of reagent received, separate the shipment if multiple lot numbers and expiration dates were received.
> 3. Take one kit from shipment for verification. If more than one lot number or expiration date was received, test one from each (if so desired).
> 4. Prepare the reagent according to manufacturer's instruction of unit procedure.
> 5. Test reagent against a known positive control and record the observed result.
> 6. Test reagent against a negative control (reagent blank) and record the observed result.
> 7. If the reagent is verified, store or stage shipment according to procedure.
> 8. If the reagent is not verified, take appropriate actions.

If reagents are mixed from stock chemicals, the components used should be documented at the time of mixing in a similar manner. An expiration date should be assigned to reagents mixed by the unit in accordance with accepted forensic practices and should be clearly marked on the container. These reagents should also be verified after mixing and prior to use in the field. Records, similar to those outlined above should be kept.

Standards should be handled similarly. There will be a fundamental difference however. Standards will not be verified upon arrival in the same manner that the reagents are. They are verified via documentation from the company that created the standard. Standards should be logged in, the documentation reviewed and then filed in a logical manner. A basic outline may look like this:

Upon receipt of a standard, perform the following tasks:

1. Inspect standard and ensure it is received in good condition.
2. Record the lot number and expiration date if applicable.
3. Inspect documentation verifying standard.
4. File document (perhaps with the log).

Standards are very often purchased in bulk quantities and it makes sense to create single-use sized items for use in the field. For example, a unit might purchase animal blood as a standard for verifying catalytic presumptive blood tests. Often, this comes in a bottle that would be too large to easily transport in the field. Also, it is usually best to refrigerate this to prevent it from smelling. Single-use dry stains can be created on filter paper that is much easier to manipulate, use at the scene and store (as it can be stored dry at room temperature). When this action is taken, there should be a method of tracking them. This is easy to do by creating an in-house serial or lot number that ties all of them together. This way, if there is a problem down the road, they can be recalled from service if necessary.

Procedures for verification in the field will mimic those used when reagents are received by the unit. As previously mentioned, it is desirable to know the reagent is going to work before it used in a scene as a way to prevent false negatives. To this end, investigators should verify that the reagent is working before use, outside of the crime scene. In order to do this, the investigator will need to have the reagent and a known standard with them in the field. A basic outline for this procedure may look like this:

Prior to using the reagent in the field:

1. Open reagent kit and verify the contents are complete.
2. Verify and record the expiration date and lot number. If the expiration date has passed, do not use the reagent.
3. Record the standard used for verification.
4. Prepare/mix the reagent according to manufacturer's instruction or unit procedure.
5. Apply the reagent to the known standard and record observations (e.g. immediate color change).
6. Apply the reagent to the negative control (blank) and record observations (e.g. no immediate color change).
7. Record conclusions (reagent working properly).

Obviously, if the reagent is not working properly, it will be discarded and a new kit or new reagent will be verified for use. If for some reason this occurs, a review for possible causes should be performed. One of the first things that might be checked is the storage conditions. Sometimes, reagents or kits are brought to the crime scene in expectation that they will be used. If they are not used and left in a vehicle that becomes very hot or very cold, the reagent can be undermined. If this happens, the malfunctioning reagents may be a singular occurrence. Quality assurance personnel may want to go back to the storage location and test reagent or kits of the same lot number, expiration date or shipment as a way to eliminate general storage as the problem. If more kits are found to be defective then more drastic actions may be warranted. It is likely that this won't happen if reagents are handled properly, but there is a method for investigating just in case.

Materials with Shelf Life

Another area of some concern are items that have a shelf life. Because a shelf life is akin to an expiration date, management should strongly consider treating them the same. The main difference that the unit may encounter is that there may be no specific expiration date attached to these items. In this case, the best option may be to simply put one on the item with permanent marker and track the location of these items, both deployed and in storage.

Decontamination

For the protection of investigators and for the protection of evidence, the crime scene unit may want to have very specific procedures outlining how and when decontamination will be performed. There should be, at the least, two specific procedures.

Routine Decontamination

The unit's quality assurance manual should have a routine cleaning schedule that enumerates what to clean, when to clean and how to clean. No one is perfect. Things get missed and forgotten. Not every tool used at a crime scene will always get cleaned before it is put away. It is just the nature of things. But remember, as soon as a tool is put away dirty (contaminated), everything it comes into contact with is now also dirty (contaminated). So, a schedule should be devised for cleaning. It can be a simple directive that after every scene, fresh bodies perform certain tasks. On a weekly basis all tasks are performed. The more detailed the procedure is, the more likely a thorough job will be performed.

As-Needed Decontamination

This procedure should simply incorporate the methods and materials that will be used when tools and surfaces come into contact with evidence. This usually includes 10 percent bleach and an alcohol wash.

STANDARD LOG (COMMERCIALLY PURCHASED STANDARDS)

STANDARD:

IDENTITY OF STANDARD	DATE RECEIVED AT UNIT	SUPPLIER'S NAME	MANUFACTURER'S NAME	UNIQUE ID NUMBER/ LOT NUMBER	VERIFICATION METHOD	EXPIRATION DATE	PREPARER'S NAME AND SIGNATURE

REAGENT VERIFICATION LOG (INITIAL)

REAGENT:

DATE RECEIVED AT UNIT	EXPIRATION DATE	SUPPLIER'S NAME	MANUFACTURER'S NAME	UNIQUE ID NUMBER/ LOT NUMBER	DATE OF RELIABILITY CHECK	OBSERVATION & CONCLUSIONS	VERIFICATION PERFORMED BY (NAME & SIGNATURE)

FIGURE 10.4 Quality assurance log examples. An agency can use logs to create their own. However, keep in mind the basic information that must be captured in these logs

Conclusions

Quality assurance will be an area of scrutiny for any crime scene unit. The responsibility for this will fall squarely on those in charge. One must recognize that in order to have quality throughout the whole forensic process, it must start at the crime scene. Investigators should be educated in, and understand the reasons for, and philosophies behind, all quality assurance procedures. Only then can they act independently when situations arise that are not codified in a manual.

Note

1 NAS Report, p.26.

11

PRE-EVENT/INCIDENT PLANNING AND CONTINUITY OF OPERATIONS

How many of you can remember your parents giving you advice to the effect of, "Don't put all your eggs in one basket?" When it comes to a crime scene investigation unit's (CSIU) preparedness and response to major incidents, nothing can be more accurate. In order for the CSIU to maintain its continuity of operations (con-ops), during a high consequent event (HCE), that is to say an incident or event beyond the CISU's normal response capabilities, there must be pre-incident planning, preparation and preparedness, which includes back-up facilities, equipment, and other assets. First the CSIU's management has to understand and prioritize the possible HCE threats to their jurisdiction, such as those events that are announced and planned well in advance, for example the Super Bowl, a Political Event/Convention, a Thanksgiving Day Parade or New Year's Eve Celebration. In addition to the planned events, let us not forget those unannounced incidents that take us by surprise, such as terrorist attacks involving a weapon of mass destruction (WMD), transportation incidents (plane or train crash), with or without mass injuries or mass fatalities, and construction incidents involving the collapse of structures (buildings/bridges) or equipment (cranes) with or without mass injuries or mass fatalities, to name a few. Once this has occurred, the CSIUs have to understand how each of the identified HCE threats will impact their day-to-day operations. From this a needs assessment is developed and prioritized, so that that the jurisdiction can begin its preparations and preparedness. Some of the con-ops' areas of concern are:

1. Personnel
2. Protocols and procedures
3. Equipment
4. Training
5. Facilities
6. Vehicles

At a major incident, such as a terrorist attack, no one law enforcement agency may ever have enough qualified CSIs, especially if we are dealing with an attack involving chemical, biological, radiological, nuclear, and/or explosives (CBRNE) or multiple, simultaneous attacks in one jurisdiction. And, remember, while your agency may be busy dealing with the HCE(s), the everyday crimes that we CSIs respond to, will still be occurring in your jurisdiction and will require the CSIU's response. This being said, start thinking regionally. Identify your jurisdiction's neighboring law enforcement agencies with crime scene investigative capabilities then identify:

1. The other agency's CSIU management
2. The number of CSIs
3. The CSI's:
    a. Certifications
    b. Training and capabilities
    c. Protocols and procedures
    d. Equipment
4. The CSIU's budget
5. The CSIU's facilities
6. Their willingness to:
    a. Enter into mutual aid agreements (MAAs) for CSI incident response or form a forensic regional response task force
    b. Cross train CSIs
    c. Share:
        i. Personnel
        ii. Facilities
        iii. Equipment
        iv. Expenditures

After all the above has been identified and the agencies involved have entered into the preliminary written agreements, then these agencies will need to fully develop their responsibilities, protocols, procedures, training, response triggers, notifications, and mobilization plans for the various HCEs that they have identified for their jurisdictions. All of this has to be in writing, with signed agreements, which for all intents and purposes, are contracts. Since we are speaking about developing protocols and procedures, don't develop these protocols and procedures in a vacuum. This is to say, if your protocols and procedures require support, assistance, involvement or interaction with other law enforcement assets, such as special weapons and tactics (SWAT) teams, bomb squads/explosive ordnance disposal units (EODs), or a law enforcement hazardous materials team (Hazmat), or, non-law enforcement emergency response agencies, such as fire departments, hazmat, emergency medical services (EMS), office of emergency management (OEM), medical examiner's/coroner's office, death investigators, or non-response agencies, such as hospital emergency rooms or public health laboratories, to name just a few of the possibilities, then make contact with them and involve them in the development of your protocols, procedures and response plans. Do not assume any outside agency's capabilities or cooperation. Once your protocols and procedures have been developed, they need to be validated by a subject matter expert (SME), peer reviewed and tested. The testing can easily be accomplished by conducting drills to help identify if any problems with the protocols and procedures exist. If issues are identified, then the protocols can be tweaked, to make corrections if needed. Once the protocol changes have been accomplished, more drills are required to ensure the changes work.

When developing protocols, procedures, or plans, for HCEs, make them as flexible as possible. Mike Tyson is credited with saying, "Everybody has a plan until they get hit." Nothing could more true and for anyone who has ever developed protocols, procedures and plans for HCEs and responded to actual HCEs, you learn very quickly that your protocols, procedures, and plans have to be able to roll with the punches. Since we are discussing not developing protocols, procedure and plans in a vacuum, it also should be stated in the strongest of terms, that if the CSIU is being asked to support a large-scale event, then the CSIU needs to have a direct seat at the planning table. The CSIU doesn't speak for or make representations of the capabilities of any other emergency agencies or units; therefore no other units or agencies should make the assumption that they can reasonably speak on behalf of the CSIU's operational capabilities, its needs, and its potential roll to support the large-scale event being planned. We all know the cliché about making assumptions, but in fact the CSIU would not be made an ass, because the "planners' lack of proper planning" does not become the CSIU's emergency.

Typically when the CSIU is being asked to support a large-scale event, such as a political party's national convention or a World Series baseball game, it will be tasked as a rapid forensic investigative support element of what is known in New York City as an arch-angel package, consisting of units from multiple emergency response agencies: law enforcement, fire, emergency medical services (EMS), and office of emergency management (OEM), to name a few. The law enforcement component typically consists of personnel from the crime scene investigations unit (CSIU), bomb squad or explosive ordnance disposal (EOD) unit, arson and explosives unit (A&E), emergency service unit (ESU is NYC's SWAT), technical assistance response unit (TARU), hazmat/WMD team, highway units (for escorts) and disorder control unit (DCU, also known as the riot team). The arch-angel package will be staged off site from the event, at a location that is protected and secured and has rapid access to events site.

With large scale events, as listed previously, an Emergency Operations Center (EOC), will be opened in support of the event and an Incident Command System (ICS) will be established. The CSIU will fall under the Intelligence and Investigation Section, attached to the Forensic Investigations Branch as the CSIU Group.

This will typically be the case for all events and or incidents, where ICS is set up and the CSIU will be utilized.

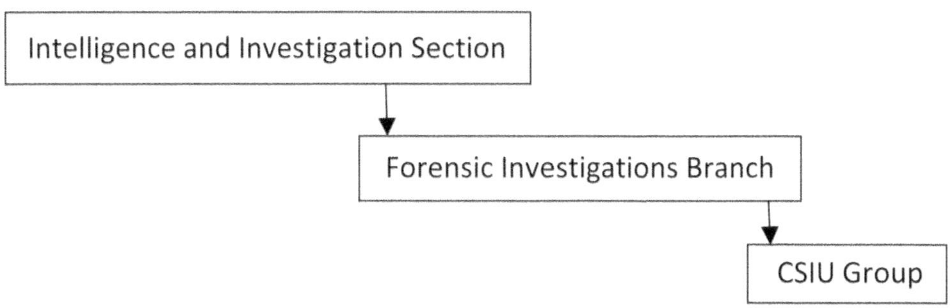

FIGURE 11.1 ICS Org Chart for the CSIU

If your CSIU is to be a part of something like an arch-angel package, then during the planning for the event you should ask for and obtain plans of the venue, such as site plans, elevation plans, floor plans, cross-sectional plans, utility plans, and public work plans. By no means is that a complete list, but you get the idea. Also if your CSIU has 3D laser scanning/measuring technology, 360 degree automated photography capabilities, and aerial photography assets, it's a good practice to scan and photograph the entire venue before the event, to be able to show how this site appeared before anything possibly happens. The point is to have these plans, scans and photographs, hard copies and digital versions, at the ready so that should something happen requiring the CSIU to go operational at the event, you can expedite the CSIU's response and documentation of the crime scene. If your CSIU doesn't have these capabilities, see if other agencies in your jurisdiction have them, and, if they do, request their assistance to support your mission at this event. Many jurisdictions' OEMs, have geographical information systems (GIS), that have this type of information. Remember, "Work smarter, not harder." Also, when the CSIU is obtaining these plans, scans and photographs from other agencies or units, then before they can be used the CSIU has to go to the venue's site and verify if all the plans, scans, and photographs are accurate, before they can be used. The authors have documented numerous examples where plans were obtained from; the New York City Buildings Department, the New York City Parks Department, the New York City Housing Authority, the New York City Transit Authority, and the Port Authority of New York and New Jersey, in connection with high profile criminal investigations in New York City, only to bring these plans to the crime scenes and find that they were not accurate AND did not depict what was actually built, constructed or in place at the scene. Most of the times the reasons for these discrepancies were due to these city agencies issuing contracts to contractors to construct alterations to these locations and the plans hadn't been updated properly back at their offices. Other times the residents and commercial tenants, of these properties had performed illegal alterations to the locations which were not identified by these city agencies. Whatever the reasons, this problem would cause us to modify the plans in the field to make them represent what is actually at the scene. And, if the plans were so far off and couldn't be effectively altered in the field, then we would have to produce our own plans in the field and go back to the CSIU's main office to draft and plot them with our computer aided Design and drafting (CADD) programs and print them on our plotters.

Continuing with planning for major (large scale) events/incidents, CSIU's must understand that these events/incidents are very attractive targets for terrorists who wish to create mass fatalities by utilizing weapons of mass destruction (WMDs), such as Chemical, Biological, Radiological, Nuclear, and Explosive Agents (CBRNE), armed assaults such as the 2008 Mumbai attack by Lashkar-e-Taiba. This being said, all CSIU's should be trained and certified a hazardous materials technicians. CSIU will also require: personal protective equipment (PPE), detection, monitoring, screening and analytical field equipment, specialized crime scene documentation, collection, processing, and packaging equipment. The CSIU will also need specialized equipment for decontamination of their equipment and evidence. The preparations and validations of extensive protocols and procedures will be required to ensure the CSIUs' are processing these scenes correctly. This will require for the CSIU's to identify the appropriate laboratories which will conduct the analysis of these types of evidence and to work with them in the development and validation of the required protocols and procedures. Once these protocols are validated, then the CSIU's should identify all the other units, and agencies that they will be required to work with or will be needed to support the CSIU's operations and train with them in preparation for a response to such scenes. In addition to the hazardous material training, certification and equipment, all CSIU's should be trained and certified in post blast investigations, fire investigations and major transportation incidents. And, just as with hazmat, the CSIU's should plan, develop protocols and train with all the units and agencies (local, state, and federal) that they will be required to work with or support their operations. With attacks such as these, the probability of mass fatality is high. CSIU's will need to plan, develop protocols and procedures to work with the death investigators of the various medical examiner's and coroner's offices, as the dead fall under their jurisdiction.

Revisiting con-ops, and not putting all your eggs in one basket, it's best to understand that while the CSIU may work out of a central location, be that the forensic laboratory or some other police facility, the CSIU's vehicles, equipment and some personnel, should be spread out or staged, across your jurisdiction at pre-identified satellite or back-up facilities. To do otherwise is to court disaster. Thinking strategically, if your central location becomes the victim of a natural disaster such as a hurricane, a tornado, an earthquake or a flood, or manmade disaster, such as a terrorist attack on your facility, your agency's crime scene investigative capabilities may just have been greatly diminished or totally destroyed. The authors would like to relate the true story of what happened to the New York City, Mayor's Office of Emergency Management (OEM), during the September 11, 2001 terrorist attack. The NYC OEM office was located in number Seven World Trade Center (WTC) at the time

FIGURE 11.2 3D laser scanning of Jefferson Memorial pre-event (Leica C-10)

FIGURE 11.3 3D laser scanning of stadium pre-event (Leica C-10)

of the attack. Seven WTC was a 50-story office building, north-east of Tower One. While this building wasn't directly impacted by any of the two planes utilized in the attack, building and plane debris from the North Tower impact and collapse, crashed through the roof and facade of Seven World Trade Center, which was evacuated. These materials made their way through the building where it caused fires on multiple floors. Theses fire continued, unabated, until the fire softened the steel, causing it to fail and number Seven World Trade Center would collapse hours after Towers One and Two collapsed. This collapse wiped out the NYC OEM's office and their capabilities to effectively support New York City's emergency response to the 9/11 attacks for some period of time. Having no back-up locations, NYC OEM scrambled to set up a temporary OEM at one of Manhattan's, west side piers, Pier 92, used by the cruise industry. This was a lesson learned the hard way, and will never happen again, as the NYC OEM has set up numerous back-up facilities within New York City and outside of New York City, to support their vital operations. The key to con-ops is redundancy.

The authors know what some of you are saying right about now, "My agency doesn't have the budget or logistics to do this!" We could answer this with any number of clichés: "You can pay me now or you can pay me later and later always cost more." Or how about, "Penny wise, dollar foolish."

You choose. We prefer this cliché: "Better to have it and not need it, then to need it and not have it." In most cases your agency may not have the budget or logistics, may be an accurate statement, but does that mean you throw your hands up and surrender? No, you don't. You look for monies from any and all legitimate sources you can find. There are grants from: the US Department of Homeland Security (DHS), the US Department of Justice (DOJ), the US Department of Energy (DOE), the US Environmental Protection Agency (EPA) and the US Department of Transportation (DOT), to name a few. There are US Drug Enforcement Administration (DEA) Drug forfeiture monies, and many more sources, that can assist your agency with obtaining funding and facilities for con-ops, planning, development and implementation. Also as stated early think regionally, pool your resources to share the expenses and strategically place your equipment and assets around your jurisdictions.

Once your agency makes the commitment to develop and implement a con-ops plan, your agency must identify the correct satellite or back-up locations to stage your assets. This will require very thorough analysis of the threats, natural and manmade, for which you are planning to respond to and for which the locations you are considering to utilize may encounter. Your agencies' assessment of these locations should include, amongst other criteria, your agency's ability to secure and protect these locations from the natural and manmade threats whether or not public works and utilities can support the planned operations at these facilities and whether the transportation infrastructure supports the fast and efficient movement of materials, equipment and personnel, to and from these locations. All these physical locations should require electronic employee identification access cards to make entry and only employees assigned to these locations will be granted access. All other employees not assigned to these sites and non-employees, seeking access to these sites will require: proper identification, legitimate business at the site, must sign in, be escorted throughout the facility, and never left unattended. In addition to physical security of the site, all computer, digital data, IT, and communications will require redundancies in the equipments': data security/storage, power supply, HVAC systems and fire protection. The HVAC and fire protection systems must be appropriate for protection of these types of electronic equipment.

In Chapter 7, we spoke of "Investigative Equipment," As we stated, it is important to have someone from the CSIU in charge of maintaining all the equipment for the CSIU operations. This is critical for the CSIU's con-ops, especially for response to large-scale events or incidents, such as those involving mass fatalities or the use of chemical, biological, radiological, nuclear, or explosives (CBRNE), agents. The "equipment manager or equipment custodian," is responsible to ensure all of the investigative support equipment, such as generators, batteries, power tools, lights, forensic light sources, HVAC equipment, tents, ladders, tables, chairs, trash containers (standard and hazardous), communications, computers, plotters, printers, personal protective equipment (PPE), decontamination equipment, hazardous material equipment, instruments, meters, monitors, chemicals/reagents, presumptive field tests, and equipment for documentation, collection, processing, and packaging, are maintained, operational, calibrated, not expired, certified chemically clean, sterile, not contaminated/cross contaminated, and inventoried in sufficient quantities to support all of the CSIU response operations. The equipment manager or equipment custodian, is also one of the main persons responsible for ensuring the con-ops for the CSIU by maintaining stock piles of equipment at the satellite or back-up locations, in response vehicles and at the CSIU's main facility. The equipment manager or equipment custodian should also have an assistant and multiple trained back-up equipment managers or equipment custodians. Remember, "One is None and Two is One," redundancy! A question that typically arises about the equipment manager or equipment custodian is whether the equipment manager or equipment custodian need to be sworn or civilian and whether they need to be a trained, certified CSI? The answer about sworn or civilian is that it really doesn't matter, unless this person will be responsible to protect and safeguard the equipment at a major incident deployment, then that person, whoever it is, may need to be armed. Many law enforcement agencies don't allow their civilian CSIs to be armed while working; however other law enforcement agencies do allow civilian CSIs to be armed while working. As for the question of whether or not the equipment manager or equipment custodian needs to be a trained certified CSI, the answer is no, but it indeed helps if they have a CSI/forensic background. Remember this person will have tremendous amounts of quality assurance/quality control (QA/QC) responsibilities for the CSIU's equipment and should meet the American Society of Crime Laboratory Directors' (ASCLAD) and the International Organization for Standardization's (ISO) accreditation requirements for these issues.

Since we were speaking of CSIUs' response vehicles, let's continue with vehicles and who is responsible for their maintenance and readiness. There are several schools of thought or models for this. One model has the equipment manager or equipment custodian responsible for this and the other model has another member of the CSIU as the "CSIU's fleet manager." Some of the factors in determining which model to use are the manpower of the CSIU, the size of the CSIU's fleet, and as always, the budget. If your CSIU has the manpower to have a 24/7 dedicated equipment manager or equipment custodian then let this person handle it as it is just a natural extension of their current duties. As stated in Chapter 8, the day-to-day crime scene vehicles should be well designed to carry all the required equipment, to assist in the processing, packaging, and storage of the forensic evidence recovered from conventional crime scenes, as well as to act as a mobile field office for these scenes. For the more complicated scenes, or shall we say the "unconventional crime scene," such as scenes involving CBRNE, plane crashes, building collapses, and the like, the CSIU will need, in addition to the daily response vehicles, specialty vehicles such as panel trucks with hydraulic lift gates, to store and haul the specialty equipment, which can be quite heavy and bulky, a mobile lab or crime scene evidence processing truck, and a CSIU "command and control" truck. A quick note on storing equipment in CSIU vehicles: if your vehicles are being stored or parked in non-climate control environments, and or their interiors are not being climate controlled (temperature and humidity) when not in use, thus making them susceptible, to extreme swings in temperature and humidity, the CSIU equipment manager or equipment custodians and the various crime scene investigators (CSIs) must understand which equipment can and cannot be stored in the vehicles. Many of the forensic chemicals, electronic equipment (battery powered or AC powered), as well as, collection and packaging equipment, can be rendered unusable, damaged or destroyed by exposure to these extreme temperature and humidity swings. This being the case, all equipment identified as having these issues should be stored in some sort of portable case to easily be transported from its climate controlled storage environment, the CSIU office or other CSIU facility, to the CSIU response vehicles for use in the field, and then returned to the climate controlled storage environment from the response vehicles upon returning from the field.

FIGURE 11.4 CSIU standard response vehicle, left side

FIGURE 11.5 CSIU standard response vehicle, right/rear

FIGURE 11.6 CSIU standard response vehicle, right entrance to work area (photo courtesy of Specialty Vehicle Solutions)

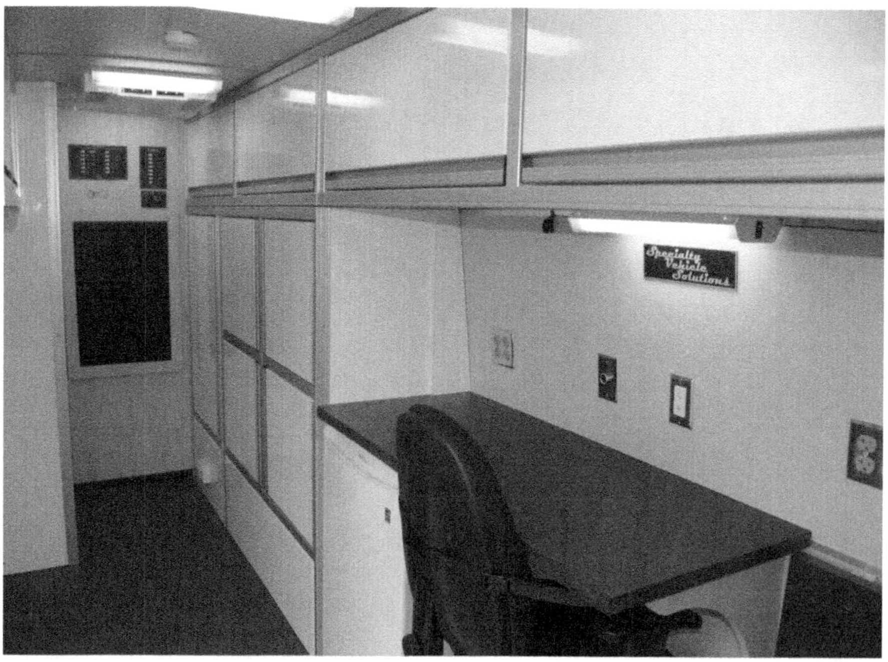

FIGURE 11.7 CSIU standard response vehicle, interior of work area, front right to back left (photo courtesy of Specialty Vehicle Solutions)

FIGURE 11.8 CSIU standard response vehicle, interior of work area, front to back (photo courtesy of Specialty Vehicle Solutions)

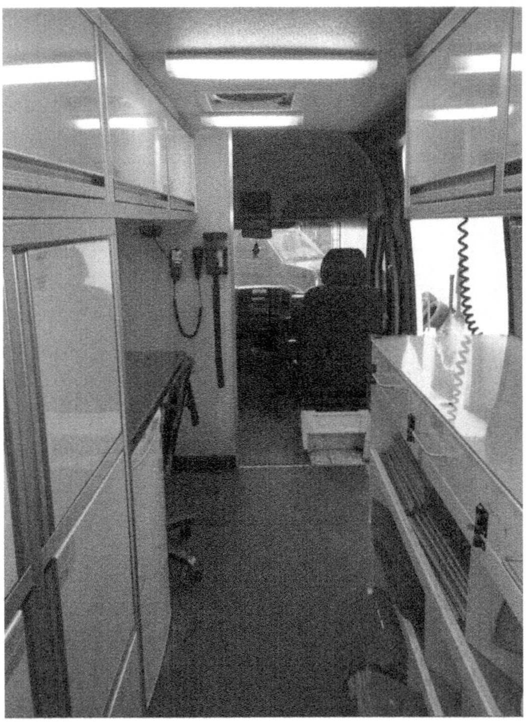

FIGURE 11.9 CSIU standard response vehicle, interior of work area, back to front (photo courtesy of Specialty Vehicle Solutions)

FIGURE 11.10 CSIU standard response vehicle, interior of rear storage area (photo courtesy of Specialty Vehicle Solutions)

FIGURE 11.11 Right side of mobile lab (photo courtesy of Agilent Technologies and ENG Mobile System)

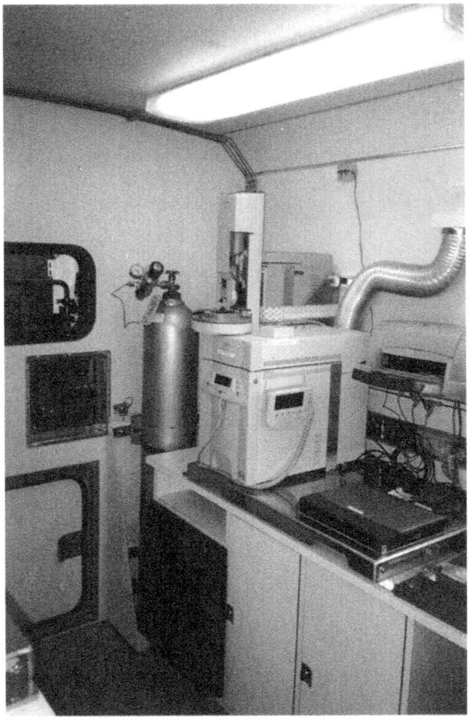

FIGURE 11.12 Interior left rear analytical compartment showing GC/MIDI (photo courtesy of Agilent Technologies and ENG Mobile Systems)

FIGURE 11.13 Interior right rear analytical compartment showing GC/MS (photo courtesy of Agilent Technologies and ENG Mobile Systems)

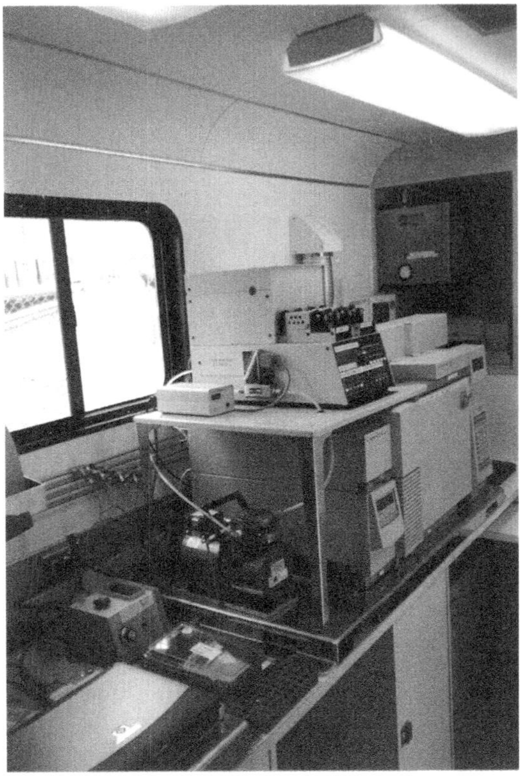

FIGURE 11.14 Interior left front analytical compartment showing GC/IR (photo courtesy of Agilent Technologies and ENG Mobile Systems)

FIGURE 11.15 Interior rear preparation compartment showing glove box and sample portal (photo courtesy of Agilent Technologies and ENG Mobile Systems)

FIGURE 11.16 Interior rear preparation compartment showing safety cabinet (photo courtesy of Agilent Technologies and ENG Mobile Systems)

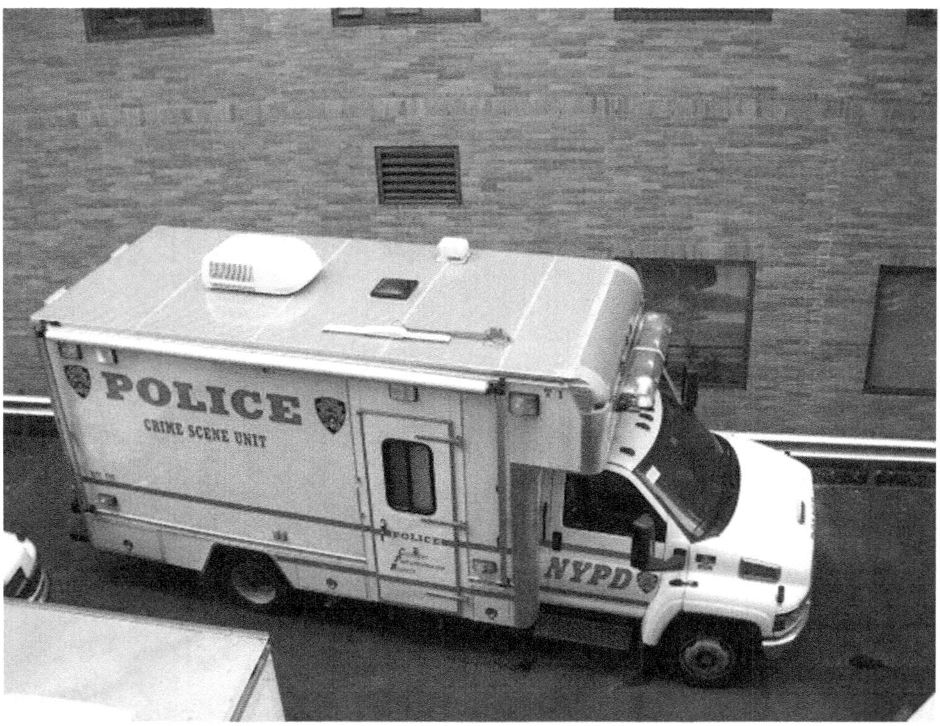

FIGURE 11.17 CSIU major incident response vehicle, right side

FIGURE 11.18 CSIU major incident equipment transport vehicle with hydraulic lift, left rear side

FIGURE 11.19 CSIU major incident equipment transport vehicle with hydraulic lift, left side

FIGURE 11.20 CSIU major incident equipment transport vehicle with hydraulic lift, front left side

FIGURE 11.21 Rolling cage of self contained breathing apparatus (SCBA) which can be transported on the CSIU major incident equipment transport vehicle when needed

FIGURE 11.22 Rolling cage of self contained breathing apparatus (SCBA) interior

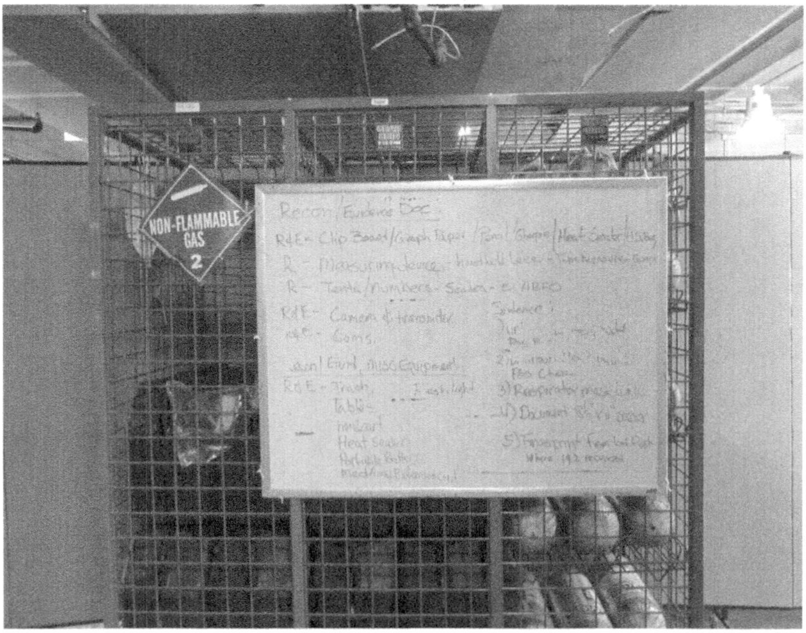

FIGURE 11.23 Rear of rolling cage of self contained breathing apparatus (SCBA) with white board attached

FIGURE 11.24 Rolling cage of personal protection equipment (nitrile gloves and chemical protection suits) which can be transported on the CSIU major incident equipment transport vehicle when needed

FIGURE 11.25 Rolling cage of personal protection equipment (chemical protective boots and SCBA masks) which can be transported on the CSIU major incident equipment transport vehicle when needed

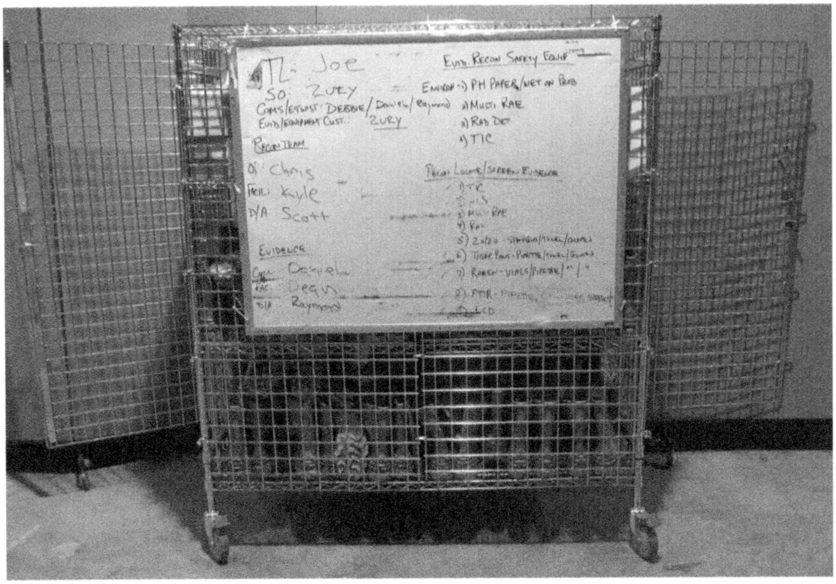

FIGURE 11.26 Rear of rolling cage of personal protection equipment (chemical protective boots and SCBA masks) which can be transported on the CSIU major incident equipment transport vehicle when needed, with white board

FIGURE 11.27 Rolling cage of forensic collection, processing, and packaging equipment which can be transported on the CSIU major incident equipment transport vehicle when needed

FIGURE 11.28 Interior of rolling cage of various forensic evidence collection, processing, and packaging equipment which can be transported on the CSIU major incident equipment transport vehicle when needed

FIGURE 11.29 Interior of rolling cage of serology evidence collection, processing, and packaging equipment which can be transported on the CSIU major incident equipment transport vehicle when needed

FIGURE 11.30 Interior of rolling cage of hair and fiber evidence collection, processing, and packaging equipment which can be transported on the CSIU major incident equipment transport vehicle when needed

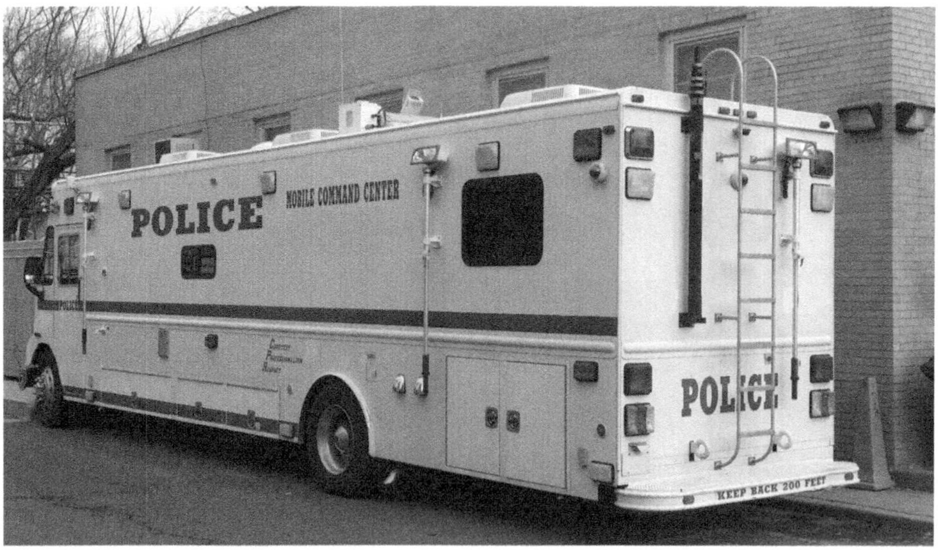

FIGURE 11.31 Forensic investigation division major incident command and control vehicle, left rear side

Our response vehicles are no different from our other equipment in terms of con-ops and as such should not all be kept in one location. Staying with the redundancy theme, your CSIU should have some back-up CSIU response vehicles, spread out at your satellite or back-up facilities. A huge lesson learned from the authors' response to the 9/11 attacks in New York City, is that we should not be driving our response vehicles directly into and or through such contaminated scenes and that after working such scenes we and our equipment need to be decontaminated before allowing either to enter a clean response vehicle. For the CSIU personnel this also includes a change into clean, uncontaminated clothing, post decontamination. Our CSIU vehicles will need to be parked at designated, uncontaminated staging areas to ensure they don't become contaminated. In the case of our 9/11 response, our vehicles became contaminated, inside and out. This caused the authors' and co-workers' continued exposure to the toxic cocktail in that dust/debris, who were utilizing these vehicles for transportation to and from our offices. This mistake continued to snowball because we drove those contaminated vehicles back to our main office and our satellite offices, transferring the contamination from our vehicles and clothing to our offices, locker rooms, bathrooms/showers and co-workers. And, if we didn't change our clothes and wash up at our offices we transferred the contamination to our private vehicles, then to our homes and families. This can never happen again. If our response vehicles do get contaminated, they need to be immediately taken out of service and decontaminated. If the response vehicles were exposed to materials that can't be properly or effectively decontaminated then these vehicles pose a health and safety risk. They then need to be condemned, treated as hazardous waste and properly disposed of in accordance with all applicable laws and replaced.

It is the authors' hope that after reading this chapter that you review your CSIU's day-to-day operations with an eye towards the CSIU's continuity of operations, planning, preparedness, and response to support HCEs and the investigation of unconventional high profile crime scenes.

References

Popular Mechanics Magazine, Hearst Communications, Inc www.popularmechanics.com/technology/engineering/architecture/4278874

New York City Amateur Radio Emergency Communications Service www.nyc-arecs.org/911.html

The Center For Court Innovation, A Public/Private Partnership with the New York State Unified Court System www.courtinnovation.org/sites/default/files/emergencyplanning.pdf

12

REPORTS AND RECORDS MANAGEMENT

The Crime Scene Report

In the end all of the effort expended by the CSI team boils down to several pages of reports and accompanying images. Most of the entities who will review the CSI's work will never actually witness the work in progress, or visit the scene, or even have the opportunity to meet face to face with the CSI team. Instead they will read the reports and view the accompanying documentation and infer from it whether a proper job was done during the crime scene processing. Therefore it behooves the CSI to write a complete and concise report including not only all of the work that was done at the scene but also the decisions and considerations that were made during the scene processing. The main goal of crime scene processing is to maximize the collection of probative forensic evidence. This goal and all of the steps taken to reach it must be communicated to the reader of the crime scene report. Once the report is completed it should be subjected to administrative and possibly technical review procedures as described in Chapter 10 Ensuring.

A well written crime scene report should be:

- Concise
  - The report must contain all of the required detail but be presented in as short and simple form as practical
- Accurate
  - The facts are reported based on the physical evidence, results of processing activity, personal observations, and conferrals
- Objective
  - No conclusions are made in a crime scene report and no theories are presented. The evidence speaks for itself once the analysis is concluded. (Note: when crime scene reconstruction is carried out it may result in conclusions but this should be reported separately from the crime scene investigation report even if it is completed by the same individual.)

- Complete
  - The facts as known, scene considerations, physical forensic evidence recovered and processing activity must be presented in their entirety

During crime scene processing CSIs make many careful decisions about how the scene will be handled and how the evidence will be processed. It is critical that *all* of this information is conveyed in the report in order to prevent someone from inferring that something was either completely overlooked or not given proper consideration. The report must include processes that were met with negative results during processing as well as the ones that produce positive results; the fact of the matter is that they may be equally important.

In the authors' experience CSIs often fail to take credit for their efforts in the report when they are met with negative results. For instance, if a CSI uses a forensic light source to search for biological stains at a crime scene but fails to locate any evidence it is not uncommon for the fact that the search was done to be left out of the report. This is unfortunate since the absence of biological stains may be just as important to finding out the truth about what occurred as if the stains were present. It also fails to allocate the credit deserved for a thorough job by the CSI team and can lead the person reviewing the report to wrongly conclude that the forensic light was not used when it should have been. Even though the fact that the forensic light was used may be in the field notes it should not be assumed that anyone will read through the notes before playing Monday morning quarterback and assuming that something was overlooked. Experience teaches that they usually won't. In short, as the old saying goes, if it's not in the report it wasn't done (at least in the mind of the reader).

The crime scene reports produced by a unit must also be consistent in presentation, style and format from one CSI to the next. The audience of readers is limited and the same people will repeatedly need to read and understand the reports that are produced for the various cases that different members of the unit handle. This audience includes, detectives and criminal investigators, lab technicians, scientists, forensic experts, prosecutors and defense attorneys. They will all have experience in reading these types of reports and consequently will have expectations about what the report should contain and how the material should be presented. This is just the normal course of business. Consistency is expected and is required in order to remain efficient and prevent errors or miscommunication. Imagine an attorney presenting a written brief to the court and writing it freehand in their own personal style instead of in the format that is expected by the court. Regardless of the merits of the brief the court would not entertain the matter as it would not conform to what is normal business practice in the legal community. The same holds true for crime scene reports as they are also business records prepared to create a permanent record of events and communicate findings.

Although the reports should be consistent within a unit they will undoubtedly vary in style from agency to agency. This may be acceptable when it comes to style and format but we must at least strive for consistency in content throughout the CSI field.

Crime Scene Report Formats

The crime scene report may be a single document that covers all of the activities involved in the crime scene processing or it may be a collection of individual documents each covering a single activity or process. Some CSI units may prefer to write reports that include in the body a narrative description of activities and processing tasks while others may use a format that follows a chronological timeline of activities and processes. The timeline begins when the call is received and continues until the scene investigation is concluded and the evidence is delivered to its destination. It may also include follow up work and conferrals that occur in the interim between the conclusion of scene activities and the time the report is written.

The benefit to a narrative report over a chronological report is the ability to use headings and sub-headings to make it easy to locate and read specific topics of information. However, writing a good narrative report takes good writing skills and can be a lengthy process. The benefit to a chronological report is that it creates an understanding of the larger process and helps to prevent omissions since it follows the contemporaneous notes taken at the scene. The downside to this type of report is that it may be difficult to locate specific facts without reading through the entire report.

A good solution to effective report writing and for maintaining consistency is to use templates that are created and pre-approved for use throughout the unit. This type of force captioned reporting has become more common as computer software has advanced allowing for the creation of customized forms that can be used to record and report information.

Report templates can be created in word processing software and there are some software applications that offer off the shelf reports for crime scene investigation many of which are integrated into photo management software. Since each agency has unique policies and each case is different it is difficult to develop a one-size-fits-all report for CSI work. If off the shelf software is used it should have the capability to be customized in order for it to be truly valuable.

A narrative crime scene report may contain the following sections as they apply to the case:

Case Information Section

The case information section of the report is used to record the basic information regarding the crime scene investigation assignment including its location and time and the persons handling the CSI work. The section also provides an opportunity to cross reference the case to any other related cases and make the reader aware of the fact that there may be additional information involved with the case when inter-related cases exist. For instance the case being reported may be for a homicide incident that involved a motor vehicle and a different CSI team may have processed the vehicle at a separate location. That information would obviously be important to a reader but without a cross reference in the case information section it may go undiscovered.

The following should be reported in the case information section of the report:

- Case number
- Related case numbers
- Type of incident or crime under investigation
- Date of occurrence of the incident
- Date of the crime scene investigation
- Location of the scene
- CSI team members
    - Primary investigator
    - Assisting investigator(s)
    - Technical assistants

    - Crime scene supervisor
    - Crime scene case manager (if applicable)
- Arrests
    - Arrestee's name and pedigree information
- Suspects
    - Name and pedigree information of any identified suspects
    - Description of any unidentified suspects

Victim(s) Information Section

The victim section includes in-depth information about the victim and their condition. If the victim is deceased at the scene then an on-scene examination by the medico-legal investigator will be conducted and should be attended by the CSI primary investigator. During this process information about the victim and injuries will be obtained and photographs should be taken by the CSI team. During and following the examination, steps may be needed to safeguard potential evidence on the body of the victim. These potential steps include wrapping bags around the hands of the victim if contact between the suspect and victim is suspected and using new body bags to wrap the body. The details of this process should be recorded in the report.

Elimination samples of fingerprints and DNA may be required to be collected from the victim in order to compare any fingerprint or DNA evidence against and identify any evidence that matches the victim. Whether the samples are needed and whether they were, or were not, collected needs to be documented in the report. This information will be very important when submitting DNA samples to the CODIS database.

The following should be reported in the victim information section of the report:

- Name and pedigree information
- Clothing description
- Physical status
    - Uninjured
    - Injured
        - Description of injuries
            - Evidence of bleeding
            - Anatomical wound chart
    - Deceased
        - Medical examiner or coroner information
        - Description of injuries
            - Evidence of bleeding
            - Anatomical wound chart
        - Personal property list
        - Steps to preserve evidence on body
            - Bag hands
            - Bag body
- Location
    - On scene

    - Hospital
        - Hospital and doctor's information
        - Condition and diagnosis
- Processing
    - Was victim processed by CSI team?
        - Photographs
        - Interview
        - Evidence collected
        - Elimination fingerprints collected
        - Elimination DNA samples collected

Scene Information Section

The scene information section reports on observations made by the CSI team upon arrival at the scene, such as weather and lighting, and records people who are involved in the incident either in an official capacity or as a suspect, arrestee, or witness.

After arriving at the scene the CSI team will conduct conferrals and a walk-through of the crime scene. The information gathered during this time begins to present a picture of what occurred and this information is written into the incident summary. At this point in the investigation no conclusions can be drawn so the incident summary simply lists the facts as known. Theories or conclusions should not be included in the report since they are likely to change as the investigation continues. The CSI should report observations and facts while refraining from prematurely diagnosing a cause for what is observed. For instance after observing a pocket knife on the sidewalk at a crime scene the CSI may infer that it was dropped by a fleeing suspect only to be proven wrong later when its learned that it was actually tossed by another individual when the police arrived and started questioning people. The report should simply state that a pocket knife was observed on the sidewalk without prematurely concluding how it got there.

The following should be reported in the scene information section of the report:

- Time of arrival at scene
- Time of departure from scene
- Location type
    - Indoor residential premise
    - Indoor commercial premise
    - Outdoor public space
    - Outdoor private space
    - Government facility
    - Transportation facility
- Environmental factors
    - Outdoor weather and temperature
    - Indoor temperature at scene (if applicable)
    - Lighting conditions
        - Daylight or darkness
        - Artificial lighting types

- Scene security upon arrival
    - Name of police officer(s) safeguarding the scene
    - Methods used to secure scene
        - Scene roped off
        - Indoor scene secured at entryways
        - Other
    - Measures employed by CSI team to secure scene
- Persons present upon arrival or involved in incident
    - Police officers
    - Investigators
    - Medical or coroner personnel
    - Fire and ambulance personnel
    - Suspects or arrestees
    - Witnesses
        - Fingerprint elimination samples
        - DNA elimination samples
- Summary of incident
    - Concise written statement about the facts of the incident as they are known at the time. Do not include any theories or preliminary conclusions.

Crime Scene Images Section

The crime scene images section reports on the details of the efforts put forth to document the scene using photography and, if applicable, video. If film photography is used, additional detail is required in written form. If digital photography is used then the electronic file will record camera information, such as setting, flash use, field of view, and so on, in the metadata attached to the file. When digital photography is used then a statement as to how the images have been stored and archived should be included.

The photos should be individually listed in a photo log. The photo log records each exposure by stating the following: the type of photo (overview, mid-range or close-up), the location that the photographer was positioned when the photo was taken, the direction that the camera was pointed and the subject of the photo. It seems that as digital photography is implemented into crime scene operations there is a tendency to eliminate the photo log. A written photo log can be very helpful to the investigation as it provides the written description of what the photographer was intending to reveal in the photo. When looking at crime scene photos it is not always apparent as to what is shown. Imagine being blindly handed a close-up photo of a 1-inch long tool mark impression on a door jamb. Since the close-up photo does not reveal the surroundings, it may be nearly impossible to decipher what is shown in the image but as soon as you read a written description in the photo log it becomes very clear to you what is shown. Of course if you didn't have the written description you could just ask the photographer to explain what is depicted but we have to remember that crime scene photos are used by many people who never get to meet and talk with the CSI team. Also the photos may be needed well into the future when the photographer may no longer be available.

The following should be reported in the crime scene imaging section of the report:

- Photographer's name
- Videography used to supplement photos
- Time photography began
- Camera information (may be embedded in meta data if digital photography is used)
- Total number of images captured at scene
- Method used to store images if digital photography was used
- Photo log
    - Description of each photo
        - Photo type
            - Overall view
            - Mid-range view
            - Close-up view
    - Description of subject of the photo
    - Photographer's location when capturing the photo
    - Direction camera facing when capturing the photo

Crime Scene Search Section

The crime scene search section covers one of the more important aspects of the crime scene process but one that is often overlooked when it comes to report writing. It is often just assumed that the reader will know that a search was conducted since it is such an obvious activity that takes place at the crime scene. Including details of the search however can be very important for a reader to understand the effort and level of thoroughness that went into completing the search. This information may become important later on in cold case investigations as new information becomes available and the initial scene processing needs to be reviewed. This was the case recently at an infamous 35-year-old missing child case in New York City where a six-year-old boy named Etan Patz was reported missing. New information became available decades later that led to the arrest of an individual for the murder of the child in 1979. After the arrest the subject reportedly gave information about the crime scene which prompted a return to the scene. To verify the validity of the statements regarding where some of the child's belongings were placed it became important to ascertain what areas were searched back in 1979. It is believed that a very thorough search was conducted back then but the specific facts of the search were not recorded as part of the written reports at that time.

The following should be reported in the crime scene search section of the report:

- Search team members
    - Name and title of all persons participating in the search
- Legal basis for search
    - Search warrant
    - Consent
    - Search warrant exception
- Time of crime scene search
- Areas included in the search
- Search method used
- Search tools utilized

- Lighting and oblique lighting
- Ladders and tools
- Forensic lights
    - Wavelength settings
    - Barrier filters employed
    - Results (both negative and positive)

Forensic Evidence Section

The forensic evidence section of the report details all of the items of evidence that were discovered and were photographed and/or collected. This section of the report can be divided into subsections for each different type of evidence. Physical evidence types are dictated by either their physical characteristics or their primary value for forensic testing. Therefore an item like a bullet would be listed as firearms' related evidence because of its characteristics but a drinking straw may be listed as DNA evidence if it is believed that the suspect's mouth had contact with it or it may be listed as controlled substance evidence if its primary value is as drug paraphernalia.

Evidence listed in the report should be presented along with information about its context and probative value. Each entry should include the unique identifier assigned to the item, its location within the scene, fixed measurements, person recovering the evidence, and probative value for forensic testing.

The following should be reported in the forensic evidence section of the report:

- Item type
- Unique identifier
- Description of the item
    - Physical characteristics
    - Functional characteristics
    - Operational characteristics
- Location at the scene
- Fixed position measurements
- Person recovering evidence
- Packaging and marking information
- Probative value for forensic testing

The forensic evidence section may be sub-divided based on the following evidence types:

- Firearms and related evidence
    - Firearms
        - Type, make, caliber
        - Serial number
    - Firearm components and accessories
    - Ammunition cartridges
    - Cartridge cases
    - Fired bullets and fragments

    - Items bearing suspected ballistic damage
        - Ballistic damage at scene
            - Description and location
            - Fixed measurements
            - Angle of impact (if applicable)
        - Bullet hole confirmation
        - Muzzle to target distance determination
- Weapons (other than firearms)
    - Knives and edged weapons
    - Blunt instruments
    - Other weapons
- DNA Evidence
    - DNA swab samples
        - Suspected blood stains
        - Suspected semen stains
        - Suspected saliva
        - Suspected touch DNA (skin cells)
    - Cuttings containing suspected DNA
    - Physical items suspected to contain DNA
    - Buccal swabs
        - Victim elimination
        - Other person elimination
        - Suspect
        - Arrestee
    - Sexual assault evidence kits
- Fingerprint evidence
    - Latent print lifts
    - Items suspected to bear latent prints
    - Items bearing patent or plastic prints
    - Latent, patent or plastic print images
- Impression evidence
    - Footwear impressions
        - Physical items bearing footwear impressions
        - Two dimensional lifts
        - Three dimensional casts
        - Footwear impression images
        - Known comparison footwear samples
    - Tire tread impressions
        - Physical items bearing tire tread impressions
        - Two dimensional lifts
        - Three dimensional casts
        - Tire tread impression images
        - Known tire tread comparison impressions
    - Tool marks

        - Three dimensional casts
        - Tool mark impression images
        - Known comparison tools
- Criminalistics evidence
    - Hairs and fibers
        - Hair from scene
        - Fibers from scene
        - Adhesive tape lifts from scene
        - Trace evidence vacuum samples
        - Known comparison samples
    - Glass evidence
        - Glass fragments from scene
        - Items bearing glass fragments
        - Plate glass
            - Direction of force determinations
            - Fracture analysis (bullet hole sequence)
            - Headlights and taillights
    - Paint evidence
        - Items containing paint transfer
        - Known paint scraping samples
    - Soil evidence
    - Jigsaw fit evidence
    - Plastic bags (striations)
    - Questioned documents/handwriting
    - Chemical unknowns
    - Arson and explosives evidence
- Chemical, biological, radioactive materials
    - Poisons
    - Contaminated food
    - Chemical threats
    - Biological threats
    - Radiological threats
- Controlled substances
    - Suspected controlled substance recovered from the scene
    - Suspected controlled substance recovered from the arrestee
    - Drug paraphernalia
- Computer, digital and multimedia evidence
    - Computers, tablets, personal digital devices
    - Cell phones
    - Surveillance images and video
    - Data from IT devices
- Other physical evidence
    - Physical evidence with demonstrative value

Crime Scene Processing Section

The crime scene processing section reports the steps used at the crime scene to process it and maximize the recovery of probative evidence. The processing steps must be reported regardless of the results since positive and negative results can be equally important. Reporting all activities also conveys to the reader that a methodical and systematic approach was used to thoroughly process the scene.

The following should be reported in the crime scene processing section of the report:

- Latent print processing
  - Areas processed for latent prints
  - Methods and products utilized
  - Results of processing
- Presumptive blood testing
  - Test utilized, lot number, expiration date
  - Results of control tests
  - Description of areas of application at scene
  - Results of application (positive and negative results)
- Acid phosphatase testing
  - Test utilized, lot number, expiration date
  - Results of control tests
  - Description of areas of application at scene
  - Results of application (positive and negative results)
- Chemi-luminescent search for blood (Luminol or Blue Star)
  - Product information, lot number, expiration date
  - Results of positive and negative control tests
  - Description of areas of application at scene
  - Results of application (positive and negative results)
- Bloodstain enhancement
  - Reagent utilized (LCV, Amido Black) lot number, expiration date
  - Description of areas of application at scene
  - Results of application
- Bullet hole confirmation testing
  - Presumptive lead testing (sodium rhodizonate)
    - Test utilized, lot number, expiration date
    - Results of control tests
    - Method utilized
    - Description of areas of application at scene
    - Results of application (positive and negative results)
  - Presumptive test for copper (2NN)
    - Test utilized, lot number, expiration date
    - Results of control tests
    - Description of areas of application at scene
    - Results of application (positive and negative results)

Bloodstain Pattern Section

Bloodstain pattern analysis is a sub-specialty in forensic investigations and is frequently conducted by experienced and properly trained CSIs. This work should only be done by persons who are qualified and meet the requirements recommended by the Scientific Working Group on Bloodstain Pattern Analysis (SWGSTAIN) and all work should conform to the units written quality assurance program for bloodstain pattern analysis. When bloodstain pattern analysis is done the report issued should be able to stand on its own without the reader having to reference other sections of the crime scene report.

SWGSTAIN.QA.DOC4 recommends the following report elements are included in a bloodstain pattern analysis report:

Report Elements

2.1 Title – This section of the report must identify the subject matter of the document.

2.2 Case Identifier – The report must have a unique case identifier which is clearly displayed on each page of the report. It is recommended the requesting agency's case identifier be displayed on the first page.

2.3 Name and Address of Reporting Agency – The name and address of the reporting agency must be included.

2.4 Date of Report – The date of the report must be included.

2.5 Case Information – This section of the report should outline the background information supplied or question(s) posed to the analyst during the course of the investigation and analysis. This may include, but is not limited to:

- Information supplied by investigating officers
- Medical/DNA reports
- Environmental conditions
- Conditions surrounding the author's involvement in the case
- Summary of case background
- Name and address of the submitting agency or requesting officer

2.6 Description of Items – The report must include a description of the items of evidence or materials received which are relevant to the bloodstain pattern analysis.
At minimum, this should include:

- Physical description (e.g., size, color, etc.)
- Unambiguous identification (e.g., item number, serial number, etc.)
- Recovery location, if known

2.6.1 The extent to which the items are further described within the report may be case dependent (e.g., damp condition, moldy, soiled, fabric damage, fabric type, etc.)

2.6.2 It is recommended the date and manner of receipt of items be included.

2.7 Location of the Tests or Examinations – The report must identify the locations where examinations took place.

2.8 Methods – This section of the report should define the techniques utilized in the examination. The extent to which the method is described (or referenced) in the report is agency and jurisdiction dependent.
2.9 Limitations and Assumptions – Statements of evidence limitations and assumptions (e.g., photographic review, evidence condition, lack of DNA profiling testing, etc.) should be included in the report.

For example:

- *"Limitations may exist when basing any conclusions on photographic evidence alone. From a technical perspective, the photographic record of the scene and exhibits specific for conducting a bloodstain pattern analysis is partly inadequate and as such, has restricted a more comprehensive interpretation."*
- *"The contamination caused by multiple items packaged together limited the bloodstain pattern examination."*
- *"Numerous sampled bloodstains failed to yield DNA profiles and as such, have restricted a more comprehensive examination."*

2.10 Observations and Examinations – This section of the report must include the observations and examinations recorded in the course of the BPA which provide the basis upon which subsequent conclusions will be made.
2.10.1 Each general location where observations are recorded should be separately addressed in this section. The subsections defined here will be case dependent.

For example:

- Crime scene divided into logical subsections (e.g., room by room, areas within a room, etc.)
- Victim/Deceased
- Physical evidence (e.g., victim's clothing, suspect's clothing, etc.)

2.10.2 Descriptors of the reported stains and stain patterns should be included. The extent and manner the stains or patterns are described is agency dependent.

For example:

- *"Numerous bloodstains less than "x" millimeters in size were present…"*
- *"Elliptical shaped bloodstains were present…"*
- *"Directionality was present that indicated direction of travel upwards…"*
- *"A linear distribution of bloodstains was present…"*

2.10.3 Compass points – When describing scene observations, it is recommended that compass points be incorporated into the description for accuracy in referencing the location.
2.10.4 Measurements – Measurements should be included in this section of the report and may be reported using the system commonly employed in that jurisdiction; however, it is recommended measurements are reported using the metric system. Due to their size, individual spatter stains should be reported using the metric system. Measurement examples include but are not limited to:

- Area(s) of origin
- Room size
- Locations of bloodstains
- Dimensions of a bloodstain pattern

2.10.5 Terminology – Bloodstain pattern analysis terminology must be defined and referenced. This may be accomplished by the use of footnotes, an appendix or glossary, or defining within the body of the report.
2.10.6 Photographs – Photographs should be utilized to assist in the reporting of stain observations. If used, these must be identified and referenced. Photographs may be annotated.
2.10.7 Sketches – It is recommended sketches, scene diagrams and plans are included.
2.10.8 Chemical applications – The results of any chemical application (e.g., chemical enhancements, presumptive blood testing, etc.) must be reported.

For example:

- *"Leuco Crystal Violet (LCV) was applied to (location or item) and this revealed…"*
- *"Presumptive testing for blood was positive on the stains located on…"*

2.10.9 Negative Findings – It may be appropriate to combine negative findings for ease of reporting. When reporting a negative finding, the basis for this should be indicated.

For example:

- *"No blood-like stains were visibly or chemically detected on (list of items)"*
- *"No apparent bloodstaining was visible on (list of items)"*

2.10.10 Collected Samples – The location(s) of collected stain sample(s) relevant to the bloodstain pattern analysis must be reported with reference to their unique identifier(s).
2.11 Conclusions – This section must include a collation of the findings drawn from the analysis and based on the information and observations previously presented in the body of the report. This section of the report must be clear and concise. Observations previously stated in the report must be referenced within the wording of the conclusion.

For example:

- *"The directionality of the drip stains and flow patterns of blood observed on the clothing worn by the deceased indicated he was in an upright position while bleeding."*

2.11.1 Opinion – When an opinion is reported, it must be clearly marked as such. The basis upon which the opinion has been made must be documented and if applicable, referenced.
2.12 Qualifying Statements – A statement must be included that acknowledges if information changes, the conclusions rendered in the original report may be affected.

For example:

- *"This report is based solely on the information and materials made available at this time and may be modified with the submission of new information."*

- *"This statement is based on information provided to me during this investigation. If further information becomes available, I may need to reappraise my findings and conclusions. If such a reappraisal were required, it would be more effective carried out in advance of any trial."*

2.13 Signature – Each report must have the name and signature of the reporting analyst(s) and, when appropriate, a co-signature. Consideration should be made to placing a signature or initials on each page of the report.

Vehicles Section

Vehicles frequently become part of a crime scene investigation. They are often used in the commission of the crime or to provide transportation to or from the scene. Sometimes they are simply located in the vicinity of the crime and become inert victims when their surfaces bear ballistic damage or fingerprint and DNA evidence. Whatever the connection to the crime it is important to document specific information about vehicles in the crime scene report when they become involved in the crime scene process.

Involved vehicles are often documented in place at the scene and then removed to a vehicle processing facility to be examined. In this case it is important to record the vehicle information at both locations to show the chain of custody of the vehicle. When a vehicle is transported off scene to a processing facility it must be reported how the vehicle was transported and what steps were taken to safeguard potential evidence during the transport.

The following should be reported in the vehicle section of the report:

- Vehicle's relationship to incident
  - Used during commission of crime
  - Used to travel to or from the crime scene
  - Victim's vehicle
  - Suspect's vehicle
  - Parked at scene
- Make, model, color, VIN number and year of vehicle
- Condition of vehicle and damage (if applicable)
- Tire information (if applicable)
- Location and position of vehicle
- Consent to search or search warrant information if applicable
- Details of examination and processing
- Processing location if different from primary scene
  - Transport means of vehicle
  - Procedures used to safeguard vehicle
- Storage location

Crime Scene Sketch and Diagram Section

The sketch and diagram section of the report records whether or not a sketch was prepared and if it was then who prepared it. Since some crime scenes will require more than a single sketch to be prepared, the number of sketches prepared is also documented.

Measurements go hand in hand with preparation of the sketch so details regarding the measurement process can also be recorded in this section. Although it is not necessary to include a list of measurements since they are located elsewhere in the report, it should indicate the methods for measuring the scene and the tools that were employed. If electronic tools were used then a statement of how and where the data was stored and archived should also be included. A copy of the sketch should be attached to the report.

Finished diagrams are prepared in some cases to present professional appearance and for use in briefings and court testimony. If diagrams have been prepared it should be reported here. If software was used to create the diagrams then information about how the files have been stored and archived should also be included. A copy of the diagram should be attached to the report.

The following should be reported in the crime scene sketch and diagram section of the report:

- Rough sketch
  - Indicate if rough sketch was prepared
    - Name of preparer and measuring assistant
    - Number and type of sketches prepared and attached to report
    - Method and tools used to record measurements
      - Measurement tool validation (if applicable)
      - Method used to record data if electronic instrument used
- Finished diagram
  - Indicate if finished diagram was prepared
    - Name of preparer
    - Method used
    - Number of diagrams prepared and attached to report
    - Method used to store data if software was used

Additional Reports

Additional reports will often be required during the crime scene process. These forms include checklists, wound charts and those reports needed to invoice the items collected as evidence, deliver them to a laboratory intake facility and request testing to be done.

Evidence Invoice Reports

Evidence invoicing reports will vary by agency but are required to intake and track evidence and to maintain a record of the chain of custody or each item. Many agencies utilize inventory management systems to intake and track evidence and the forms required to utilize the process are unique to the system. Many of these systems take advantage of barcoding so it may become necessary to attach barcode labels to the evidence packaging. Regardless of the system utilized a description of the item on the evidence invoice will be required. Here the item should be described consistent with the way it is described in the crime scene case documents in order to avoid confusion. Copies of any property invoices should be maintained in the crime scene case folder.

When laboratory testing is desired for the items of evidence the request will typically need to be a formal written request. Some laboratories may have pre-printed forms for this use. A copy of all requests for laboratory services made by the CSI team should be maintained in the crime scene case file.

As per the FBI Handbook of Forensic Services all requests for evidence examinations at the FBI laboratory must contain the following information:

- The submitting contact person's name, agency, address, and telephone number.
- Previous case-identification numbers, evidence submissions, and communications relating to the case.
- Description of the nature and the basic facts of the case as they pertain to evidence examinations.
- The name(s) of and descriptive data about the individual(s) involved (subject, suspect, victim, or a combination of those categories) and the agency-assigned case-identification number.
- The name of the prosecutor assigned, if available.
- A list of the evidence being submitted "herewith" (enclosed) or "under separate cover."
    - *Herewith* is limited to small items of evidence that are not endangered by transmitting in an envelope. Write on the envelope before placing evidence inside to avoid damaging or altering the evidence. The written communication should state: "Submitted herewith are the following items of evidence."
    - *Separate cover* is used to ship numerous or bulky items of evidence. Include a copy of the communication requesting the examinations. The written communication should state: "Submitted under separate cover by [list the method of shipment] are the following items of evidence."
- What type(s) of examination(s) is/are requested.
- Where the evidence should be returned and where the laboratory report should be sent. A street address must be included.
- A statement if the evidence was previously examined, if there is local controversy, or if other law enforcement agencies have an interest in the case.

Latent fingerprint lifts are typically not invoiced the same way as physical evidence. Instead these are usually delivered along with a latent print lift report to a fingerprint examiner who analyzes compares, evaluates the impressions and validates any identification. The fingerprint lifts are typically stored in a paper case folder by the fingerprint examiner. A copy of the latent print lift report should be maintained in the crime scene case folder.

Information typically included on a latent fingerprint report includes:

- Case information
- Total number of lifts recovered
- Description of each lifted latent print impression
    - Lift number (1 of x)
    - Method used to develop print
    - Exact location print was obtained
    - Orientation of the print on the surface
- Description of any additional items submitted for laboratory development of latent prints
- Elimination prints from victims or other involved parties
- Suspect's or arrestee's information

Checklists

Checklists can be very helpful to ensure all of the required tasks for an investigation have been completed without missing any steps and also to ensuring that the contents of the case folder are complete.

The case completion checklist is a multi-column document that has a pre-printed entry for each major step in the process along with a column to enter the time the step was completed and space for remarks. As each step is completed the corresponding box is checked on the list thus ensuring a thorough process is completed.

	TASK	REMARKS
☐	**Secure and protect the scene**	
	Conduct interviews and conferrals	
☐	First officer	
☐	Investigators	
☐	Victims and witnesses	
☐	**Walk-through scene**	
	Document scene	
☐	Notes	
☐	Images and photo log	
☐	Rough sketch	
☐	Examination quality images captured	
☐	**Search the scene**	
	Process and visualize	
☐	Latent fingerprints	
☐	Forensic light source	
☐	Reagent applications	
☐	Blood spatter analysis/documentation	
☐	Ballistic trajectory analysis/documentation	
	Evidence collection	
☐	DNA swabs	
☐	DNA evidence	
☐	Firearms related evidence	
☐	Weapons (other than firearms)	
☐	Impressions	
☐	Photographed	
☐	Casted	
☐	Lifted	
☐	Trace evidence (criminalistics)	
☐	Sexual assault kits	
☐	Digital and multimedia evidence	
☐	Controlled substance evidence	
	Elimination samples	
☐	Fingerprint eliminations	

- ☐ DNA eliminations
- ☐ **Evidence marked**
- ☐ **Evidence packaged**
- ☐ **Evidence sealed**
- ☐ **Final search conducted**
- ☐ **Scene released**
- ☐ **Evidence invoiced**
- ☐ **Evidence preliminary probative value determined**
- ☐ **Photos developed/printed/archived**
- ☐ **Diagrams prepared/printed and archived**
- ☐ **Chain of custody documented**

Charts

Charts are used as a supplement to the crime scene report. Charts can be very helpful for a reader to comprehend details about specifics discussed in the case report particularly when it comes to understanding written descriptors of positions such as where a wound is located on the body. Charts can usually be read and understood much more quickly than the written data.

The following charts are often used to supplement a crime scene report:

- Wound charts
  The wound chart is an anatomical chart showing the human body and is used by the CSI to illustrate the position on the body of wounds, injuries or marks. The chart shows all sides of the body including the hands and feet. Separate charts should be used for male and female victims. Captions should be included to record pertinent case information, victim's information, and the preparer's information.
- Vehicle charts
  Pre-drawn vehicle charts provide an effective way to illustrate the positions of items of evidence such as latent prints or DNA swabs and damage, including bullet damage, on motor vehicles. Generic charts are used for different vehicle types including, passenger vehicles, sport utility vehicles, trucks, and motorcycles.

Records Management

The records associated with a crime scene case, including; reports, notes, sketches, diagrams, charts, and images need a system of management. These records must be stored in a way that protects them from loss or damage and makes them easy to locate and retrieve when they are needed. The crime scene unit managers must work to develop a robust system that as much as is humanly possible guarantees the records' posterity, security, and accessibility over many years.

Case records can exist and be created in two main classifications: physical records and electronic records. Physical records are those that exist on paper; they have form and can be held in the hand and observed. Electronic records are those that exist in digital form. Either type of case record can be converted into the other. Physical records can be digitized through scanning and electronic records can be printed to become physical records. These two types of case records require different standard operating procedures to be properly managed. The duty to preserve these records is universally expected and is mandated by state law in over half on the United States. This duty exists in large part to protect a defendant's rights to due process and a fair trial under the sixth and fourteenth Amendments to the US Constitution.

In the course of operation the crime scene unit also creates enterprise records which require records management although possibly not as robustly as case records require. These records include personnel records, attendance rosters and assignments, SOPs, training records, purchasing records, communications, vehicle and facility records and plans.

According to ISO 15489-1:2001 records management includes:

- Setting policies and standards
- Assigning responsibilities and authorities
- Establishing and promulgating procedures and guidelines
- Providing a range of services relating to the management and use of records
- Designing, implementing and administering specialized systems for managing records; and integrating records management into business systems and processes

In 2012 Hurricane Sandy struck the New York area with a devastating blow and in the process created a hard lesson learned regarding records management. Included in the hurricane's path of destruction were two warehouses where forensic evidence and old crime scene records were stored. In New York City large warehouses are often located along the waterfront, a fact connected to the city's past status as one of the busiest shipping ports in the world. These two large city owned locations were utilized to store thousands of items of evidence, vehicles, and paper records from past crime scene investigations. When the storm hit, the facilities were secured to the extents possible but there was nothing that could stop the storms force from flooding and destroying the warehouses and much of their contents. Owing to safety concerns and contamination issues even the evidence that was not washed away became inaccessible. There are criminal prosecutions that are in jeopardy due to the fact that the evidence was lost, became contaminated or is still inaccessible. Similar situations occurred in New Orleans in 2005 when Hurricane Katrina struck and they are reportedly still dealing with the issues that resulted.

Disasters on such a massive scale are difficult to plan for when devising record management systems but these cases illustrate the need for management to consider all of the possibilities and put plans and policies in place to maintain records. The records created by a crime scene unit have a very significant impact on people's lives and the responsibility is on crime scene management to maintain them as pristinely as is reasonably possible.

What constitutes an acceptable system is one that conforms to some accepted standard such as the ISO guidelines in ISO 15489. There is not a simple solution but clearly if the unit is to be successful a record management solution must be implemented.

In today's digital age information technology (IT) can be leveraged to manage records and to create redundant systems for recovery in the event that a disaster strikes one of the records management sites. As time moves on, this will be more of a permanent solution but currently most agencies who employed such systems still must deal with managing the pre-existing paper records. Electronic record management systems can also be employed to digitize pre-existing case files but the process of converting physical records into electronic records is labor intensive.

Once an IT system for records management has been implemented, the management of electronic records becomes integrated into the operation and is automated. The system still needs management and oversight but the process is much easier then maintaining large storage space for physical files. The amount of data created and stored by crime scene units has grown exponentially over the years and that phenomenon should be expected to continue at huge rates as digital devices expand in the roles of the CSI.

Crime scene managers need to consider the following when developing records management policy:

- **Identifying what information requires capture and storage**
  Some of the data created obviously requires capture but not everything is black and white. It seems obvious that the scene documentation including the report, photographs and diagrams require capture but what about other case related materials such as emails regarding the investigation? In today's age email is even becoming too slow for some to embrace and they prefer instant messaging (IM). When IM is used in the process of a crime scene investigation, does it require capture? This may seem far-fetched to some but it is not unheard of for a CSI to communicate with a first officer through these methods. Products are also available on the market today that can record a scene so the walk-through process can be accomplished in a virtual environment on smart devices rather than physically entering the scene or even being in the vicinity. All of these technologies bring benefits to the table but they all create data and whether or not that data requires capture must be considered.
- **Creating and approving SOPs regarding records**
  All of the policies for records management should be formally contained in an SOP on Records management. The SOP should include policy for the creation, storage, retrieval, distribution, and eventual disposition of records.
- **Developing a records storage plan, which includes the short and long-term housing of physical records and digital information**
  The space required to store physical records should be designated in the SOP along with the method for securing the space and maintaining it in environmental condition that promotes the longevity of the records. Security includes controlling access to the records and tracking a record's movement. Digital information will require support from IT professionals to develop a storage plan. Larger agencies will typically have IT departments that must be brought into the process as they must understand the policies required for crime scene records management.
- **Identifying, classifying, and storing records**
  What exactly constitutes a record must be defined. Once a record is created it must be classified so that the storage requirements can be applied. Physical case records, electronic case records and enterprise records will all have different policies for storage.
- **Coordinating access to case records internally and externally, maintaining confidentiality, privacy, and access**
  The records were originally created to be shared. A CSI does not take photographs or draw sketches of a crime scene for their own benefit; it is for the benefit of others. However this sharing must be properly coordinated and controlled due to the sensitive and confidential nature of the material. There have been cases where crime scene records were inappropriately disseminated and agencies found themselves in hot water because of it. In the end there is a responsibility to the victims and our justice system to maintain access to the records properly.

Another issue that should be of concern to crime scene unit managers is abiding by court orders to seal records. An order to seal records is often issued by the court when, charges are dismissed, plea bargains are agreed upon or a person is exonerated. It may become necessary to seal crime scene records in some cases particularly when the suspect or arrestee is named in the case records. This can be a tricky area and sealed crime scene records should not necessarily be destroyed since there may be a later prosecution of another individual requiring the records to be distributed. A policy and mechanism for sealing records should be developed.

- **Executing a retention policy on the handling of records which are no longer required for normal operational activity**

The retention policy dictates how long the records will be maintained in a manner that they are immediately accessible and when they may be migrated to an archive system or eventually destroyed. Case records are normally held for very long periods and in some cases indefinitely; however, this may vary by crime type. The crime scene managers may consider statute of limitations for different crimes and maximum sentencing periods for convicted offenders.

In the case of burglary the statute of limitations may be six years in a given state making it unnecessary to have immediate access to the case records after this period of time expires. However, the maximum sentence may be 25 years. So it is possible that a defendant was prosecuted near the end of the statute of limitations and sentenced to the maximum sentence. Appeals usually occur shortly after sentencing but can happen at any point if new evidence is discovered and in cases such as deportation it may occur even after the sentence is served. Therefore the records may be moved to a long-term storage archive after the statute of limitations but they still must be maintained. At some point though it becomes unlikely that crime scene records for a burglary investigation will be required. In the above scenario it may be after a 30- or 35-year period following the occurrence.

Murder and crimes punishable by life imprisonment or the death penalty typically do not have a statute of limitations. These cases sometimes go cold for several decades before information develops to solve the case. Since the widespread use of DNA testing was introduced to identify suspects in past crimes there have been an extraordinary number of cold cases solved and each one requires access to old records.

Perhaps most important when it comes to records management is the wrongful convictions that have been identified since forensic DNA testing became available. Well over a thousand wrongfully convicted persons have been exonerated since DNA first brought the issue to light in 1989; some of them were on death row. The number of wrongfully convicted persons is a stark reality that is astonishing to most in law enforcement and it was the impetus behind the National Academy of Science Report recommending a new path forward.

The crime scene profession and all involved must face these facts about wrongful conviction and not bury their head in the sand. One of the most common causes that have been identified as leading to wrongful convictions is invalidated or improper forensic science. This is one of the most pressing issues facing the US system of justice and one that must be fixed not through fault-finding activities but through problem-solving solutions. One part of that solution involves the creation of quality crime scene cases and their proper maintenance so, when necessary, the facts surrounding the scene can be reviewed.

Many states now have laws that provide access to evidence for post-conviction testing where the state has an obligation to produce exculpatory evidence in criminal cases so that a defendant may inspect and test it. Included in these laws are requirements for maintaining crime scene evidence and that includes the crime scene documentation. Crime scene managers are managers of government entities and therefore are expected to know and conform to the laws of their state.

> As an example, Massachusetts General Law chapter 278A provides a comprehensive framework for criminal defendants who have been found guilty to gain access to evidence and forensic testing to support a claim of factual innocence in the Post-Conviction Access to Forensic and Scientific Analysis Act.
>
> - The act creates statewide statutory duty for governmental entities in possession of materials collected during an investigation that resulted in a criminal conviction to systematically retain those materials for the duration of a convicted defendant's sentence, including any term of parole or probation.
> - The act mandates, "Any governmental entity that is in possession of evidence or biological material that is collected for its potential evidentiary value during the investigation of a crime, the prosecution of which results in a conviction, shall retain such evidence or biological material … without regard to whether the evidence or biological material was introduced at trial."

Records Management Systems

Perhaps the best practical way for a modern crime scene unit to develop and maintain quality management systems for records management is to employ an enterprise wide computerized case management solution. Applications are available for this purpose and they are typically run through the agency IT structure. A centralized server is used to deploy an application across the unit's network and users are given role based access to utilize the system. Even with a computerized case management system there still may be a need for a physical paper case folder to hold things such as hand written notes, sketches, discs, and printed materials.

Intake

All crime scene cases start with the receipt of a request for service. Crime scene investigators do not self-initiate investigations but instead play a support role in the criminal investigation process and must be requested to participate before they become involved. Not all requests for service will result in the intake of the case. Some calls will not meet the criteria to generate a response of a CSI team and instead of being routed through an intake process are instead recorded as inquiries. The intake process signals the decision to investigate the scene. Once a case intake is completed a case number is assigned and a case folder is created where all of the records for the case are to be stored. Intake should be available to users at various locations since a crime case investigation may need to be initiated from locations other than at the crime scene unit offices.

- Intake requires the following fields of information
  - Date and time of request for service
  - Type of incident or crime to be investigated

- Location of the scene
- Basic details of the incident
- Person requesting CSI response
- Phone number at the scene
- Nature of the evidence in plain view at the scene
- Date and time of occurrence of the incident
- Victim(s) preliminary information
    - Victim's location
- CSI team members being dispatched to the scene
    - Primary investigator
    - Assisting investigator(s)
    - Technical assistants
    - Crime scene supervisor
    - Crime scene case manager (if applicable)
- Unit vehicles being dispatched to the scene
- Suspect information
- Arrest information

Casework

Casework is input into the case folder by the CSI's completion of various forms. The forms may contain captioned fields and space for writing free-form narratives. It is important when procuring case management software to make sure the ability for complete customization of forms is available. Pre-canned reports will not serve every agency and can lead to issues later on when captions that don't apply to the unit's workflow are left blank leading the reader of the reports to conclude that there was an omission. Terminology and abbreviations may also be unit specific requiring customization of the case management system.

Reporting will need to be developed for the following sections of the case file:

- Scene and victim information
- Crime scene search report
- Crime scene images
- Sketch and diagramming
- Scene processing report
- Forensic evidence
- Vehicles

Photo Management

A well designed case management system can integrate the reporting with photo management for crime scene images into a single application. This allows for a training, operation and maintenance of only a single application and all of the case records are stored in a single case folder. The photo manager component should handle the upload, annotation, and storage of the working copies of images. Redundant archives may be handled separately.

Photo management capability should enable the user to upload photos in batches while also storing the meta data and exif files attached to photos. The upload process should be password protected and be subjected to audit. After upload the ability to create a photo log and add a description for each photo is needed. The system should also have the ability to print photos without the need for exporting to external applications and should track and record all activity.

In the event that film photography is utilized then the film will require developing and the negatives should be stored in the paper case folder. The images should also be recorded to digital media to allow for electronic management of the case images.

External Attachment Management

The ability to attach external files and digitized documents to the case file will definitely be necessary. This material is either created or received by the crime scene unit during the course of an investigation.

- Created files
  External files will be created for investigations in the form of CADD diagrams, maps, charts, 3D models and point clouds.
- Digitized files
  Digitized files are created when paper documents are scanned or faxed. This will be required for any handwritten documents created during the crime scene investigation. Digitizing these documents presents a method to memorialize them and create a permanent record. Depending on the content and agency policy the originals may still need to be maintained in paper form in a physical case folder.
- Received files
  Files may be received by the crime scene unit in many instances. These files include surveillance images and video, electronic records such as information from plate readers or police computer checks, recorded data from vehicle data recorders or security systems and communication data from cell phones and PDAs.
- Instrument data
  The CSI team will utilize various forms of electronic instruments which generate instrument data. These include total stations, laser scanners, laser distance meters, temperature probes and analytical equipment. The data generated may be used to write reports or create exhibits in a CAD program but the raw data generated by the instrument may also require storage.

Case Review

Every case submitted by the CSI will require a review process before it is considered completed and approved. Crime scene cases may be subjected to administrative and technical reviews. Administrative reviews ensure that the work conforms to policy and is free from grammatical errors and omissions. Administrative reviews should be conducted on every case. Technical reviews are done to ensure that the work is technically sound and that the data contained in the report supports any conclusions that were made. Technical reviews should be done on any case where conclusions are made which typically involves crime scene reconstruction techniques such as trajectory analysis, bloodstain pattern analysis or where some form of crime scene processing was performed requiring technical expertise. Technical reviews may be done on a certain percentage of randomly selected cases or on all cases involving certain techniques.

Reviews should be done in the electronic form whenever possible to prevent the creation of physical copies of reports which would then need to be controlled or destroyed as the work is a only draft and is still subject to revision. If the reviewer recommends corrective actions prior to the report being approved then there should be an electronic method to alert the CSI who prepared the report of what revisions are suggested. The CSI can then make any revisions and re-submit the report for approval.

The case management system must be designed to facilitate both the administrative and technical review processes. It should have the capability to record reviewer's notes along with the date and time and identity of the reviewer. The system must also prevent the external distribution of cases that have not been reviewed and approved. In the event that an incomplete report is released it must be clearly marked to communicate that the work is a draft version only and is subject to revision. Releasing draft copies of reports should be avoided except in the event of exigent circumstances.

Distribution

The report and its attachments are in reality the final product that the crime scene unit is in business to deliver to the customer. The customer of course is the various people who rely on the crime scene report to help make their own decisions. Many people rely on the report to further their own work. Scientists use the report to facilitate laboratory analysis. Investigators use the report to make decisions about what actually occurred at the crime scene and who is responsible for the crime. The prosecutor uses the report to help make decisions about whether or not a charge can be proven, and if so then how the facts should be presented in court. Defense attorneys use the report to find areas where doubt may exist that could result in a finding of not guilty. The jury uses the report to help make decisions about guilt and innocence and the judge uses it to assure a fair trial is held and to help make decisions about sentencing. All of these people and more will require distribution of the crime scene records but it must be done in a prescribed and controlled manner.

It is the responsibility of the crime scene unit managers to develop a sound distribution policy to ensure that the records are made readily available to the people who need them providing that they have valid permission and authority to possess them. A crime scene supervisor should review and authorize the distribution of records prior to the release of any records.

Case records may be distributed in the following incidents:

- To personnel within the crime scene unit
- To the lead investigator assigned to the case
- To laboratory personnel assigned to analyze evidence upon a written request
- To the prosecutor assigned to the case upon written request
- To defense attorneys upon court order
- To individuals resultant to court order
- To authorized investigative bodies
- In compliance with freedom of information laws as applicable to each case

When case records are distributed a record of the request and distribution should be kept with the case folder. Distribution of physical records should only be done through hand delivery or certified mail type services. Distribution of electronic records should only be done through secure transmission services and not by personal email accounts (except exigent circumstances).

Electronic case management systems allow for this type of control and tracking. Users can be given access passwords and the level of access can be governed according to their role. A supervisor within the unit may be able to access all materials while another CSI may only have access to certain reports. Persons outside the immediate agency can also be given access through password protection but a vetting process should be required and this should be done on a very limited basis.

Footprints are created by users when they log into a system and access records. Audit reports can be generated on a case level to see a report of who accessed the case record, when they accessed it and what actions they took. Audit reports can also be generated to see a report of all activity for a particular user. These auditing functions may deter but cannot completely protect case records from unauthorized access but when unauthorized access occurs they do allow for identification and remedial actions.

Conclusion

Reporting and records management is a critical aspect of crime scene investigation management. This is certainly not the fun part of the job but it is required to maintain quality. The crime scene report is what most people see and use to judge a crime scene unit's work. The quality of the report reflects on the entire unit not only on the individual CSI that prepares it. Well-developed policy on crime scene reports and records management should result in a high quality product. Good reports though are only useful if they are managed in a system where they can be stored and protected and then retrieved when needed. Quality management requires that a records management system be developed and maintained. Out of 73 assessments reported by ASCLD/LAB under ISO 17025:2005 during 2013, the number one issue reported for non-conformance was non-conformance with section 5.10 Reporting the Results. This means the work was done properly but the reports were not handled correctly.

In today's technology driven society, computer managed data is the only practical way to do business. In New York City an investigative case management system was developed that spans the entire agency. The system was originally developed under chief of detectives Phil Pulaski and has grown to be a tremendous success. This system presents an example for the development of case management systems for law enforcement agencies. The system ties all aspects of an investigation into a single electronic case folder. When a homicide occurs, many different people may contribute to the investigation. A homicide detective may locate witnesses and conduct interrogations of suspects and the CSI will process the scene. Computer specialists may recover and analyze electronic devices. Scientists may analyze crime scene evidence, and fingerprint examiners may identify prints and so on. With an agency wide case management system, all of the investigative data is funneled into a single case folder so the people that need it can access it in a timely and efficient manner. The enterprise case management system enables intake, reporting, photo management, file attachment, archiving, review, approval and distribution all in a single system. The system also allows for messaging and alerts. Alerts can be used to send notification when a specific action occurs or at specific times in the investigations progress. When messaging is used, the messages can be saved as part of the case record. In short the system presents an all-encompassing solution for investigative case reporting and management.

Other agencies have also had success with investigative case management systems and laboratory information management systems. When designing a case management system all aspects of the unit's operations will need to be considered. Choosing applications that allow for full customization and future expansion are critical. New systems need to be able to communicate with pre-existing systems so data can be exchanged without having to enter it multiple times into various systems throughout the agency. The goal is to input data once, review it and then manage it for use where it is needed. A well designed system takes a great deal of effort to implement but once it is in place it makes management of the unit a much more efficient process.

INDEX

For Product Safety Concerns and Information please contact our EU representative GPSR@taylorandfrancis.com Taylor & Francis Verlag GmbH, Kaufingerstraße 24, 80331 München, Germany

Batch number: 10732706

Printed by Printforce, the Netherlands